LESSON PLANS

Prepared by

CAROLE M. CASTEN

California State University, Dominguez Hills

DYNAMIC PHYSICAL EDUCATION

FOR SECONDARY SCHOOL STUDENTS

Fifth Edition

PEARSON

Benjamin
Cummings

San Francisco Boston New York
Cape Town Hong Kong London Madrid Mexico City
Montreal Munich Paris Singapore Sydney Tokyo Toronto

Senior Acquisitions Editor: Deirdre Espinoza
Project Editor: Laura Stone
Editorial Assistant: Sabrina Larson
Managing Editor: Wendy Earl
Production Editor: Leslie Austin
Composition: Carole M. Casten
Manufacturing Buyer: Stacy Wong
Executive Marketing Manager: Lauren Harp
Cover Designer: Yvo Riezebos

ISBN : 0-8053-7883-9
1 2 3 4 5 6 7 8 9 10—TCS—09 08 07 06 05
www.aw-bc.com

Contents

Preface

Using *Lesson Plans for Dynamic Physical Education for Secondary School Students*

Lesson Plans for Dynamic Physical Education for Secondary School Students is designed for use with the textbook *Dynamic Physical Education for Secondary School Students, Fifth Edition, (DPESS)* by Robert P. Pangrazi and Paul W. Darst. Most of the activities in the lesson plans are covered in detail in the textbook. Reference pages are noted in the lesson plans. The lesson plans provide a guide for teachers presenting lessons in a well-ordered, sequential manner, to students from 7th grade through high school. These lesson plans should be regarded as an aid in curriculum and instructional planning. The lessons can serve as a framework for developing a curriculum to meet the needs of the students being served and the teachers.

Many teachers take the activities from the lesson plans and write them on 3" X 5" index cards. Having notes helps teachers mentally organize the lesson and results in a more effective presentation. All lesson presentations should be mentally rehearsed to prevent wasted time and excessive use of written notes. Notes relieve the teacher of the burden of trying to remember the sequence of activities and the worry of forgetting the main elements of each lesson.

Format of the Lesson Plans

Three-week, two-week, and one-week units are presented for each topic. The movement experiences are for the beginning learner. Each lesson plan is divided into four instructional parts as described in Chapter 4 of *DPESS,* plus a concluding evaluation and a cheer. The instructional parts of the lesson plan and the major purposes of each are as follows:

1. **Introductory Activity:** Introductory activities are used to physiologically prepare youngsters for activity when entering the activity area. They can serve as a gross motor warm-up as well as a time to practice and reinforce class management skills. Descriptions of introductory activities can be found in *DPESS*, Chapter 14.

2. **Fitness Development Activity:** Fitness activities should be allocated 8–12 minutes in a 30–35 minute activity period. The length of the fitness section of class varies depending on the time frame of each scheduled class and the developmental level of the students. The activities should be personalized, progressive in nature, and exercise all parts of the body. Brief discussions should be included in the lessons about the values of fitness for a healthy lifestyle. A comprehensive discussion of physical activity and fitness principles and activities is found in *DPESS*, Chapters 15 and 16.

3. **Lesson Focus Activities:** The purpose of the lesson focus is to help youngsters attain major program objectives, body management competency, fundamental and specialized skills. The lesson focus uses 15–20 minutes of the daily lesson depending on the length of the teaching period. While the lesson plan activities are organized into three-week, two-week, and one-week units in this book, the instructor may adapt and expand the lessons to any length to fit the organizational needs of the school. The content of each unit is presented in a developmental sequence ensuring that students can be successful and that material will be presented in a progressive manner.

4. **Game Activity:** This part of the lesson uses the last 5–7 minutes of the period. Games can be used as the culminating activity for practicing skills presented in the lesson focus or can be unrelated to the lesson focus. This portion of the lesson is presented for the purpose of completing

the lesson with a fun and enjoyable activity. The game portion of each lesson should leave students with positive feelings toward movement.

5. **Evaluation/Review:** Good instruction puts closure on a lesson by conducting an evaluation/review requiring active involvement of the students. The instructor should end each lesson asking students pertinent questions evaluating elements of the day's activities and introducing activities for the next period.

6. **Cheer:** Athletic teams build spirit and bonding by ending each practice or entering each competition with a cheer. This practice applied to physical education classes can have the same result. Ending the class with a cheer can produce enthusiasm, bonding, and spirit. While the lesson plans include cheers, students really enjoy creating them. Allow students the opportunity to demonstrate their creativity by creating their own cheers. Try to end the classes with a cheer and see the spirit and enthusiasm blossom.

Orientation and Class Management Games

During the first lesson with new students, the instructor should teach and reinforce class management rules and games. Following are elements of instruction you might find useful in establishing the class format, routines, and expectations.

1. **Class rules, format, objectives, and expectations:** Discuss class rules, format, objectives, and expectations with the class the first day you meet the students to assure their understanding. Explain what the consequences are when rules are not followed. Explain that the format of each lesson will include an introductory activity, fitness development, lesson focus, and finish with a game activity.

2. **Grading:** Explain the course grading policies and grading scale the first day of each unit.

3. **Entry and exit behaviors:** Demonstrate and explain entry and exit behaviors for the physical education class. Establish a policy for obtaining equipment.

4. **Nonparticipation:** Explain how excuses for nonparticipation will be handled. Establish guidelines for making up missed material or lost points.

5. **Safety:** Describe safety procedures for physical education classes. Explain that each unit will have unique rules that you will explain at the onset of the unit.

6. **Distribution of equipment:** Make students responsible for acquiring equipment and returning it at the end or appropriate portion of the lesson. Place equipment around the perimeter of the teaching area for easy and safe distribution of equipment.

7. **Starting and stopping class:** In general, a whistle, a drum beat, and a raised hand are effective signals for stopping the class. A voice command should be used to start the class. Use the phrase: "When I say go" or "When I say begin" followed by what you want executed to assure that students do not begin before instructions are finished.

8. **Formations:** Practice various teaching formations such as scattered, moving into a circle, and grouping. Transitions between formations should be done while moving, i.e., jogging from scattered formation into a circular formation. Refer to *DPESS* Chapter 7 for class management details.

- **Creating partners:** Use the Back-to-Back, or Elbow-to-Elbow, or Toe-to-Toe technique for creating groups of 2. All students not finding an elbow to touch should move toward a marker in the center of the room and raise a hand to find a partner. Emphasis should be on finding a partner near them, not searching for a friend, and taking a different partner each time.

- **Forming a circle:** Use the technique of moving around the room with a locomotor movement and direct students to follow the back of someone's neck and fall-in to a circle.

- **Groups of 3 or more:** Use the Whistle Mixer to create groups of 3 or more. Students move around the area with a locomotor movement, the teacher whistles (or claps, etc.) a given number of times and raises the same number of fingers above his or her head to signal the group size. Students move together to create groups of the size matching the number of whistles signaled. Groups not complete should raise arms identifying the need for additional members and move toward the center of the area. Students needing to join a group should move toward the center of the area toward the established marker and raise their hand to facilitate finding others needing a group. The goal is to find the correct number of students as quickly as possible.

9. **Freeze positions:** To establish and focus attention on instructions, it is valuable to establish a "freeze" position for students to assume whenever you signal a stop via whistle, drum, etc. A commonly used freeze position is that similar to the "ready" position in sports with the hands on the knees. Equipment is placed between the feet.

Notes of Appreciation

Acknowledgments and appreciation go to my husband, Rich, for his computer expertise, perfectionist nature, and endless hours spent on the compilation of this textbook. Sincere thanks are extended to Dr. Robert P. Pangrazi for his continued support, feedback, friendship, and confidence in my writing. Additional thanks are extended to both Dr. Pangrazi, professor emeritus, and Dr. Paul Darst, professor at Arizona State University, and co-authors of the textbook *Dynamic Physical Education for Secondary Students* for the opportunity to write this lesson plan book. Laura Stone, Benjamin Cummings, deserves special thanks for her support and assistance in the writing of this textbook.

Some of the information shared in this textbook was motivated or gathered from the innovative and creative thinking of a number of professors and teachers in the greater Los Angeles area and graduate and senior students at California State University Dominguez Hills (CSUDH). Dr. Reginald Price, professor at California State University San Bernardino, contributed the lesson focus, Task Sheets, and exam portion of the Racquetball Unit. To him I owe sincere gratitude for his hard work in a timely manner. Thank you to all of the following people for contributing ideas or materials to the lesson plans: Janice Manion and Kathy Odorico—Tennis Unit; Nick Carr, and Dr. John Johnson, professor, CSUDH—Golf Unit; Anthony Quiarte contributed the "written lesson" and "programmed instruction"—Weight Training Unit; Diana Vance—Volleyball Unit; Joanna Enserro Natividad—Soccer Unit; Alicia Megofina and Eric Calhoun—Orienteering Unit; Barry Barnes and Alan Ransom—Rock Climbing Unit; Neftali Rivera and Wilma Uy—Team Handball Unit; Grace Dacanay and Luis Gomez—Table Tennis Unit; John Noble and Arturo Gutierrez—Frisbee Golf; Irene Flores and Stephanie Rodriguez—Flag Football Unit; and Wendy Bogdanovich, Mike Cota, John Ramirez and Carrie Reeder—Softball Unit. To Maria Medina, Sabrina Larson, and Amy Yu, thank you for assistance in page referencing the 5th edition of this lesson plan book. To Melissa Acosta, Kevin Geddes, and Lisa Goldschein, thank you for field-testing the lessons at the California Academy of Mathematics and Science. To the other teachers in the greater Los Angeles area, thank you for field-testing items from the textbook. To Beverly Francis, secretary, California State University Dominguez Hills, thank you for your continued encouragement.

To **all** the contributors to this textbook, I offer sincere gratitude and a big THANK YOU.

Badminton

OBJECTIVES:

The student will:
1. Juggle one, two, or three scarves as directed by the instructor.
2. Work cooperatively with peers during the High Five Introductory Activity.
3. Demonstrate agility and speed in the Triangle Tag Game.
4. Demonstrate balancing in a variety of positions during the Balance Tag.
5. Demonstrate cooperation with peers during the Snowball Relay game.
6. Demonstrate agility, starting, stopping, and stretching skills during the Move and Stretch Activity.
7. Demonstrate agility and dodging skills during the introductory activities.
8. Demonstrate cooperation and agility during the Pentabridge Hustle Introductory Activity.
9. Execute balancing positions, running, and dodging skills during the Balance Tag Introductory Activity.
10. Participate in strengthening and stretching exercises, in the Fitness Challenge Course Circuit, Fitness Obstacle Course, Parachute Rhythmic Activities, Interval Training Activities, Four Corners Fitness activities, Continuity Exercises, and jump roping activities to improve their overall fitness levels.
11. Participate in "Marking" demonstrating agility and quickness.
12. Play Tug-of-War challenge with a partner.
13. Participate in Back-to-Back Take Down with a partner following the rules and playing cooperatively.
14. Execute forehand and backhand strokes.
15. Execute proper form of the forehand clear shot demonstrated by the teacher.
16. Demonstrate the forehand smash and drop shots using form demonstrated in class.
17. Execute the backhand clear shot on the court using form demonstrated in class.
18. Execute the backhand drop shot on the court using form demonstrated in class.
19. Execute the forehand shots on the court using form demonstrated in class.
20. Perform the Badminton Forehand Clear Shot as demonstrated by the instructor.
21. Demonstrate forehand net drop using form taught by instructor.
22. Demonstrate serving on the court aiming for the hoops on the floor and using form demonstrated in class.
23. Demonstrate the forehand drive and drop shot during a rally activity with classmates.
24. Read the Rules Handout distributed by the instructor.
25. Practice underhand, forehand, and backhand shots on a court using appropriate Task Sheets.
26. Practice the forehand smash to a target on the court using appropriate Task Sheets.
27. Execute skills and knowledge of rules while playing Badminton Doubles.
28. Play Singles Badminton with a partner demonstrating knowledge of rules of the game.
29. Play Badminton in a Round Robin Tournament during class executing skills and rules demonstrated in class.
30. Complete a Badminton Written Knowledge Exam during class and score 70% or better.
31. Complete a Badminton Skills Test working cooperatively with a partner during the class period.

BADMINTON BLOCK PLAN
3-WEEK UNIT

Week #1	Monday	Tuesday	Wednesday	Thursday	Friday
Introductory Activity	Juggling Scarves	Weave Drill	Triangle Plus 1 Tag	Balance Tag	Running High Fives
Fitness	Challenge Course	4-Corners	Continuity Exercises	Challenge Course	General Movements
Lesson Focus	Forehand Grip Backhand Grip	Underhand Serve, Review Forehand & Backhand Grip	Forehand Clear Forehand Drop Forehand Smash	Backhand Shots, Clear and Drop Review Forehand	Review Skills Forehand Backhand Serve
Game	Frisbee 21	Partner Tug-of-War	Hoops on the Ground	Hoops and Plyometrics	Circle Hook On

Week #2	Monday	Tuesday	Wednesday	Thursday	Friday
Introductory Activity	Marking	Move and Stretch	Fastest Tag	Vanishing Bean Bags	Zipper
Fitness	Continuity Exercises	Interval Training	Challenge Course	4-Corners	Challenge Course
Lesson Focus	Review: Forehand Net Drop, Backhand Net Drop, Underhand Long Serve	Rules Skills Review Play Drive Rally	Play Doubles Badminton Games	Station Skill Review	Play Badminton Games
Game	Fetch Relay	Mixed Doubles Games	Snowball Relay	Over and Under Ball Relay	Frozen Tag

Week #3	Monday	Tuesday	Wednesday	Thursday	Friday
Introductory Activity	Pentabridge Hustle	Juggling Scarves	Move and Perform a Stretch	Eliminate today	Balance Tag
Fitness	Parachute Rhythmic Aerobic Activities	Stations	Continuity Exercises	Parachute Rhythmic Aerobic Activities	4-Corners
Lesson Focus	Play Badminton Games	Play Badminton Games	Written Exam	Skills Partner Testing	Round Robin Tournament
Game	Partner Tug-of-War	Back-to-Back Take Down	Round Robin Tournament	Round Robin Tournament	Round Robin Tournament

Badminton Lesson Plan 1

EQUIPMENT:

1 badminton racquet per student	Music CD/tape, CD/cassette player
2 shuttlecocks per student	3 juggling scarves per student

INSTRUCTIONAL ACTIVITIES	TEACHING HINTS

INTRODUCTORY ACTIVITY (2–3 MINUTES)

Juggling Scarves

Scarves are held by the fingertips near the center. To throw the scarf, it should be lifted and pulled into the air above eye level. Scarves are caught by clawing, a downward motion of the hand, and grabbing the scarf from above as it is falling.

DPESS page 392

Scattered formation

Place scarves along perimeter of teaching area.

Cascading Activities: One scarf; two scarves; three scarves

FITNESS DEVELOPMENT (8–12 MINUTES)

Challenge Course

Agility run between and around cones.
Hop through hula hoops.
Hurdle over 3 benches set up with space between them.
Leap/jump over ropes set up on a diagonal.
Crab walk (feet first) length of a mat.
Log roll down the length of a mat.
Jump rope 10 times using "Hot Peppers."
Skip around cones set-up.
Crab walk (hands first) between markers/cones.
Curl-ups
Jog around the area.
Push-ups
Stretching activities

DPESS page 351

Use music to motivate moving through obstacle course.

LESSON FOCUS (15–20 MINUTES)

Forehand Grip
Backhand Grip

Demonstrate grips

Forehand Grip = thumb and forefinger should form a V. This points toward shoulder of opposite stroking arm when held in front of body.

Backhand Grip = thumb should be resting on the flat side behind the handle. The thumb is further up on the handle than the index finger.

DPESS page 412

No courts are needed for this lesson.

Scattered formation

Direct students to pick up a racquet and return to space.

Practice grip using forehand grip, hit birdie with the palm of racquet face up. Bounce birdie on racquet into air 20 times.

Bounce birdie to self 20 times using backhand grip.

Bounce birdie using forehand grip while changing levels. Repeat with backhand.

Bounce birdie to self in air while walking.

In place, keep birdie in air switching alternately from forehand to backhand.

Direct students to bounce birdie at different heights.

GAME (5 MINUTES)

Frisbee 21

Players stand 10 yards apart and throw the disc back and forth. The throws must be accurate and catchable. One point is awarded for a 2-handed catch and 2 points for a 1-handed catch. A player must get 21 points and win by 2 points.

DPESS page 465

Use "elbow-to-elbow" to make pairs.

Direct students to area having 1 student pick up Frisbee before going.

EVALUATION/REVIEW AND CHEER

Ask students questions reviewing elements of forehand and backhand grip.

Cheer: 2, 4, 6, 8, P.E. is really great!

Badminton Lesson Plan 2

EQUIPMENT:

1 Tug-of-War rope per 2 students
1 badminton racquet per student
2 shuttlecocks per student
Cones, bean bags, jumping boxes

Courts and nets
CD/cassette player
Music CD/tape for fitness

INSTRUCTIONAL ACTIVITIES	TEACHING HINTS

INTRODUCTORY ACTIVITY (2–3 MINUTES)

Weave Drill
Students are in ready position. They will shuffle left, right, forward, backward, over, and around obstacles on signal by the teacher's hand motion.

DPESS page 306
Scattered formation in front of teacher
Mark area with cones

FITNESS DEVELOPMENT (8–12 MINUTES)

Four-Corners
On signal, each student will move around the perimeter counter-clockwise. As students pass the corner they change the movement they are doing based on the instructions posted on each cone.

DPESS pages 347–348
Set up a rectangle boundary with cones.
Use music for continuous motivation.

Examples of movements listed at each cone:
Crab walk, hopping, bear crawl, jogging, skipping, galloping, curl-ups, reverse curl-ups, push-ups, jump roping, etc.

LESSON FOCUS (15–20 MINUTES)

Underhand Serve

DPESS pages 412–413
Scattered formation
Racquets and shuttlecocks around perimeter of teaching area
Direct students to pick up a racquet and a shuttlecock and return to demonstration area. Shuttlecock placed on floor between feet

Demonstrate Serve
Students should use their shuttlecock and their partners to serve twice into the correct service court. Then change servers.

Student practices serve motion in own space.
Use management technique "Back-to-Back" to make partners. Assign 4 students to each serving area.
Rotate positions on court.
Each student should serve 8 times per service court.

Review Forehand and Backhand Grips
Demonstrate and review

Student bounces birdie to self 10 times using forehand and then backhand grip.
Alternate bouncing to self using forehand and backhand.

GAME (5 MINUTES)

Partner Tug-of-War Activities
Different Positions
Pick-up and Pull

DPESS page 401
Create partners.
1 rope per 2 students

EVALUATION/REVIEW AND CHEER

Ask students "What are the important parts of the serve?"
"Where should you serve from?"
"Where do you serve to?"
Cheer: P.E., P.E., What does it mean? Pretty exciting physical education!

Badminton Lesson Plan 3

EQUIPMENT:

1 badminton racquet per student
2 shuttlecocks per student

Continuity music CD/tape, CD/cassette player
Hula hoops for 1/2 class size

INSTRUCTIONAL ACTIVITIES	TEACHING HINTS

INTRODUCTORY ACTIVITY (2–3 MINUTES)

Triangle Plus 1 Tag
Three students hold hands to form a triangle. One person in the triangle is the leader. The fourth person outside the triangle tries to tag the leader. The triangle moves around to avoid getting the leader tagged. Leader and tagger are changed often.

DPESS page 312
Use Whistle Mixer to make groups of 3.

FITNESS DEVELOPMENT (8–12 MINUTES)

Continuity Exercises
These exercises are a type of interval training. Create a CD/cassette tape with 30–35 seconds of music and 20 seconds of silence. During the music, the students will jump rope.

DPESS pages 349–350
Scattered formation

Direct students to pick up a rope and move to their own space.

During each silence instruct the students to do a different exercise, i.e., push-ups, curl-ups, reverse push-ups, side leg lifts on each side, coffee grinder, arm circling, crab walks forward and backward, etc.

1 individual jump rope per student

When the music resumes, the students jump rope again.

LESSON FOCUS (15–20 MINUTES)

Forehand Clear Shot

DPESS page 413
Direct student to pick up racquet and 2 shuttlecocks. Return to demonstration area.

Demonstrate Forehand Clear Shot
Practice hit four shuttlecocks in a row to partner over net. Change roles. Repeat.

Student practices with shuttlecocks on floor.
Use elbow-to-elbow to create pairs.
Direct students to courts.

Demonstrate Forehand Drop Shot

Bring students together.
Assign students to hit 4 drop shots over net to partner. Change roles. Repeat.

Demonstrate Forehand Smash

Bring students together.
Assign practice: Forehand clear/drop shot. Return with a smash.
Repeat.

Rally
Use all strokes and keep the shuttlecock in place as much as possible.

Assign students to court.

GAME (5 MINUTES)

Hoops on the Ground
Students run around the area where hoops are spread. When the teacher calls a number, that number of students must get inside 1 hoop in 5 seconds or less.

DPESS page 313
Spread hoops around floor.

Repeat and vary challenges.

EVALUATION/REVIEW AND CHEER

Name one forehand shot. Where should the shuttle land in a drop shot?
Where should the shuttle land on the court when using the forehand clear shot?
Cheer: 5, 4, 3, 2, 1. Badminton is lots of fun!

Badminton Lesson Plan 4

EQUIPMENT:

1 hoop per person	Obstacle course markers
2 shuttlecocks per student	CD/cassette player
1 badminton racquet per student	Music CD/tape

INSTRUCTIONAL ACTIVITIES	TEACHING HINTS

INTRODUCTORY ACTIVITY (2–3 MINUTES)

Balance Tag
To be safe, balance in a stipulated position.

DPESS page 312
Scattered formation; select several "its."

FITNESS DEVELOPMENT (8–12 MINUTES)

Challenge Course
Agility run between and around cones.
Hop through hula hoops.
Hurdle over 3 benches set up with space between them.
Leap/jump over ropes set up on a diagonal.
Crab walk (feet first) length of a mat.
Log roll down the length of a mat.
Jump rope 10 times using "Hot Peppers."
Skip around cones set up.
Crab walk (hands first) between markers/cones.
Curl-ups
Jog around the area.
Push-ups
Stretching activities

DPESS page 324
Use music to motivate moving through obstacle course.

LESSON FOCUS (15–20 MINUTES)

Backhand Clear Shot
Demonstrate
Practice
Partner stands on same side of court and tosses shuttles to
   backhand side. Change roles after 4 shots. Repeat.

DPESS page 413
Direct students to pick up racquet and 2 shuttlecocks;
   then go to demonstration area.
Scattered formation
Shuttlecocks on floor between feet
Practice movement following demonstration.
Use elbow-to-elbow to create pairs.
Assign 2 pairs to each court.

Backhand Drop Shot
Demonstrate
Practice
Partner stands on same side of court and tosses shuttles to
   backhand side. Change roles after 4 shots. Repeat.

DPESS page 413
Same groups as in Clear Shot practice

Review Forehand Shots

Bring students together to review all shots.
Assign students to play and keep shuttlecock in play
   using all strokes practiced.

GAME (5 MINUTES)

Hoops and Plyometrics
Student rolls or carries the hoop while jogging.

DPESS page 309
On signal student drops hoop on floor.
Challenge student to move in and out of as many hoops
   as possible during given time period. Change
   challenges frequently.

EVALUATION/REVIEW AND CHEER

Ask questions of the day's lesson.
1. Where does the hitting point during the Backhand Shots?
2. Where should the shuttlecock land when using the Backhand Drop?
Cheer: 3, 2, 1. Badminton is really fun!

Badminton Lesson Plan 5

EQUIPMENT:

1 badminton racquet per student	CD/cassette player
2 shuttlecocks for student	Music CD/tape to direct fitness
1 clipboard and pencil per 3 students	1 Forehand Clear and 1 Serving Task Sheet per student

INSTRUCTIONAL ACTIVITIES	TEACHING HINTS

INTRODUCTORY ACTIVITY (2–3 MINUTES)

Running High Five's
Students use a locomotor movement (run, skip, slide, gallop) to move around. When whistle is blown, students run to a partner and jump in air and give each other a "high five" and then continue moving until whistle is blown again.

DPESS page 314
Scattered formation in area marked off by cones

Alternate locomotor movements.

FITNESS DEVELOPMENT (8–12 MINUTES)

Jump Rope
Students perform different styles of jump roping as instructed by teacher.
Forward in place and while traveling; backward in place and traveling; alternating feet/leg swings
Hot Peppers

DPESS pages 480–482
Scattered formation

Create a routine to music.

Stretching Exercises
Stretch entire body, particularly leg muscles worked.

DPESS pages 342–344

Strengthening Exercises
Focus on upper body development exercises.

DPESS pages 344–346

LESSON FOCUS (15–20 MINUTES)

Forehand Clear Shot and Serve Practice
Explain Reciprocal Task Sheet for Badminton Skills.

DPESS pages 412–413
Use Whistle Mixer to create groups of 3.
Identify a Doer, Tosser, and Observer in each group.
Assign students to courts.

Practice
Use Task Sheets.

GAME (5 MINUTES)

Circle Hook-On
1 student plays against 3 students with joined hands. Lone student tags a designated student in circle. The other 2 students maneuver to keep tagger away from designated student.

Use Whistle Mixer to create groups of 4.
Rotate roles as players are tagged.
Circle may move in any direction but must not release hands.

EVALUATION/REVIEW AND CHEER

Review main elements of shots practiced.
Cheer: 2, 4, 6, 8. The weekends are really great!

BADMINTON RECIPROCAL TASK SHEET: FOREHAND CLEAR SHOT AND SERVE

Doer's Name: _____

Tosser's Name: _____

Observer's Name: _____

Directions:	This task is performed in groups of three: Doer, tosser, and observer.
The tosser:	Throw a high, clear service to the doer.
The observer:	Read the tasks below to the doer. Analyze the doer's form comparing the performance to the criteria listed below. Offer feedback about what is done well and what needs to be corrected. Rotate roles after the doer hits 2 Forehand Clear Shots and 2 Serves.
The doer:	Perform the tasks read to you by the observer.

ROTATION: Doer   Tosser   Observer   Doer

Please note: Each person in your group needs a Task Sheet, 1 pencil, and 1 clipboard per group. If you hold the racket in your right hand, your right foot is dominant, vice versa.

TASKS	DATES									
(Record date of practice)										
A. Ready Position for Forehand Clear	Y	N	Y	N	Y	N	Y	N	Y	N	Feedback
1. Keep feet square.										
2. Keep toes straight.										
3. Feet are shoulder width apart.										
4. Knees are slightly bent.										
5. Weight on balls of feet.										
6. Hold racket in front of body.										
7. Hold racket with handshake grip.										
8. Keep your eyes on the shuttlecock.										
B. Foot Work for Forehand Clear										
1. Lead with dominant foot.										
2. Pivot on nondominant foot.										
3. Hit shuttlecock.										
4. Recover to ready position.										
5. Maintain balance.										
6. Transfer weight from nondominant foot to dominant foot.										
C. Serving										
1. Ready position: dominant foot is behind nondominant foot.										
2. Use forearm rotation and wrist action.										
3. Contact shuttlecock below the waist.										
D. Change Roles										
E. Repeat										

Badminton Lesson Plan 6

EQUIPMENT:

Continuity music CD/tape
CD/cassette player
1 individual jump rope per student

2 shuttlecocks per student
Badminton courts and nets
1 badminton racquet per student

INSTRUCTIONAL ACTIVITIES	TEACHING HINTS

INTRODUCTORY ACTIVITY (2–3 MINUTES)
DPESS page 310

Marking

Scattered formation

FITNESS DEVELOPMENT (8–12 MINUTES)
DPESS pages 349–350

Continuity Exercises

Jump Rope
Sit-ups (15)
Jump Rope
Push-ups (15)
Jump Rope
Double Crab Kick (20)
Side Leg Flex (12 ea. side)
Jump Rope
Reclining Partner Pull-up (10 times ea.)
Jump Rope
Curl-ups
Jump Rope
Reverse Curl-ups
Jump Rope
Stretch all body parts

Scattered formation

Alternate jumping rope and performing 2 count exercises. Rope jumping is done to prerecorded music (40 seconds) and exercise done on silence prerecorded to 30 seconds.

DPESS pages 342–344

LESSON FOCUS (15–20 MINUTES)
DPESS pages 412–413

Stations:

1. Forehand Net Drop
   Demonstrate aiming to hoops.
2. Backhand Net Drop
   Demonstrate aiming to hoops.
3. Underhand Long Serve
   Demonstrate aiming to hoops set on court.
4. Forehand Clear Shot
   Demonstrate aiming to hoops set in backcourt.
5. Backhand Clear Shot
   Demonstrate aiming at hoops set in backcourt.
6. Forehand Clear, Smash Return
   Demonstrate skill.
7. Rally shuttlecock using all strokes.

Hit over net aiming for hula hoops placed across court, near net.
Move students from station to station as you demonstrate.
Can repeat stations on courts if desired.
Following all demonstrations, use "Toe-to-Toe" to make partners.
1 partner gets equipment.
Assign other partner to court.
Partners go to court to practice.
Each student hits 4 shots and then changes roles.
Signal when to rotate.

GAME (5 MINUTES)

Fetch Relay

DPESS page 406

Squads line up and place 1 member at the other end of the playing area, 10 to 20 yards away. This person runs back to the squad and fetches the next person. The person who has just been fetched in turn runs back and fetches the next person. The pattern continues until all members have been fetched to the opposite end of the playing area.

Use Whistle Mixer to create groups of 4–5.

Create lines/squad formation with each group.

Identify first player to go to opposite end of playing area.

EVALUATION/REVIEW AND CHEER

Discuss skills necessary for accuracy.
Cheer: 2, 4, 6, 8. What do we appreciate? Drop shot!

Badminton Lesson Plan 7

EQUIPMENT:

1 badminton racquet per person	Rules handout
2 shuttlecocks per person	Music tape/ CD and player

INSTRUCTIONAL ACTIVITIES	TEACHING HINTS

INTRODUCTORY ACTIVITY (2–3 MINUTES)

Move and Stretch

Students run within set perimeter and perform stretches upon designated signal. Use flash cards to signal stretches.

Both Arms Up: stretch high

Touch Toes

Hamstring Stretch: Right leg forward, left back with heel on ground. Hold 30 seconds and switch.

Standing Hip Bend: Both sides. Hold 20 seconds each side.

Wishbone Stretch: Hands clasped behind back and lean forward.

DPESS pages 308–309
Scattered formation

FITNESS DEVELOPMENT (8–12 MINUTES)

Continuous Movement Activities:

Interval Training

Brisk Walk; Rope Jumping; Brisk Walking; Jog in Place; Brisk Walking; Jump Rope in Place; Brisk Walk

Hot Peppers Rope Jumping; Slow Jog; Jump Rope Quickly; Brisk Walking; Jog

DPESS page 347
Scattered formation
Object is to monitor heart rate, first warming up to 120–140 beats per minute music. Then strenuous activity is alternated with rest interval; 45 seconds for strenuous activity followed by 30 seconds rest period. Heart rate is taken before and after rest period.

Strength Exercises

Curl-ups; Push-ups; Reverse Push-ups

DPESS pages 344–346

Stretching

Lower Leg

Bear Hug

Hurdler's Stretch

Sitting Side Stretch

Back Bender

Stretch Arms Up Going Up on Toes

DPESS pages 342–344

LESSON FOCUS (15–20 MINUTES)

Explain badminton rules and strategies.

DPESS pages 412–413
Distribute rules handout.

Review skills by demonstration.

Doubles Drop

Game played between the net and short service line. Keep track of the number of rallies and increase the number of hits.

DPESS page 416

Use Whistle Mixer to create groups of 4.

Assign to courts to play Lead-Up games using rules.

Drive Rally

DPESS page 416

```
      X   X

o---------------------o

      O   O
```

Played with 4 players; drive crosscourt and down the alley; if shot is too high, smash return it.

GAME (5 MINUTES)

Mixed Doubles Games

DPESS pages 414–415
Using Whistle Mixer, create groups of 4.
Follow rules while playing.

EVALUATION/REVIEW AND CHEER

Review and discuss rules and strategies.

Cheer: 2, 4, 6, 8. Badminton is really great!

BADMINTON RULES HANDOUT

Games and Match: Eleven points make a game in women's singles. All doubles and men's singles games are 15 points. A match constitutes two games out of three. As soon as a side wins two games, the match is over. The winner of the previous game serves the next game. Players change courts after the first and second games. In the third game, players change after 8 points in a 15-point game and after 6 points in an 11-point game.

Scoring: Only the serving side scores and continues to do so until an error is committed.

Setting: If the score becomes tied, the player or side first reaching the tied score may extend the game. In a 15-point game, the set may occur at 13-13 (setting to 5 points) or 14-14 (setting to 3 points). In an 11-point game, the score may be set at 10-10 (setting to 2 points) or 9-9 (setting to 3 points). A set game continues, but the score called is now 0-0, or "Love all." The first player or side to reach set score wins. If a side chooses not to set, the regular game is completed.

Singles Play: The first serve is taken from the right service court and received cross court (diagonally) in the opponent's right service court. All serves on 0 or an even score are served and received in the right-hand court. All serves on an odd score are served and received in the left service court.

Doubles Play: In the first inning, the first service is one hand only. In all other innings, the serving team gets to use two hands. At the beginning of each inning, the player in the right court serves first. Partners rotate only after winning a point.

     Even and odd scores are served from the same court as in singles play. If a player serves out of turn or from the incorrect service court and wins the rally, a let will be called. The let must be claimed by the receiving team before the next serve.

     If a player standing in the incorrect court takes the serve and wins the rally, it will be a let, provided the let is claimed before the next serve. If either of the above cases occurs and the side at fault loses the rally, the mistake stands, and the players' positions are not corrected for the rest of the game.

Faults: A fault committed by the serving side (in-side) results in a side out, while a fault committed by the receiving side (out-side) results in a point for the server. A fault occurs in any of the following situations.
1. During the serve, the shuttlecock is contacted above the server's waist, or the racquet head is held above the hand.
2. During the serve, the shuttlecock does not fall within the boundaries of the diagonal service court.
3. During the serve, some part of both feet of the server and receiver do not remain in contact with the court, inside the boundary lines, until the shuttlecock leaves the racquet of the server. Feet on the boundary lines are considered out-of-bounds.

Badminton Lesson Plan 8

EQUIPMENT:

1 badminton racquet per student
2 shuttlecocks per student
CD/cassette player
Individual jump ropes for fitness
4 individual mats for fitness

Music for fitness circuit
Challenge Course station instructions
4 wands for challenge course
Cones
Balance bench

INSTRUCTIONAL ACTIVITIES	TEACHING HINTS

INTRODUCTORY ACTIVITY (2–3 MINUTES)

Fastest Tag
Object is to tag other players without being tagged. Players that get tagged must sit where they are and wait for 10 seconds. They can rejoin game. If two people tag each other at the same time both must sit down.

DPESS page 312
Scattered formation

Every player is a tagger.

FITNESS DEVELOPMENT (8–12 MINUTES)

Challenge Course Circuit
Set up 3–4 parallel (side-by-side) courses in one-half of the area.
Course 1. Crouch jumps; pulls, or scooter movements; or balance down a bench; agility hop through two hoops on floor. Skip, slide, or jog to a cone.
Course 2. Weave in and out of four wands held upright by cones. Crab walk between two cones: lead with feet once, hands once. Gallop to a cone.
Course 3. Do a tumbling activity length of mat; agility run through hoops; leap frog over partner alternating roles between cones.
Course 4. Curl-ups and push-ups on a mat. Sitting stretches. Jump rope in place.

DPESS page 351

Movement should be continuous.

Arrange three or four courses with a group at each course. Students perform the challenges from start to finish and jog back to repeat the course. On signal, groups move to a new course.

Rotate groups to each course after a specified time. Music can be used for motivation and to signal changes.

LESSON FOCUS (15–20 MINUTES)

Play Doubles Badminton
Review Doubles rules and strategy.
Rotate positions on court after each point.

DPESS pages 414–415
Use Whistle Mixer to make groups of 4.
Assign to courts.
Mix-up players on teams after each game.

GAME (5 MINUTES)

Snowball Relay
This relay is similar to the fetch relay, except that after 1 person has been fetched, both players run back and pick up another player. The pattern continues until the majority of squad members are running back and forth, picking up the remaining members. This relay can be exhausting for the first few people in line.

DPESS page 406
Use Whistle Mixer to create line/squads of 5–6.

Place lines at one end of area with one person opposite line at other end of area.

EVALUATION/REVIEW AND CHEER

Ask how games went and if there were any rule questions needing clarification.
Cheer: Badminton, Cooooo-ol!

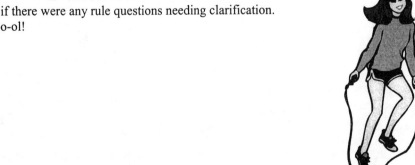

Badminton Lesson Plan 9

EQUIPMENT:

Task Sheets, 1 per student: Forehand/Backhand; Smash
1 badminton racquet per student
2 shuttlecocks per student
1 ball per 4 students for game

Fitness station instructions
Mats
8 cones

INSTRUCTIONAL ACTIVITIES	TEACHING HINTS

INTRODUCTORY ACTIVITY (2–3 MINUTES)

Vanishing Bean Bags

Spread bean bags throughout the area to allow 1 per student. Students move around the area until a signal is given. On the signal, they find a bean bag and sit on each. Each round, direct a new locomotor movement task and take away a bean bag.

DPESS page 309
Scattered formation

FITNESS DEVELOPMENT (8–12 MINUTES)

Four Corners

Outline a large rectangle with 4 cones. Place signs with tasks on both sides of the cones. Students move around the outside of the rectangle and change their movement pattern as they approach a corner sign.
The following movement tasks are suggested:
1. Jogging
2. Skipping/Jumping/Hopping
3. Sliding/Galloping
4. Abdominal strengthening exercises
5. Upper body strengthening exercises
6. Side leg work
7. Full body stretches

DPESS pages 347–348
Use Whistle Mixer to create 4 equal groups.

Assign each group a corner to begin at.

LESSON FOCUS (15–20 MINUTES)

3 Stations:
1. Underhand, Forehand, and Backhand Shot
2. Forehand Smash to Target Area
3. Singles Badminton

DPESS pages 413–414
Review skills.
Explain Task Sheets.
Explain stations.
Review Singles rules.
Using a management game, divide the class into 3 groups.
Assign each group to a station.
Describe rotation procedures.
Distribute equipment and Task Sheets.

This lesson focus may take two class periods to complete.

GAME (5 MINUTES)

Over and Under Ball Relay

Distribute 1 ball per group.

DPESS page 405
Use Whistle Mixer to create lines/squads of 5–6.
Assign spaces for lines leaving room between lines.

EVALUATION/REVIEW AND CHEER

Discuss singles rules and any questions that may have arisen.
Review elements of skills taught in class today.
Cheer: P.E. is great for me!

RECIPROCAL TASK SHEET: UNDERHAND SHOT–FOREHAND

Name of Doer: _____

Directions: You will work with two partners on this Task Sheet. The roles are:
Doer: Using the Forehand hit the shuttle 6 times in a row between the two lines on the wall.
Score Keeper: Count how many times the shuttle lands in the target area. Report score to recorder.
Recorder: Observe doer and record elements performed.

(Record date of practice)	DATES									
	Y	N	Y	N	Y	N	Y	N	Y	N
1. Stand 6' from the wall. Drop the shuttle and hit it underhand to the target area.										
2. Shuttlecock held at chest height.										
3. Shuttle contacted below waist level.										
4. Racquet head below wrist level.										
5. Wrist cocked throughout the stroke.										
6. Repeat until hit wall 6 times.										
7. Accuracy: Hit in target area.										
8. Change roles: Doer Recorder Scorekeeper Doer										

RECIPROCAL TASK SHEET: UNDERHAND SHOT–BACKHAND

Name of Doer: _____

Directions: You will work with two partners on this Task Sheet. The roles are:
Doer: Using the Backhand hit the shuttle 6 times in a row between the 2 lines on the wall.
Score Keeper: Count how many times the shuttle lands in the target area. Report score to recorder.
Recorder: Observe doer and record elements performed.

(Record date of practice)	Dates									
	Y	N	Y	N	Y	N	Y	N	Y	N
1. Stand 6' from the wall. Drop the shuttle and hit it underhand to the target area.										
2. Shuttlecock held at chest height.										
3. Shuttle contacted below waist level.										
4. Racquet head below wrist level.										
5. Wrist cocked throughout the stroke.										
6. Repeat until hit wall 6 times.										
7. Accuracy: Hit in target area.										
8. Change roles: Doer Recorder Scorekeeper Doer										

RECIPROCAL TASK SHEET: FOREHAND SMASH TO TARGET

Name of Doer: _____

Directions: You will work with two other people on this Task Sheet. One will be the Doer, one the Recorder/Observer, and the third the Tosser/Hitter.

Tosser/Hitter: Hit 4 high serves to your partner
Doer: Stand between the centerline and the short service line. Smash the serves into your partner's court. Try and call the location you are aiming towards.
Observer: Check the doer for the elements listed below.
Rotation: Doer   Tosser   Observer   Doer

(Record date of practice)	DATES							
	Yes	No	Yes	No	Yes	No	Yes	No
1. Shuttle hit with racquet face square to shuttle's flight.								
2. Shuttle contacted 12–18" in front of body.								
3. Arm straight at impact.								
4. Continual racquet acceleration throughout swing, impact and follow through.								
5. Did the smash land where doer called it?								
6. Change roles after 4 tries.								

Badminton Lesson Plan 10

EQUIPMENT:

Task Sheets, 1 per student; Forehand/Backhand; Smash
1 badminton racquet per student
2 shuttlecocks per student
Obstacle course instructions

CD/cassette player
Music CD/tape for fitness
Mats, cones, benches

INSTRUCTIONAL ACTIVITIES	TEACHING HINTS

INTRODUCTORY ACTIVITY (2–3 MINUTES)

Zipper

Each student bends over, reaches between the legs with the left hand, and grasps the right hand of the person to the rear. This continues on down the line until all hands are grasped. On signal, the last person in line lies down, the next person backs over the last person and lies down, and so forth until the last person lies down, and then immediately stands and reverses the procedure. The first team to zip and unzip the zipper is declared the winner.

DPESS page 407

Divide class into lines of 7–9.

Players make a single-file line.

Space lines out in area.

FITNESS DEVELOPMENT (8–12 MINUTES)

Challenge Course

DPESS page 351

See Lesson 1 of this unit for details.
Use music to motivate moving through obstacle course.
Create a CD/tape with 30 seconds of music and 5 seconds of no sound to indicate a change of stations.
Or, just use music and allow students to progress around the Challenge Course at their own pace.

LESSON FOCUS (15–20 MINUTES)

Continue with stations, wherever students left off after previous lesson.

GAME (5 MINUTES)

Frozen Tag

When tagged, the person must freeze with the feet in straddle position. To be able to resume play, 3 people must move under and through a "frozen" person's legs.

DPESS page 312

Scattered formation
Select several "its" to start the tag game.

EVALUATION/REVIEW AND CHEER

Cheer: Badminton, F–U–N !

Badminton Lesson Plan 11

EQUIPMENT:

Parachute
1 Partner Tug-of-War rope per 2 students
Round Robin Tournament Chart

1 badminton racquet per student
2 shuttlecocks per student

INSTRUCTIONAL ACTIVITIES	TEACHING HINTS

INTRODUCTORY ACTIVITY (2–3 MINUTES)

Pentabridge Hustle

DPESS page 310
Use Whistle Mixer to create groups of 4–5.
Students move continuously under bridges made by group.

FITNESS DEVELOPMENT (8–12 MINUTES)

Parachute Rhythmic Aerobic Activity
Skip both directions.
Slide both directions.
Run both directions.
Jump to center.
Hop backward.
Lift parachute overhead.
Lower parachute to toes.
Repeat above.
Run CW with chute overhead.
Make a dome.
Strengthening and stretching exercises.

DPESS page 352

Direct locomotor movements while holding parachute.

Use music to motivate.

Alternate locomotor movements with seated strength and stretching exercises.

LESSON FOCUS (15–20 MINUTES)

Round Robin Badminton Tournament

Explain tournament.
Explain how chart is used.
Students not interested in the tournament can play singles or doubles.

GAME (5 MINUTES)

Partner Tug-of-War

DPESS page 401
Use management game to create pairs.
1 rope per 2 students

EVALUATION/REVIEW AND CHEER

Discuss tournament play. Review rules.
Cheer: 2, 4, 6, 8. Badminton is really great!

Badminton Lesson Plan 12

EQUIPMENT:

Music for fitness
CD/cassette player
1 badminton racquet per student

2 shuttlecocks per court
Round Robin Tournament Chart
3 juggling scarves per person

INSTRUCTIONAL ACTIVITIES	TEACHING HINTS

INTRODUCTORY ACTIVITY (2–3 MINUTES)

Juggling Scarves
Scarves are held by the fingertips near the center. To throw the scarf, it should be lifted and pulled into the air above eye level. Scarves are caught by clawing, a downward motion of the hand, and grabbing the scarf from above as it is falling.

DPESS page 392
Scattered formation
Place scarves along perimeter of teaching area.
Cascading Activities: One scarf; two scarves; three scarves

INSTRUCTIONAL ACTIVITIES	TEACHING HINTS

FITNESS DEVELOPMENT (8–12 MINUTES)

Station Fitness
Partner resistance exercises
Jump Rope
Crab walks and Body Twist
Curl-ups, push-ups, reverse curl-ups
Stretching
Treadmills
Jumping Jacks
Running in Place

DPESS pages 342–347 and 350–351

Use management game to divide class into 8 groups.
Assign each group to a station to begin.
Explain stations.
Explain rotation.
Use music to motivate and musical silences to signal station rotation.

LESSON FOCUS (15–20 MINUTES)

Continue Round Robin Tournament.

GAME (5 MINUTES)

Continue Tournament or Play Back-to-Back Take Down

DPESS page 401

EVALUATION/REVIEW AND CHEER

Cheer: Badminton... FUN!

Badminton Lesson Plan 13

EQUIPMENT:

Continuity Exercise Music CD/tape
CD/cassette player
1 written exam per student

1 racquet per student
2 shuttlecocks per court

INSTRUCTIONAL ACTIVITIES	TEACHING HINTS

INTRODUCTORY ACTIVITY (2–3 MINUTES)

Move and Perform a Stretch

DPESS pages 308–309
See Lesson Plan 7, this unit: Introductory Activity

FITNESS DEVELOPMENT (8–12 MINUTES)

Continuity Exercises

DPESS pages 349–350
See Lesson Plan 6, this unit: Fitness Development.

LESSON FOCUS (15–20 MINUTES)

Written Exam

GAME (5 MINUTES)

Play Badminton Singles or Doubles

Allow students to play or rally upon completion of written exam.

EVALUATION/REVIEW AND CHEER

Discuss questions from exam.
Cheer: 3, 2, 1, Badminton is fun!

BADMINTON KNOWLEDGE TEST

NAME: _____

Part I.   **True/False.** If the statement is true mark it with a +. If it is false mark it with a 0.

_____ 1.   A women's singles game consists of 11 points. A doubles game is 15 points.

_____ 2.   After the serve is made, either side can score a point.

_____ 3.   The backhand grip is different from the grip for the forehand.

_____ 4.   The server serves 5 times and alternating courts for each serve.

_____ 5.   In men's singles, if the score is 14 all, it may be set at 3 points.

_____ 6.   In doubles, after the serve is returned, the partner can cross the mid-court line.

_____ 7.   In doubles play, the up and back formation is weak in covering side line shots.

_____ 8.   In singles, the server will serve from the right-hand court when his score is an odd number.

_____ 9.   In singles play, the long service line is not used.

_____10.   If the shuttlecock is struck above the waist on the serve, it is a fault.

Part II.   **Best Answer.** Select the best answer for the statement.

_____11.   If the serving side touches the net during play it is
a.   a point for the server   c. a let
b.   a side out   d. played over

_____12.   In general, when playing a backhand stroke, the best position is to have the
a.   left side toward the net   c. body face the net
b.   right side toward the net   d. none of the above

_____13.   In doubles, the most effective defensive formation is the
a.   up-and-back position   c. combination
b.   rotation   d. side-by-side

_____14.   In doubles, the basic serve is the
a.   high clear   c. drive
b.   smash   d. low and short

_____15.   The around-the-head stroke is used as a
a.   substitute for all backhand strokes   c. in place of a high backhand stroke
b.   drop shots   d. a recovery stroke

_____16.   If the shuttlecock flight is high and it falls sharply near the baseline it is a
a.   high clear   c. drop
b.   smash   d. drive

_____17.   In doubles, the combination formation should be changed from an up-and-back to a side-by-side formation if the shuttlecock is returned by a
a.   clear   c. drop
b.   smash   d. drive

_____18.   The best stroke for returning a shuttlecock, if you are in doubt, during singles play is the
a.   drive   c. lob
b.   drop   d. smash

_____19.   In doubles, when the serving team is playing in the up-and-back formation, the short serve is returned
a.   with a drive cross the court   c. clear to the backhand corner of the court
b.   down the side boundary line   d. with a drop to the server's backhand

_____20.   If the receiver steps out of his receiving court after the shuttle is served and before it crosses the net, it is
a.   a point for the server   c. a side out
b.   a let   d. served over

Part III.   **Matching**. Match the statements in Column B to the terms in Column A.

Column A Strokes		Column B Bird Flight
_____ 21.	Smash	a. Upward and back to the baseline.
_____ 22,	Hairpin	b. Flat flight and very near to the top of the net.
_____ 23.	Drop shot	c. Straight up and straight down over the net.
_____ 24.	High clear	d. Falls close to the net between the net and short service line.
_____ 25.	Drive	e. Sharply downward.

BADMINTON KNOWLEDGE TEST ANSWERS

I.   True-False

1.	+	6.	+
2.	0	7.	+
3.	+	8.	0
4.	0	9.	+
5.	+	10.	+

II.   Best Answer

11.	b	16.	a
12.	b	17.	a
13.	d	18.	c
14.	d	19.	b
15.	c	20.	a

III.   Matching

21.	e
22.	c
23.	d
24.	a
25.	b

Badminton Lesson Plan 14

EQUIPMENT:

1 Skills Test Score Sheet per student
1 badminton racquet per student
1 clipboard and pencil per 3 students

5 shuttlecocks per group
Music for fitness (optional)
CD/cassette player for fitness (optional)

INSTRUCTIONAL ACTIVITIES	TEACHING HINTS

INTRODUCTORY ACTIVITY (2–3 MINUTES)

Eliminate today to allow extra time for skill tests.

FITNESS DEVELOPMENT (8–12 MINUTES)

Parachute Rhythmic Aerobic Activities

DPESS page 352
See Lesson Plan 11, this unit, for details.

LESSON FOCUS (15–20 MINUTES)

Partner Skills Test

Use Whistle Mixer and create groups of 3.
Explain Skills Test Task Sheets.

GAME (5 MINUTES)

Badminton
Play Singles or Doubles

Allow students to play upon completion of exam.

EVALUATION/REVIEW AND CHEER

Discuss element of skills test.
Students create cheer.

Badminton Lesson Plan 15

EQUIPMENT:

Four Corners Fitness Instructions
Cones
Mats
Music for fitness

CD/cassette player
1 badminton racquet per student
2 shuttlecocks per court
Tournament Chart

INSTRUCTIONAL ACTIVITIES	TEACHING HINTS

INTRODUCTORY ACTIVITY (2–3 MINUTES)

Balance Tag

DPESS page 312
See Lesson Plan 4, this unit: Introductory Activity.

FITNESS DEVELOPMENT (8–12 MINUTES)

Four Corners

DPESS pages 347–348
See Lesson Plan 9, this unit: Fitness Development.

LESSON FOCUS AND GAME (15–25 MINUTES)

Round Robin Badminton Tournament

EVALUATION/REVIEW AND CHEER

Review unit. Introduce next unit.
Cheer: The Weekend's here. Yeah! -Or-
    Badminton was fun!

BADMINTON SKILLS TEST

Name of Doer, Partner,
Recorder_____

Directions:	Work with two other people on this self-test: **Doer:** Complete elements on exam; **Partner:** Toss/Hit to doer as listed; **Recorder:** Read instructions, observe doer, and record results.
Equipment:	Clipboard and pencil; 2 badminton racquets per group; 1 Skill Test per person; 5 shuttlecocks per group

Serves	Score Out of 5
1. Standing behind the short service line on the right side of the court, serve the shuttlecock crosscourt over the net 5 times.	
2. Standing behind the short service line on the left side of the court, serve the shuttlecock crosscourt over the net 5 times.	
3. Standing behind the short service line, next to the centerline in the right court, serve the shuttlecock crosscourt over the net, between the net and a rope 1 foot above it. Repeat 5 times in a row from the right.	
4. Standing behind the short service line, next to the centerline in the right court, serve the shuttlecock crosscourt over the net, between the net and a rope 1 foot above it. Repeat 5 times in a row from the left.	
Underhand Clears: Forehand and Backhand	
5. Standing between the net and the short service line, drop the shuttlecock and underhand clear on the forehand side, 5 clears in a row to the back 4 feet of the court marked for doubles.	
6. Standing between the net and the short service line, drop the shuttlecock and underhand clear on the backhand side, 5 clears in a row to the back 4 feet of the court marked for doubles.	
7. Standing 6 feet behind the short service line, underhand clear on the forehand side, 5 clears in a row to the back 4 feet of the doubles court.	
8. Standing 6 feet behind the short service line, underhand clear on the backhand side, 5 clears in a row to the back 4 feet of the doubles court.	
Drops	
9. Standing just behind the short service line on the right court, underhand drop on the forehand side a tossed shuttlecock from your partner. Return 5 drops in a row from the forehand side.	
10. Standing just behind the short service line on the right court, underhand drop on the forehand side a tossed shuttlecock from your partner. Return 5 drops in a row from the backhand side.	
Long Serves	
11. Standing to the right of and next to the centerline, 12 feet from the net, serve 5 long serves in a row to the opposite court.	
12. Standing to the left of and next to the centerline, 12 feet from the net, serve 5 long serves in a row to the opposite court.	
Overhead Clears: Forehand	
13. Standing within 12 feet of the net, a partner underhand clears the shuttlecock. Return 5 shuttlecocks in a row with an overhead forehand clear into the doubles court, at least 10 feet from the net.	
14. Standing within 12 feet of the net, a partner underhand clears the shuttlecock. Return 5 shuttlecocks in a row with an overhead forehand clear into the doubles court, to the back 4 feet of the doubles court.	
15. A server sets up short, high shots 6 to 8 inches from the net. Standing 6 feet from the short service line, smash 5 in a row within 15 feet of the net.	
16. Standing within the last 5 feet of the backcourt, overhead drop opponent's clears to you. Drop 5 shuttlecocks to the right courtside between the net and the short service line.	
17. Standing within the last 5 feet of the backcourt, overhead drop opponent's clears to you. Drop 5 shuttlecocks to the left courtside between the net and the short service line.	
18. Stand on the centerline, 6 feet from the short service line. Partner set up low, flat serves down the forehand alley. Hit 5 forehand drives in a row down that alley.	
19. Stand on the centerline, 6 feet from the short service line. Partner set up low, flat serves down the forehand alley. Hit 5 forehand drives in a row down that alley.	
20. Standing within 12 feet of the net, from a high clear set-up by a partner, backhand 5 overhead clears in a row to the back 6 feet of the doubles court.	

Basketball

OBJECTIVES:

The student will:
1. Participate in the Over, Under, and Around #1, and Hula Hoop Circle Pass activities demonstrating cooperation and agility.
2. Execute scarf juggling skills juggling 2 or 3 scarves using skills demonstrated in class.
3. Demonstrate cooperation developing partner stunts during the Introductory Activity.
4. Demonstrate agility and cooperation during the Vanishing Bean Bags Activity.
5. Play Addition Tag demonstrating dodging and sprinting skills.
6. Participate in Blob Tag demonstrating cooperation with classmates, dodging, and starting and stopping skills.
7. Participate in partner mirroring activities demonstrating cooperation and creativity.
8. Improve cardiovascular and physical fitness levels during the Continuity Exercise Fitness Activities.
9. Execute a variety of fitness exercises and aerobic movements during the Rhythmic Parachute Activities.
10. Improve their fitness levels while participating in the Fitness Scavenger Hunt Activities as demonstrated by the instructor.
11. Complete the Fitness Challenge Course to improve all levels of fitness.
12. Jump rope to improve cardiovascular endurance.
13. Participate in Circuit Training to improve his overall fitness.
14. Participate in dribbling and passing drills using skills demonstrated by the instructor.
15. Execute defensive dribbling activities.
16. Demonstrate defensive footwork using techniques demonstrated by the instructor.
17. Perform the following footwork: jump stop pivot, v-cuts, inside turns, defensive slide with head up, and good balance.
18. Perform the Chest pass and the Overhead pass with accuracy and follow through.
19. Demonstrate lay-up shots from the center and each side of the basket 5 times.
20. Perform 5 jump shots 15 feet from the center and the sides of the court.
21. Demonstrate offensive basketball skills using form demonstrated in class by the instructor.
22. Perform dribbling skills during the Dribble Relay game.
23. Demonstrate an understanding of basketball rules strategy while playing basketball in class.
24. Participate in the Round Robin Tournament executing cooperation, teamwork, and basketball skills learned during the unit.
25. Execute basketball skills of dribbling, shooting, passing, offense, and defense as demonstrated throughout the unit during the skill testing.
26. Complete a written exam scoring 70 % or better.

BASKETBALL BLOCK PLAN
3-WEEK UNIT

Week #1	Monday	Tuesday	Wednesday	Thursday	Friday
Introductory Activity	Move and Change Direction	Juggling Scarves	Over, Under and Around #1	Parachute Activities	Run and Lead
Fitness	Rope Jumping	Aerobic Workout	Fitness Scavenger Hunt	Jog and Stretch	Continuity Exercises
Lesson focus	Ball Handling Dribbling	Dribbling Passing	Dribbling Passing	Shooting Rebounding Dribbling	Passing Shooting
Game	Triangle Plus One Tag	Spider Tag	Hula Hoop Pass	Wand Activities	Hoops and Plyometrics

Week #2	Monday	Tuesday	Wednesday	Thursday	Friday
Introductory Activity	Individual Stunts	Jog Around Obstacles	Vanishing Bean Bags	Pentabridge Hustle	Blob Tag
Fitness	Parachute Activities	Stretch and Strengthening Exercises	Continuity Exercises	Circuit Training	Fitness Scavenger Hunt
Lesson focus	Defensive Footwork and Skills	Stations: Lay-Ups; Free Throws; Dribbling; Guarding; Rebounding	Stations: Footwork; Dribbling; Passing; Shooting; Guarding	Offensive Skills Jump Stop Pivoting Dribbling and Stopping	Rules and Strategy Player Positions
Game	Horse	Individual Tug-of-War	Dribble Relay	Sideline Basketball	5 on 5 Half Court Basketball

Week #3	Monday	Tuesday	Wednesday	Thursday	Friday
Introductory Activity	Mirroring	Musical Hoops	Addition Tag	Eliminate, Allowing Time for Tournament	Move and Perform Stretch
Fitness	Challenge Course	Walk, Jog, Sprint	Aerobic Workout	Challenge Course	Walk, Jog, Sprint
Lesson focus	Play Basketball	Skill Testing	Written Exam	Round Robin Tournament	Round Robin Tournament (Cont.)
Game	Play Basketball	Dribble Relay	Play Basketball	Tournament (Cont.)	Tournament (Cont.)

Basketball Lesson Plan 1

EQUIPMENT:

Basketball courts	CD/cassette player
1 basketball per student	Rope jumping exercise music CD/tape
1 individual jump rope per student	

INSTRUCTIONAL ACTIVITIES	TEACHING HINTS

INTRODUCTORY ACTIVITY (2–3 MINUTES)

Move and Change Direction	DPESS page 308
Students run in any direction; change directions on signal	Scattered formation
	Reverse; 45 degrees; Left turns

FITNESS DEVELOPMENT (8–12 MINUTES)

Rope Jumping	DPESS pages 480–482.
Students jump rope until command given to change activities. Create a music CD/tape with 1minute of music, 30 seconds silence. Alternate jumping with exercise.	Push-ups; Bend and Stretch; Curl-ups; Reverse Curl-ups; Treadmill

LESSON FOCUS (15–20 MINUTES)

Drills to use ball comfortably in place	DPESS pages 418–423.
Ball around waist	Scattered formation
Ball around right, left knee	Demonstrate
Ball around right, left ankle	1 ball per student for practice
Figure 8 around legs both directions	
Ball between legs switching arm from front to back	
Walking and passing alternately under each front leg	Demonstrate
Dribbling	Practice length of court
In place; Walk; Jog; Stop and go	1 ball per student

GAME (5 MINUTES)

Triangle Plus 1 Tag	DPESS page 312
Person outside triangle tries to tag leader. Leader and tagger change places when tagged.	Create groups of 4 using management game. 3 make triangle formation holding hands. Select leader in group.

EVALUATION/REVIEW AND CHEER

Review elements of dribbling and ball handling.
Cheer: Yeah, basketball is here this year!

Basketball Lesson Plan 2

EQUIPMENT:

1 basketball per student	Aerobic workout music CD/tape
3 juggling scarves per student	CD/cassette player

INSTRUCTIONAL ACTIVITIES	TEACHING HINTS

INTRODUCTORY ACTIVITY (2–3 MINUTES)

Juggling Scarves	DPESS pages 392–394
Column juggling; Cascading	Scattered formation; 3 scarves per student

FITNESS DEVELOPMENT (8–12 MINUTES)

Aerobic Workout	DPESS pages 358–359
	See Lesson 7, Racquetball Unit for details

LESSON FOCUS (15–20 MINUTES)

Review Dribbling Skills	DPESS pages 418–423
Passing Skills	Scattered formation for reviewing dribbling.
Bounce pass; Chest pass; Overhead pass	Set up passing activities in lines or scattered formation

INSTRUCTIONAL ACTIVITIES	TEACHING HINTS

GAME (5 MINUTES)

Spider Tag
Pairs work together to tag other pairs
When tagged, they become "its."

DPESS page 312
Using a management game, create partners
Select one pair to be the "its."

EVALUATION/REVIEW AND CHEER

Discuss important elements of passing skills.
Have students create the cheer.

Basketball Lesson Plan 3

EQUIPMENT:

1 basketball per student
1 hula hoop per 5 students

Fitness Scavenger Hunt Instruction Cards
Music and CD/cassette player for fitness activities

INSTRUCTIONAL ACTIVITIES	TEACHING HINTS

INTRODUCTORY ACTIVITY (2–3 MINUTES)

Over, Under, and Around #1

DPESS page 310
Using Toe-to-Toe, create groups of 2.

FITNESS DEVELOPMENT (8–12 MINUTES)

Fitness Scavenger Hunt
See Golf, Lesson 7 for details

DPESS page 356

LESSON FOCUS (15–20 MINUTES)

Dribbling
Two hand V; One hand V
Dribbling with: Crab turn; Crab slide; V-Cut;
Reverse pivot
Reviewing Passing Skills

DPESS pages 418–423
Demonstrate each skill followed by practice in scattered
  formation.
Practice in formations.
Demonstrate each skill followed by practice.
Practice in scattered formation, then in set formations.

GAME (5 MINUTES)

Hula Hoop Circle Pass

DPESS page 314
See Golf Unit, Lesson 2 for details.
Use Whistle Mixer to make 4 groups of students.

EVALUATION/REVIEW AND CHEER

Review major elements of dribbling skills presented in class.
Cheer: 3, 6, 8, basketball is great!

Basketball Lesson Plan 4

EQUIPMENT:
1 basketball per student
1 large parachute
1 wand per student

INSTRUCTIONAL ACTIVITIES	TEACHING HINTS

INTRODUCTORY ACTIVITY (2–3 MINUTES)

Parachute Activities	DPESS page 351

FITNESS DEVELOPMENT (8–12 MINUTES)

Jog and Stretch	
Lower leg stretch (Stand facing a wall with feet shoulder width apart)	Scattered formation
Achilles tendon stretch; Bear hug stretch; Hurdlers stretch; Groin stretch, Ankle stretch; Standing hip bend;	Jog around gym several times, then stretch.
Elbow puller; Wishbone stretch; Push ups; Curl-ups; Reverse Curl-ups	

LESSON FOCUS (15–20 MINUTES)

Shooting	DPESS pages 418–423
Free Throws	Demonstrate each shot then practice first without ball and
Lay-ups; Jump Shots; Set Shot	then with one at courts.
Rebounding	Assign to baskets. Set up challenging drills for small
Dribbling challenge drills	groups of students.

GAME (5 MINUTES)

WAND ACTIVITIES	DPESS page 401
Wand Whirl	Scattered formation
Stand wand in front of body. Balance it with 1 finger. Release, turn, and catch the wand.	
Wand Kick over Begin same as Whirl, but leg kick over the wand before turning.	Work with a partner.
Wand Wrestle Goal: move the wand to a horizontal plane.	Wand is held in vertical position by opponent.

EVALUATION/REVIEW AND CHEER

Review main points presented in basketball shooting.
Cheer: We love basketball!

Basketball Lesson Plan 5

EQUIPMENT:

Basketball courts	CD/cassette player
1 basketball per student	Continuity Exercise Music CD/tape
1 individual jump rope per student	1 hoop per student

INSTRUCTIONAL ACTIVITIES	TEACHING HINTS

INTRODUCTORY ACTIVITY (2–3 MINUTES)

Run and Lead (Similar to File Running)	DPESS page 354
Students jog in formation. Last person sprints to front of line to become leader.	Line or circle formation

FITNESS DEVELOPMENT (8–12 MINUTES)

Continuity Exercises	DPESS page 349
See Badminton Unit, Lesson 3 for complete details.	Scattered formation

INSTRUCTIONAL ACTIVITIES	TEACHING HINTS

LESSON FOCUS (15–20 MINUTES)

Passing Skills Review
- Chest
- Overhead

DPESS pages 418–423
Create Task Sheets covering these passing skills.
Allow students to work together and check form on Task Sheets.

GAME (5 MINUTES)

Hoops and Plyometrics
Spread hoops around the area and give directions to move around using locomotor movements and freeze inside a hoop.

DPESS pages 309–310
Scattered formation

EVALUATION/REVIEW AND CHEER

Review elements of passing skills taught.
Cheer: 2, 4, 6, 8, Basketball is really great!

Basketball Lesson Plan 6

EQUIPMENT:

1 parachute
Music CD/tape for fitness activities

1 basketball per student
CD/cassette player

INSTRUCTIONAL ACTIVITIES	TEACHING HINTS

INTRODUCTORY ACTIVITY (2–3 MINUTES)

Individual Stunts
Leg dip; Behind Back Touch; Double Heel Click

DPESS page 398
Scattered formation
Explain stunts and student practices.

FITNESS DEVELOPMENT (8–12 MINUTES)

Rhythmic Parachute Activities
See Lesson 11, Badminton for details.

DPESS pages 351–352
Use a music CD/tape for added motivation and enthusiasm.

LESSON FOCUS (15–20 MINUTES)

Defensive Footwork
Jump stop pivots; V-Cuts; Defensive slides
One-on-One Defense
Defensive player keeps offensive player in front of her using defensive slides.

DPESS pages 418–423
Body position; good footwork; balanced pivot
Create pairs.
Student with ball is defensive player.

GAME (5 MINUTES)

Horse

DPESS page 421
Use a management game to create groups of 4.

EVALUATION/REVIEW AND CHEER

Review defensive skills taught during the class.
Cheer: Playing basketball is great!

Basketball Lesson Plan 7

EQUIPMENT:

1 basketball per student
16 cones

1 Tug-of-War rope per 2 students

INSTRUCTIONAL ACTIVITIES	TEACHING HINTS

INTRODUCTORY ACTIVITY (2–3 MINUTES)

Light Jog Around Cones

DPESS page 347
Allow students to "fall in" line behind a leader moving around cones.

FITNESS DEVELOPMENT (8–12 MINUTES)

Calf Stretch; Hamstring Side Stretch; Jump in place; Groin stretches; Jog, Sprint, Jog; Curl-ups; Push-ups; Reverse curl-ups

DPESS page 348
Scattered formation. Instructor leads activities.
Use music CD/tape for interest and fun.

LESSON FOCUS (15–20 MINUTES)

Station Work:
Lay-ups; One-on-One Rebounding; Dribbling Review; Free Throws

DPESS pages 418–423
Create stations.
Demonstrate movements of each station.
Assign groups of 4–5 to each station.

GAME (5 MINUTES)

Partner Tug-of-War Activities
• **Different Positions**
• **Pick-up and Pull**

DPESS page 401
Create partners using Back-to-Back with someone your own size.
1 rope per 2 students

EVALUATION/REVIEW AND CHEER

Ask questions regarding skills used in lay-ups and free throws.
Students create cheer.

Basketball Lesson Plan 8

EQUIPMENT:

1 basketball per student
Continuity Exercise Music CD/tape

Station Instruction Charts
Cones to mark stations

INSTRUCTIONAL ACTIVITIES	TEACHING HINTS

INTRODUCTORY ACTIVITY (2–3 MINUTES)

Vanishing Bean Bags

DPESS page 309
See Lesson 3, Golf Unit for complete details.

FITNESS DEVELOPMENT (8–12 MINUTES)

Continuity Exercises
These exercises are a type of interval training.

DPESS pages 348–349
See Lesson Plan 3, Golf Unit for complete details.

LESSON FOCUS (15–20 MINUTES)

5 Station Practice:
Write instructions for each station on Station Cards.
Demonstrate activities for each station.
• **Footwork Review Activities**
• **Dribbling Review Activities**
• **Passing Review Activities**
• **Shooting Review Activities**
• **Guarding Activities Introductory Activity:**
Demonstrate skills as each group comes to the station.

DPESS pages 418–423
Use Whistle Mixer to create even groups to distribute to each station.
Assign groups to begin at each station.
Explain rotation procedures.

INSTRUCTIONAL ACTIVITIES	TEACHING HINTS

GAME (5 MINUTES)

Dribble Relay	DPESS page 421
	Create even groups of 5–6.
Students dribble around cone and return to line.	
When all have dribbled, group sits down.	Assign to starting position.
Can vary dribbling challenge each round.	

EVALUATION/REVIEW AND CHEER

Review elements of each station. Discuss areas of difficulty or concern.
Cheer: 2, 4, 6, 8, basketball is great!

Basketball Lesson Plan 9

EQUIPMENT:
1 basketball per student
CD/cassette player and music CD/tape for Circuit Training

INSTRUCTIONAL ACTIVITIES	TEACHING HINTS

INTRODUCTORY ACTIVITY (2–3 MINUTES)

Pentabridge Hustle	DPESS page 310
Students move continuously under bridges created by group members.	Using Whistle Mixer, create groups of 5. 4 members of group make bridges that 1 must go under. Movement flows continuously.

FITNESS DEVELOPMENT (8–12 MINUTES)

Circuit Training	DPESS page 357
Create 9–10 different fitness circuit stations.	Distribute students evenly throughout circuit. Explain rotation. Give a locomotor movement to execute between stations.
Use a music CD/tape for interest and motivation.	

LESSON FOCUS (15–20 MINUTES)

Offensive Footwork and Skills	DPESS pages 418–423
Demonstration followed by practice in scattered formation.	Scattered formation
Jump Stop	Create groups of 4 for line drills.
• Jump stop and hold	Assign group a line placement on courts. Two-foot jump, stop, jog forward, take short jump, and land on both feet. Hands up ready to receive ball. Call out ball when landed.
Pivoting	Pivot and jog forward, jump stop, pivot backward (180 degrees), then pivot forward on same foot. Continue down practice area.
• Jump stop, front pivot each foot	
• Jump stop, back pivot each foot	
Dribbling and Stopping	Dribble forward until hear whistle, stop. Dribble again on signal.

GAME (5 MINUTES)

Sideline Basketball	DPESS page 421
	Divide class into 2 teams per court. Select 4 players for center court work. Sideline players pass to court players. Game continues until a team scores a point.

EVALUATION/REVIEW AND CHEER

Review elements of skills taught.
Let students create the cheer for the day.

Basketball Lesson Plan 10

EQUIPMENT:

Fitness Scavenger Hunt Cards

Basketball rules information handout

1 basketball per student

CD/cassette player and music CD/tape for exercising

INSTRUCTIONAL ACTIVITIES	TEACHING HINTS

INTRODUCTORY ACTIVITY (2–3 MINUTES)

Blob Tag

Person at end of line tags and holds hands of those tagged.

DPESS page 309

Using a management game, create pairs. Select several "its." "its" hold hands.

FITNESS DEVELOPMENT (8–12 MINUTES)

Fitness Scavenger Hunt

Have cards made directing groups to a particular fitness activity area. Each area has fitness activity/exercise instructions.

DPESS page 356

Create groups of 4–5 using Whistle Mixer. Direct each group to begin at a particular area for the Scavenger Hunt.

LESSON FOCUS (10–15 MINUTES)

Basketball Rules, Strategy, Player Positions

Have handouts ready for homework reading assignment.

DPESS pages 418–423

Explain and demonstrate rules, player positions, and game strategy. Have students set up situations you direct and practice player positions and rules.

GAME (10 MINUTES)

Play 5 on 5 Half Court Basketball

Use regulation rules.

DPESS page 423

Using Whistle Mixer, create groups of 5. Assign to courts for half-court games.

EVALUATION/REVIEW AND CHEER

Discuss rules and situations needing clarification. Explain upcoming Round Robin Tournament.

Cheer: 4, 3, 2, 1, basketball is really fun!!!

Basketball Lesson Plan 11

EQUIPMENT:

Obstacle course instruction sheets

Mats

Cones

Music CD/tape and CD/cassette player

1 basketball per person

INSTRUCTIONAL ACTIVITIES	TEACHING HINTS

INTRODUCTORY ACTIVITY (2–3 MINUTES)

Mirror Drill in Place

DPESS page 313

Students work with a partner.

FITNESS DEVELOPMENT (8–12 MINUTES)

Challenge Course

DPESS page 351

See Badminton Unit, Lesson 1 for details.

LESSON FOCUS AND GAME COMBINED (20–25 MINUTES)

Play 5 on 5 Half Court or Full Court Basketball

Use regulation rules. Groups that are ready can play full court basketball.

DPESS pages 421–422

Using Whistle Mixer, create groups of 5. Assign to courts for half-court games.

EVALUATION/REVIEW AND CHEER

Review rules of basketball. Ask questions regarding rules application observed during game.

Cheer: 1, 2, 3, we all agree on PE!

Basketball Lesson Plan 12

EQUIPMENT:

Music CD/tape

CD/cassette player

1 clipboard and pencil per 2 students

1 basketball per student

1 Skill Test Sheet per student

INSTRUCTIONAL ACTIVITIES	TEACHING HINTS

INTRODUCTORY ACTIVITY (2–3 MINUTES)

Musical Hoops (Variation of Hoops on the Ground)

Create a music CD/tape with 10-second pauses.

Have 1 less hoop than number of students

Call out a different locomotor movement after each pose.

DPESS page 310

When music stops, students must be in a hoop. Call out positions they must stop/pose in during each break of the music.

FITNESS DEVELOPMENT (8–12 MINUTES)

Walk, Jog, Sprint

DPESS page 354

See Golf Unit, Lesson 12 for details.

LESSON FOCUS (15–20 MINUTES)

Skill Testing

DPESS page 422

Use "Core Objectives" to create a skill exam.

Students can work in partners and test each other.

GAME (5 MINUTES)

Dribble Relay

See Lesson 8 for details.

EVALUATION/REVIEW AND CHEER

Review material for written exam.

Cheer: 1, 2, 3, 4, Give me more of basketball!

Basketball Lesson Plan 13

EQUIPMENT:

CD/cassette player

Aerobic Exercise Music CD/tape

1 written exam per student

1 basketball per student

INSTRUCTIONAL ACTIVITIES	TEACHING HINTS

INTRODUCTORY ACTIVITY (2–3 MINUTES)

Addition Tag

Select 2–3 "its." They run and try to tag others. Each line grows as outside person tags and picks up other line "members." The longest line at the end is the winner.

DPESS page 312

FITNESS DEVELOPMENT (8–12 MINUTES)

Aerobic Workout

DPESS pages 348–349

See Racquetball Unit, Lesson 7 for details.

LESSON FOCUS (15–20 MINUTES)

Written Exam

GAME (5 MINUTES)

Full Court Basketball

Allow students to play upon completion of exam.

EVALUATION/REVIEW AND CHEER

Discuss Round Robin Tournament.

Cheer: Basketball, yes!

BASKETBALL EXAM

Directions: Fill in the letter matching the most appropriate response on your answer sheet. True = A; False = B

True/False

_____ 1. There are 7 players plus substitutes on an official basketball team.
_____ 2. A field goal is worth 2 points.
_____ 3. A free throw is worth 2 points.
_____ 4. After making a field goal, the team that made the goal takes the ball out at the end line.
_____ 5. Blocking is stopping the progress of a person with or without the ball.
_____ 6. Faking or feinting is a defensive technique.
_____ 7. A bounce pass is rarely effective near the goal.
_____ 8. A player should use the dribble to cover the ground.
_____ 9. Man-to-man defense means that the guards move with the ball.
_____10. It is legal to hand the ball to another player.
_____11. On a jump ball, a player may <u>not</u> tap the ball until it reaches "its" highest point.
_____12. A jump ball is taken in the center-restraining circle <u>only</u> at the beginning of each quarter.

Multiple Choice

13. ____ is called by the referee if while dribbling you drop the ball, stop and pick it up, and then begin dribbling again.
    a. Traveling
    b. Double dribbling
    c. Free throw
    d. a & b
    e. all of the above

14. How long may a player of the offensive team stand in the free throw lane?
    a. indefinitely
    b. 5 seconds
    c. 3 seconds
    d. 10 seconds

15. The penalty for two players on opposite teams holding the ball at the same time is
    a. a free throw for the first player that got the ball
    b. a jump ball for the two players involved in the tie ball
    c. the ball is taken out of bounds at the sideline
    d. all of the above

16. After 5 team fouls, the penalty for unnecessary roughness or overguarding is
    a. ball taken out of bounds at the sidelines by the team that was fouled
    b. free throw for the team making the foul
    c. free throw for the team that was the victim of a foul
    d. all of the above

17. Which of the following is the easiest to intercept?
    a. long pass
    b. low bounce
    c. dribble
    d. any of the above

18. How long may a player in bounds hold the ball when <u>not</u> being closely guarded?
    a. 3 seconds
    b. 5 seconds
    c. indefinitely
    d. 10 seconds

19. Which of the following is illegal?
    a. striking the ball with the fists
    b. holding the ball for six seconds when closely guarded
    c. using both hands on the first dribble
    d. all of the above

20. How long may a player stand in the free throw lane if her team does not have possession of the ball?
    a. 3 seconds
    b. 5 seconds
    c. 10 seconds
    d. indefinitely

Basketball Lesson Plan 14

EQUIPMENT:
Fitness Challenge Course Instructions (see Badminton Unit, Lesson 1 for details)
Round Robin Tournament chart
1 ball per court

INSTRUCTIONAL ACTIVITIES	TEACHING HINTS
INTRODUCTORY ACTIVITY AND FITNESS COMBINED (15 MINUTES)	
Challenge Course	DPESS page 351
	See Badminton Unit, Lesson 1 for details.
LESSON FOCUS AND GAME COMBINED (20 MINUTES)	
Round Robin Tournament	Create teams and chart for tournament.
EVALUATION/REVIEW AND CHEER	

Discuss issues that may have arisen during tournament.
Students create cheer.

Basketball Lesson Plan 15

EQUIPMENT:
Round Robin Tournament Chart   1 basketball per court

INSTRUCTIONAL ACTIVITIES	TEACHING HINTS
INTRODUCTORY ACTIVITY (2–3 MINUTES)	
Move and Perform a Stretch	DPESS pages 308–309
	See Lesson 13, Badminton for details.
FITNESS DEVELOPMENT (8–12 MINUTES)	
Walk, Jog, Sprint	DPESS page 354
	See Lesson 12 for details.
LESSON FOCUS AND GAME COMBINED (20–25 MINUTES)	
Round Robin Tournament Conclusion	
EVALUATION/REVIEW AND CHEER	

Discuss tournament and introduce next unit.
Students create cheer.

Golf

OBJECTIVES:

The student will:
1. Participate in gross motor movements, isometrics, plyometrics, and cardiovascular activities.
2. Participate in Continuity Exercise activities to increase cardiovascular endurance, strength, and flexibility.
3. Execute Formation Rhythmic Running to increase the circulation and generally warm the body up while reinforcing the following of a beat while moving.
4. Demonstrate starting, stopping, and running skills in Bean Bag Touch and Go and Ball activities.
5. Read the class safety rules hand-out and sign the cover sheet indicating understanding.
6. Demonstrate and use the proper grip 100% of the time.
7. Demonstrate the proper address of the ball 100% of the time.
8. Execute the chip, pitch, and drive shots using form demonstrated in class.
9. Demonstrate the stance, grip, and address routine used in putting a golf ball.
10. Putt the ball on the practice greens.
11. Demonstrate the basics of the full swing.
12. Review chipping using a self-check Task Sheet.
13. Identify etiquette and rules on Task Sheets 15–17.
14. Demonstrate the golf full swing using the 5 iron and skills demonstrated in class.
15. Using the full swing, practice hitting into a net and at targets.
16. Execute form taught in class for Sand Trap Shots.
17. Complete a written exam covering rules, etiquette, and skills techniques scoring at least 70%.
18. Work with a partner and complete the "Golf Rating Scale" to receive a skill exam grade.
19. Play Frisbee Keep Away demonstrating throwing, catching, and jumping skills.
20. Play Tug-of-War with a team.
21. Demonstrate dodging, running, and agility during Push-Up Tag.
22. Play "Frisbee 21" with a partner demonstrating 1- and 2- hand catching and throwing accuracy.
23. Play a game of simulated golf demonstrating skills, rules, and etiquette studied during the unit.

GOLF BLOCK PLAN
3-WEEK UNIT

Week #1	Monday	Tuesday	Wednesday	Thursday	Friday
Introductory Activity	Blob Tag	Parachute Routine	Vanishing Bean Bags	Parachute Locomotor Routine	Ball Activities
Fitness	Continuity Exercise	Parachute Activities	Continuity Exercises	Parachute Fitness Activities	Walk, Jog, Sprint
Lesson Focus	Putting	Chip Shot	Chip Shot Review Pitch Shot	Full Swing	Review Address Routine Swings
Game	Frisbee Catch	Hula Hoop Pass	Football Pass Relay	Reverse Hula Hoop Spin	Pentabridge Hustle

Week #2	Monday	Tuesday	Wednesday	Thursday	Friday
Introductory Activity	Over, Under, Around	Formation Rhythmic Running	Bean Bag Touch and Go	Mirror Drill in Place	Partner Tug-of-War
Fitness	Continuity Exercise	Fitness Scavenger Hunt	Continuity Exercise	Stretching Four Corners Partner Resistance	Circuit Training
Lesson Focus	Full Swing	Pitch Shot Chip Shot Full Swing	Sand Trap Stunts Full Swing	Putting	Full Swing
Game	Frisbee Keep Away	Team Tug-of-War		Frisbee Freedom	Nine Lives

Week #3	Monday	Tuesday	Wednesday	Thursday	Friday
Introductory Activity	Mirror Drill in Place	Follow the Leader	Flag Chase	Eliminate Today	Formation Rhythmic Running
Fitness	Exercise to Music	Walk, Jog, Sprint	Fitness Challenge Course	Stretching	Golf Game
Lesson Focus	Pitch Shot	Pitch and Run Putting	Pitching Rules and Etiquette	Written and Skill Exam	Golf Game
Game	Musical Hoops	Frozen Tag	Frisbee 21	Putting Practice	Golf Game

Golf Lesson Plan 1

EQUIPMENT:

1 putter per student	1 frisbee per 2 students
5 golf balls per student	1 individual jump rope per student
1 putting green per 2 students	1 CD/cassette player
1 whistle	Continuity music CD/tape
1 clipboard and pencil per green	2 Putting Task Sheets per pair placed on clipboard

INSTRUCTIONAL ACTIVITIES	ORGANIZATION TEACHING HINTS
INTRODUCTORY ACTIVITY (2–3 MINUTES)	
Blob Tag	DPESS page 312
Select 2–3 "its"	Change "its" 1 or 2 times during activity.
FITNESS DEVELOPMENT (8–12 MINUTES)	
Continuity Exercises	DPESS pages 349–350
These exercises are a type of interval training. Create a CD/cassette tape with 30–35 seconds of music and 20 seconds of silence. During the music the students will jump rope.	When the silence begins, instruct the students to do an exercise, i.e., push-ups, curl-ups, reverse push-ups, etc. When the music resumes, the students jump rope. During each silence direct a difference exercise.
Stretching	DPESS pages 342–344
During the last silence, conduct stretching exercises to stretch the areas worked, i.e., calves, quadriceps, etc.	Slower and lower-volume music should be added to this portion of the CD/tape for enjoyable stretching.
Bear Hug	DPESS page 342
Lunge Forward: Achilles and calf stretch	Attempt to place the rear foot flat on the floor. Hands on front thigh for support. Back flat and on upward diagonal.
Lunge forward and extend rear leg straight back.	
Hamstring Stretch-Reverse Lunge: From the lunge position, shift lunge and weight to rear leg, extend front leg. Keep heel on ground, toe flexed and pointing to sky.	Hold stretch for 30 seconds. Change legs. Hands on front thigh for support, back flat but on upward diagonal.
Standing Hip Bend (Both sides)	DPESS page 343
Hold the position for 20–30 seconds.	
Elbow Puller and Pusher (Both sides)	DPESS pages 343–344
Wishbone Stretch	DPESS page 344
Hold position for 10–20 seconds	
LESSON FOCUS (15–20 MINUTES)	
Putting	DPESS page 472
Teach putting at a carpeted green. Use the "green" for your demonstration area.	Direct each student to pick up a putter and bring it to the demonstration area. Scattered formation around demonstration area.
Reverse Overlap Grip	Demonstrate, then students practice the grip.
Stance	Demonstrate, then have students practice the stance.
Aiming	Line up sight line with club. Imagine a line to the hole.
Address Routine	Demonstrate, then practice Address Routine.
Practicing putting	Direct students to get elbow-to-elbow to select a partner. Ask each pair to pick up 5 golf balls and then go to a putting green. Students practice putting 5 balls and then change roles. Repeat.
Putting Task Sheet	Direct students to pick up a clipboard with attached Task Sheet 1 and a pencil and come to the demonstration area. Explain the Task Sheet. One student is the "doer." One student is the "observer." Observer reads Task Sheet to doer, records results, and offers feedback. Change roles as directed on Task Sheet.
If students complete Task Sheet quickly, they can play a putting game. See how many points can be earned when a person earns 1 point for each putt made.	

INSTRUCTIONAL ACTIVITIES	**ORGANIZATION TEACHING HINTS**

GAME (3–5 MINUTES)

Frisbee Catch

Partners can keep score or just free throwing and catching.

1-hand catch = 2 points

2-hand catch = 1 point

Keep score to 20 points and then start over.

DPESS pages 464–465

Demonstrate throwing and catching a Frisbee.

Use Back-to-Back with a new person to create partners.

One person puts a hand on their head. The person with his hand on his head is to go and get a Frisbee for the pair and return to the partner.

EVALUATION/REVIEW AND CHEER

Have students take home "Golf Safety Rules," read it, sign it and return "cut off" to class on the next day.

Cheer: 2, 4, 6, 8, Playing golf is really great!

Bring students together and review learning experiences of the day.

RECIPROCAL TASK SHEET 1: ADDRESSING AND PUTTING THE BALL

Name: _____

Name: _____

Directions: Work with a partner. Place both of your names on each Task Sheet. One person is the "doer" while the other person is the "observer." Observer reads information/instructions to the doer, offers verbal feedback, and places a check in the "yes" or "no" column recording the performance of their partner. Record the date of the practice. Complete the Task Sheet until you are directed to "change roles." Then, the "doer" becomes the "observer." Each person has his/her own Task Sheet.

ADDRESS ROUTINE	DATES							
(Record date of practice)								
	Yes	No	Yes	No	Yes	No	Yes	No
1. Assume the grip you have selected to use.								
2. Stand behind the ball and sight the hole.								
3. Move up to the side of ball; with arms extended place the club head down directly behind the ball so the clubface is "square" to the intended line of the putt.								
4. Place your feet so the ball is in front of the left foot about one putter blade length in front of the toe. Feet about 12" apart.								
5. Knees slightly bent.								
6. Weight mainly on left foot.								
7. Head over the ball. Eyes on ball.								
PUTTING								
8. Partner should place his club right above toes of partner making a straight line toward the target.								
9. Point both elbows out slightly.								
10. Swing the club back 12"–18." Swing forward and through the ball. The follow through should be about the same distance as the BACKSWING. Accelerate through the ball in a smooth motion.								
11. BACKSWING and follow through make a straight line parallel to partners club.								
12. Change roles.								
13. Repeat 1–12.								

GOLF SAFETY RULES

1. Follow all rules set by your instructor.
2. Do not swing a golf club until you have been instructed to do so. Always look around to see that no one is close by and within range of your swing.
3. Be careful where you walk while other people are taking practice swings.
4. Stand well away and out of range of a player taking a swing.
5. Do not swing a golf club so the follow through of the swing is traveling toward anyone.
6. If you hit a golf ball that is traveling toward someone, call "FORE."
7. Wait for the signal from your instructor before retrieving balls.
8. Accidents occur because of carelessness, lack of awareness, or lack of knowledge. Always look around and practice safely.

Please cut off at the dashed line, sign, date, and return below to your instructor.

CUT OFF AND RETURN TO INSTRUCTOR

I, _____, have read and understand the golf safety rules. I agree to follow the rules of the class.

_____ Date _____

(Signature)

Golf Lesson Plan 2

EQUIPMENT:

Whistle	#7 iron
6 whiffle balls per student	5 hula hoops
Individual jump ropes	15 bean bags
1 parachute	CD/cassette player
Bag of golf tees, 5 of each color	6 cones
Easel chalkboard or diagram of setups on field	

INSTRUCTIONAL ACTIVITIES	ORGANIZATION TEACHING HINTS

INTRODUCTORY ACTIVITY (2–3 MINUTES)

Parachute (Locomotor) Routine with Music	DPESS pages 351–352
Define clockwise and counter-clockwise.	Explain routine, then turn on music.
Ask "What are locomotor movements?"	
Routine example:	Locomotor Routine to a popular tape/CD:
16 Runs clockwise (CW)	"Run left!"
16 Runs counterclockwise (CCW)	"Run right!"
16 Jumps to center	"Jump to center!"
16 Jumps back	"Jump back and tighten chute!"
8-count lift overhead	"Lift overhead!" (8 counts)
8-count lower to toes	"Lower to toes"
4-count lift	"Again!" "Up! Down!"
4-count lower	"Hold overhead and run left!" (32 counts)
	"Hold at waist and run right!"
Repeat all, but increase difficulty by holding chute overhead on CW run.	"Lift overhead!" (16 counts)
Release on last lift.	"Lower to toes!"
	"Lift and release!"

FITNESS DEVELOPMENT (8–12 MINUTES)

Parachute Fitness Activities	DPESS pages 351–352
Toe Touches	Hold parachute sitting while in extended leg position around the parachute.
Explain isometrics. Lift chute taut to chin. Bend forward and touch grip to toes. Hold taut to chin.	16 repetitions
Curl-Ups: Curl-up, bend knees, lie back, extend legs. Repeat 16 times.	Hold parachute sitting position in a circle. Curl-up, bent knees. Extended legs under chute and lie on back.
Dorsal Lifts	Lying prone, head toward chute, arms straight, chest taut.
	Lift arms and chest, lower, repeat 8 times.
Sitting leg lift: Sit—legs under chute, on signal lift a leg off ground for 6 to 10 seconds. Try to keep leg straight. Alternate legs.	When blow whistle: Freeze.
	Try variation: Side leg lefts. Lie on side. Lift top leg and lower.
Jump rope in place.	Scattered formation
Travel while rope jumping.	Move around carefully while rope jumping.
Hot Peppers	Jump as fast as you can until I blow the whistle.
Skip rope at a comfortable pace.	

LESSON FOCUS (15–20 MINUTES)

Chip Shot	DPESS page 472
Each student gets a 7 iron.	Explain purpose.
Demonstrate grip.	Practice grip.
Demonstrate stance: Forward foot open toward target.	Practice stance.
Demonstrate swing.	Have students spread out to safe location to swing.
Practice swing aiming at target.	Set cones approximately 10' from chipping area. Cones mark the target.
Hit balls to target.	Have students get balls.
Repeat practice.	Signal to retrieve balls.
Count # balls stopping close to target.	Try to have ball stop rolling close to cone.
Complete activity.	Collect equipment.

INSTRUCTIONAL ACTIVITIES	ORGANIZATION TEACHING HINTS

GAME (5 MINUTES)

Hula Hoop Circle Pass

Place a hula hoop over the clasped hands of two members of each circle. On signal—pass the hoop around the circle without releasing handgrips.

DPESS page 314

Use Whistle Mixer to form groups of 5 holding hands in a circle.

EVALUATION/REVIEW AND CHEER

Review elements of swing.

Students create cheer.

Golf Lesson Plan 3

EQUIPMENT:

Self-check Task Sheets	Whistle
Clipboards	Pencils
Parachute	15 hula hoops
6 whiffle balls per student	90 bean bags
4 chip nets	#7 irons
Rope	1 football per 5 students
CD/cassette player	Continuity Music CD/tape

INSTRUCTIONAL ACTIVITIES	ORGANIZATION TEACHING HINTS

INTRODUCTORY ACTIVITY (2–3 MINUTES)

Vanishing Bean Bags

DPESS page 309

Spread bean bags out in area. Begin with 1 bag/student. Have students begin by moving around the area until you give a signal.

FITNESS DEVELOPMENT (8–12 MINUTES)

Continuity Exercises — DPESS pages 349–350

Stretch — DPESS pages 342–344

Bear Hug — DPESS page 312

Standing Hip Bend. Be sure not to bounce. — DPESS page 343 Hold the position for 10–20 seconds.

Arm and Shoulder Stretch — DPESS page 344

Elbow Puller and Pusher — DPESS page 344 Both sides in each exercise.

Wishbone stretch — DPESS page 344 Hold position for 10–20 seconds.

LESSON FOCUS (15–20 MINUTES)

Review Chip Shot

Review basic elements.

DPESS page 472

Have students complete the Self-Check Task Sheet: Golf Chip Shot.

Pitch Shot

Demonstrate grip.
    Practice grip.
Demonstrate stance.
    Practice stance.
Demonstrate swings:
    1/2 swing
    3/4 swing
    Full swing

DPESS page 472

Demonstrate and discuss difference in loft of 9 iron, 7 iron, and pitching wedge. Describe purpose and effectiveness of each club in reaching the green or getting out of bunkers. Students pick up a club. Spread students out to practice swings. Use hula hoops and "chip nets" as targets.

Hint: Long jump ropes can be stretched to indicate swing area.

Direct students to the practice area. 6 balls per student are needed.

Hula hoops   Chip Nets
O   O
  O O   o o o o

Safety Reminder

Practice each type of swing 6 times before trying to aim at the target.

Whistle to indicate when to retrieve balls and when practice can resume. Return equipment.

INSTRUCTIONAL ACTIVITIES	ORGANIZATION TEACHING HINTS

GAME (5 MINUTES)

Football Pass Relay

Leader hands off football turning right with torso rotation similar to the "take away" of the golf club.

Each student receives the pass and hands off. Last person runs with ball to the head of the squad.

Organize lines of 5–6 students using Whistle Mixer.
Explain that students freeze when they hear the whistle.

Repeat relay until all have finished. Then group sits down.

EVALUATION/REVIEW AND CHEER

Review main elements of pitch and chip shots.
Cheer: 2, 4, 6, 8, Golf is really, really great!

SELF-CHECK TASK SHEET: GOLF CHIP SHOT

Name: _____

Objective: The student will demonstrate the grip, the stance, the ball alignment, and the chipping stroke.

Directions: Record date of practice. Record all components followed for each section: grip, stance, ball alignment, and stroke.

1st: Two Shots   Chip 15'
2nd: Two Shots   Chip 30'

(Record date of practice)	DATES							
GRIP	Yes	No	Yes	No	Yes	No	Yes	No
1. The most common grip is started with the palm of right hand facing the target.								
2. The back of the left hand faces the target with the left thumb on top of the club (for left handers the reverse is done).								
STANCE								
1. Place feet on both ends of 12" strip set parallel to target line.								
2. Knees are bent.								
3. Eyes on ball.								
BALL POSITION								
1. Ball slightly in front of left foot.								
STROKE								
1. Keep your head perfectly still and your eyes directly over the ball.								
2. Swing arms in a pendulum action from your shoulders around the pivot of your immobile head.								
3. Point both elbows outward slightly.								
4. Club should end facing in the direction you are hitting the ball.								

Golf Lesson Plan 4

EQUIPMENT:

CD/tape	CD/cassette player
1 weighted scarf per student	#9 iron for each student
Tees for each student	8 hoops
10 whiffle balls per student	3 chipper nets
Rope	2 cones
Bucket of 10 hard golf balls	Parachute

INSTRUCTIONAL ACTIVITIES	ORGANIZATION TEACHING HINTS

INTRODUCTORY ACTIVITY (2–3 MINUTES)

Parachute Locomotor Routine	**DPESS pages 351–352**
Popular music	Whistle to change action.
16 runs CW	"Tighten chute!"
16 runs CCW	Hold chute overhead on CW run.
8 jumps in place	
16 skips forward	
8-count lift overhead	
8-count lower to toes	
4-count lift	
4-count lower to toes	
Repeat all.	
Face chute and hold with 2 hands:	Whistle to signal direction change.
slide CW; slide CCW.	

FITNESS DEVELOPMENT (8–12 MINUTES)

Parachute Fitness Activities	**DPESS pages 351–352.** Hold chute with left hand.
Skip forward CCW; skip CW; run CCW; run CW	Change hands on chute to change directions.
	Whistle signals "stop." Give directions.
Slide right, slide left	Place two hands on chute; hold chute tautly.
	Put chute down.
	Sprint around room.
	Whistle to return to spot around chute.
Stretching Exercises	**DPESS pages 342–344**
Overhead; standing hip bend; wishbone stretch	
Toe Toucher	**DPESS page 351**
Lift to taut—chin level	Sitting, legs under chute
	Bend to touch grip to toes; lift to taut—chin level.
	Repeat 16 times.
Curl-Ups	Taut to chin. Hold. Curl-up—bend knees. Touch edge of
Legs under chute—lie on back, curl-up—bend knees, lie back—extend legs. Repeat total 4 times.	chute to toes.
Parachute Drills	Lying prone
Dorsal lifts	Head toward chute
Lift arms and chest, hold, lower.	Arms straight
Repeat 8 times total.	Chute taut
Sitting Leg Lifts	Sit, legs under chute
Lift legs straight, hold 6-8 sec. Variation: lying supine lift torso and straight legs to a "V" sit position, hold.	Whistle; "Lift & Hold"
	Whistle; "Lower"
Sitting Pulls	Sit with back to chute.
Hold chute overhead, on signal try to pull to knees.	Whistle; "Up and Hold"
All Fours Pull	Sitting facing chute hands and knees hold chute with one
Hold overhead, 6-8 sec to eye level, 6-8 sec to waist, etc.	hand.
On signal, pull and hold 6-10 sec. Repeat other hand.	Whistle; "Pull and Hold"
Roll parachute tightly.	Everyone walks to center to fold up chute.

INSTRUCTIONAL ACTIVITIES	ORGANIZATION TEACHING HINTS
Sprint-Jog File Run All students in each line jog around area. Last runner in each line sprints to weave in and around each of the people in the line until he gets to front. Then last person in line repeats.	**DPESS page 354** Organize groups of 5 using Whistle Mixer. Make lines.

LESSON FOCUS (15–20 MINUTES)

Full Swing Demonstrate grips: baseball, overlapping, interlocking.	**DPESS page 471** Direct student to pick up a club— #9 or #7 iron. Practice grips.
Address the ball: Body position; Weight; Knees; Shoulders and Arms; Lining up club head and feet	Practice.
Demonstrate Full Swing Practice 3/4 swing and full swing 10 times without ball.	Review safety rules. Direct students to go to practice area and place club down. Pick up practice balls.
Practice full swing with Whiffle balls.	Direct starting and ball collection.
Use of the tee	Practice with hard golf balls and tee.
When used?	Change balls.
How high is ball on tee?	Put equipment away.

GAME (5 MINUTES)

Reverse Hula Hoop Spin Squad leaders: Roll hoop forward with a reverse spin. When it returns, pass it over your body to the ground, step out of it, and pass it to the next person in squad line. (Winning squad is first to finish.)	**DPESS page 390** Squads of 5-6 people. Leader takes a hoop. Leader collects hoops.

EVALUATION/REVIEW AND CHEER

Review elements of the full swing. Students create cheer.

Golf Lesson Plan 5

EQUIPMENT:

1 rubber ball per student	1 clipboard per 2 students
1 #9 iron per student	Reciprocal Task Sheets 2–4
6 whiffle golf balls per student	15 hula hoops for shooting targets

INSTRUCTIONAL ACTIVITIES	ORGANIZATION TEACHING HINTS

INTRODUCTORY ACTIVITY (2–3 MINUTES)

Ball Activities

DPESS page 309
Scattered formation

FITNESS DEVELOPMENT (8–12 MINUTES)

Walk, Jog, Sprint
1 Whistle = Walk
2 Whistles = Jog
3 Whistles = Sprint

DPESS 354
Direct moving around track and varying activity with whistle signal for 10 minutes.
Watch students' response to vigorous movement and adjust directions accordingly.

Strength Exercises
Push-ups; Inclined wall push-ups; Curl-ups; Curl-ups with twist; Reverse push-ups

DPESS pages 344–346

LESSON FOCUS (15–20 MINUTES)

Review following skills:
  Grips
  Addressing ball
  Review safe practice techniques.
  Practice will take place with Task Sheets.

DPESS pages 470–472
Scattered formation
Have students practice without ball following each review. Demonstration
Direct students to get "Toe-to-Toe" with someone to create partners.

Explain each Task Sheet

Direct students to get a 7 or 9 iron, a clipboard with pencil, and Task Sheets 2, 3, and 4.

Demonstrate swings:
  1/2 swing
  3/4 swing
  Full swing

Student picks up a 9 iron and 6 Whiffle balls.
Scattered formation directed by teacher
Practice each swing without ball following demonstration.
Practice each swing with each set of balls at practice area.

Review/Demonstrate Pitch Shot

Direct students to re-group for demonstration.
Assign to practice alone with 6 balls and then re-group.

Review/Demonstrate Chip Shot

Following demonstration, assign to practice alone with 6 balls.

GAME (5 MINUTES)

Pentabridge Hustle

DPESS page 310
Play Whistle Mixer to create groups of 5. 4 students make bridges that the others go under. As soon as a student exits the last bridge they form a new one. Then the first "bridge" becomes the "hustler." You can add locomotor challenges before creating a new bridge.

EVALUATION/REVIEW AND CHEER

Discuss main elements of swings practiced during the class period.
Cheer: Give me a "G"; Give me an "O"; Give me an "L"; Give me an "F"; What does that spell? Golf! Yeah!

RECIPROCAL TASK SHEET 2: GRIPS

Name: _____

Name: _____

Directions: Work with a partner. Your partner will read the Task Sheet to you. Record dates and check appropriate response for each checkpoint for the grip. Complete the grip practice with your partner a minimum of five times.

GRIPS* Check hand positions	DATES							
(Record date of practice) **BASEBALL GRIP**								
LEFT HAND	Yes	No	Yes	No	Yes	No	Yes	No
1. Hand placed so only cap of club is extended beyond palm								
2. Club head is resting flat on "its" sole and is squarely aligned with target								
3. Back of hand facing toward target								
4. Fingers gripped around club so the grip of the club lies diagonally across the second joint of the index finger								
5. No spaces between fingers								
6. Thumb positioned slightly to right of the top of the grip								
7. V formed by thumb and index finger points to right shoulder when club placed squarely in front of body								
RIGHT HAND								
1. Place right hand on grip as though you were slapping grip (palm facing target).								
2. Grip fingers around club so left thumb fits snugly in palm of right hand.								
3. Little finger touches index finger of left hand								
4. No spaces between fingers								
5. V formed by thumb and index finger points to right of chin								
OVERLAPPING OR VARDON GRIP (Same as above except:)								
1. Little finger of right hand overlaps the index finger of left hand								
INTERLOCKING GRIP (Same as 10-finger or baseball grip except:)								
1. Little finger of right hand interlocks the index finger of left hand								

* The checkpoints refer to right-handed golfers.

RECIPROCAL TASK SHEET 3: ADDRESS

Name: _____

Name: _____

Directions: Work with a partner. Your partner will read the Task Sheet to you as you perform the address. Record the dates and check the appropriate response for each checkpoint for the address. Execute the address by yourself and with your partner reading to you a minimum of 5 times. Rotate after 5 times.

ADDRESS ROUTINE	DATES							
(Record date of practice)								
ADDRESS (Address routine)	Yes	No	Yes	No	Yes	No	Yes	No
1. Assume correct grip. (Review Task Sheet)								
2. Stand behind ball and sight target. (Choose a tree, post, etc. to act as target).								
3. Move up to side of ball; with arms extended, place the club head down directly behind the ball so the club head is perpendicular or "square" to the intended line of flight.								
4. Place your feet so the ball is opposite the center of your stance.								
5. Weight is evenly distributed through feet.								
6. Knees relaxed–not hyper-extended								
7. Body bent slightly forward from hips								
8. Shoulders relaxed so arms hang freely from body								
9. Arms and shoulders form triangle with hands as the apex of the triangle.								
10. Feel comfortable.								

Do you look like this?

RECIPROCAL TASK SHEET 4: STANCES

Name: _____

Directions: Work with a partner. Partner reads Task Sheet as you perform. Record the dates and check the appropriate response for each checkpoint for the stances. Perform each task 5 times alternating practice turns with your partner.

STANCE	DATES							
(Record date of practice)								
SQUARE OR PARALLEL	Yes	No	Yes	No	Yes	No	Yes	No
1. Feet approximately shoulder-width apart								
2. Weight evenly distributed								
3. Knees relaxed–not hyper-extended								
4. Toes pointed toward intended line of flight								
Square								
OPEN								
1. Feet 8-10 inches apart								
2. Weight evenly distributed								
3. Knees relaxed–not hyper-extended								
4. Toes pointed toward intended line of sight								
Open								
CLOSED								
1. Feet slightly more than shoulder-width apart								
2. Weight evenly distributed								
3. Knees relaxed–not hyper-extended								
4. Toes pointed toward intended line of flight								
Closed								

Golf Lesson Plan 6

EQUIPMENT:
1 frisbee per student
1 #9 iron per student
1 #5 iron per student

CD/cassette player
Continuity Exercise CD/tape
Reciprocal Task Sheet 5
5 whiffle balls per student

INSTRUCTIONAL ACTIVITIES	ORGANIZATION TEACHING HINTS

INTRODUCTORY ACTIVITY (2–3 MINUTES)

Over, Under, and Around

DPESS pages 310–311
Use elbow-to-elbow or Back-to-Back to form partners.
Scattered formation with partner

FITNESS DEVELOPMENT (8–12 MINUTES)

Continuity Exercises
Create a CD/cassette tape with 30–35 seconds of music and 20 seconds of silence. During the music, the students will jump rope. When the silence begins, instruct the students to do an exercise, i.e., push-ups, curl-ups, etc.

DPESS pages 349–350
Use a CD/cassette tape to direct movements.
When the music resumes, the students jump rope. During each silence direct a different exercise.

LESSON FOCUS (15–20 MINUTES)

Reciprocal Task Sheet Activities
For Full Swing

Distribute Task Sheets.

GAME (5 MINUTES)

Frisbee Keep Away
Change places when center player catches Frisbee or on the teacher's signal.

DPESS pages 463–464
Use the Whistle Mixer to create groups of 3.

EVALUATION/REVIEW AND CHEER

Discuss elements of the full swing.
Cheer: We love to play golf!

RECIPROCAL TASK SHEET 5: FULL SWING

Name: _____

Directions: Work with a partner. Record the dates and check the appropriate response for each checkpoint for the full swing. Have your partner check you a minimum of 5–10 times. See your instructor for additional Task Sheets. Each person needs his or her own Task Sheet. Partner (observer)–try to observe no more than two checkpoints at one time.

(Record date of practice) **BACKSWING** (As club begins to move back)	DATES							
	Yes	No	Yes	No	Yes	No	Yes	No
1. Head–head down, eyes on ball								
2. Club–brushes back against ground in an arc								
3. Arms–left arm straight, right elbow begins to bend, wrists begin to cock								
4. Trunk–inclined forward, gives naturally in direction of BACKSWING								
5. Legs–left knee turns inward, right leg straight								
TOP OF BACKSWING								
1. Head–head down, eyes looking over left shoulder at ball								
2. Arms–left elbow remains extended (relaxed) while right elbow is pointing down, wrists are cocked								
3. Trunk–inclined forward, rotated to right from hips								
4. Feet–most weight is on right foot and only left heel has lifted slightly								
5. Grip–firm grip maintained–last 3 fingers of left hand squeezed around club grip								
DOWNSWING								
1. Head–head down								
2. Arms–left arm remains extended, right elbow coming into side, wrists remain cocked as trunk uncoils								
3. Trunk–uncoils and turns to left, weight shifting to left foot								
4. Legs–left knee straightens and right knee begins to turn inward								
CONTACT								
1. Head–head down and eyes on ball								
2. Arms–elbows straight								
3. Trunk–rotated slightly left								
4. Club–clubface contacting ball squarely								
FOLLOW-THROUGH								
1. Head–head down until right shoulder hits chin								
2. Arms–right arm is extended and left arm bent, hands high								
3. Trunk–body remains balanced as hips and shoulders (center of waist) turn to face target								

RECIPROCAL TASK SHEET 6: FULL SWING–#5 IRON
WITH PLASTIC BALLS

Name: _____

Directions: You and your partner each need your own Task Sheets to write on. Go to the field together and take a #5 iron and 10 plastic balls. You will take turns hitting 10 balls. Record the number of balls you hit up in the air out of 10. Each day you and your partner should hit a minimum of 30 shots each. If you swing and miss you need not count it. Each person needs his or her own Task Sheet. You may record your progress or have your partner record this.

Date	# Out of 10	# Out of 10	# Out of 10	# Out of 10	# Out of 10	# Out of 10	# Out of 10	Total
1.								
2.								
3.								
4.								
5.								
6.								
7.								
8.								
9.								
10.								

BE CAREFUL WHERE YOU WALK------------------------------PEOPLE ARE SWINGING!

NO ONE RETRIEVES BALLS UNTIL EVERYONE HAS HIT AND SIGNAL IS GIVEN

Golf Lesson Plan 7

EQUIPMENT:
1 #9 iron per student
6 whiffle golf balls per student

15 hula hoops
Scavenger Hunt Instructions
2 Tug-of-War ropes

INSTRUCTIONAL ACTIVITIES	ORGANIZATION TEACHING HINTS

INTRODUCTORY ACTIVITY (2–3 MINUTES)

Formation Rhythmic Running

DPESS page 313
Scattered formation.

FITNESS DEVELOPMENT (8–12 MINUTES)

Fitness Scavenger Hunt
Each group is given a list directing them to designated areas to find directions for exercise/activity at that location.

DPESS page 356
Use Whistle Mixer to create groups of 3.
Each group is assigned a different starting point.
Each station lists exercises that work the entire body.

LESSON FOCUS (15–20 MINUTES)

Practice:
 Pitch Shot
 Chip Shot
 Full Swing

DPESS pages 471–472
Scattered along safe zone
Set up targets to hit towards:
 Hoops
 Flags
 Ropes
 Cones

GAME (5 MINUTES)

Team Tug-of-War

DPESS page 401
Use management game to create 4 teams.

EVALUATION/REVIEW AND CHEER

Review elements of chip, pitch, and full swing.
Discuss Tug-of-War games. Students create cheer.

Golf Lesson Plan 8

EQUIPMENT:
Task Sheets: Sand Traps, Full Swing
Pencils
#9 iron or pitching wedge for 1/2 class
Continuity Exercise CD/tape

Clipboards
#5 iron or wood for 1/2 class
CD/cassette player
Distance markers/flags

INSTRUCTIONAL ACTIVITIES	ORGANIZATION TEACHING HINTS

INTRODUCTORY ACTIVITY (2–3 MINUTES)

Bean Bag Touch and Go
On signal, run to bean bag, touch it and run again.
Increase challenges with instructions during "Freeze."

DPESS page 309
Scattered formation. Establish "Freeze."
Examples: Touch 5 blue bean bags and sprint; touch 3 bean bags and skip; etc

FITNESS DEVELOPMENT (8–12 MINUTES)

Continuity Exercises

DPESS pages 349–350

LESSON FOCUS AND GAME COMBINED TODAY (20 MINUTES)

Sand Trap Shots
Full Swing Review

Demonstrate hitting from sand using "Running Long Jump Area."

DPESS pages 471–472. Divide group in half.
Group 1: Use Reciprocal Task Sheet 7: Full Swing 5 iron. Explain Task Sheet. Direct to area setup.
Group 2: Use Sand Trap Reciprocal Task Sheet 8 working in pairs.

EVALUATION/REVIEW AND CHEER

Review Sand Trap techniques.
Cheer: Sand traps... Oh, dear!

RECIPROCAL TASK SHEET 7: FULL SWING #5 IRON

Name: _____

Directions: You and your partner each need your own Task Sheets to write on. Go to the field together and take a #5 iron and 10 balls. You will take turns hitting 10 balls and recording the spot where the ball hit for each shot. Designate where the ball hits by placing the number of the shot on the Task Sheet. Each day you and your partner should hit a minimum of 20 shots each so numbers 1–20 should show on your Task Sheet. If you swing and miss you need not count it.

120 yards _____

100 yards _____

80 yards _____

60 yards _____

40 yards _____

20 yards _____

Hitting line _____

BE CAREFUL WHERE YOU WALK -----------------------------------PEOPLE ARE SWINGING!

NO ONE RETRIEVES BALLS UNTIL EVERYONE HAS HIT AND SIGNAL IS GIVEN

RECIPROCAL TASK SHEET 8: SAND TRAPS

Name: _____

Directions: Work with a partner. Each person has his or her own Task Sheet. One person is the "doer" while the other person is the "observer." Observer reads information/instructions to the doer, offers verbal feedback and places a check in the "yes" or "no" column recording the performance of their partner. Record the date of the practice. Complete the Task Sheet until you are directed to "change roles." Then, the "doer" becomes the "observer." Each person has his/her own Task Sheet.

(Record date of practice)	DATES							
	Yes	No	Yes	No	Yes	No	Yes	No
1. Use open stance.								
2. Keep hands ahead of ball at Address.								
3. Hit down on ball, do not scoop it up.								
4. Execute chip shot with arms and shoulders— no body motion.								
5. Ball hit out of trap on first contact.								
6. Change roles with partner.								

Golf Lesson Plan 9

EQUIPMENT:

Putting greens

1 putter per student

1 golf ball per student

1 Task Sheet per student

4 cones

Exercise Station Task Sheets for cones

1 clipboard and pencil per 2 students

INSTRUCTIONAL ACTIVITIES	ORGANIZATION TEACHING HINTS

INTRODUCTORY ACTIVITY (2–3 MINUTES)

Mirror Drill in Place

DPESS page 313

Scattered formation with a partner.

FITNESS DEVELOPMENT (8–12 MINUTES)

Stretching

  Lower Leg Stretch

  Achilles Tendon Stretch

  Balance Beam Stretch

  Side Leg Stretch

  Groin Stretch

  Cross-Legged Stretch

  Body Twist

  Standing Hip Bend

  Elbow Grab Stretch

DPESS pages 342–344

Students scattered.

Place arms on wall or fence for support.

Make Task Sheet for each cone.

Aerobic Activity

Four Corners

  Skipping

  Jogging

  Sliding

  Running backwards

  Jumping

  Leaping

  Hopping

  Galloping

DPESS pages 347–348

Set up 4 cones creating a square. Each cone should list two locomotor activities.

Student executes the movement listed on the Task Sheet on the cone until she gets to next cone.

Music CD/tape directs length of aerobic exercising.

Stretch Activities

Partner Resistance Exercises

DPESS pages 350–351

LESSON FOCUS (15–20 MINUTES)

Putting

Review Technique

  Grip; Stance

  Address; Aiming

Explain Putting Task Sheet

DPESS pages 470–472

Scattered formation

Use Management Game (i.e., Back-to-Back/elbow-to-Elbow) to make pairs.

GAME (5 MINUTES)

Putting Challenge

1. Pick a spot to putt from.
2. Challenge your partner and see who can get the ball into the hole in the least number of putts.
3. Let your partner select a point to put from. Same rules.
4. Repeat.

High-5 your partner upon completion.

Frisbee Freedom

Play Frisbee toss with partner.

With partner on putting carpet/green

Return equipment.

DPESS pages 463–465

Select a safe place to play.

EVALUATION/REVIEW AND CHEER

Review elements involved in putting.

Cheer: Golf swings!

RECIPROCAL TASK SHEET 9: PUTTING

Name: _____

Name: _____

Objective: The student will putt the ball from various distances using technique demonstrated in class.

Instructions:
1. You will work with a partner and check each other off on this Task Sheet.
2. Read the instruction to your partner.
3. Give your partner verbal feedback on the task.
4. Change roles upon completion of each task.
5. Go to a putting green for your practice.

TASKS	PARTNER			
	1		2	
	Yes	No	Yes	No
1. Address the ball.				
2. Aim at hole. Begin each shot with #1 and #2.				
3. Stand 5 feet from the hole and putt. Repeat 5 times. Record number of times ball goes into hole on 1 putt.				
4. Stand 10 feet from hole and putt. Record how many holes you make in 3 or less putts.				

Turn in Task Sheet and Clip Board.

Golf Lesson Plan 10

EQUIPMENT:

1 partner Tug-of-War rope per 2 students
1 #9 iron per student
1 clipboard, pencil per 2 students
Continuity CD/tape for circuits (35 seconds music, 15 seconds silence)

CD/cassette player
10 golf balls per student
Task Sheets 10 and 11 per student

INSTRUCTIONAL ACTIVITIES	ORGANIZATION TEACHING HINTS

INTRODUCTORY ACTIVITY (2–3 MINUTES)

Partner Tug-of-War Activities
Partner pulls: Side to side; Facing; Crab position hooked
    on foot; Back-to-Back

DPESS 401

Use elbow-to-elbow to make pairs.

FITNESS DEVELOPMENT (8–12 MINUTES)

Circuit Training
Activities include:
Jump Rope
Chair Squats
Posterior Shoulder Stretch
Should Extension
Trunk Rotation Stretch
Shoulder Abduction/Flexion/Rotation
Trunk Forward Flexion Stretch
Push-ups
Back Arch and Sag
Abdominal Crunches
Hamstring Stretch
Bent-over Row
Jogging

DPESS page 348

Use Whistle Mixer to create groups of 4-5.

Continuity CD/tape to signal the duration of exercise at
    each station. Station work: 1 minute of exercise
    followed by 10-second interval for rest and preparation
    for the next station.

It is important if circuit training is to be effective that
    quality exercise be performed at each station.

This circuit is designed specifically for golf.

LESSON FOCUS (15–20 MINUTES)

Full Swing
Go over instructions on each Task Sheet.
Have students take: Two golf clubs (9 iron and 3 wood), a
    clipboard, Task Sheets, and 10 golf balls each. Go to
    the practice area.

DPESS page 471
Explain Reciprocal Task Sheets 10 and 11.
Review elements of full swing. Demonstrate with the
    wood.
Use Back-to-Back to create pairs.

GAME (5 MINUTES)

Nine Lives
Any number of fleece balls can be used—the more the
    better. At a signal by the instructor, players scramble
    for a ball and hit as many people below the waist with
    it as possible. Once a player has been hit 9 times,
    he/she leaves the game and stands out of bounds for a
    count of 25.

Scattered formation
Cone off 50' area. Place 10 fleece balls around perimeter
    of area.
Remind the students about fair play and the importance of
    keeping an accurate count of the number of hits they
    have received. Compare the experience to keeping a
    golf score.
A player may have only one ball at a time.
A hit above the shoulders eliminates the thrower.

EVALUATION/REVIEW AND CHEER

Discuss: Importance of a one piece take-away.
What may happen if the swing goes past parallel at the
    top of the full swing?
Cheer: 2...4...6...8...Hitting a golf ball can be great.

RECIPROCAL TASK SHEET 10: FULL SWING #9 IRON

Name: _____

Directions: You and your partner take a Task Sheet for yourself and go to the field with a #9 iron and 10 balls. You will take turns hitting 10 balls and recording the spot where the ball hit for each shot. Designate where the ball hits by placing the number of the shots on the Task Sheet. Each day you and your partner should hit a minimum of 20 shots each so numbers 1–20 should show on your Task Sheet. If you swing and miss you need not count it.

Dates			
125 yards			
90 yards			
80 yards			
70 yards			
60 yards			
50 yards			
40 yards			
30 yards			
20 yards			
10 yards			
Hitting line			

BE CAREFUL WHERE YOU WALK ----------------------------------PEOPLE ARE SWINGING!

NO ONE RETRIEVES BALLS UNTIL EVERYONE HAS HIT AND A SIGNAL IS GIVEN

Signature of partner: _____

RECIPROCAL TASK SHEET 11: FULL SWING #3 WOOD

Name: _____

Directions: Use your own Task Sheet and have your partner watch you and record the results. You and your partner go to the field and take a #3 wood and 10 balls. You will take turns hitting 10 balls and recording the spot where the ball hit for each shot. Designate where the ball hits by placing the number of the shot on the Task Sheet. Each day you and your partner should hit a minimum of 20 shots each so numbers 1–20 should show on your Task Sheet. If you swing and miss you need not count it.

120 yards _____

100 yards _____

80 yards _____

60 yards _____

40 yards _____

20 yards _____

Hitting line _____

BE CAREFUL WHERE YOU WALK ----------------------------------PEOPLE ARE SWINGING!

NO ONE RETRIEVES BALLS UNTIL EVERYONE HAS HIT AND A SIGNAL IS GIVEN

Signature of partner: _____

Golf Lesson Plan 11

EQUIPMENT:

1 clipboard and pencil per 2 students	Task Sheet 12 and 13 for each student
1 #9 and #7 iron per 2 students	5 balls per student
Marked area for "Pitch and Run" station	Marked area for "Pitch Shot"
CD/cassette player	12-minute music CD/tape 120–150 beats per min.
Music CD/tape 5 minutes long with 10 seconds of silence following 30 seconds of music	

INSTRUCTIONAL ACTIVITIES	ORGANIZATION TEACHING HINTS

INTRODUCTORY ACTIVITY (2–3 MINUTES)

Mirror Drill in Place

DPESS page 313

Use a management game to make pairs. Identify first leader/follower. Signal time for leader and follower to change roles after approximately 30-40 seconds.

FITNESS DEVELOPMENT (8–12 MINUTES)

Rhythmic Aerobic Exercise to Music

Create a music CD/tape 120-150 beats per minute or use Aerobic Exercise CD/tape.

DPESS pages 346–347

Scattered formation within a coned area in the teaching area

Standing Hip Bend	40 seconds
Trunk Twist	30 seconds
Slides each direction	30 seconds
Skip around cones	30 seconds
Jumping Jacks	30 seconds
Triceps Push-Ups	30 seconds
Curl-Ups	30 seconds
Knee Touch Curl-Ups	30 seconds
Push-Ups	30 seconds
Gallop around cones	30 seconds
Jump Rope	1 minutes
Lower Leg Stretch	30 seconds
Balance Beam Stretch	30 seconds
Rocking Chair	30 seconds
Carioca around cones	1 minutes
Jog in place	
Calf Stretch	

DPESS pages 342–346

LESSON FOCUS (15–20 MINUTES)

Pitch Shot

Review the Pitch Shot.

Review safety rules.

Instruct students how and when to change stations.

Collect Task Sheets upon completion of activity.

DPESS page 472

Use management game to divide class in half. Assign group 1 to begin with Task Sheet 12. Group 2 should begin with Task Sheet 13.

Direct students to take 9 and 7 irons, 10 balls, Task Sheets 12 and 13 and clipboard to their assigned area.

GAME (5 MINUTES)

Musical Hoops (Variation of Hoops on the Ground)

Hoops, one fewer than the number of students, placed on the floor. Players are given a locomotor movement to do around the hoops while the music is played.

DPESS page 313

Scattered formation.

When the music stops, the students step inside and empty hoop. One student per hoop. Repeat with another locomotor movement. Examples are: slide, gallop, run, skip, leap, and carioca.

EVALUATION/REVIEW AND CHEER

Discuss success of students during Pitch and Run Activities.

Cheer: Give me a par, par, par; Give me a birdie, birdie, birdie; Give me an Eagle, Eagle, Eagle; Give me an H, O, L, E, (2 times) I, N, ONE!

OR...

Cheer: Hole in one (clap, clap) All of us! (Baseball cheer take-off.)

RECIPROCAL TASK SHEET 12: PITCH AND RUN - #7 IRON

Name: _____   Date: _____

Directions: You and your partner go to the area marked for the "Pitch and Run" and take a #7 iron and 10 balls. Stand anywhere around the 30 foot circle (starting line) and record where the ball comes to rest by writing the number of the shot on the target. Each practice must consist of a minimum of 20 shots for each person.

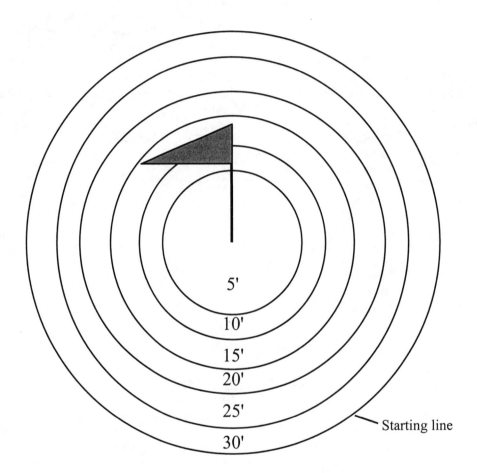

NO ONE RETRIEVES BALLS UNTIL EVERYONE HAS HIT!

Partner's signature: _____

RECIPROCAL TASK SHEET 13: PITCH SHOT - #9 IRON

Name: _____   **Date:** _____

Directions: You and your partner go to the area marked for the "Pitch Shot" and take a #9 iron and 10 balls. Stand anywhere around the 75-foot circle (starting line) and record where the ball comes to rest by writing the number of the shot on the target. The ball must carry in the air to the 50-foot restraining line before it is considered a pitch shot.

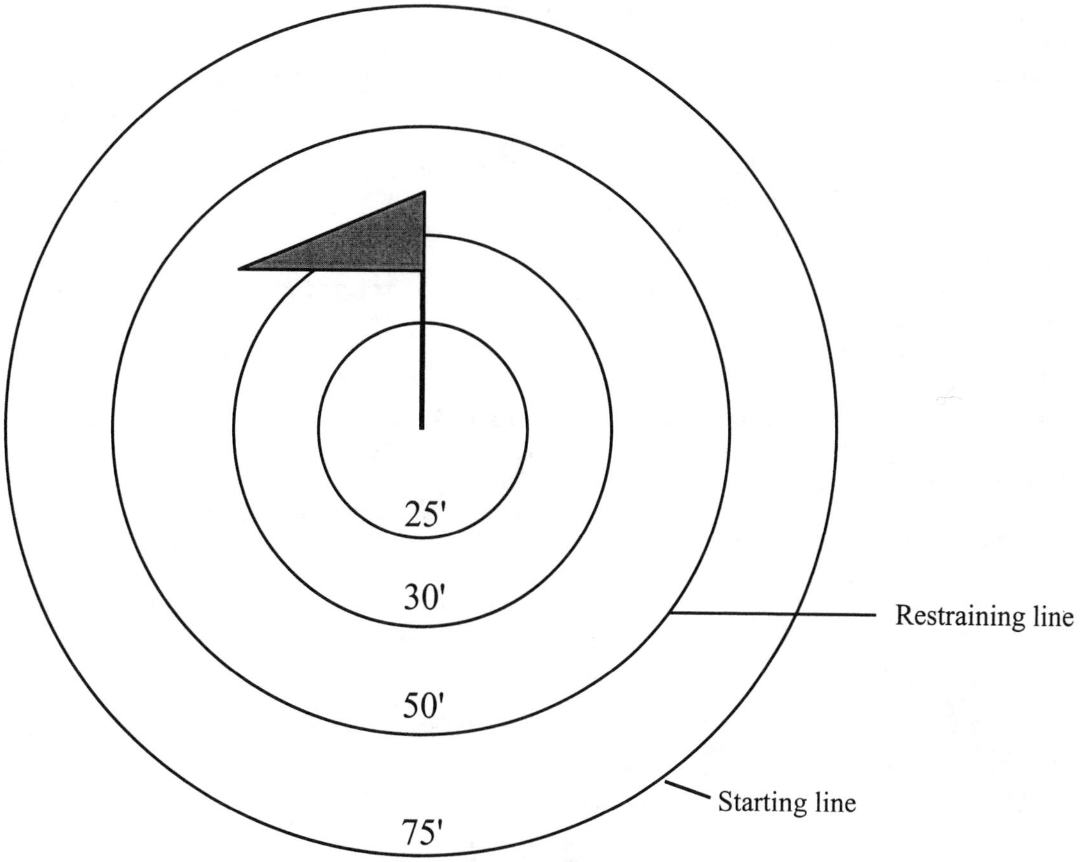

25'

30'

50'

75'

Restraining line

Starting line

BE CAREFUL THAT NO ONE IS ON THE OPPOSITE SIDE OF THE TARGET WHEN HITTING. YOU MAY GET HIT.

NO ONE RETRIEVES BALLS UNTIL EVERYONE HAS HIT!

Partner's signature: _____

Golf Lesson Plan 12

EQUIPMENT:

1 #7 iron per 2 students
Clipboard and pencil per 2 students
5 balls per student

1 putter per 2 students
Task Sheets 14, 15, and 16 for each student
Whistle

INSTRUCTIONAL ACTIVITIES	ORGANIZATION TEACHING HINTS

INTRODUCTORY ACTIVITY (2–3 MINUTES)

New Leader

DPESS page 311
Create pairs by playing "Back-to-Back."

FITNESS DEVELOPMENT (8–12 MINUTES)

Walk-Jog-Sprint
1 Whistle = Sprint
2 Whistles = Walk
3 Whistles = Jog

DPESS page 354
Scattered formation within boundaries
Teacher directs length of time for each activity by
   monitoring class. Progressively increase the time of
   each activity.

Stretch
Achilles Tendon; Lower Leg; Balance Beam; Bear Hug;
Leg Pick-Up; Side Leg; Hurdler's; Groin Stretch; Sitting
   Toe Touch; Body Twist

DPESS pages 342–344

Scattered formation

Strength
Crab Walk; Push-ups; Reclining Partner Pull-ups; Curl-
   ups; Reverse curls; Curl-ups with twist

DPESS pages 344–346

LESSON FOCUS (15–20 MINUTES)

Pitch and Run Game
Putting Station
Explain Task Sheets 14 and 15 and Score Card.
Pitch and Run Game Equipment
10 balls per 2 students
1 #7 iron per 2 students
2 Task Sheet 14s, clipboard and pencil
Putting
10 balls
1 putter per 2 students
Task Sheet 12 and 13 for each student
Clipboard and pencil

DPESS page 472
Stations
Use management technique to divide class in half.
Play elbow-to-elbow to create pairs in each group.

Assign groups to begin at Putting or Pitch and Run Game.
   Explain how and when to change stations. Explain
   Score Card.

Direct students to pick up equipment needed for their first
   station.

GAME (5 MINUTES)

Frozen Tag

DPESS page 312
Scattered formation. Select several "its."

EVALUATION/REVIEW AND CHEER

Discuss results of day's activities.
Cheer: 2, 4, 6, 8, playing golf is really great!

TASK SHEET 14: PITCH AND PITCH AND RUN GAME

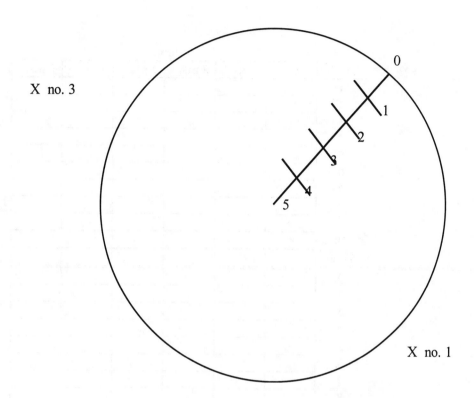

Instructions: Report to the Pitch, and Pitch and Run game station on the field with your partner. Standing at position number 1 (no. 1), each person hits 10 balls and partner records scores. Standing at position number 2 (no. 2), each person hits 10 balls and partner records scores. Stand at position number (no. 3). Each person hits 10 balls and records the scores. To score, your partner takes rope around to each ball hit, and measures the distance from the stake to decide your score. Scores are 5 points, 4 points, 3 points, 2 points, 1 point, 0 points, successively, from each stake. The highest score of all 10 balls wins the round for that position.

SCORE CARD

Name: _____

Directions: Check the appropriate column for the number of points you score on each ball. Do this for each position.

	Trials	\multicolumn{6}{c}{Points}

	Trials	5 pts.	4 pts.	3 pts.	2 pts.	1 pt.	0 pts.
	1						
	2						
	3						
	4						
	5						
Position No. 1	6						
	7						
	8						
	9						
	10						
	Total						
	1						
	2						
	3						
	4						
	5						
Position No. 2	6						
	7						
	8						
	9						
	10						
	Total						
	1						
	2						
	3						
	4						
	5						
Position No. 3	6						
	7						
	8						
	9						
	10						
	Total						
	Grand Total						

Winner's Name: _____

Partner's Name: _____

RECIPROCAL TASK SHEET 15: PUTTING
SHORT PUTTS

Directions: You and your partner go to the area set up for short putts and take 5 balls and a putter with you. Take 10 trials each from a distance of 1', 3', 5', 7', and 10' and record the number made.

	1'	3'	5'	7'	10'	Total
1st trial						
2nd trial						
3rd trail						
4th trial						
5th trial						
6th trial						
7th trial						
8th trial						
9th trial						

RECIPROCAL TASK SHEET 16: PUTTING
LONG PUTTS

Directions: You and your partner go to the indoor area set up for long putts and take 5 balls and a putter with you. Take 10 trials each and record the number of putts it took you to get the ball into the cup from a distance of 15', 20', 25', and 30'.

Distance	1	2	3	4	5	6	7	8	9	10
15'										
20'										
25'										
30'										

Golf Lesson Plan 13

EQUIPMENT:

Flag football belts for 1/2 class	Clipboard and pencils for 3/4 class
CD/cassette player	10 hoops
Long rope and 2 standards	Horizontal climbing ladder
Low balance beam/bench	Cones
Station instructions for Challenge Course	#7 irons for 1/2 class
10 golf balls for 1/2 class	Task Sheets 17–20 for each student

15 minutes music CD/tape for fitness Challenge Course activities

INSTRUCTIONAL ACTIVITIES	ORGANIZATION TEACHING HINTS

INTRODUCTORY ACTIVITY (2–3 MINUTES)

Flag Grab and Chase

One team wears flags positioned in the back of the belt. On signal, the chase team captures as many flags as possible within a designated amount of time. The captured flags are counted. The teams switch positions and the team that captures the most flags wins.

DPESS page 314

Scattered formation inside large boundary area

Split class into using a management game such as Back-to-Back; Toe-to-Toe; or elbow-to-elbow to make two groups by then directing one in the group to put hand on hips. Then separate the two groups into teams.

Direct one team to pick up belts with flags attached.

FITNESS DEVELOPMENT (8–12 MINUTES)

Fitness Challenge Course

Design a course using the following components:

- Agility run through hoops
- Log rolls
- Run and weave through a coned course.
- Leap over a taut rope.
- Cross a horizontal ladder (or hang for 5–10 seconds).
- Power jump onto and off of 3 jumping boxes.
- Walk the length of a balance beam.
- Run high knees for 50 yards.
- Curl-ups
- Crab walks from one cone to another
- Stretching exercises
- Rope jumping
- 10–20 push-ups

DPESS page 351

Divide class into groups of 4–5 using Whistle Mixer. Assign each group a starting point on the Challenge Course. Use music to motivate.

Course should be created to exercise all parts of the body

All students should be able to run the Challenge Course 3 times.

Allow students to develop new challenges for the course.

Music can be used for fun and to motivate students.

Students will travel the course at their own pace. Have a passing lane to the right.

LESSON FOCUS (15–20 MINUTES)

Pitching Practice

Task Sheet 17
Explain organization to switch stations.
Explain Task Sheets 18-20.

DPESS pages 471–472

Use a management technique to create 2 groups. Within the groups play "Back-to-Back" to create partners.

Assign one group to the Pitching Practice area. Direct them to take a clipboard with pencil, 2 copies of Pitching Task Sheet 17, a 7 iron, and 10 balls.

The other group picks up a clipboard for each person with a pencil and Task Sheets 18–20.

GAME (5 MINUTES)

"Frisbee 21"

Game Rules:

- Players stand 10 yards apart.
- Throw disc back and forth. Throws must be catchable.
- 1 point = 1-hand catch
- 2 points = 2-hand catch

DPESS page 465

Create partners using "elbow-to-elbow" technique.

Have 1 person kneel. The standing partner gets a Frisbee from perimeter of area and brings to partner.

Player must get 21 points to win and win by 2 points.

EVALUATION/REVIEW AND CHEER

Review rules and etiquette of golf.
Students create cheer.

RECIPROCAL TASK SHEET 17: PITCH SHOT

Name: _____

Directions: You and your partner go to the marked area. Stand anywhere behind the starting line and record where the ball comes to rest by writing the number of the shot on your chart. The ball must carry in the air 50' to be considered a pitch shot.

_____ **75'** _____

_____ **50'** _____

_____ **30'** _____

_____ **25'** _____

_____ **Starting Line** _____

TASK SHEET 18: RULES AND ETIQUETTE

Name: _____

Unplayable Lie

One of these four options is illegal:

a) Two club-lengths from the ball

b) Point on extension of line from ball to cup 10 yards away

c) Anywhere on line from tee to ball

d) Spot from which original ball was hit

Which one of the above is illegal? (See diagram below.)
Circle the correct answer.

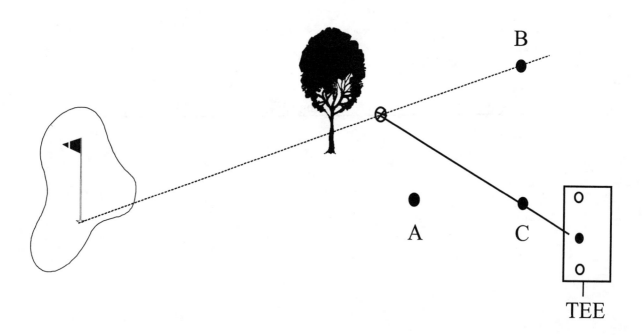

TASK SHEET 19: RULES AND ETIQUETTE

Name: _____

Lateral Water Hazard

Four options are given below as possible points from which to play a ball entering a lateral water hazard:

a) Teeing ground

b) Within 5' of the margin of the water where the ball entered

c) Within 3' of the margin of the water on the other side of the hazard opposite where the ball entered

d) 30' in the adjacent fairway, on a line drawn between the point where the ball crossed the margin of the water and the hole

How many of the above choices are legal? Which one(s)? (See diagram below.)
Circle legal choices.

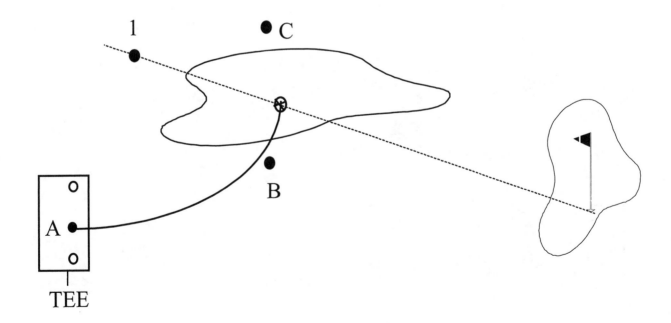

TASK SHEET 20: RULES AND ETIQUETTE

Name: _____

Direct Water Hazard

Only two of the five options described below are points from which a ball entering a water hazard from the tee may be played:

a)   From teeing ground

b)   45 yards in front of the tee in line of entry

c)   90 yards in front of the tee in line of entry

d)   75 yards behind water on line from entry to hole

e)   5' from point of entry in line to hole

Which are the two alternatives? (See diagram below.)
Circle the two alternatives.

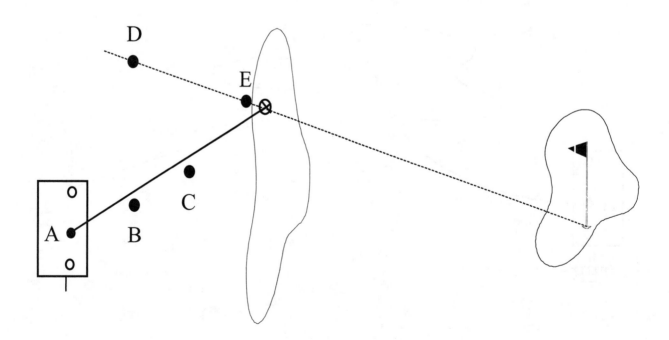

Golf Lesson Plan 14

EQUIPMENT:

1 #9 iron per student

Whiffle golf balls

6 flag markers

Golf Rating Scale Skill Exam (**DPESS page 474**)

Golf Score Cards

15 hula hoops

Written exam

INSTRUCTIONAL ACTIVITIES	ORGANIZATION TEACHING HINTS

INTRODUCTORY ACTIVITY (5 MINUTES)

Eliminate today to allow time for Game and Exam.

FITNESS DEVELOPMENT (5 MINUTES)

Student directed stretching

LESSON FOCUS (15–20 MINUTES)

Distribute Written Exam.

Give instructions.

When exam is completed, student should begin the Golf Rating Scale activity.

Distribute Golf Rating Scale.

Assign student a partner to complete rating scale.

Turn in rating scale upon completion.

GOLF RATING SCALE (DPESS page 474)

Name: _____   Class Period: _____

1. **Grip** (4 points -- 1 each)

   _____ Right-hand V is straight up or slightly right

   _____ Two knuckles of left hand showing

   _____ Grip tension is correct

   _____ Hands completely on grip of club

2. **Stance** (4 points -- 1/2 each)

   _____ Feet proper width apart

   _____ Standing proper distance from ball

   _____ Weight even over feet (ask)

   _____ Knees bent properly

   _____ Proper bend from waist

   _____ Arms hanging naturally

   _____ No unnecessary tension in arms and hands

   _____ No unnecessary tension in legs

3. **Alignment** (3 points -- 1 each)

   _____ Not left of target

   _____ Not right of target

   _____ Proper sequence of address
   (Draw imaginary line and pick a spot on the line. Set club square, feet together. Place right foot first on parallel line. Take last look at target.)

4. **Swing** (10 points -- 1 each)

   _____ One piece take away

   _____ Head did not move up and down.

   _____ Head did not move back and forth.

   _____ Left arm extended.

   _____ A complete coil is present.

   _____ Club toe up to target -- BACKSWING -- at parallel level

   _____ Club toe up to target -- forward swing -- at parallel level

   _____ Club accelerates through ball.

   _____ Club continues after contact.

   _____ Facing target at the finish

Points	Performance
10	Good contact, good trajectory, good direction
9	Good contact, good trajectory, fair direction
8	Good contact, fair trajectory, fair direction
6	Fair contact, fair trajectory, fair direction
4	2 items fair, 1 item barely acceptable
2	1 item fair, 2 items barely acceptable
0	Miss or near miss

Golf Lesson Plan 15

EQUIPMENT:

1 #9 iron per student	Golf Score Cards
Whiffle golf balls	15 hula hoops
6 flag markers	Written exam
Drum/tambourine	

INSTRUCTIONAL ACTIVITIES	ORGANIZATION TEACHING HINTS

INTRODUCTORY ACTIVITY (2–3 MINUTES)

Formation Rhythmic Running
Run 3 times.
Run in a small circle 4 times.
Jump in place 8 times.
Run 8 times and clap on counts 1, 4, 5, 7, and 8.

Repeat above.

DPESS page 313
Give instructions to "fall in" to a circle or lines.
Play drum or tambourine to set rhythm.

Increase tempo.

Format change for this lesson to allow time for game.

LESSON FOCUS/GAME (35–40 MINUTES)

Golf Game on Field

Explain Golf Game

DPESS page 473
Use Whistle Mixer to create teams of 4–5.
Distribute score cards for each group.
Start groups at different holes.

GOLF GAME SETUP ON FIELD

CHIPPING

SAND TRAP

PUTTING IN SAFE LOCATION

GOLF GAME SCORE CARD

Names	Holes					
	1	2	3	4	5	6

Exam and Supplemental Task Sheets

RECIPROCAL TASK SHEET 21: THE CHIP SHOT

Name: _____

1. **Student Information**: 60%–70% of all shots taken during a golf round are taken within 100 yards of the pin. The chip shot is a short accurate shot, used when just off the green.
2. **Objectives**: The student will demonstrate the skills of a short chip shot, from about 20 yards distance.
3. **Directions**: Chip 20 balls onto a green stopping the ball within 3' of a target located about 30' away. Have your partner record date and check appropriate response for each checkpoint for the chip shot.

(Record date of practice)	DATES							
Address	Yes	No	Yes	No	Yes	No	Yes	No
1. Take a narrow stance (feet within shoulder width) that is slightly open (lead foot just off the target line).								
2. 60% of weight on lead foot, toe slightly pointed out								
3. Knees slightly bent								
4. Bent over the ball from the waist								
5. Head down, over the ball								
6. Hands slightly in front of the ball, lead arm and club forming a straight line to the ball.								
7. The wrist of the trail hand forms a reverse "C" at address.								
BACKSWING								
1. Weight stays on lead foot.								
2. Keep head, hips, and knees level throughout swing.								
3. Bring the club back smoothly, using the arms and shoulders.								
4. Keep the hands and wrists quiet.								
5. Preserve the reverse "C" in the wrist of the trail hand.								
6. Make a compact swing. The club head should stay below the knees.								
Downswing								
1. Weight stays on lead foot through impact.								
2. Keep head, hips, and knees level throughout swing.								
3. Control the club using arms and shoulders through impact.								
4. Keep hands and wrists quiet.								
5. Preserve the reverse "C" in the wrist of trail hand.								
6. Brush the grass through impact.								

(Record date of practice)	DATES							
Follow-Through	Yes	No	Yes	No	Yes	No	Yes	No
1. Weight stays on lead foot.								
2. Keep head, hips, and knees level.								
3. Preserve the reverse "C" in the wrist of the trail hand.								
4. Change roles with partner.								
5. Repeat until you complete all three columns on this Task Sheet.								

RECIPROCAL TASK SHEET 22: SCORING

Directions: Two girls, Jane and Nancy, are playing a game of golf. The scores for each hole are listed as follows. Fill in the score card completely on the answer sheet; Jane is keeping score.

Hole 1 - Jane shot a 4 and Nancy took a bogey.

2 - Jane made a 6 and Nancy a 7.

3 - Jane shot ladies' par for the hole and Nancy made a birdie.

4 - Jane and Nancy both shot a 6.

5 - On the drive, Jane swung at the ball and missed it. Her second attempt was good and after 6 more strokes, her ball was in the cup. Nancy made the hole in 7.

6 - Both players made the hole in even par.

7 - Jane made an eagle. Nancy sliced her drive; her second shot was short of the green, but with two approach shots and two putts the ball was in the cup.

8 - Jane had a lot of hard luck and ended up with a 13. Nancy took 6 strokes.

9 - Jane made a 6 and Nancy a 7.

SCORE CARD

Hole	Yards	Men's Par	Women's Par	Handicap	Jane	Nancy			W + L- H O
1	345	4	4	10					
2	410	4	5	1					
3	474	4	5	6					
4	229	3	4	14					
5	396	4	4	4					
6	159	3	3	16					
7	552	5	5	5					
8	316	4	4	13					
9	367	4	4	17					
Out	3218	35	38						

1. What is Jane's medal score?

2. What is Nancy's medal score?

3. Who is the winner by medal play?

4. Who is the winner by match play?

5. What is the score by match play for Jane?

6. What is the score by match play for Nancy?

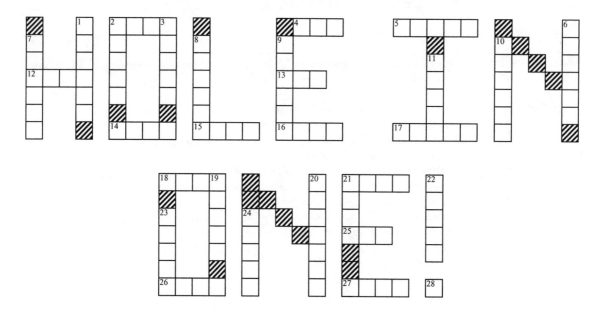

Across

2. The player farthest from the _____ should shoot first during play.
4. Players should begin play from between _____ markers.
5. Keep _____ when another player is preparing to shoot.
12. When you lift your ball from the green, _____ the ball's position with a coin.
13. The high side of a bunker is the _____.
14. The _____ marks the spot on the green where the cup is located.
15. The _____ of a coin may be used to decide who shoots first off the first tee.
16. When you remove the flagstick from the hole, don't drop it on the green; instead, lay it down gently on the _____ of the green.
17. Before teeing off, the golfer may practice at the driving _____.
18. A #1 _____ club is also called a driver.
21. The club shaft is parallel or almost parallel to the ground at the top of the backswing during a(n) _____ swing.
25. Players should tee up within _____ club lengths behind the tee markers.
26. The basic rule in golf is to play the ball where it _____.
27. Call "_____" if your ball is heading toward other players.
28. When gripping the club, the _____ formed by the thumb and index finger should point to the center of the body.

Down

1. A _____ shot is used to hit the ball out of a sand trap.
2. Playing first off the tee is call the _____.
3. A score of two under par for the hole is a(n) _____.
6. When leaving a sand trap, be sure to _____ your tracks.
7. Be careful not to _____ the green.
8. The person with _____ score on the preceding hole tees off first.
9. A score of one under par is a(n) _____.
10. An obstacle that interferes with the flight or roll of the ball is a(n) _____.
11. The putting surface is called the _____.
19. A _____ is a piece of turf removed by the club in making a shot, and should be replaced immediately.
20. A _____ of one stroke is counted when a ball is hit into a pond.
21. Stand with _____ shoulder width apart when swinging a driver.
22. The _____ is the unmowed area to the side of the fairway.
23. In _____ play, a golfer does not return to the original spot to shoot another ball if his is lost because it slows play.
24. Record your _____ at the next tee, not while you are still on the green. This allows the group behind you to start play.

ANSWER SHEET

Across

2. The player farthest from the <u>hole</u> should shoot first during play.
4. Players should begin play from between <u>tee</u> markers.
5. Keep <u>quiet</u> when another player is preparing to shoot.
12. When you lift your ball from the green, <u>mark</u> the ball's position with a coin.
13. The high side of a bunker is the <u>rim</u>.
14. The <u>flag</u> marks the spot on the green where the cup is located.
15. The <u>toss</u> of a coin may be used to decide who shoots first off the first tee.
16. When you remove the flagstick from the hole, don't drop it on the green; instead, lay it down gently on the <u>edge</u> of the green.
17. Before teeing off, the golfer may practice at the driving <u>range</u>.
18. A #1 <u>wood</u> club is also called a driver.
21. The club shaft is parallel or almost parallel to the ground at the top of the backswing during a <u>full</u> swing.
25. Players should tee up within <u>two</u> club lengths behind the tee markers.
26. The basic rule in golf is to play the ball where it <u>lies</u>.
27. Call "<u>FORE</u>" if your ball is heading toward other players.
28. When gripping the club, the <u>V</u> formed by the thumb and index finger should point to the center of the body.

Down

1. A <u>bunker</u> shot is used to hit the ball out of a sand trap.
2. Playing first off the tee is call the <u>honor</u>.
3. A score of two under par for the hole is an <u>eagle</u>.
6. When leaving a sand trap, be sure to <u>smooth</u> your tracks.
7. Be careful not to <u>damage</u> the green.
8. The person with the <u>lowest</u> score on the preceding hole tees off first.
9. A score of one under par is a <u>birdie</u>.
10. An obstacle that interferes with the flight or roll of the ball is a <u>hazard</u>.
11. The putting surface is called the <u>green</u>.
19. A <u>divot</u> is a piece of turf removed by the club in making a shot, and should be replaced immediately.
20. A <u>penalty</u> of one stroke is counted when a ball is hit into a pond.
21. Stand with <u>feet</u> shoulder width apart when swinging a driver.
22. The <u>rough</u> is the unmowed area to the side of the fairway.
23. In <u>medal</u> play, a golfer does not return to the original spot to shoot another ball if his is lost because it slows play.
24. Record your <u>score</u> at the next tee, not while you are still on the green. This allows the group behind you to start play.

GLOSSARY OF TERMS

Address: Taking the grip, stance, and proper body position in preparation to making a stroke.

Approach shot: A stroke played to approach putting green, i.e., pitch, chip.

Apron: The grass area around green.

Away: The ball farthest from hole.

Birdie: A score of one under par for a hole.

Bogey: A score of one over par for a hole.

Break of green: The slant of the green.

Bunker: A hazard, usually a depressed area covered with sand or a grassy mound.

Bye: The holes remaining to be played to determine the winner of the match.

Caddie: A person who carried the golfer's clubs and who can give her advice in regard to the course.

Casual water: Water, which accumulates on a course after a storm, not always present--not part of a hazard.

Chip shot: A short, low shot played to the green.

Closed stance: The left foot slightly in advance of the right--the player tends to face slightly away from the line of flight of the ball.

Club: The implement with which the ball is struck.

Course: The area within which play is permitted.

Cup: The hole sunk in the green into which the ball must be played in order to terminate play on that hole.

Dead: A ball is said to be "DEAD" when it lies so near the hole that the putt is a dead certainty. A ball is also said to "FALL DEAD" when it does not run after slighting.

Divot: A piece of turf removed by the club in making a shot.

Dogleg: A hole in which the fairway curves to the right or to the left.

Double bogey: Two strokes over par for a hole.

Driver: #1 wood.

Drop the ball: The player stands facing the hole and drops the ball over her shoulder.

Eagle: A score of two under par for the hole.

Face: The striking surface of the club.

Fade: A shot that slightly curves to the right in flight.

Fairway: The mowed grassy area between the tee and the putting green.

Flag: Marks the spot on the green where the cup is located.

Flagstick: The marker indicating the location of the hole.

Flight: Division of players according to ability for tournament; also, the path of the ball in the air.

Fore: A warning cry to any person in the line of the play.

Four-ball match: Two players play their better ball against the better ball of their opponents.

Foursome: Two players playing one ball on each side; partners alternate hitting the ball.

Green: The putting surface.

Grip: That part of the club that is grasped and the grasp itself.

Gross score: The total number of strokes taken to complete a round of golf.

Grounding the club: Placing the sole of the club on the turf in preparation for making the stroke.

Half-shot: A stroke that is less than a full swing.

Halved: Each side makes the same score on a hole.

Handicap: The approximate number of strokes one shoots over par, or the allowance of strokes to equalize players of different ability.

Hanging lie: The ball lies on a downward slope.

Hazard: Any obstacle that interferes with the free flight or roll of the ball (National; trees, natural water, rocks and so forth; made hazards; bunkers, sand traps; and so forth).

Head of the club: The heavy part of the club, used for striking the ball.

Heel of the club: The part of the club head below the point where the shaft and the head meet.

Hole: One unit of the course including the playing tee, fairway, hazards, green, and cup.

Holing out: Sinking the ball in the cup.

Honor: The privilege of playing first, acquired by winning the preceding hole.

Hook: A flight of the ball curves to the left.

Impact: The contact of the club with the ball.

Irons: A graded series of metal-headed clubs.

Lie: The position of the ball on the ground.

Like: A player is playing "the like" when she makes an equal number of strokes to that just played by her opponent.

Links: The golf course.

Loft: To elevate the ball; also, the angle of pitch of the face of the club.

Loft of the club: The angle of pitch of the clubface.

Loose impediments: Objects such as dead grass, fallen leaves, pebbles, worms, fallen twigs, etc.

Mashie: A five iron used in golf.

Match Play: Competition by holes; the player winning the most holes wins the match.

Match: The game itself.

Medal Play: A competition by total scores for all holes; the player with the lowest total score wins the match.

Medalist: The low score player in a medal tournament.

Nassau: A system of scoring awarding one point for the winning of each "nine" and an additional point for the match.

Net score: The score resulting from subtracting handicap from gross score.

Niblick: An iron-headed golf club with the face slanted at a greater angle than any other iron except a wedge; a nine iron.

Nook: The point at which the shaft joins the head of the club.

Obstruction: An artificial object on the course, which may be movable or fixed.

Odd: A player is playing "odd" when on a given hole she is making a stroke one more in number than that last played by her opponent.

Open stance: The left foot is drawn back so that the player tends to face somewhat in the direction of the flight of the ball.

Out-of-bounds: The area outside the proper course, from which balls may not be played.

Par: An arbitrary standard of scoring excellence based on the length and difficulty of a hole.

Pitch shot: A shot played to a putting green that travels in a high trajectory.

Press: Trying to hit the ball beyond one's normal power.

Provisional ball: A second ball played in case it is undetermined if the first ball is lost or out-of-bounds.

Pull: A ball that travels in a straight line to the left of the intended line of flight.

Push: A shot that travels in a straight line to the right of the intended line of flight.

Rough: The areas to the right or left of the fairway in which weeds and grass are allowed to grow.

Slice: A shot that curves in flight to the right, caused by the ball spinning in a horizontal, clockwise manner.

Stance: The position of feet in addressing the ball.

Stroke: Any forward motion of the club head made with intent to strike the ball.

Stroke play: Competition based on the total number of strokes taken.

Tee: The starting place for the hole or the peg on which the ball is placed for driving.

Tee markers: The markers placed on the tee to indicate limits of the teeing area.

Trajectory: The line of flight the ball takes when hit.

Whiff: When you swing and miss the ball.

GOLF QUIZ

TRUE/FALSE SECTION: Mark an A on the answer sheet if the statement is true. If the statement is false or partially false, mark B on the answer sheet.

1. A ball is said to have "hooked" when it curves off to the right.
2. The body should be facing the target at the end of the follow-through.
3. If a divot is taken, the player should not take the time to replace it.

MULTIPLE CHOICE: Place the corresponding letter of the best answer on the answer sheet.

4. What term is used to refer to the first shot on each hole?
    a. The drive
    b. The pitch and run
    c. The approach
5. In order to best sight the line of a putt, how should the player stand?
    a. With eyes to the right of the ball
    b. With eyes directly over the ball
    c. With eyes to the left of the ball
6. What is the last stroke necessary to reach the green called?
    a. Approach shot
    b. The drive
    c. The putt
7. What determines the amount of height a club gives to a ball?
    a. Length of the club
    b. Slant of the club head
    c. Weight of the head
8. In the grip, the little finger of the right hand overlaps or interlocks with what other finger?
    a. The forefinger of the left hand
    b. The middle finger of the left hand
    c. The little finger of the left hand
9. The part of the swing that allows the golfer to assume a comfortable position in relation to the ball is
    a. The follow-through
    b. The downswing
    c. The address
10. What do you call out loudly if there is any chance that your ball may hit someone?
    a. Fore
    b. Look-out
    c. Heads-up

TRUE/FALSE: Read each question carefully and circle the correct answer. Good luck!

11.	The part of the club between the grip and the head is known as the shaft.	T	F
12.	The club head should rest on the ground on the sole of the club rather than the heel.	T	F
13.	Golf clubs, classified as woods and irons, vary primarily in loft angle and shaft length.	T	F
14.	As loft increases, shaft length decreases.	T	F
15.	In regulation play, the golfer is allowed to carry 14 clubs: #2 through #9 irons; 1, 2, 3, and 4 woods, a putter, and a wedge.	T	F
16.	A pitching and sand wedge is used primarily to hit out of a sand trap.	T	F
17.	All golf holes are the same length, but bunkers, sand traps, etc. are used to create variety.	T	F
18.	After the drive, the person whose ball is farthest from the hole should play first.	T	F
19.	One should not play an approach shot to the green until the players ahead have left it.	T	F
20.	A ball that falls off the tee may not be re-teed without a penalty stroke.	T	F
21.	Whenever a player hits a ball that he feels may hit or come close to another golfer, he should yell "Fore!"	T	F
22.	At the beginning of the swing, the club should be drawn back slowly rather than rapidly.	T	F
23.	Rhythm in the golf swing is more important than speed.	T	F
24.	The stance has much to do with the direction the ball takes when hit.	T	F
25.	The center of your waist should be facing the target at the end of the follow-through.	T	F
26.	A ball is said to have "hooked" when it curves off to the right.	T	F

MULTIPLE CHOICE: Circle the best answer.

27. What term is used to refer to the first shot on each hole?
    a.   The drive
    b.   The pitch and run
    c.   The approach

28. What is the last stroke necessary to reach the green called?
    a.   The putt
    b.   The approach shot
    c.   The fairway shot

29. What is the standard of scoring excellence based on the length of a hole and allowing two putts on the putting green called?
    a.   Birdie
    b.   Bogey
    c.   Par

30. What is the mowed grassy area between the tee and putting green called?
    a.   The fairway
    b.   The rough
    c.   The green

31. The term "foursome" refers to:
    a.   The number of strokes taken on the fairway
    b.   Four players playing together
    c.   The only number of players allowed to play together on a golf course

32. What term refers to the position of the ball on the ground?
    a.   Flat
    b.   Lie
    c.   Set

33. What is the starting place for a hole or the peg on which the ball is placed for driving?
    a.   Tee
    b.   Marker
    c.   Pin

34. In finishing the swing, where should the weight be?
    a.   On the right foot
    b.   On the heels
    c.   On the left foot
    d.   On the toes

35. What will lifting one's head on a swing cause?
    a.   Topping ball
    b.   Lifting ball
    c.   Hooking ball
    d.   Slicing ball

36. Which is common to all stances?
    a.   Weight on toes
    b.   Weight back toward heels
    c.   Weight on whole foot

37. In the interlocking or overlapping grip, the little finger of the right hand interlocks or overlaps with which finger?
    a.   Index or forefinger of the left hand
    b.   Middle of left
    c.   Little finger of left

RECIPROCAL TASK SHEET 23: SCORING

Directions: Two girls, Jane and Nancy, are playing a game of golf. The scores for each hole are listed as follows. Fill in the scorecard completely, on the answer sheet; Jane is keeping score.

Hole 1 - Jane shot a 4 and Nancy took a bogey.

2 - Jane made a 6 and Nancy a 7.

3 - Jane shot ladies' par for the hole and Nancy made a birdie.

4 - Jane and Nancy both shot a 6.

5 - On the drive, Jane swung at the ball and missed it. Her second attempt was good and after 6 more strokes, her ball was in the cup. Nancy made the hole in 7.

6 - Both players made the hole in even par.

7 - Jane made an eagle. Nancy sliced her drive; her second shot was short of the green, but with two approach shots and two putts the ball was in the cup.

8 - Jane had a lot of hard luck and ended up with a 13. Nancy took 6 strokes.

9 - Jane made a 6 and Nancy a 7.

SCORE CARD

Hole	Yards	Men's Par	Women's Par	Handicap	Jane	Nancy			W + L- H O
1	345	4	4	10					
2	410	4	5	1					
3	474	4	5	6					
4	229	3	4	14					
5	396	4	4	4					
6	159	3	3	16					
7	552	5	5	5					
8	316	4	4	13					
9	367	4	4	17					
Out	3218	35	38						

1. What is Jane's medal score?
2. What is Nancy's medal score?
3. Who is the winner by medal play?
4. Who is the winner by match play?
5. What is the score by match play for Jane?
6. What is the score by match play for Nancy?

GOLF ETIQUETTE

1. On Tee
   a. Observe tee markers.
   b. Player with honor drives first.
   c. Don't talk or move around when another player is driving.
   d. In general, be still while person is driving.
   e. Stand diagonally in front to the right of player.

2. Fairway
   a. Player who is away plays first.
   b. Never stand in line of player's shots.
   c. Keep quiet when another player is shooting.
   d. Ball list, signal other players to go ahead.
   e. Wait until preceding players are off green before making approach shots.
   f. Replace and press down with foot all sods.
   g. Call "Fore" if ball goes near other players.

3. Sand Trap
   a. Leave bag on edge of trap.
   b. Enter and leave at nearest point.
   c. Smooth out footmarks and club marks.

4. Green
   a. Leave bag on edge.
   b. Place flag at the edge of green.
   c. Player away putts first.
   d. Keep away, out of line, of others putting.
   e. Keep still when player is putting.
   f. Avoid stepping on turf at edge of cup.
   g. Replace flag in cup.
   h. Leave green immediately after completing shots.

5. In General
   a. Wear only flat heels.
   b. When playing slowly, motion players behind to go ahead. Then wait until they are out of range before playing.

EQUIPMENT

CLUBS
Names and Uses
1. Woods
    a. (#1)–driver–120–180 yards, tee-off.
    b. (#2)–brassie–150–170 yards, tee-off, fairway-good lie.
    c. (#3)–spoon–145–160 yards, tee-off, on short holes; fairway.
2. Irons

    #1–driving iron

    #2–mid-iron, 140–150 yards, fairway long shots--poor lie, fairway long iron shots, low rough.

    #3–Mid-mashie, 125–135 yards.

    #4–Mashie iron, 115–125 yards, often used by women for tee shots on very short holes, long approach club, short roll-up approaches; more distance and less loft than mashie.

    *5–Mashie, 105–115 yards, and less; most popular approach club; rough and bed lies where distance is greater than can be obtained from lofted clubs; occasionally tee shots on very short holes.

    #6–Spade mashie; bad rough–greater distance than niblick.

    #7–Mashie niblick, 95–105 yards.

    *8–Pitching niblick, 85–95 yards.

    #9–Niblick

    *10–Putter

Woods and Iron Uses
1. The woods and first three irons are used for distance.
2. #4, 5, 6 irons are approach shots of medium distance; the ball will have a roll.
3. #7, 8, and 9 irons are used in hazards, bad rough, short approaches, and sand traps, and high pitch shots.
4. #10, the putter is used on the green.
5. Clubs marked (*) are essential for minimum set.

Racquetball

OBJECTIVES:

The student will:
1. Demonstrate agility, creativity, and cooperation while participating in the Introductory Activities.
2. Execute various locomotor movements called out by the instructor during the Rubber Band Introductory Activity.
3. Demonstrate cooperation with a partner during the Spider Tag Introductory Activity.
4. Perform locomotor movements to a beat while following the movements of a leader during the Introductory Activity.
5. Demonstrate dodging skills and the push-up position during the Introductory, Push-Up Tag Activity.
6. Demonstrate mirroring and cooperation skills while working with a partner.
7. Demonstrate leg, upper body strength, and teamwork skills while playing Crab Cage ball.
8. Demonstrate the ability to follow instructions, remember movement patterns, and simultaneously run, bend, and recover during the Introductory Activity.
9. Participate in the Fitness Cookie Jar Activities to improve all components of fitness.
10. Participate in the Partner Fitness Racetrack to improve fitness.
11. Perform the Continuity Exercises as directed by the instructor to improve his fitness level.
12. Participate in the Four Corners Fitness Activity to improve his overall fitness levels.
13. Participate in Aerobic workouts to improve her endurance, strength, and flexibility.
14. Improve her fitness level by participating in the Fitness Obstacle Course.
15. Demonstrate hoop-rolling ability while running.
16. Demonstrate agility, creativity, and cooperation during the Over, Under, and Around activity.
17. Participate in the Parachute Rhythmic Aerobic activity to improve fitness and demonstrate moving to a beat.
18. Practice the ready position and the forehand stroke as demonstrated in class by the instructor.
19. Practice the backhand stroke using form demonstrated by the instructor.
20. Practice half-lob serve using form demonstrated by the instructor in class.
21. Practice the fault and out serves using form demonstrated by the instructor.
22. Practice the back-wall return shot using form demonstrated by the instructor.
23. Practice the Power and "2" Serves using form demonstrated by the instructor.
24. Demonstrate the Pinch Shots using the Drop Hit Ball Drill demonstrated by the instructor.
25. Complete the Written Exam on Racquetball scoring 70% or better.
26. Cooperate with other students while participating in the Mass Stand Up Game.
27. Demonstrate cooperation and agility during the game "Entanglement."
28. Demonstrate agility, cooperation, and speed and dodging during the Addition Tag Game.
29. Participate in the Wheelbarrow relay demonstrating cooperation with a partner.
30. Demonstrate Frisbee throwing and catching skills during the Frisbee 21 Game.
31. Participate in Wand balancing and agility activities directed by the instructor.
32. Demonstrate skills learned in class during the Skills Test to the satisfaction of the instructor.
33. Play singles games up to 5 points using skills demonstrated in class.
34. Play racquetball demonstrating the rules and skills taught by the instructor.
35. Play in the Round Robin Racquetball Tournament using skills and rules taught by the instructor.

RACQUETBALL BLOCK PLAN
3 WEEK UNIT

Week #1	Monday	Tuesday	Wednesday	Thursday	Friday
Introductory Activity	Seat Roll and Jog	Hoops and Plyometrics	Over, Under, and Around	New Leader	Over, Under, and Around
Fitness	Fitness Scavenger Hunt	Partner Racetrack Fitness	Continuity Exercises	Parachute Rhythmic Aerobic Activity	Challenge Course
Lesson Focus	Ready Position Forehand Stroke	Court Orientation Forehand Stroke Drop Hit Ball Drill	Backhand Stroke Drop Hit Drill	Half Lob Serve	Fault and Out Serves Back Wall Return
Game	Entanglement	Mass Stand Up	Wheelbarrow Relay	Addition Tag	Frisbee 21

Week #2	Monday	Tuesday	Wednesday	Thursday	Friday
Introductory Activity	Rubber Band	Spider Tag	Formation Rhythmic Running	Push-Up Tag	Mirror Drill In Place
Fitness	Circuit Training	Aerobic (Dance) Exercises	Four Corners	Continuity Exercises	Partner Racetrack Fitness
Lesson Focus	Dead Ball Hinders Serves	Back Corner Return Shot	Passing Shots	Power Drive and "2" Serves	Shot Pinch
Game	Over and Under Ball Relay	Crab Cage ball	Addition Tag	Wand Activities	Crab Cage ball

Week #3	Monday	Tuesday	Wednesday	Thursday	Friday
Introductory Activity	Bean Bag Touch and Go	Eliminate to allow time for games	Eliminate to allow time for games	Eliminate to allow time for Tournament	Eliminate to allow time for Tournament
Fitness	Fitness Cookie Jar Exchange	Challenge Course	Continuity Exercises	Aerobic Workouts	Parachute Rhythmic Aerobic Activity
Lesson Focus	Racquetball Record of Sheets Games	Skills testing	Written Exam	Round Robin Tournament	Round Robin Tournament
Game	Play Racquetball	Play Racquetball	Play Racquetball	Round Robin Tournament	Round Robin Tournament

Racquetball Lesson Plan 1

EQUIPMENT:

1 racquet and racquetball per person	Music CD/tape
Fitness Scavenger Hunt Cards	CD/cassette player
Cones for stations	6 individual jump ropes
Station instruction cards	2 clipboards, Task Sheets, and pencils per court

INSTRUCTIONAL ACTIVITIES	TEACHING HINTS

INTRODUCTORY ACTIVITY (2–3 MINUTES)

Seat Roll and Jog
Direct students to seat roll right/left with hand signal.
   Alternate rolls with jogging in place.

DPESS page 304
Scattered formation
Student begins on "all fours" with head up looking at
   teacher for instructions.

FITNESS DEVELOPMENT (8–12 MINUTES)

Fitness Scavenger Hunt
Ideas for Fitness Hunt Cards:
1. Run to each corner of the Gym and perform 15 curl-ups at each corner.
2. Run to the bleachers and perform step-ups.
3. Carioca to cones set up and touch each cone.
4. Jog to the tumbling mats and perform stretches listed on the station cards.
5. Jog to the jump rope station, start the music tap during the entire CD/tape.
6. Jog backwards to touch 2 walls.
7. Jog forwards and touch 4 colored lines on the courts.
8. Skip to the sit-up, push-up station. Follow station card instructions.
9. Slide to the jumping jack station.
10. Skip to the jump rope station.

DPESS page 356
Use Whistle Mixer to create groups of 5.
Direct students to work as a team to "hunt" for the
   exercise space/area.
Assign each group a different starting point.
Give each group a "Fitness Hunt" Card.
Additional instructions can be added.

LESSON FOCUS (15–20 MINUTES)

Racquetball
Overview of the game of Racquetball: Court dimensions
Types of games: Singles, Cut-throat, Doubles

DPESS pages 476–479
Direct each student to pick up a racket, ball, and eye
   guards and bring them to the demonstration court.
Explain the parts of the racket and how it is to be held
   when not striking the ball.

Ready Position
Forehand Stroke
Demonstrate forehand grips and position for hitting.

Demonstrate the ready position.
Demonstrate the movement pattern from ready position to
   forehand position.
Demonstrate the back swing, forehand stroke, and follow
   through, without a ball.

Practice: Explain the Task Sheet.

Direct four students to go to each court. Equipment is
   arranged around the perimeter of each court.

GAME (5 MINUTES)

Entanglement
Each group makes a tight circle with their arms.

DPESS page 407

EVALUATION/REVIEW AND CHEER

Review elements of the Ready Position and Forehand Stroke.
Cheer: Racquetball is cool!

RECIPROCAL TASK SHEET 1

Name: Student "A": _____

Name: Student "B": _____

Directions: Two students will work together. Place both of your names on each Task Sheet. One individual is the "doer" while the other individual is the "observer." The "observer" reads information/instructions to the "doer," offers verbal feedback, and places a check in the "yes" or "no" columns recording the performance of their partner. When the "doer" has completed an item, the "doer" becomes the "observer" and the "observer" becomes the "doer."

Note: For this lesson, one pair of students will be working in one-half of the racquetball court while the other pair of student will be working in the other half of the court. In essence, the court will be divided into TWO long narrow areas. Each item is to be done five times before moving to next item.

	Student "A"		Student "B"	
	Yes	No	Yes	No
1. Demonstrate the Ready Position.				
2. Demonstrate the Forehand Grip you plan to use when hitting a forehand shot.				
3. Demonstrate the Forehand Position for hitting the ball.				
4. Demonstrate the movement pattern from the Ready Position to Forehand Position.				
5. Demonstrate the back swing, forehand stroke and follow through. "NO Ball!!"				

When both students have completed this Task Sheet, you are to return to the demonstration court and submit your Task Sheet to the Instructor.

RACQUETBALL SAFETY RULES

1. Follow all rules set by your instructor.
2. Wear protective eye wear at all times while in a racquetball court.
3. Make sure the racket wrist thong is on your wrist before swinging the racket.
4. Before swinging racket for practice drills, look around to see that no one is within range of your swing.
5. Do not stand near a player that is involved in a practice drill.
6. Limit swing of the racket to an arc of 180 degrees–half circle.
7. Do not walk into front court area to retrieve a ball while another player is involved in a practice drill.
8. Do not enter a court while players are involved in practice drills and/or a game. When play has stopped, knock on the d and wait until invited to enter the court.
9. During a game, do not turn around and look for the ball when it is behind you.
10. Do not push an opposing player during a game in order to reach the ball.
11. Accidents occur because of careless, lack of awareness, or lack of knowledge. Always follow safety rules when involve in practice drills and games.

Please cut off at the dotted line, sign, date, and return below to your instructor.

CUT OFF AND RETURN THIS SLIP TO INSTRUCTOR

I, _____, the undersigned, have read and understand the Racquetball Safety Rules. Furthermore, I agree to follow the rules of the class.

NAME: _____   DATE:_____
          (Signature)

Racquetball Lesson Plan 2

EQUIPMENT:

1 hula hoop per student	2 clipboards, Task Sheets, and pencils per court
Station instruction cards	1 pair protective eye guards per student
1 racquetball and racquet per student	

INSTRUCTIONAL ACTIVITIES	TEACHING HINTS

INTRODUCTORY ACTIVITY (2–3 MINUTES)

Hoops and Plyometrics

Each student rolls the hoop while running. On signal, the hoops are dropped. Challenge students to move in and out of a given number of hoops specified by color. State locomotor movement to use. Student then picks up the hoop and resumes rolling it.

DPESS page 309

Scattered formation.

Each student has a hoop and listens for instructions.

FITNESS DEVELOPMENT (8–12 MINUTES)

Partner Racetrack Fitness

On signal 1 partner begins the first activity on station card while other jogs around perimeter. Switch roles, then perform next task alternating positions until they complete all tasks at the station. Rotate to next station.

Task suggestions: Strengthening and stretching exercises, i.e., sit-ups, push-ups, upper and lower body stretches, etc.

DPESS pages 356–357

Use Back-to-Back to create partners.

Assign partners to a station to begin.

Explain station rotation.

LESSON FOCUS (15–20 MINUTES)

Court Orientation: Explain court markings:

- Service zone area (Service line, Short line, Drive Serve lines)
- Service boxes for doubles play; Receiving lines
- Front Court Area; Back Court Area

DPESS pages 476–479

Scattered formation

Review Forehand Stroke

Demonstrate drip hit ball drill–3 contact areas.

Demonstrate rally drill–forehand only.

Demonstrate ball contact areas:

1. Center of body
2. Front of lead leg
3. Back of lead leg

Demonstrate hitting off the lead leg.

Practice

When students complete Task Sheet, they are to continue practicing the drop hit drill and the rally drill.

Direct four students to go to each court and follow the Task Sheet instructions.

GAME (5 MINUTES)

Mass Stand Up

Start with 3 people sitting Back-to-Back. Lock elbows and try to stand up. Increase the number to 4 people, then 5, and so forth. See how many people can stand up simultaneously.

DPESS page 406

Use a management game, i.e., Whistle Mixer, to create group of 3.

Spread groups out in area.

RECIPROCAL TASK SHEET 2

Name: Student "A": _____
Name: Student "B": _____

Directions: Two students will work together. Place both of your names on each Task Sheet. One individual is the "doer" while the other individual is the "observer." The "observer" reads information/instructions to the "doer," offers verbal feedback, and places a check in the "yes" or "no" columns recording the performance of their partner. When the "doer" has completed an item, the "doer" becomes the "observer" and the "observer" becomes the "doer."

Note: For items 1–5, one pair of students will be working in one-half of the racquetball court while the other pair of students will be working in the other half of the court. In essence, the court will be divided into TWO long narrow areas. Students must stay on their side of the court during item 5.

Items 2–5 are to be done five times before moving to next item.

	Student "A"		Student "B"	
	Yes	No	Yes	No
1. Point out the following court markings: Service line, Short line, Receiving line.				
2. Demonstrate movement pattern to Forehand Position, back swing, forehand stroke, and follow through.				
3. Complete the drop hit ball drill from the Forehand Position.				
4. Using drop hit ball drill, demonstrate hitting the Forehand Stroke off the lead leg.				
5. Participate in the Rally drill. Forehand Strokes only! "Doer" hits the ball to front wall on their side of the court. When the ball rebounds from the front wall the "doer" hits the ball again (rallies) and continues to do so as long as the ball can be hit with a forehand stroke.				

When all items on Task Sheet have been completed by both students, repeat item 5 if time permits. Submit your completed Task Sheet to the Instructor.

Racquetball Lesson Plan 3

EQUIPMENT:

CD/cassette player
Continuity Exercise CD/tape
1 individual jump rope per student

1 racquetball, racquet, and eye guards per student
2 clipboards, 2 Task Sheets, and 2 pencils per court

INSTRUCTIONAL ACTIVITIES	TEACHING HINTS

INTRODUCTORY ACTIVITY (2–3 MINUTES)

Over, Under, and Around

One person gets in position on all fours while the other stands alongside, ready to begin the movement challenge. Challenge is to move over, go under, and run around partner a certain number of times. For example, move over your partner 5 times, go under 8 times, and run around 13 times.

DPESS pages 310–311

Use "elbow-to-elbow" management technique to create partners.

When the task is completed, partners change positions and the challenge is repeated.

FITNESS DEVELOPMENT (8–12 MINUTES)

Continuity Exercises

DPESS pages 349–350

LESSON FOCUS (15–20 MINUTES)

Backhand Stroke

Demonstrate backhand grips (Eastern & Continental); backhand position for hitting the ball.

Demonstrate ball contact areas:
1. Center of body
2. Front of lead leg
3. Back of lead leg

Practice

Upon completion of the Task Sheet, two students at a time are to practice the cross-court rally drill. One student hits a forehand while the other hits a backhand. The two other students are to stand outside the court.

DPESS page 476

Demonstrate the movement pattern from the ready position to the backhand position.

Demonstrate the back swing, backhand stroke, and follow through. No ball!

Review hitting off lead leg.

Demonstrate drop hit ball drill–3 contact areas.

Demonstrate rally drill–backhand only.

Demonstrate cross-court rally drill-forehand/backhand.

Direct four students to go to each court and follow the Task Sheets.

Students change roles after five rallies.

GAME (5 MINUTES)

Wheelbarrow Relay

DPESS page 405

Use "elbow-to-elbow" to create pairs. Then combine pairs to make lines/squads of 4 or 6.

Identify race area.

EVALUATION/REVIEW AND CHEER

Review elements of the backhand stroke.
Students create cheer.

RECIPROCAL TASK SHEET 3

Name: Student "A": _____

Name: Student "B": _____

Directions: Two students will work together. Place both of your names on each Task Sheet. One individual is the "doer" while the other individual is the "observer." The "observer" reads information/instructions to the "doer," offers verbal feedback, and places a check in the "yes" or "no" columns recording the performance of their partner. When the "doer" has completed an item, the "doer" becomes the "observer" and the "observer" becomes the "doer."

Note: For items 1–5, one pair of students will be working in one-half of the racquetball court while the other pair of students will be working in the other half of the court. In essence, the court will be divided into TWO long narrow areas. Students must stay on their side of the court during item 5.

Items 2–5 are to be done five times before moving to next item.

	Student "A"		Student "B"	
	Yes	No	Yes	No
1. Demonstrate the Backhand Grip you plan to use when hitting a backhand shot.				
2. Demonstrate the Backhand Position for Hitting the ball.				
3. Demonstrate the movement pattern from the Ready Position to Backhand Position.				
4. Demonstrate back swing, backhand stroke, and follow through. "NO Ball!"				
5. Complete the drop hit ball drill from the Backhand Position.				
6. Using drop hit ball drill, demonstrate hitting the Backhand Stroke off the lead leg.				
7. Participate in the Rally drill. Backhand Strokes only! "Doer" hits the ball to front wall on their side of the court. When the ball rebounds from the front wall the "doer" hits the ball again (rallies) and continues to do so as long as the ball can be hit with a backhand stroke.				

When all items on Task Sheet have been completed by both students, repeat item 5 if time permits. Submit your completed Task Sheet to the Instructor.

Racquetball Lesson Plan 4

EQUIPMENT:

1 parachute	CD/cassette player
1 racquetball, eye guards, and racquet per student	Music CD/tape
2 clipboards, 2 Task Sheets, and 2 pencils per court	

INSTRUCTIONAL ACTIVITIES	TEACHING HINTS

INTRODUCTORY ACTIVITY (2–3 MINUTES)

New Leader

The task is to continuously move in a productive fashion that will warm up the group. One person begins as the leader. When a signal is given, a new leader steps up and leads the next activity.

DPESS page 311

Use Whistle Mixer to create groups of 3–5.

FITNESS DEVELOPMENT (8–12 MINUTES)

Parachute Rhythmic Aerobic Activity

DPESS page 352

See Badminton Unit, Lesson Plan 11 for details.

LESSON FOCUS (15–20 MINUTES)

Serve: Half Lob

Demonstrate the following:

- Position in service zone from which serve is delivered.
- Stroke action when delivering (hitting) the serve.
- Flight patterns (possible) of the ball during serve.
- Follow through action after stroking the serve.
- Movement pattern to center court position after served ball crosses Short Line.

Demonstrate Serve Drill

- The role of the individual serving
- The role of the individual receiving/returning the served ball

DPESS page 477

Scattered position on court near service area

Fault and Out Serves

Describe a Fault Serve and an Out Serve.

Practice

Direct four students to go to each court. Students are to follow the instructions on the Task Sheets.

Out of Class Assignment

Handout: Fault Serves and the types of Out Serves.

Distribute handout at end of class. Students are to read information on the handout by next class period.

GAME (5 MINUTES)

Addition Tag

The "its" hold hands and can tag only with their outside hands. When they tag someone, that person must hook on. This continues and the tagging line becomes longer and longer. Regardless of the length of the line, only the hand on each end of the line is eligible to tag.

DPESS page 312

Scattered formation in area

Select several "its."

Change "its" after each tag game.

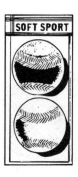

RACQUETBALL UNIT: FAULT SERVES HANDOUT

Service Faults: Result in an out if any two occur in succession.

    A. Foot Faults
    B. Short Service
    C. Three-Wall Service
    D. Ceiling Serve
    E. Long Serve
    F. Out-of-Court Serve
    G. Bouncing Ball Outside Service Zone
    H. Illegal Drive Serve
    I. Screen Serve
    J. Serving Before the Receiver is Ready

Note: When the first serve is a fault serve, the server receives a second opportunity to place the ball in play by serving.

RACQUETBALL UNIT: OUT SERVES

Out Serves: Result in loss of serve (out).

    A. Two Consecutive Fault Serves
    B. Failure to Serve Promptly
    C. Missed Serve Attempt
    D. Touched Serve
    E. Fake or Balk Serve
    F. Illegal Hit
    G. Non-Front Serve
    H. Crotch Serve
    I. Out-of-Order Serve
    J. Ball Hits Partner
    K. Safety Zone Violation

Note: When an out serve occurs, the server loses serve. They do not receive a second opportunity to place the ball in play serving.

RACQUETBALL RECIPROCAL TASK SHEET 4

Name: Student "A": _____

Name: Student "B": _____

<u>Directions</u>: Two students will work together. Place both of your names on each Task Sheet. One individual is the "doer" and one is the "observer." Then they reverse roles.

<u>Note</u>: For items 1–3, one pair of students will be working in one-half of the racquetball court while the other pair of students will be working in the other half of the court. Students must stay on their side of the court. Items 2–3 are to be done five times before moving to next item. For safety, only two individuals can be in the court for item 4: Service Drill. One pair of individuals is to wait outside the court while the other pair of individuals complete one phase of this drill, then individuals switch places.

	Student "A"		Student "B"	
	Yes	No	Yes	No
1. Demonstrate the position in the service zone from which Half Lob is delivered.				
2. Demonstrate stroke and follow through action for Half Lob serve.				
3. Demonstrate movement pattern to center court position after served ball crosses Short Line.				
4. Complete Serve Drill: Doer becomes *"Server"* and Observer becomes *"Receiver"*				
Phase 1: *<u>Server:</u>* Serve ball and watch rebound pattern. *<u>Receiver:</u>* Move to served ball and catch it.				
Phase 2: *<u>Server:</u>* Serve ball and move to center court position. *<u>Receiver:</u>* Return served ball.				
Phase 3: *<u>Server:</u>* Serve, center court position, rally return of serve. *<u>Receiver:</u>* Return serve and move to center court area.				
Phase 4: *<u>Server:</u>* Serve, center court position, rally return of serve to play out serve. *<u>Receiver:</u>* Return serve, move to center court area and play out serve.				

Submit your completed Task Sheet to the Instructor.

Racquetball Lesson Plan 5

EQUIPMENT:

Cones to mark obstacle course
Instruction cards for each station
3 mats
Benches

Hoops
Music CD/tape
CD/cassette player
1 racquetball and racquet per student

INSTRUCTIONAL ACTIVITIES	TEACHING HINTS

INTRODUCTORY ACTIVITY (2–3 MINUTES)

Over, Under, and Around

DPESS pages 310–311

FITNESS DEVELOPMENT (8–12 MINUTES)

Challenge Course

DPESS page 351
See Badminton Unit, Lesson Plan 1 for details.

LESSON FOCUS (15–20 MINUTES)

Fault and Out Serves
Demonstrate the above types of serves

DPESS page 477
Scattered formation

Shot: Back-wall Return
Demonstrate the following:
• Forehand Shot; Backhand Shot:
Demonstrate back wall drill for:
• Forehand shot; Backhand shot.

DPESS page 477
A. Movement pattern from center court area to back court area.
B. Forehand stroke ready position.
C. Movement pattern during forehand stroke.
D. Movement pattern after hitting forehand shot.

Practice
Explain Task Sheets.

Direct four students to go to each court and follow Task Sheet instructions and activities.

Out of Class Assignment: Direct students to read the information on the handout by the next class period.

At the end of class, distribute a handout on the different types of Dead-Ball Hinders.

GAME (5 MINUTES)

Frisbee 21
Throw and catch Frisbee. Keep score:
2 handed catch = 1 point
1 hand catch = 2 points

DPESS page 465
Create partners using "Toe-to-Toe."
Students stand 10 yards apart.
Must win by 2 points

EVALUATION/REVIEW AND CHEER

Review elements of faults and out serves.
Cheer: 2, 4, 6, 8, Racquetball is great!

RACQUETBALL UNIT HANDOUT: DEAD-BALL HINDERS

Dead-Ball Hinders: Result in the rally being replayed.
  A. Court Hinders
  B. Ball Hits Opponent
  C. Body Contact
  D. Screen Ball
  E. Back swing Hinder
  F. Safety Holdups
  G. Other Interference

Note:
  1. Play stops when either player calls "hinder."
  2. Five of the seven types can be placed into one of the following categories:
        a. Contact
        b. Stroke
        c. Visual
  In some instances, it is easier to remember the 3 categories.
  3. Hinder calls have been incorporated in the game of racquetball as a measure of safety.

RECIPROCAL TASK SHEET 5

Name: Student "A": _____

Name: Student "B": _____

Directions: Two students will work together. Place both of your names on each Task Sheet. One individual is the "doer" and one is the "observer." Then they reverse roles.

Note: For items 1–2, one pair of students will be working in one-half of the racquetball court while the other pair of students will be working in the other half of the court. Students must stay on their side of the court. Items 1–4 are to be done five times before moving to next item. For safety, only two individuals can be in the court for item 3–4: Back-Wall Return Drill. One individual from each pair is to wait outside the court while the other individual completes one phase of this drill then individuals switch places.

	Student "A"		Student "B"	
	Yes	No	Yes	No
1. Back-wall Return: Forehand shot. Demonstrate the following positions: A. Movement pattern from center court area to back court area B. Forehand stroke ready position C. Movement pattern during forehand stroke D. Movement pattern after hitting forehand shot				
2. Back-wall Return: Backhand shot. Repeat Items A–D above for Backhand shot				
3. Complete Back-Wall Drill: From forehand ready position: A. Toss ball onto back wall, on rebound let ball bounce on the floor then catch. B. Toss ball onto back wall. On the rebound let the ball bounce on the floor then hit it toward the front wall. C. Toss ball so it hits the floor then hits the back wall and rebounds into the court. During the flight of the rebound from the back wall, hit the ball toward the front wall before it bounces on the floor.				
4. From Backhand Ready Position: Repeat Items 3 A–3 C.				

Racquetball Lesson Plan 6

EQUIPMENT:

1 rubber ball per 5–6 students   1 racquetball, eye guard and racquet per student

Circuit Training Instructions   2 clipboards, 2 pencils, 2 Task Sheets per court

INSTRUCTIONAL ACTIVITIES   **TEACHING HINTS**

INTRODUCTORY ACTIVITY (2–3 MINUTES)

Rubber Band

On signal, the students move away from the instructor using a designated movement such as a jump, run, hop, slide, carioca, or walk. On the second signal, students sprint back to the instructor's position where the activity originated. The cycle is repeated with different movements. As a variation students can perform 1 or 2 stretching activities when they return to the teacher.

DPESS page 309

Scattered formation near teacher/leader

FITNESS DEVELOPMENT (8–12 MINUTES)

Circuit Training

DPESS page 348

See Golf Unit, Lesson Plan 10 for details.

INSTRUCTIONAL ACTIVITIES	TEACHING HINTS

LESSON FOCUS (15–20 MINUTES)

Dead-Ball Hinders
Demonstrate the different types.

Serve: Lob
Demonstrate the following:
- Position in service zone from which serve is delivered
- Stroke action when delivering (hitting) the serve
- Flight patterns of the ball during the serve
- Follow-through action after stroking the serve
- Movement pattern to center court position after served ball crosses Short Line

Review Serving

Practice

DPESS pages 476–479
Scattered in safe location on court for demonstration

Serving, receiving/returning the served ball
Fault Serves and Out Serves

Direct four students to go to each court and follow the instructions on the Task Sheets.

GAME (3–5 MINUTES)

Over and Under Ball Relay

DPESS page 405

Racquetball Lesson Plan 7

EQUIPMENT:

1 cage ball	1 racquetball, eye guards and racquet per student
Aerobic Exercise Music CD/tape	2 clipboards, pencils, and Task Sheets per court
CD/cassette player	

INSTRUCTIONAL ACTIVITIES	TEACHING HINTS

INTRODUCTORY ACTIVITY (2–3 MINUTES)

Spider Tag
Students stand Back-to-Back with a partner with the elbows hooked. The "its" chase the other pairs. If a pair is tagged (or becomes unhooked), they become "it."

DPESS page 312
Create partners using "Back-to-Back."
Select one pair to be "it."

FITNESS DEVELOPMENT (8–12 MINUTES)

Aerobic Workouts

DPESS page 358
Scattered formation

Sample 8 Count Aerobic Exercise Phrases of Movement

Jump in place 8 times.	Hit the sides of thighs with straight arms.
Walk in place 16 times.	On toes, perform 16 steps moving arms down and up on the sides or in the front of the body.
Run in place 8 times.	Lift feet high in the rear.
Run in place 8 times.	Lift knees high in front.
Perform 8 jumping jacks.	Arms move down and up with leg movements.
Perform 8 jumping jacks.	Arms move down and up to shoulder level.
Mountain Climber	Jump and land with feet separated forward and backward. Alternate which foot lands in front and in back on each jump. Arms swing high in opposition to legs.
Run in place 8 times.	Lift knees high in the front.
Run in place 8 times.	Lift feet high in the rear.
Perform 4 slides to the right.	Repeat to the left. Repeat whole phrase.
Hop on one foot and lift up the opposite knee.	Reverse.
Hop and swing kick the opposite foot forward.	Alternate.
Charleston Bounce Step	Step L, kick R foot forward, step back, and touch L toe back. Repeat 8 times. Reverse.
Schottische (Run R, L, R, Hop L. Alternate 4 X.)	Run 3 times in place or while traveling then hop (clap simultaneously).

INSTRUCTIONAL ACTIVITIES	TEACHING HINTS
Grapevine	Step to R, cross L foot over R, step to R on the R foot, cross L behind the R, and step on R while traveling to R. Repeat phrase 4 times moving to R.
Grapevine Schottische	Step to R on R, cross L behind R, step on R-to-R and hop on R. Reverse. Repeat 4 times.
Run 3 times in place.	Kick and clap on 4th count. Alternate. Repeat 4 X.
Twist the body using a bounce landing.	Swing arms in opposition overhead on each twist.
Walk in place.	To cool down
Leg Stretches & Upper Body Stretches	**DPESS pages 342–346**

LESSON FOCUS (15–20 MINUTES)

Shot: Back Corner Return	**DPESS pages 476–479**
Demonstrate the following:	A. Movement pattern from center court area to corner area.
• Right Back Corner:	B. Ready position while facing the corner (junction of side wall and back wall).
• Left Back Corner:	C. Movement pattern, including an adjustment step, for stroking a ball that rebounds from the back wall/side wall.
	D. Movement pattern, including an adjustment step, for stroking a ball that rebounds from the side wall/back wall.
	E. Movement pattern after hitting return shot.
Demonstrate Back Corner Drill:	A. Down-the Line return.
	B. Cross-Court return.
Practice. Explain the Task Sheets.	Direct four students to go to each court

GAME (5 MINUTES)

Crab Cage ball	**DPESS pages 402–403**
	Use Whistle Mixer to create 4 teams. Assign each team to a side of the square. Delineate square with cones in each corner. Assign each team a number.

EVALUATION/REVIEW AND CHEER

Review elements of the back corner return shot.
Cheer: Serving rates!

Racquetball Lesson Plan 8

EQUIPMENT:

Cones and station instruction cards	CD/cassette player
Drum and beater	1 racquetball, eye guards, and racquet per person
Music CD/tape	2 clipboards, 2 pencils, 2 Task Sheets per court

INSTRUCTIONAL ACTIVITIES	TEACHING HINTS

INTRODUCTORY ACTIVITY (2–3 MINUTES)

Formation Rhythmic Running	**DPESS page 313**

INSTRUCTIONAL ACTIVITIES	TEACHING HINTS

FITNESS DEVELOPMENT (8–12 MINUTES)

Four Corners	**DPESS page 347**
	See Badminton Unit, Lesson Plan 9 for details.

LESSON FOCUS (15–20 MINUTES)

Shot Demonstrations:	**DPESS page 477**
Passing	A. Down-the-Line shot
Forehand Stroke	B. Cross Court shot
Backhand Stroke	C. Wide Cross Court shot
Explain the purpose of Passing Shots.	A. Winning the point on the shot OR
	B. Creating a weak return from your opponent

INSTRUCTIONAL ACTIVITIES	TEACHING HINTS
	Demonstrate practice drill for Passing Shots using drop hit ball drill. Drop hit ball drill was in Lesson 2.
Practice	Direct four students to go to each court.
Explain practice with the Task Sheets.	
Out of Class Assignment	Students are to read the handout by next class period.
Handout: Avoidable Hinders	

GAME (5 MINUTES)

Addition Tag

DPESS page 312
See Lesson Plan 4 this unit for details.

RACQUETBALL HANDOUT: AVOIDABLE HINDERS

Avoidable Hinders: Result in loss of rally.
> A. Failure to Move
> B. Stroke Interference
> C. Blocking
> D. Moving into the Ball
> E. Pushing
> F. Intentional Distractions
> G. View Obstruction
> H. Wetting the Ball
> I. Apparel or Equipment Loss

Note:
> 1. In recreational type racquetball, few "avoidable hinder" situations arise.
> 2. Avoidable hinders are not replayed.

Racquetball Lesson Plan 9

EQUIPMENT:

Continuity Exercise Music CD/tape	CD/cassette player
1 racquetball and racquet per student	

INSTRUCTIONAL ACTIVITIES	TEACHING HINTS
INTRODUCTORY ACTIVITY (2–3 MINUTES)	
Push-Up Tag	**DPESS page 312**
FITNESS DEVELOPMENT (8–12 MINUTES)	
Continuity Exercises	**DPESS pages 349–350**
	See Lesson Plan 3 from the Badminton Unit for details.
LESSON FOCUS (15–20 MINUTES)	
Avoidable Hinders:	**DPESS pages 476–479**
	Demonstrate the different types.
Serves: Power (Drive) "2"	Place students in safe area on court for demonstration.
Position in service zone from which serve is delivered.	
Stroke action when delivering (hitting) the serve.	
Flight patterns of the ball during the serve.	
Follow through action after stroking the serve.	
Movement pattern to center court position after served ball crosses Short Line.	
Practice	Use a management game to make groups of four.
Explain Task Sheets.	Assign four students to go to each court.
GAME (5 MINUTES)	
Wand Activities:	**DPESS pages 401–402**
Wand Whirl	Scattered formation
Wand Kick Over	Direct students to pick up a wand and bring it to their
Thread the Needles	space.

Racquetball Lesson Plan 10

EQUIPMENT:

Partner Fitness Racetrack Instructions	Music
Station markers	CD/cassette player

INSTRUCTIONAL ACTIVITIES	TEACHING HINTS

INTRODUCTORY ACTIVITY (2–3 MINUTES)

Mirror Drill In Place

Student faces partner. One person is leader and makes a quick movement with the hands, head, legs, or body. Partner tries to mirror and perform the exact movement. Leader must pause briefly between movements. Leader and partner exchange places after 30 seconds.

DPESS page 313

Create partners using "Toe-to-Toe" technique.
Spread groups out in space.
Identify the first "leader."

FITNESS DEVELOPMENT (8–12 MINUTES)

Partner Racetrack Fitness

DPESS pages 356–357
See Lesson Plan 2 this unit for details.

LESSON FOCUS (15–20 MINUTES)

Pinch Shot
- Forehand Stroke
- Backhand stroke

Reverse Pinch Shot
- Forehand Stroke
- Backhand stroke

Review Drop Hit Ball Drill
See Lesson 2 for details.

Practice
Explain Pinch Shot Drill Task Sheets.

DPESS pages 476–479
Place students on court in safe place.
Demonstrate the following:
1. Forehand side of court
2. Backhand side of court

Explain the values of Pinch Shots and when they should be incorporated into a player's game.
Demonstrate practice drill for Pinch Shots using drop hit ball drill.
Direct four students to go to each court.

GAME (5 MINUTES)

Crab Cage ball

DPESS pages 402–403
See Lesson Plan 7 for details.

EVALUATION/REVIEW AND CHEER

Review elements of the Pinch Shot and Reverse Drop Hit.
Cheer: 2, 4, 6, 8, Racquetball is really great!

Racquetball Lesson Plan 11

EQUIPMENT:

20–30 bean bags of several colors   1 racquetball, eye guards and racquet per student

Fitness Cookie Jar Instructions   2 clipboards, 2 pencils, 2 Task Sheets per court; station markers

INSTRUCTIONAL ACTIVITIES	TEACHING HINTS

INTRODUCTORY ACTIVITY (2–3 MINUTES)

Bean Bag Touch and Go   DPESS page 309

FITNESS DEVELOPMENT (8–12 MINUTES)

Fitness Cookie Jar Exchange: Card suggestions:

1. Jog around the gym.
2. Crab walk forward and backward between cones.
3. Jog and shake hands with 8 different people.
4. Carioca (grapevine) step around a court going each direction.
5. Jog backwards around the Gym and "high 5" 4 other people.
6. Perform a mirroring activity with your partner.
7. Execute maximum number of curl-ups/push-ups.
8. Perform the coffee grinder on each side.
9. Execute maximum reverse push-ups.
10. Jump rope at a Hot Peppers rate.

DPESS page 356

Use management game to create partners.

Direct each partner set to pick a card from the "Cookie Jar."

Create a music CD/tape with 35 seconds of music for activity followed by a 10-second silence for picking a new card and changing activities.

LESSON FOCUS (15–20 MINUTES)

Record of Games Sheets

Explain the Record of Games sheet.

DPESS pages 476–477

Practice Drills: (6-8 minutes)

Students practice the following and change after 5 tries:

1. Two types of serves
2. Back-wall or Back Corner return shot
3. Passing or Pinch shot

Use a management game to create groups of 4.

Direct four students to go to each court to practice drills explained.

GAME (5 MINUTES)

Modified Racquetball

Two students (doers) play a 3-point singles game. The other two students (observers) stand outside the court.

Students change roles at the end of each 3-point game.

Explain Records of Game Sheets.

Direct students to return to same courts for games.

Each student is responsible for completing their Record of Games sheet and submitting it to the Instructor at the end of class.

EVALUATION/REVIEW AND CHEER

Review racquetball rules and the Records of Games Sheets.

Students create cheer.

RACQUETBALL RECORD OF GAMES SHEET

NAME: _____

    Game #1:   **Date**_____

        Opponent: _____

                      Score: _____–_____ Circle Your Score

    Game #2:   **Date**_____

        Opponent: _____

                      Score: _____–_____ Circle Your Score

    Game #3:   **Date**_____

        Opponent: _____

                      Score: _____–_____ Circle Your Score

Racquetball Lesson Plan 12

EQUIPMENT:

Obstacle course markers
Station instructions

1 clipboard and pencil per 2 students
1 Skills Test Sheet per student

INSTRUCTIONAL ACTIVITIES	TEACHING HINTS

INTRODUCTORY ACTIVITY (2–3 MINUTES)

Eliminate to allow more time for Skill Test.

FITNESS DEVELOPMENT (8–12 MINUTES)

Challenge Course

DPESS page 351
See Badminton Unit, Lesson Plan 1 for details.

LESSON FOCUS (15–20 MINUTES)

Skill Test
Explain Skill Test.

Use Whistle Mixer to create groups of 4.
Direct four students to go to each court.
When the Skill Test sheets are completed, students
submit them to the Instructor.

GAME (5 MINUTES)

Modified Games
Play singles games to 5 points.

Upon completion of Skills Test, students are to play.
Students change roles after each 5-point game.

EVALUATION/REVIEW AND CHEER

Discuss exam and how it went. Introduce upcoming class activities.
Cheer: Racquetball is fun!

RACQUETBALL SKILL TEST

Name: Student "A": _____

Name: Student "B": _____

Directions: Two students will work together. Place both of your names on the Skill Test sheet. One individual is the "doer" while the other individual is the "observer." The "observer" reads the skill to be demonstrated to the "doer," and places a check in the "yes" or "no" columns recording the performance of the doer. When the "doer" has completed the Skill Test, the "doer" becomes the "observer" and the "observer" becomes the "doer."

Note: Students will drop hit/toss ball to demonstrate the skills listed. Two attempts can be utilized to demonstrate each skill. If the skill is not demonstrated in the two attempts, the "NO" column is to be marked.

	Student "A"		Student "B"	
	Yes	No	Yes	No
1. *Demonstrate serves*: Select two of the following: A. Lob Serve				
B. Half Lob Serve				
C. Power (Drive)				
2. *Demonstrate the following shots:* A. Back wall Return: Forehand stroke				
B. Down-the-Line Pass: Backhand stroke				
C. Cross Court Pass: Forehand stroke				
D. Back Corner Return: Forehand stroke				
E. Back-wall Return: Backhand stroke				
F. Traditional Pinch: Backhand stroke / Backhand side of Court				
G. Reverse Pinch: Forehand side of court				
H. Back-wall Return: Backhand stroke				
Totals:				

Racquetball Lesson Plan 13

EQUIPMENT:
1 written exam and pencil per student
Continuity Exercise music CD/tape
CD/cassette player
1 individual jump rope per person
1 racquetball, racquet, and protective eye guard per student

INSTRUCTIONAL ACTIVITIES	TEACHING HINTS

INTRODUCTORY ACTIVITY (2–3 MINUTES)
Eliminate to allow more time for exam and playing.

FITNESS DEVELOPMENT (8–12 MINUTES)

Continuity Exercises	DPESS pages 349–350
	See Badminton Unit, Lesson Plan 3 for details.

LESSON FOCUS (15–20 MINUTES)

Written Exam	Distribute a copy of the exam and a pencil to each
Explain Exam Instructions.	student.
	Students complete the exam and return it and the pencil to the instructor.

GAME (5 MINUTES)

Play Racquetball	Allow students to set up games upon completion of exam.
Use 5 points as a game.	Change opponents after each 5-point game.

EVALUATION/REVIEW
Review areas students were concerned about on the written exam.
Discuss how each of the games went.

RACQUETBALL ROUND ROBIN TOURNAMENT: SINGLES

GROUP: _____   **CLASS:** _____

PLAYERS:

1.	2.
3	4.
5.	

Play one (1) game to 7 points.
When the game has been played between two players,
circle the pairing numbers of the players.

1 vs 5	2 vs 4	5 vs 4
3 vs 1	4 vs 3	5 vs 2
3 vs 2	2 vs 1	1 vs 4
3 vs 5		

RACQUETBALL UNIT: EXAM

Name: _____

TRUE/FALSE: Completely cover the T with a "dot" if the statement is TRUE or completely cover the F with a "dot" if the statement is FALSE.

T	F	1.	The game of racquetball experienced tremendous growth during the 1970's and became very popular.
T	F	2.	In a regulation game of racquetball, the first player to score 15 points (and ahead by 1 points) is the winner.
T	F	3.	The server should move to the center court area immediately after serving the ball.
T	F	4.	Short serves and long serves are the most common types of fault serves.
T	F	5.	Two types of passing shots are cross-court and down the line or wall.
T	F	6.	The individual receiving can score points.
T	F	7.	AARA rules require individuals to wear protective eye guards while playing.
T	F	8.	The player serving or the player receiving can call a hinder.
T	F	9.	A non-front serve is one type or example of a service fault.
T	F	10.	The "side-by-side" formation used in doubles play is the easier to master than the "I" formation.

FILL-IN-THE-SILENCES: Place the correct response or term in the appropriate silence(s).

1. There are three different types of games that can be played in racquetball. These involve the number of players. Name the three types of games.

   _____   _____   _____

2. Various types of serves should be used in playing the game of racquetball. Name four types of serves that have been introduced and explained during this course.

   _____   _____

3. Name four types of fault serves.

   _____   _____

4. There are seven types of Dead-Ball Hinders, which can occur during a game. Name four of these:

   _____   _____

   _____   _____

5. Name four types of out serves.

   _____   _____

   _____   _____

MATCHING: Place the letter of the best response in the silence next to the statement that best describes said response.

A. Kill Shot
D. Short Serve
G. Loss of Service
J. Ceiling Serve

B. Dead-Ball Hinder
E. Play Continues
H. Point
K. Doubles

C. Service Zone
F. Passing Shot
I. Long Serve
L. Non-Front Serve

_____ 1. Player A serves the ball, B's return of service strikes A in the back of the leg.

_____ 2. Player B attempts to serve, but the ball contacts the side wall before hitting the front wall and rebounding into the backcourt area.

_____ 3. The area bordered by the service line and the short line.

_____ 4. During play, Player A, who has served, hits a return, which rebounds off the front wall and strikes their racket.

_____ 5. Player B's serve rebounds from the front wall, bounces on the floor back of the short line and contacts the left side wall before Player A attempts to return the ball.

_____ 6. Following a legal serve by Player A, Player B's return bounces on the floor on the way to the front wall.

_____ 7. Player A serves the ball, but the rebound is not long enough to carry the ball over the short line on the fly.

_____ 8. An offensive shot which is hit low on the front wall so the rebounding will ball bounce two times very quickly.
_____ 9. A game in which the players can utilize the "side-by-side" formation.
_____ 10. Player B's serve rebounds from the front wall and contacts the sidewall and back wall before bouncing on the floor.

Racquetball Lesson Plan 14

EQUIPMENT:

Round Robin Tournament Chart	1 racquetball, eye guard, and racquet per student
1 clipboard and pencil and score sheet per 2 students	1 record of Games Sheet per student from lesson 11
Dance Exercise Music CD/tape	CD/cassette player

INSTRUCTIONAL ACTIVITIES	TEACHING HINTS

INTRODUCTORY ACTIVITY (2–3 MINUTES)

Eliminate to allow time for tournament play.

FITNESS DEVELOPMENT (8–12 MINUTES)

Aerobic Workout

DPESS 358.
See Lesson Plan 7 this unit for details.

LESSON FOCUS AND GAME (15–25 MINUTES)

2 Day Round Robin Tournament

All tournament games will be to 7 points.

Each student will record the results of their games on their Record of Games sheet and submit it to the instructor at the end of each class period.

Divide students into groups of 5 based on skill level.

Each student will play a 7-point game against each student in his group. (Each student will end up playing four different opponents during the 2-day tournament.)

EVALUATION/REVIEW AND CHEER

Discuss how each of the tournament games is going. Clarify questions regarding rules/Records of Games Sheets.
Teams create cheers.

Racquetball Lesson Plan 15

EQUIPMENT:

Round Robin Tournament Chart	1 racquetball, eye guard and racquet per student
1 clipboard and pencil and score sheet per 2 students	1 Record of Games Sheet per student
Dance Exercise Music CD/tape	CD/cassette player

INSTRUCTIONAL ACTIVITIES	TEACHING HINTS

INTRODUCTORY ACTIVITY (2–3 MINUTES)

Eliminate to allow time for tournament.

FITNESS DEVELOPMENT (8–12 MINUTES)

Parachute Rhythmic Aerobic Activity

DPESS page 352
See Badminton Unit, Lesson Plan 11 for details.

LESSON FOCUS AND GAME (15–25 MINUTES)

Continue Round Robin Tournament

Complete Round Robin Tournament.

Pickup Games

Students that complete the tournament before the end of the class period can play 5-point singles games against any other student in the class.

EVALUATION/REVIEW AND CHEER

Discuss how each of the tournament games went.
Introduce the next unit.
Students create cheer.

Soccer

OBJECTIVES:

The student will:
1. Demonstrate changing from walking to sprinting quickly when given a signal by the instructor.
2. Participate in the Four Corners Fitness Activities to improve her overall fitness levels.
3. Demonstrate proper tagging skills demonstrating safety rules explained by the instructor.
4. Demonstrate the ability to perform locomotor movements on command.
5. Rapidly change movements and count the number of repetitions performed during the Magic Number Challenge.
6. Form a variety of pyramids and demonstrate the proper points of support while performing them.
7. Demonstrate a smooth rhythmic run during the Formation Rhythmic Running Activity.
8. Space himself safely while running during Racetrack Fitness and Formation Rhythmic Running.
9. Participate in Circuit Training exercises and movements working towards performing at a higher intensity than previously.
10. Demonstrate the ability to work in groups and properly perform various exercises at each station.
11. Participate in Aerobic Exercises to improve overall fitness.
12. Perform Continuity Exercises including rope jumping for 30 seconds to improve her overall fitness levels.
13. Demonstrate the skills and techniques of passing a soccer ball in the air on the laces, as demonstrated by the teacher.
14. Demonstrate the correct techniques for dribbling a soccer ball with both inside and outside of both feet.
15. Demonstrate the ability to dribble a soccer ball for speed using outside of the foot.
16. Demonstrate control of her body and the ball while dribbling around the cones.
17. Develop ball foot and eye hand coordination using a soccer ball.
18. Demonstrate the proper techniques for passing a soccer ball short and long distances with both the inside and outside of both feet.
19. Demonstrate one and two touch passing skills using both inside and outside of both feet as demonstrated by the teacher.
20. Demonstrate the proper skills and techniques for collecting a soccer ball to themselves using their head.
21. Demonstrate quick reactions while playing soccer with classmates in a game situation.
22. Demonstrate the ability to work with a partner using a Task Sheet and during all class activities.
23. Demonstrate dribbling, passing, trapping, and heading skills using form demonstrated by the instructor during the skill test.
24. Demonstrate proper dribbling techniques in a game of Dribblerama.
25. Participate in the Soccer Tournament demonstrating skills practiced during the unit.

SOCCER BLOCK PLAN
3 WEEK UNIT

Week #1	Monday	Tuesday	Wednesday	Thursday	Friday
Introductory Activity	Fastest Tag	Move and Assume Pose	Formation Rhythmic Running	Number Challenges	Combination Movements
Fitness	Circuit Training	Mini Challenge Course	Partner Racetrack Fitness	Fitness Scavenger Hunt	Parachute Fitness Exercises
Focus	Dribbling Kick and Trap	Dribbling Kicking	Dribbling with a Defender	Dribbling High Trapping Skills	Throw-ins Instep Kick and Trap
Game	Frisbee 21	Chain Tag	Team Tug-of-War	Parachute Activities	Hacky Sack Juggling

Week #2	Monday	Tuesday	Wednesday	Thursday	Friday
Introductory Activity	Blob Tag	Hoops on the Ground	Walk, Trot, Sprint	New Leader	Move and Freeze on Signal
Fitness	Circuit Training	Aerobic Workout	Four Corners	Continuity Exercises	Parachute Fitness Activities
Focus	Passing and Trapping	Passing Combination Skills	Passing	Heel Pass Heading Dribbling	Heading Goal Kicking Goalie Defense
Game	Frisbee Keep Away	Flag Chase	Half Court Sideline Soccer	Soccer Keep Away	Dribblerama

Week #3	Monday	Tuesday	Wednesday	Thursday	Friday
Introductory Activity	Group Tag	Run, Stop, Pivot	Vanishing Bean Bags	Mini Pyramids	Ball Gymnastics
Fitness	Hexagon Hustle	Challenge Course Circuit	Parachute Aerobic Activity	Circuit Training	Fitness Scavenger Hunt
Focus	Rules Soccer Game	Play Soccer	Soccer Skill Test	Round Robin Tournament	Continue Tournament
Game	Dribbling Relays	Continue Soccer Games	Heading Game	Tournament	Tournament

Soccer Lesson Plan 1

EQUIPMENT:

20 cones	1 ball per student
Continuity music CD/tape	CD/cassette player
1 Task Sheet per 2 students	Whistle
1 pen/pencil and clipboard per 2 students	

INSTRUCTIONAL ACTIVITIES	TEACHING HINTS

INTRODUCTORY ACTIVITY (2–3 MINUTES)

Fastest Tag
Everyone is "it."

DPESS page 312
Scattered formation
See Lesson 8, Volleyball Unit for details.

FITNESS DEVELOPMENT (8–12 MINUTES)

Stations: Circuit Training
When music starts, students begin activity at the station. At pause in music they switch. Stations consist of push-ups, lunges, sit ups, flyers, etc. Include stations for aerobic activity.

DPESS page 348
Using Whistle Mixer, create groups of 7 students.
Assign each group to begin at a different station.
Go through all stations once then begin again.

LESSON FOCUS (15–20 MINUTES)

Dribbling using inside and outside of both feet.
Explain Task Sheets and rotation.
The doer will dribble the ball 10 times each with the inside, outside, left and right feet to the cone and back, then switch.

DPESS pages 435–436
Place cones on field 10 feet apart for practice areas.
Use Back-to-Back to create partners.
Assign one partner to pick up equipment:
   1 Ball, 1 Clipboard, pencil and Task Sheet.
Work with same partner.

Inside Kick and Trap: Demonstrate skill and drill.

GAME (5 MINUTES)

Frisbee 21

DPESS page 465
See Golf Unit, Lesson 13 for details.

EVALUATION/REVIEW AND CHEER

Ask students what techniques they worked on in class.
Cheer: Soccer, soccer, let's play!

Soccer Lesson Plan 2

EQUIPMENT:

20 cones	CD/cassette player
1 soccer ball per 2 students	Continuity Music Exercise CD/tape
1 Task Sheet per 2 students	Poster board for course
1 pen/pencil, clipboard per 2 students	Whistle

INSTRUCTIONAL ACTIVITIES	TEACHING HINTS

INTRODUCTORY ACTIVITY (2–3 MINUTES)

Move and Assume Pose
Students will move doing a variety of locomotor movements. Freeze on signal and assume balancing poses on various body parts.

DPESS page 308
Scattered formation

FITNESS DEVELOPMENT (8–12 MINUTES)

Mini Challenge Course
The course will consist of crab walk, weave in and out of cones, and hop over cones, skip, and jog backward.

DPESS page 351
See Lesson 6, Volleyball for details
Students will be in groups and each group will start at different times to allow for space.

INSTRUCTIONAL ACTIVITIES	TEACHING HINTS

LESSON FOCUS (15–20 MINUTES)

Dribbling for speed

The student will run and dribble ball between 2 cones 10 times. Both partners can practice at once with adequate spacing.

Kicking and Trapping

Repeat drill used yesterday, but increase distance.

Combination Dribbling and Kicking Drill

Student dribbles toward partner 1/2 distance between the cones set up, then passes to partner who must trap the ball and begin the drill himself. Alternate turns.

DPESS pages 435–436

Set cones up 20 feet apart.

Using a management technique, create partners.

1 ball per person

Use same partners.

Use same partners and cones set up for dribbling drill.

GAME (5 MINUTES)

Chain Tag

Two parallel lines 20 feet apart. 3 people in center between the lines form a chain. The players on the end can tag people. On signal the center says "come" and the 2 lines run across, if tagged they join the chain.

Select 3 to be in center.

EVALUATION/REVIEW AND CHEER

Talk about skills practiced today. Ask if there were any particular areas needing clarification.
Cheer: 2-4-6-8, Dribblin's great!

Soccer Lesson Plan 3

EQUIPMENT:

20 cones	Tug-of-War rope
1 soccer ball per person	Whistle

INSTRUCTIONAL ACTIVITIES	TEACHING HINTS

INTRODUCTORY ACTIVITY (2–3 MINUTES)

Formation Rhythmic Running

Run on signal, run in direction led.

DPESS page 313

Scattered formation inside a coned off area

See Lesson 5, Volleyball Unit for complete details.

FITNESS DEVELOPMENT (8–12 MINUTES)

Partner Racetrack Fitness

DPESS page 356

See Lesson 6, Tennis Unit for complete details.

LESSON FOCUS (15–20 MINUTES)

Dribbling through cones

Stations set up with cones simulating defenders

Each station will have more cones than the previous with a tighter area. Each student will dribble through each station 2 times once with left foot and once with right foot.

Object is to not knock down cones.

DPESS pages 435–436

Use Whistle Mixer to create groups of 3–4.

Assign groups of 3–4 to each station.

On signal, change stations. Keep head up and the ball close to body.

Use both inside and outside of foot. Maintain control.

Dribbling with a defender

Demonstrate methods of "stealing" ball from dribbler.
Dribble toward defender who tries to take ball away.

Same groups

1 dribbler to 1 defender or 2 dribblers to 1 defender if in groups of 3.

GAME (5 MINUTES)

Team Tug-of-War

There are 2 even teams each team on each half of the rope. On signal teams begin pulling and first team to pull the other over the line wins.

DPESS page 407

Use a management game, i.e., Back-to-Back, to create two groups.

EVALUATION/REVIEW AND CHEER

Review skills taught by asking questions.
Cheer: We love soccer!

Soccer Lesson Plan 4

EQUIPMENT:

Magic number cards

1 jump rope per student

1 soccer ball per student

30 cones

Whistle

INSTRUCTIONAL ACTIVITIES	TEACHING HINTS

INTRODUCTORY ACTIVITY (2–3 MINUTES)

Number Challenges

Hold up a card with 3 numbers on it (i.e., 8,10,5). The students must then perform 3 selected movements the specified number of times.

DPESS page 309

Scattered formation

Students put together a series of movements based on the magic numbers given.

FITNESS DEVELOPMENT (8–12 MINUTES)

Fitness Scavenger Hunt

DPESS page 356

See Golf Unit, Lesson 7 for details.

LESSON FOCUS (15–20 MINUTES)

Dribbling with Defensive Pressure

First each student will dribble in coned area with 1 defender using skills learned, then 2 defenders. After going through coned area once, change roles. Repeat 3 X per student.

DPESS pages 435–436

Using Whistle Mixer, create groups of 3.

Identify coned off area.

High Trapping Skills

Demonstrating trapping with thigh.

Practice: Toss ball toward thigh of partner. Trap with thigh and dribble 5 feet forward,

Use same groups as above, or switch to groups of 2 for this practice. Can rotate roles if groups of 3 used and 2 balls.

GAME (5 MINUTES)

Parachute Activities

DPESS page 351

See Weight Training Unit, Lesson 15 for details.

EVALUATION/REVIEW AND CHHER

Review elements involved in trapping and defense.

Cheer: 2, 4, 6, 8, Soccer's Great!

Soccer Lesson Plan 5

EQUIPMENT:

1 parachute

1 hacky sack/bean bag per student

Whistle

1 soccer ball per student

2 cones per 2 students

INSTRUCTIONAL ACTIVITIES	TEACHING HINTS

INTRODUCTORY ACTIVITY (2–3 MINUTES)

Combination Movements

Teacher will call out movements and students will follow. Movement suggestions: hop, turn around and shake; jump, make shape in air balance; skip, collapse and roll; curl, roll, jump with 1/2 turn; whirl, skip, sink slowly; hop, collapse, creep; kneel, sway, jump to feet.

DPESS page 308

("Move and Change the Type of Locomotion")

Scattered formation

After each movement phrase, student will skip while waiting for next instruction.

INSTRUCTIONAL ACTIVITIES	TEACHING HINTS

FITNESS DEVELOPMENT (8–12 MINUTES)

Parachute Fitness Exercises

Student will hold a handle and begin either running, hopping, skipping, etc. On 1 whistle signal they will change directions. On 2 whistles they will lower chute quickly and do the exercise specified by teacher.

DPESS page 351

Scattered around parachute, holding edge of chute

LESSON FOCUS (15–20 MINUTES)

Throw-in, Thigh Trap

Demonstrate overhand throw-in.
Demonstrate thigh trap, to foot trap.

Throw-in, Thigh Trap, and Dribble

Demonstrate skill and practice drill a given distance.

Instep Kick and Trap

Demonstrate Instep Kick to partner, foot trap.

DPESS pages 435–436

Use Elbow-to-Elbow technique to create partners.
Direct students to practice throw in and trapping skills.
Same partners
Both partners practice.
Same partners
Alternate roles. Each person practices 10 times.

GAME (5 MINUTES)

Hacky Sack/Bean Bag Juggling

Student juggles bag on knees, thighs, and feet only. Strives to keep bag in action.

Scattered formation

Can challenge to count how many repetitions are possible before losing control. Identify class champion.

EVALUATION/REVIEW AND CHEER

Review trapping and throw in skill elements.
Cheer: 2, 4, 6, 8, Jugglin's really great!

Soccer Lesson Plan 6

EQUIPMENT:

2 cones per 3 students
1 soccer ball per 3 students
1 Task Sheet per student
1 pencil and clipboard per 3 students

Continuity Music Exercise CD/tape
CD/cassette player
6 hula hoops
6 jump ropes

INSTRUCTIONAL ACTIVITIES	TEACHING HINTS

INTRODUCTORY ACTIVITY (2–3 MINUTES)

Blob Tag

DPESS page 312

FITNESS DEVELOPMENT (8–12 MINUTES)

Circuit Training

DPESS page 348
See Lesson 5, Golf Unit for details.

LESSON FOCUS (15–20 MINUTES)

Passing and Trapping Skills using Task Sheets

Explain Task Sheets and demonstrate skills to practice
Each group will be at a cone with another cone 10 ft. away.

Using Whistle Mixer, make groups of 3.
Direct students to take 1 clipboard, pencil and 1 Task Sheet per person to assigned areas.

GAME (5 MINUTES)

Frisbee Keep Away

DPESS pages 463–465
See Lesson 1, Golf Unit for details.

EVALUATION/REVIEW AND CHEER

Discussion on skills practiced today.
Cheer: On 3, "PE's great"

RECIPROCAL TASK SHEET: SOCCER PASSING

Name: _____

Directions: Work with two other people. One person is the "doer," one person is the pass receiver, while the other person is the "observer." The observer reads the information/instructions to the doer, offers verbal feedback and places a check in the "yes" or "no" column recording the performance of the "doer." Record the date of the practice. After 5 practices, rotate roles. The "doer" becomes the "observer," the "observer" becomes the receiver. Each person has his/her own Task Sheet.

PASSING	DATES							
(Record date of practice)								
	Yes	No	Yes	No	Yes	No	Yes	No
1. Use the inside of your foot and pass the ball to your partner standing 10' away from you. Partner returns ball to you. Repeat 5 times.								
2. Use the outside of your foot and pass the ball to your partner standing 10' away from you. Repeat 5 times.								

ROTATE ROLES

FOOT TRAPPING	Yes	No	Yes	No	Yes	No	Yes	No
1. Repeat # 1 above and foot trap the ball.								
2. Repeat # 2 above and foot trap the ball.								
ROTATE ROLES								
THROW IN, THIGH TRAP, FOOT TRAP	Yes	No	Yes	No	Yes	No	Yes	No
1. Throw-in ball to partner, trap with thighs, drop ball to foot trap. Repeat 5 times.								

ROTATE ROLES

Turn Completed Task Sheets in to Instructor								

Soccer Lesson Plan 7

EQUIPMENT:

Cones to mark off dribbling area
1 soccer ball per 2 students
CD/cassette player

Aerobic Exercise Music CD/tape
1 flag for each student
1 hula hoop per 2 students

INSTRUCTIONAL ACTIVITIES	TEACHING HINTS

INTRODUCTORY ACTIVITY (2–3 MINUTES)

Hoops on the Ground

Students run around the area where hoops are on ground.
Teacher calls a number and that number of students
must fit inside a hoop in 5 seconds or less.

DPESS page 313
Scattered formation

FITNESS DEVELOPMENT (8–12 MINUTES)

Aerobic Workout

DPESS page 358
See Lesson 7, Racquetball Unit for details.

LESSON FOCUS (15–20 MINUTES)

Passing: Top of Foot

Demonstrate passing the ball in the air with top of foot
Head should be down, toe down, and ankle locked.

Combination Drills:

- **Dribbling, Instep Pass**
  Demonstrate dribbling down the field 15', instep pass
  to lead partner. Continue.
- **Throw in, Top of Foot Pass**
  Demonstrate throw in, top of foot pass to partner.
- **Dribbling, Outside Foot Pass**
  Repeat drill used performing with the Instep pass.

DPESS pages 435–436
Use elbow-to-elbow to create pairs.
1 ball per two students

Toss ball to partner at foot. Partner passes using top of
foot. Have doer face a fence so pass won't go too far.
Repeat 5 times then switch roles (contact the ball with
laces).
Pass ball to lead partner down field.

GAME (5 MINUTES)

Flag chase (Variation of Flag Grab)

On signal students run around and try to pull flags off. If
flag is pulled you sit down. The one with the most
flags after a given short period wins. Repeat.

DPESS page 314
Scattered formation
Each student has a flag tucked into his or her shorts.

EVALUATION/REVIEW AND CHEER

Ask questions regarding the proper form used for passing the ball in the air.
Cheer: Exercise...yeeaah!

Soccer Lesson Plan 8

EQUIPMENT:

2 cones per 2 students	Pinnies
Whistle	1 soccer ball per 2 students
	Poster board

INSTRUCTIONAL ACTIVITIES	TEACHING HINTS

INTRODUCTORY ACTIVITY (2–3 MINUTES)

Walk, Trot, Sprint	**(Similar to Walk, Jog, Sprint)**
1 whistle = run; 2 whistles = trot; 3 whistles = sprint; 4 whistles = stop and perform a stretch demonstrated. If the teacher claps = change directions.	Scattered formation Teacher directs the changes.

FITNESS DEVELOPMENT (8–12 MINUTES)

Four Corners	**DPESS page 347**
There will be groups of students at each corner, with a sign with different movements on it at each corner. On signal students begin activity, on second signal they skip, jog, etc. to next station.	See Lesson 9, Golf Unit for complete details. Use Whistle Mixer to create even numbers of people to begin at each corner.

LESSON FOCUS (15–20 MINUTES)

Passing (1 touch, 2 touch passing)	**DPESS pages 435–436**
Students will be 5 yards apart. On each signal students will continue passing but move back to be next cone. On signal they will move back to last cone marker while still passing the ball. They will do the same thing with the 2 touch (start at 1 ft. and move to 20).	Use Toe-to-Toe to create partners. 1 ball per 2 students Partners stand opposite each other at cone markings.
2 touch: Same techniques but stop the ball with the inside of the foot first, then pass it back. Repeat drill.	

GAME (5 MINUTES)

Half Court Sideline Soccer	**DPESS page 437**
Divide field in half. Follow rules of Sideline Soccer, but on 1/2 of field.	Create even teams using a management game.

EVALUATION/REVIEW AND CHEER

Discuss skills practiced during the day and Sideline Soccer game.
Cheer: We love soccer!

Soccer Lesson Plan 9

EQUIPMENT:

1 jump rope per student	20 cones
1 soccer ball per 2 students	CD/cassette player
Continuity Exercise Music CD/tape	Whistle

INSTRUCTIONAL ACTIVITIES	TEACHING HINTS

INTRODUCTORY ACTIVITY (2–3 MINUTES)

New Leader	**DPESS page 311**
The first person in line is the first leader. On signal leader executes a movement, the rest of the line must follow. On the next signal the leaders switch.	Use Whistle Mixer to create groups of 3–5.

FITNESS DEVELOPMENT (8–12 MINUTES)

Continuity Exercises	**DPESS page 349**
See Lesson 1, Golf for complete details.	Scattered formation

INSTRUCTIONAL ACTIVITIES	TEACHING HINTS

LESSON FOCUS (15–20 MINUTES)

Heel Pass

Demonstrate the heel pass. Goal: pass to a player behind you. Toe up and ankle are up and you pass the ball with the heel to a person behind you.

DPESS pages 435–436
Partner formation with a ball
Students will be 10' apart and pass.
This is a blind pass.

Heading

Demonstrate heading to a partner. May use rubber balls to begin with.

Same partner formation

Dribble Through Cones (Review)

Same partners. Use drill taught on previous day.

GAME (5 MINUTES)

Soccer Keep Away

Use all skills taught to keep ball from middle person. Rotate when middle person intercepts ball or after a given time limit.

DPESS page 437
Use Whistle Mixer to create groups of 3.

EVALUATION/REVIEW AND CHEER

Ask students which passing skill worked best for them and why.
Cheer: 3, 2, 1, Soccer is really fun!

Soccer Lesson Plan 10

EQUIPMENT:

Whistle	Parachute
20 cones	1 soccer ball per student

INSTRUCTIONAL ACTIVITIES	TEACHING HINTS

INTRODUCTORY ACTIVITY (2–3 MINUTES)

Move and Freeze on Signal
(Variation of Change, Move, and Quickly Stop)
Students move throughout the area using a variety of locomotor movements, on signal they freeze quickly.

DPESS page 308
Object is to try to reduce the response latency.
Scattered formation

FITNESS DEVELOPMENT (8–12 MINUTES)

Parachute Fitness Activities

DPESS page 351
See Lesson 4, Golf Unit for details.

LESSON FOCUS (15–20 MINUTES)

Heading

Drill: toss ball 10 times and partner will head it back, then switch.
Repeat trying to increase distance. Switch after 10 X. Demonstrate power obtained by bending legs and jumping, to push the ball high and long.

DPESS pages 435–436
Students will be in pairs with a ball.

Goal Kicking and Goalie Defense
Demonstrate skills.

Use Whistle Mixer to make groups of 3.
Assign 3 students to areas on field with cones marked simulating goals.

GAME (5 MINUTES)

Dribblerama

On signal students will dribble using skills learned and try to kick other persons balls out of the area. If ball goes out person must retrieve it. 1 point per ball intercepted and kicked out of boundaries.

Each student will have a ball and be inside a coned area.

EVALUATION/REVIEW AND CHEER

Discuss heading, goal kicking and defense skills.
Cheer: Soccer, yes!

Soccer Lesson Plan 11

EQUIPMENT:

20 cones	Poster board
1 ball per 2 students	CD/cassette player
Music CD/tape for fitness activities	Whistle

INSTRUCTIONAL ACTIVITIES	TEACHING HINTS

INTRODUCTORY ACTIVITY (2–3 MINUTES)

Group tag (Variation of Blob Tag)

There are 3 students designated "it." They try and tag others; if you are tagged you help the group tag others. Last one not tagged wins.

DPESS page 312

Scattered formation

FITNESS DEVELOPMENT (8–12 MINUTES)

Circuit Training: Hexagon Hustle

Make a hexagon with 6 cones. Place signs with directions on both sides of cone. The signs identify the hustle activity.

Assign groups to begin at each cone.

Use music for activity during silence perform flexibility, stretching and strengthening activities.

LESSON FOCUS (15–20 MINUTES)

Soccer Game and Rules

Show a videotape of soccer and explain rules.

Play Soccer

DPESS pages 436–437

Give students a rules handout to read.

Create teams ahead of time.

Assign students to playing field.

GAME (5 MINUTES)

Dribbling Relays

1. Dribble the ball with speed to the cone and back; then next person goes.
2. Dribble in and out of the cones and back to the line, then next person goes, sit when done.
3. Dribble to cone; leave ball at cone and run back. The next person runs to cone and dribbles ball back and so on. First line done wins.

Use Whistle Mixer to create groups of 5–6.

Lines of 5–6 students

EVALUATION/REVIEW AND CHEER

Discuss how short Soccer Games went. Ask if any questions over the rules.

Cheer: Soccer's great!

Soccer Lesson Plan 12

EQUIPMENT:

Cones for marking boundaries and stations	Instructions for Challenge Course Stations
6–8 jump ropes	CD/cassette player for Fitness Music
1 soccer ball per student	Music CD/tape for Fitness Stations
Pinnies for 1/2 class	Whistle or Drum
Goals	

INSTRUCTIONAL ACTIVITIES	TEACHING HINTS

INTRODUCTORY ACTIVITY (2–3 MINUTES)

Run, Stop, Pivot (Similar to Move, Stop, Pivot)

Students run, stop then pivot on signal. Vary activity by directing pivot on alternate feet and to increase the circumference of the pivot.

DPESS page 308

Scattered formation

FITNESS DEVELOPMENT (8–12 MINUTES)

Challenge Course Circuit

Arrange three or four courses with a group at each course.

DPESS page 351

See Lesson 8, Badminton Unit for complete details.

INSTRUCTIONAL ACTIVITIES	TEACHING HINTS

LESSON FOCUS (15–20 MINUTES)

Play Soccer
Review rules.

Use same teams as yesterday, but rotate opponents.

GAME (5 MINUTES)

Continue games.

Rotate after each game won.

EVALUATION/REVIEW AND CHEER

Discuss how games went. Ask questions to review important rules.
Cheer: We love soccer!

Soccer Lesson Plan 13

EQUIPMENT:

1 bean bag per student
1 soccer ball per student
1 Reciprocal Task Sheet Skill Test per student
1 clipboard, pencil per 2 students

1 parachute
Music CD/tape for fitness
CD/cassette player

INSTRUCTIONAL ACTIVITIES	TEACHING HINTS

INTRODUCTORY ACTIVITY (2–3 MINUTES)

Vanishing Bean Bags
Have students begin by moving around the area until you give a signal.

DPESS page 309
Spread bean bags out in area. Begin with 1 bag/student.

FITNESS DEVELOPMENT (8–12 MINUTES)

Parachute Rhythmic Aerobic Activity

DPESS page 351
See Lesson Plan 11, Badminton Unit for complete details.

LESSON FOCUS (15–20 MINUTES)

Soccer Skill Test
Explain Task Sheet for Reciprocal Exam.

Create groups of students.
Distribute clipboards, pencils, and Task Sheets.
Assign students to areas for testing.

GAME (5 MINUTES)

Soccer Heading Game
Object of game: pass the ball with hands to teammates who try to score by heading the ball into the goal. No goalie. Can take only 2 steps with the ball. If ball hits the ground during passing it becomes the other teams ball. First to score 3 goals wins

DPESS page 437 to create teams.
Use Soccer Field with goals at each end of field.

EVALUATION/REVIEW AND CHEER

Discuss skill exam, Heading Game, and upcoming tournament.
Cheer: Tournament play, HOORAY!

RECIPROCAL TASK SHEET: SOCCER SKILLS TEST

Name: _____

Observer's Name: _____

Directions: Work with 2 partners. Place the name of your observer on your Task Sheet. One person is the "doer," one-person rolls, tosses, or retrieves the ball, while the other person is the "observer." Observer reads information/instructions to the doer, offers verbal feedback and places a check in the "yes" or "no" column recording the performance of their partner. Complete the Task Sheet and then "change roles" within your group. Then, the "doer" becomes the "observer," the "observer" becomes the "retriever" and the "retriever" becomes the "observer." Each person has his/her own Task Sheet.

DRIBBLING	Yes	No	Yes	No	Yes	No	Yes	No
1. Dribble the ball using both feet through the cones and back to starting point.								
2. Repeat # 1.								
3. Dribble and inside pass ball to partner.								
4. Repeat using other foot.								
ROTATE POSITIONS								
PASSING								
1. Inside foot pass ball to partner.								
2. Repeat with other foot.								
3. Outside foot pass ball to partner.								
4. Repeat pass with other foot.								
ROTATE POSITIONS								
TRAPPING								
1. Trap passed/rolled ball with sole of foot.								
2. Repeat on other foot.								
3. Trap tossed ball with chest.								
4. Trap tossed ball with thigh.								
5. Repeat # 4 with other thigh.								
6. Repeat # 1 but dribble after trapping.								
HEADING								
1. Head tossed ball to target identified by instructor.								
ROTATE POSITIONS								
THROW-IN								
1. Throw ball to partner as demonstrated by instructor.								
GOAL KICKING								
1. Demonstrate an instep goal kick.								
2. Demonstrate a penalty kick								
ROTATE POSITIONS								

TURN IN THIS EXAM TO YOUR INSTRUCTOR WHEN YOU HAVE COMPLETED TAKING IT.

Soccer Lesson Plan 14

EQUIPMENT:

Cones for Circuit Training markers
Whistle
1 soccer ball per student

Circuit Training instructions
Music CD/tape for fitness
CD/cassette player

INSTRUCTIONAL ACTIVITIES	TEACHING HINTS

INTRODUCTORY ACTIVITY (2–3 MINUTES)

Mini Pyramids

On signal they find a partner and build a simple pyramid (table, statue). On the next signal, pyramids are quickly and safely dismantled and students move again.

DPESS page 399
Scattered formation
Students move throughout the area until signal is given.

FITNESS DEVELOPMENT (8–12 MINUTES)

Circuit Training

DPESS page 348
Whistle Mixer to create groups of 4–5.
See Lesson 10, Golf Unit for complete details.

LESSON FOCUS (15–20 MINUTES)

Round Robin Soccer Tournament
Explain tournament, chart, and teams.

Assign teams to field areas.

GAME (5–10 MINUTES)

Continue Soccer Tournament Play

EVALUATION/REVIEW AND CHEER

Discuss how tournament games are going.
Cheer: We love playing soccer!

Soccer Lesson Plan 15

EQUIPMENT:

20 cones
Whistle

Fitness Scavenger Hunt instruction cards
1 soccer ball per student

INSTRUCTIONAL ACTIVITIES	TEACHING HINTS

INTRODUCTORY ACTIVITY (2–3 MINUTES)

Ball Gymnastics

On signal begin activity directed by teacher. Activities: tap ball with feet; jump over ball side to side; jump over ball front and back. On signal, get with a partner and have 1 ball (Back-to-Back). Hand ball over and under, around the sides, etc. Toss 1 ball to partner. Simultaneously toss a ball to partner, alternating who begins.

Every student will have a ball.
Scattered formation

FITNESS DEVELOPMENT (8–12 MINUTES)

Fitness Scavenger Hunt

Each group is given a list directing them to designated areas to find directions for exercises/activities at that location. Create exercises at each station work entire body.

DPESS page 356
Use Whistle Mixer to create groups of 3.
Each group is assigned a different starting point.

LESSON FOCUS AND GAME COMBINED (15–25 MINUTES)

Continue Round Robin Soccer Tournament

EVALUATION/REVIEW AND CHEER

Discuss tournament games. Introduce next unit.
Students create cheer.

Tennis

OBJECTIVES:

The student will:

1. Demonstrate agility while shuffling between cones set up on a court and by participating in the Running Weave Drill during the Introductory phase of class.
2. Demonstrate movement control by changing movement patterns from skipping, to running, to galloping to side shuffles.
3. Participate in static stretching activities demonstrated in class.
4. Participate in the Flash Drill.
5. Participate in grass drills and strengthening exercises including push-ups, curl-ups, reverse push-ups, etc. for cardiovascular fitness, agility, and strength development.
6. Participate in an Aerobic Rhythmic Exercise Routine to develop cardiovascular fitness and upper body strength.
7. Improve strength and fitness by participating in the Partner Resistance Exercises and the Knee High Running.
8. Demonstrate agility and quick responses to instructions during the Quick Draw McGraw activity.
9. Demonstrate jump-roping skills during a variety of fitness activities such as Continuity Exercises.
10. Complete a Task Sheet on the Forehand Stroke while working with a partner.
11. Demonstrate a forehand drive stroke with follow through with and without a ball.
12. Demonstrate the volley across the net to a partner.
13. Identify parts of the tennis racquet when asked to point at their location.
14. Demonstrate the grip used for the volley and forehand stroke.
15. Demonstrate the ready position.
16. Perform backhand ground strokes using proper technique.
17. Demonstrate the volley to a partner while in the service box.
18. Demonstrate Forehand and Backhand Lob Shots and Forehand and Backhand Ground Strokes.
19. Demonstrate the overhead smash, lob, and ground strokes using form demonstrated by the instructor.
20. Execute serving and ground strokes following the instructions on the Task Sheets using form demonstrated by the instructor.
21. Practice accuracy while hitting the tennis ball into hoops on the court.
22. Study the rules and etiquette of the game by reading the handout and listening to the lecture given by the instructor.
23. Rally the ball on the court using the ground strokes, lob, overhead, and serve demonstrated in class by the instructor.
24. Play Tennis Doubles using rules learned and skills demonstrated by the instructor during the unit.
25. Participate in the Round Robin Tournament playing Tennis Doubles using rules learned and skills demonstrated by the instructor during the unit.

TENNIS BLOCK PLAN
3 WEEK UNIT

Week #1	Monday	Tuesday	Wednesday	Thursday	Friday
Introductory Activity	Lateral Shuffle	Square Drill	Flash Drill	Running Weave Drill	Individual Rope Jumping
Fitness	Astronaut Drills	Continuity Exercises	Partner Resistance	Aerobic Workout	The 12 Ways of Fitness
Focus	Grip, Stance Ready Position Volley	Forehand Drive Stroke	Short Court Volley Forehand Volley	Forehand Stroke	Backhand Stroke Forehand Stroke
Game	Back-to-Back	Midnight	Blob Tag	Frisbee Toss	Circle Bowling

Week #2	Monday	Tuesday	Wednesday	Thursday	Friday
Introductory Activity	Red Light Bean Bag Catch	Knee High	Quick Draw McGraw	Move, Stop, Pivot	Flash Drill
Fitness	Partner Racetrack Fitness	Partner Resistance Exercises	Continuity Exercises	Partner Resistance	Aerobic workout
Focus	Forehand Task Sheet Backhand Task Sheet	Lob Shot	Overhead Shot	Serve Lob Review Overhead	Station Review: Serve, Lob Overhead, Ground Strokes
Game	Over & Under	Fugitive Tag	Tennis Horse	Blob Tag	Alley Rally

Week #3	Monday	Tuesday	Wednesday	Thursday	Friday
Introductory Activity	In the Hoop	Eliminate	Eliminate	Eliminate	Eliminate
Fitness	Exercise Routine	Continuity Exercises	Exercise Routine	Aerobic Workout	Exercise Routine
Focus	Rules Rally and Play	Play Doubles Tennis	Written and Skills Exam	Round Robin Tennis Tournament	Round Robin Tennis Tournament
Game	Four Player Figure 8 Rally	Play Doubles Tennis	Continue Exams	Continue Tournament	Continue Tournament

---
Tennis Lesson Plan 1

EQUIPMENT:

20 cones	2 tennis balls per student
Whistle	1 racquet per student

INSTRUCTIONAL ACTIVITIES	TEACHING HINTS

INTRODUCTORY ACTIVITY (2–3 MINUTES)

Lateral Shuffle

Shuffle between the cones.

DPESS page 305

See how many times you can touch the cones.
Stay low to the ground by bending your knees.

FITNESS DEVELOPMENT (8–12 MINUTES)

Partner Resistance Exercises

DPESS pages 350–351

Use Back-to-Back finding someone the same size to
   create partners.

LESSON FOCUS (15–20 MINUTES)

Grip, Stance, Ready Position

DPESS page 489

Shake hands with racquet hands technique.
Weight on balls of feet, knees bent
Racquet gripped with dominant hand and neck
Cradled with non-dominant hand

The Volley (no bounce) Drill

Begin next to the net and hit tennis ball over the net to
   partner without letting the ball bounce.

```
            X X X
_____          Net
            X X X
```

Tennis Courts

Four people to a court; if not enough courts, then 6
   students to a court.
Ready position, knees bent, wrists ready to rotate, and
   eyes on the ball

The Volley (with bounce)

Same drill, except with one bounce in the serving court,
   while standing near the serving court line

GAME (3–5 MINUTES)

Back-to-Back

Scattered formation

Students jog around randomly; when signal is given, they
   will quickly get with someone Back-to-Back. The one
   left out will call the next activity, such as skipping,
   hopping, jogging, galloping.

EVALUATION/REVIEW AND CHEER

What is different between a volley and forehand drive shots?
Cheer: 2, 4, 6, 8 Volleying is really great!

Tennis Lesson Plan 2

EQUIPMENT:

1 tennis racquet per student	CD/cassette player
2 tennis balls per student	Continuity music CD/tape
Cones with movement instruction cards	1 individual jump rope per student

INSTRUCTIONAL ACTIVITIES	TEACHING HINTS

INTRODUCTORY ACTIVITY (2–3 MINUTES)

Square Drill

When signal is given student will begin moving in one direction. At each cone will be a sign listing movement to perform to next cone:

1 = Skipping; 2 = Running; 3 = Galloping;
   4 = Side shuffle

DPESS page 305

Play Whistle Mixer to make 4 even groups.
Cones in large square.

FITNESS DEVELOPMENT (8–12 MINUTES)

Continuity Exercises

Create a music CD/tape with 45 seconds of music and 30 seconds of silence for 10 minutes. During silence, instruct students to perform an exercise, i.e., push-ups, curl-ups, reverse push-ups, side leg lifts, arm circling, crab walks, coffee grinder, etc.

DPESS page 349

Scattered formation
Follow routine on page 322.
End music CD/tape with slower paced music appropriate for static stretches to stretch the muscles used.

LESSON FOCUS (15–20 MINUTES)

Toss ball to a partner

DPESS page 489

Forehand drive practice. Partner receives 4 tossed balls and they change roles.

Rally ball over net to partner

Rally ball over net with partner.

GAME (5 MINUTES)

Midnight (Fox in the den)

The chickens need to stay away from the foxes.
Chickens approach den asking, "What time is it?" The fox may answer any clock time. When she answers "midnight" the chickens are chased.

Select several "foxes" and "mark" them with pennies. The rest of the class are "chickens."
At the signal the chickens run for safety. The chickens are safe when they reach a specified area or goal line at the opposite end of the play area. Anyone caught is taken to the den and then assists in helping the fox.

Tennis Lesson Plan 3

EQUIPMENT:

1 tennis racquet per student

2 tennis balls per student

Music CD/tape for grass drills

CD/cassette player

INSTRUCTIONAL ACTIVITIES	TEACHING HINTS

INTRODUCTORY ACTIVITY (2–3 MINUTES)

Flash Drill

DPESS pages 307–308

FITNESS DEVELOPMENT (8–12 MINUTES)

Partner Resistance Exercises

(See Lesson 7 for details)

DPESS pages 350–351

Use Back-to-Back to select a partner the same size.

LESSON FOCUS (15–20 MINUTES)

Forehand Volley

Demonstrate volley and practice drills

Short Court Volley

Forehand Volley from Service Line

Short court—from the service square, students will volley the ball to one another. Play all 4 balls before retrieving. Then start again.

Forehand Sideline Drill

DPESS page 489

Play Whistle Mixer to create groups of 4–6. Assign 4–6 students to each court.

Bring students together to demonstrate.

Demonstrate. Explain each of the follow cues:

* Set up with the side of the body to the net.
* Contact the ball even with the front foot.
* Make sure you run to meet the ball.
* Early backswing–get the racquet back as soon as possible.
* Keep the knees bent throughout swing.

Demonstrate using the forehand stroke and aiming to hit between the singles and doubles boundaries.

Use Whistle Mixer to create groups of 4–6.

If 6 students to a court, rotate pairs from left to right on the court.

GAME (5 MINUTES)

Blob Tag

Explain that two people begin by being "it." When they tag someone, they hold hands. As a number of people are tagged, the chain becomes long, and only those at the ends are eligible for tagging.

The team(s) with the longest line wins.

DPESS page 312

Scattered formation on 1 side of tennis net.

Select 2 "its." (Can select 4)

Repeat with new "its" if time permits.

EVALUATION/REVIEW AND CHEER

Evaluate skills practiced during the lesson

Cheer: 3, 2, 1, Tennis is really fun!

Tennis Lesson Plan 4

EQUIPMENT:

1 tennis racquet per student
2 tennis balls per student
4 cones per group of 4 students for Running Weave Drill

1 Task Sheet on Forehand Stroke per student
1 clipboard with pencil attached per 2 students

INSTRUCTIONAL ACTIVITIES	TEACHING HINTS

INTRODUCTORY ACTIVITY (2–3 MINUTES)

Running Weave Drill

Leader first runs through maze and others follow. Leader can change the locomotor movement used.

DPESS page 306

Create groups of 4 using the Whistle Mixer. Assign each group to a set of cones arranged in a maze.

FITNESS DEVELOPMENT (8–12 MINUTES)

Aerobic Workout

You don't have to be a dancer to create an enjoyable, high-energy routine. An example of 4 phrases of movement identified as A, B, C, D is described.

The A, B, C, D phrases can be performed first as listed, then combined in any order that works well with the movement and the music. A simple way to add variety to the routine you have created is to add different arm movements each time you repeat the phrase. Then the original 4 phrases of movement can be repeated as originally choreographed.

DPESS pages 358–359

Create an Aerobic Rhythmic Exercise Routine lasting 8–10 minutes. The CD/tape you make should be 120 to 150 beats per minute. A pre-recorded Aerobic Dance Exercise CD/tape allowing the last two minutes to be used for a short cool down activity and approximately 5 minutes for abdominal and upper body strengthening, as well as stretching.

A: Hop on the left foot 8 times while pointing and tapping the right foot forward and then to the side (e.g., forward, side, forward, side, forward, side). Repeat the entire phrase while hopping (bouncing) on the right foot 8 times and tapping the left foot forward and to the side as described.

B: Run in place 8 times and clap on each run.

C: 8 jumping jacks using full arm movements.

D: Slide to the right 8 times and clap on the 8th slide. Repeat to the left.

LESSON FOCUS (15–20 MINUTES)

Forehand Stroke Review

Explain Task Sheets.
Pairs who complete the Task Sheets can turn materials in and rally using the Ready Position and Forehand Stroke.

DPESS page 489

Use the elbow-to-elbow or Back-to-Back technique to create pairs of students.

Have one person kneel. The person standing should pick up a clipboard with pencil and Task Sheets. The person kneeling should pick up a racquet and two tennis balls and return to partner. Assign students to courts to work on Task Sheets.

GAME (5 MINUTES)

Frisbee Toss to Partner

DPESS pages 463–465

Play "Toe-to-Toe" to select new partners.
Students should be directed to safe direction to toss Frisbee to partner and toss and catch the Frisbee over the Tennis net.

EVALUATION/REVIEW AND CHEER

Bring students together to review and discuss elements of the lesson.
Cheer: Tennis, yes!

TENNIS RECIPROCAL TASK SHEET: FOREHAND STROKE

Name: _____

Name: _____

Directions: Work with a partner. Place both of your names on each Task Sheet. One person is the "doer" while the other person is the "observer." Observer reads information/instructions to the doer, offers verbal feedback and places a check in the "yes" or "no" column recording the performance of their partner. Record the date of the practice. Complete the Task Sheet until you are directed to "change roles." Then, the "doer" becomes the "observer." Each person has his/her own Task Sheet.

READY POSITION	DATES							
(Record date of practice)								
	Yes	No	Yes	No	Yes	No	Yes	No
1. Assume the handshake grip.								
2. Non-dominant hand supports neck of racquet.								
3. Knees bent.								
4. Weight on balls of feet and ready to move.								
5. Eyes looking across net at imaginary opponent.								
FOREHAND STROKE								
6. Side to net.								
7. Drop ball in front of foot closest to net.								
8. Racquet moves back into back swing of stroke.								
9. Steps forward toward direction of net while swinging.								
10. Follows through with swing and weight change.								
11. Repeat 1–10 above, pick up balls and change roles.								

Tennis Lesson Plan 5

EQUIPMENT:

1 jump rope per student	4 cones
1 tennis racquet per student	Clubs
2 tennis balls per student	Rubber balls
1 hoop per student	Whistle

INSTRUCTIONAL ACTIVITIES	TEACHING HINTS

INTRODUCTORY ACTIVITY (2–3 MINUTES)

Individual Rope Jumping	**DPESS page 309**
Tell the students to begin traveling while rope jumping when the music begins.	Set up cones marking the boundaries.
When music stops–freeze.	Scattered position
	Emphasize jump roping as a tool that athletes use to achieve fitness.

FITNESS DEVELOPMENT (8–12 MINUTES)

The 12 Ways of Fitness	**DPESS page 357**
Explain singing tune to lead the exercise.	Using Whistle Mixer, create groups of 12.
Explain add-on fitness instructions.	Scattered formation
Execute 2–3 times through.	Identify the first student leader through the twelfth.

LESSON FOCUS (15–20 MINUTES)

Backhand Stroke	**DPESS page 489**
Grip	Scattered formation
Ready position, grip change, and backhand stroke.	
Student Trial of Backhand	Direct students to pick up a racquet and bring to area.
	Practice ready position to grip without ball.
	Practice side to net, back swing, and follow through.
Practice Backhand on Court	Use elbow-to-elbow technique to create pairs.
	Assign pairs to an area.
	Let each student hit 2 balls over net, then retrieve balls.
Forehand to Backhand	Demonstrate ready position, to forehand, to ready position, to backhand.
	Students practice.
	Students go to court and rally using this technique.

GAME (5 MINUTES)

Circle Bowling	
Four clubs or bowling pins are placed in center of circle. A guard is chosen for each club. Two of the players in the circle have a ball. The object is to knock down one of the other person's clubs. If successful then the person may change places with the one guarding it.	Circle formation Select several "its" to be first guards of clubs. Switch places if club knocked down.

EVALUATION/REVIEW AND CHEER

Review major elements of backhand stroke and other skills covered in class.
Students create cheer.

Tennis Lesson Plan 6

EQUIPMENT:

1 tennis racquet per 3 students	Clipboard with pencil and Task Sheets per 3 students
4 tennis balls per 3 students	6–8 rubber balls

INSTRUCTIONAL ACTIVITIES	TEACHING HINTS

INTRODUCTORY ACTIVITY (2–3 MINUTES)

Red Light

Scattered formation

Each student balances a bean bag or a tennis ball on his or her racquet. On "Green Light" students move in general space around other people. On "Red Light" each student stops without dropping object off racquet.

Bean Bag Catch

DPESS pages 389–390

Play "racquet to racquet" or Toe-to-Toe to make pairs.

Toss bean bag/ball to partner 3 times in a row. If successful take a large step away from partner. Repeat.

FITNESS DEVELOPMENT (8–12 MINUTES)

Partner Racetrack Fitness

Set up 5–6 stations in working area. Each station has a Task Card listing 6–8 exercises to perform. List the locomotor movement to be performed by partner during each exercise.

DPESS pages 356–357

Use Whistle Mixer to create groups of 6–10. Then use elbow-to-elbow within the group to make pairs.

Example Task Card	
10	Jumping Jacks
	Jog around perimeter of area
20–30	Curl-Ups
	Slide around perimeter of area
15–20	Reverse Push-Ups
	Skip around perimeter
10–25	Push-Ups
	Gallop around perimeter of room
30–40	Treadmills alternating feet
	Run backwards around perimeter
30–40	Treadmills moving feet simultaneously
	Jog around perimeter
15	Second standing hip bend/stretch each side
	Skip
15–30	Second Lower Leg Stretch

Use a music CD/tape to make fitness fun and motivated movement.

LESSON FOCUS (15–20 MINUTES)

Forehand and Backhand Stoke Using Task Sheets

Can rally in groups when complete Task Sheets

DPESS page 489

Play Whistle Mixer to create groups of 3.

Direct students to pick up a Clipboard and Pencil with 3 Forehand and Backhand Task Sheets, 1 racquet, 4 balls per group.

Identify first Doer, Tosser and Observer.

Explain Task Sheets.

Assign groups to courts.

GAME (5 MINUTES)

Over and Under Ball Relay

DPESS page 405

EVALUATION/REVIEW AND CHEER

What were the main points to remember in the forehand ground stroke? How do you quickly switch from a forehand to a backhand?

Cheer: Tennis is the game to play!

TENNIS RECIPROCAL TASK SHEET: FOREHAND

Doer's Name: _____

Observer's Name: _____

Directions: Work in a group of 3. One student is the "doer", one person is the "observer", one is the ball tosser.

    Doer: Complete tasks read to you.

    Observer: Read Task Sheet to partner and place a check in the appropriate box looking at 1–2 points at a time. Offer feedback.

    Tosser: Toss the ball to the forehand side of "doer."

FOREHAND	DATES							
(Record date of practice)								
	Yes	No	Yes	No	Yes	No	Yes	No
1. Assume ready position.								
2. Execute an early backswing getting racquet back as soon as possible.								
3. Quickly move to ball.								
4. Set up with the side of the body to the net.								
5. Step onto left leg (R handed players) before contact. Transfer weight to that leg.								
6. Contact the ball in front of the left leg.								
7. Contact the ball with the racquet perpendicular to the ground.								
8. Strong follow through. Right shoulder should almost touch your chin.								
9. Recover to ready position to receive another ball.								
10. Repeat Task Sheet hitting 4 balls in a row.								
11. Rotate. Tosser to Observer Observer to Doer Doer to Tosser								
12. After everyone in your group completes the Task Sheet, move on to the Backhand Task Sheet.								

TENNIS RECIPROCAL TASK SHEET: BACKHAND

Doer's Name: _____

Observer's Name: _____

Directions: Work in a group of 3. One student is the "doer", one person is the "observer", one is the ball tosser.

Doer: Complete tasks read to you.

Observer: Read Task Sheet to partner and place a check in the appropriate box looking at 1–2 points at a time. Offer feedback.

Tosser: Toss the ball to the backhand side of "doer."

BACKHAND	DATES							
(Record date of practice)								
	Yes	No	Yes	No	Yes	No	Yes	No
1. Assume ready position.								
2. Execute an early backswing getting racquet back as soon as possible.								
3. Quickly move to ball.								
4. Set up with the side of the body to the net.								
5. Step onto right leg (R handed players) before contact. Transfer weight to that leg.								
6. Contact the ball in front of the right leg.								
7. Contact the ball with the racquet perpendicular to the ground.								
8. Strong follow through.								
9. Recover to ready position to receive another ball.								
10. Repeat Task Sheet hitting 4 balls in a row.								
11. Rotate. Tosser to Observer Observer to Doer Doer to Tosser								
12. After everyone in group completes the Task Sheet, rally with your group on the court.								

Tennis Lesson Plan 7

EQUIPMENT:
1 tennis racquet per student
2 tennis balls per student

INSTRUCTIONAL ACTIVITIES	TEACHING HINTS

INTRODUCTORY ACTIVITY (2–3 MINUTES)

Knee High Running
Students will run in place knee high and alternate with jogging in place.

DPESS page 353
Scattered formation
Use verbal or whistle signal "knees high", "knees low."

FITNESS DEVELOPMENT (8–12 MINUTES)

Partner Resistance Exercises
Arm Curl-Ups
Forearm Flex
Fist Pull-Apart
Butterfly
Back Builder

DPESS pages 350–351
Play elbow-to-elbow with someone to make pairs.
Scattered formation, standing next to partner

Stretch and Pull
Seated straddle position while facing partner with feet touching ankles of partner. Hold hands and very slowly one student will lean back while the other student is being pulled forward. Reverse directions.

Explain importance of stretching.

Scissors

May use a carpet square to lie on

Bear Trap

Knee Bender

Resistance Push-Up

Reverse Push-Up
Sit with feet flat on ground near buttocks, knees bent. Place hands beneath shoulders, fingers facing heels. Support body weight on hands and feet. Bend at elbows to lower body near ground. Straighten arms. Repeat.

Both partners can perform this simultaneously or resistance can be placed by the partner pressing down on shoulders as doer straightens arms.

Jog

Jog around the area several times.
Use music to motivate fitness section.

LESSON FOCUS (15–20 MINUTES)

Lob Shot
Practice:
Toss balls to partner's forehand lob side.
Complete activity using all 4 balls. Change starter.
Repeat 3 times.
Demonstrate:
Forehand Ground stroke; Backhand Ground stroke Lob

DPESS page 490
The teacher will explain and demonstrate the lob.
Create pairs using Toe-to-Toe.
Direct each student to pick up racquet and 2 balls.
Assign students to courts.
Bring students together.
Practice rallying with forehand, to backhand, to lob as demonstrated.

Backhand Lob
Practice by tossing ball to partner's backhand side 4 times in a row. Change roles.

Bring group together for demonstration.

Rally

Students rally using the 4 skills practiced in class.

GAME (5 MINUTES)

Fugitive Tag
One person is identified as fugitive and is given head start. Switch roles when tagged.

DPESS page 312
Create partners using management game.
Scattered formation

EVALUATION/REVIEW AND CHEER

What angle should the racquet be held at to perform a lob?
What will the trajectory of the ball be at that angle?
Students create cheer.

Tennis Lesson Plan 8

EQUIPMENT:

Continuity Exercise Music CD/tape
CD/cassette player

1 tennis racquet per student
2 tennis balls per student

INSTRUCTIONAL ACTIVITIES	TEACHING HINTS

INTRODUCTORY ACTIVITY (2–3 MINUTES)

Quick Draw McGraw

Instructor faces student in "Ready Position."

Instructor holds tennis ball at "gunbelt" level and performs dramatic gestures with ball to right or left side.

Students respond by demonstrating forehand or backhand stroke.

Scattered formation with imaginary racquet.

FITNESS DEVELOPMENT (8–12 MINUTES)

Continuity Exercises

DPESS page 349

LESSON FOCUS (15–20 MINUTES)

Overhead

Practice by tossing ball high to self and execute overhead stroke.

DPESS page 490

Scattered formation

Demonstrate.

Arrange students on court facing fence.

Student works alone and practices self-toss and overhead into fence 10 times.

Lob Skill Review

Drill: Partner hits overhead shot from net, return with lob. Each person practices 4 times in a row.

Create partners using management game.

Assign groups to courts.

Review Ground strokes

Rally with 1 or 2 other students on court.

GAME (5 MINUTES)

Tennis Horse

Player 1 calls hit and attempts to hit it there. Others in line try to duplicate shot. If miss shot, player gets an "H," etc. until HORSE is spelled. If fail to make shot, player is assigned an "H." Second failure = "O." Last to spell "HORSE" is the winner.

DPESS page 421

Create groups of 4 in lines at baseline.

As soon as 1 person spells "HORSE," game starts over.

EVALUATION/REVIEW AND CHEER

Review the elements of all strokes played today.

Students create cheer.

Tennis Lesson Plan 9

EQUIPMENT:

1 tennis racquet per student	Music for fitness
2 tennis balls per student	CD/cassette player

INSTRUCTIONAL ACTIVITIES	TEACHING HINTS

INTRODUCTORY ACTIVITY (2–3 MINUTES)

Move, Stop, Pivot
Teacher blows whistle:
  once = jog
  twice = stop and pivot

DPESS page 308
Scattered formation

FITNESS DEVELOPMENT (8–12 MINUTES)

Partner Resistance Exercises
  Arm Curl-Ups
  Forearm Flex
  Fist Pull-Apart
  Butterfly
  Back builder

Seated Stretch and Pull

Scissors

Bear Trap

Knee Bender

Resistance Push-Up

Reverse Push-Up
Sit with feet flat on ground near buttocks, knees bent. Place hands beneath shoulders, fingers facing heels. Support
  body weight on hands and feet. Bend at elbows to lower body near ground. Straighten arms. Repeat. Both partners
  can perform this simultaneously or the partner can press down on shoulders as doer straightens arms to create
  additional resistance.

Jog

DPESS pages 350–351
Play elbow-to-elbow with someone to make pairs.
Scattered formation, standing next to partner
Use music to motivate fitness section.

See Lesson 7 for complete details.
May use a carpet square to lay on

Jog around the area several times.

LESSON FOCUS (15–20 MINUTES)

Serve Motion
Demonstrate serve.

DPESS page 490
Student picks up racquet.
Students practice motion spread out safely in area without
  a ball.

Serve Toss
Demonstrate the toss.

Serve With Toss
Demonstrate serve with toss.

Serve Into Serve Box
Demonstrate serving into service area.

Direct students to bring 2 balls to area.
Practice toss and catch several times.
Assign students to areas facing fence.
Serve practice-using balls.
Create Partners and assign to courts.
Serve into service box 2 times then partner serves.
Allow 10 practices per person.

Lob-Overhead Review
Demonstrate Lob and Overhead Return.

DPESS page 490
Scattered formation
Practice.

GAME (5 MINUTES)

Blob Tag

DPESS page 312
Scattered formation
Select several "its."

EVALUATION/REVIEW AND CHEER

What are the similarities between the overhead and the serve?
Students create cheer.

Tennis Lesson Plan 10

EQUIPMENT:

1 Task Sheet per person	1 tennis racquet per student
Clipboard and pencil per 2 students	2 tennis balls per student

INSTRUCTIONAL ACTIVITIES	TEACHING HINTS

INTRODUCTORY ACTIVITY (2–3 MINUTES)

Flash Drill
Teacher uses hand signals to direct movements.

DPESS pages 307–308
Scattered formation
Students jog in place or "stutter" while waiting for hand signal.

FITNESS DEVELOPMENT (8–12 MINUTES)

Aerobic Workout

DPESS pages 358–359
See Lesson 4, this unit for details.

LESSON FOCUS (15–20 MINUTES)

Skill Review Task Sheets
Serve
Ground strokes
Explain Task Sheets.

DPESS pages 489–490
Create groups of 3 using Whistle Mixer.
Assign 2 groups per court.
Determine first doer, tosser, and observer.
Explain rotation. Assign each group to a station. One person in the group picks up a clipboard and pencil plus Task Sheets for each person.

GAME (5 MINUTES)

Alley Rally
Each student must alternate forehand and backhand shots over net.
Each player is responsible for making calls on balls that land on his or her side of the net. The hitter is not allowed to question the calls that the opponent makes.

Explain game.
Use Whistle Mixer to create groups of 4.
Assign groups to courts.
Alley Rally over Net (Alternate Forehands and Backhands)

EVALUATION/REVIEW AND CHEER

Discuss elements of skills practiced.
Cheer: Rallying is really fun!

TENNIS RECIPROCAL TASK SHEET: FOREHAND AND BACKHAND STROKE

Name: _____   **Name:** _____

Directions: Work with a partner. Place both of your names on each Task Sheet. One person is the "doer" while the other person is the "observer." Observer reads information/instructions to the doer, offers verbal feedback and places a check in the "yes" or "no" column recording the performance of their partner. Complete the Task Sheet until you are directed to "change roles." Then, the "doer" becomes the "observer." Each person has his/her own Task Sheet. Practice this Task Sheet once using Forehand, once using Backhand–then change roles with your partner.

	Forehand		Backhand		Forehand		Backhand	
I. SET POSITION	Yes	No	Yes	No	Yes	No	Yes	No

A. Grip
    1. Shaking hands (forehand)
        Palm on top (backhand)
    2. Fingers spread								

B. Stance
    1. Feet spread; knees bent
    2. Weight on balls of feet								

C. Racquet
    1. Parallel to ground
    2. Standing on edge
    3. Left hand, cradling racquet								

II. BACKSWING								

A. Pivot
    1. Step promptly toward ball with nearest foot
    2. Side turned completely								

B. Racquet
    1. Backswing; begun early
    2. Racquet head back first, with firm wrists (left hand helps backhand)								

C. Run to Ball
    1. Move quickly to ball
    2. Sets on rear foot								

III. FORWARD SWING								

A. Ready position
    1. Racquet head drops below point of contact
    2. Racquet nearly parallel to ground, extends toward back fence								

B. Weight Transfer
    1. Front foot steps into line of shot
    2. All weight on ball of front foot
    3. Knees bent; good balance								

C. Point of Contact
    1. Ball contacted well in front of body
    2. Wrist firm; racquet parallel								

D. Follow-Through
    1. Racquet head continues out through line of shot
    2. Racquet standing on edge
    3. Forehand: wrist eye level; looking over elbow
    4. Backhand: wrist above head; racquet nearly vertical to ground
    5. Pose								

Repeat Task Sheet								

TENNIS RECIPROCAL TASK SHEET: THE SERVE

Name: _____   Name: _____

Directions: Work with a partner. Place both of your names on each Task Sheet. One person is the "doer" while the other person is the "observer." Observer reads information/instructions to the doer, offers verbal feedback and places a check in the "yes" or "no" column recording the performance of their partner. Complete the Task Sheet until you are directed to "change roles." Then, the "doer" becomes the "observer." Each person has his/her own Task Sheet. Practice serving four times in a row and then change roles. Observer: Watch for only one section on each serve practice.

	Yes	No	Yes	No	Yes	No	Yes	No
I. SET POSITION								
A. Grip 1. Continental grip 2. Fingers spread								
B. Stance 1. Side toward net 2. Weight on rear feet; feet spread								
C. Racquet 1. Pointing to serve area 2. Standing on edge 3. Left hand cradling								
II. BACKSWING (Ball Toss)								
A. Ball Toss 1. Ball thrown to correct height 2. Ball thrown above left foot								
B. Racquet Arm 1. Both arms work smoothly together 2. Racquet raises almost to shoulder level 3. Racquet head drops well behind back (wrist touches shoulder)								
C. Weight Transfer 1. Weight shifts to front foot 2. Balance maintained by front knee bend								
III. FORWARD SWING								
A. Throwing Motion 1. Smooth, continuous motion 2. Elbow leads wrist and racquet forward and up								
B. Contact 1. Highest point above left foot 2. Adequate wrist action 3. Adequate Spin								
C. Follow Through 1. Racquet head leads through line of shot 2. Racquet finishes on left side of body 3. Right foot comes through to help regain balance								

Tennis Lesson Plan 11

EQUIPMENT:
2 tennis balls per student
1 tennis racquet per student

12 hoops per court available
Tennis rules handout: 1 per student

INSTRUCTIONAL ACTIVITIES	TEACHING HINTS

INTRODUCTORY ACTIVITY (2–3 MINUTES)

In the Hoop

Place hoops on the ground on different places on the court.

Using Whistle Mixer or squads make groups of 3.
Place 2–3 groups of 3 at each baseline.
Each student drop hits a ball using a forehand drive and tries to place ball in any hoop.
Collect balls after each student hits their two.
Student selects own hoop(s) to use as target.

FITNESS DEVELOPMENT (8–12 MINUTES)

Run, Stop, Stretch and Strengthen Exercise Routine

Stretches
Lower leg stretch (with partner, or wall)
Balance beam stretch
Sit and reach
Side leg stretch
Groin stretch
Body twist
Ankle hold, or hand down
Squat stretch
Standing hip stretch
Elbow grab stretch

Strengthening
Push-ups
Curl-ups
Rocking Chair
Reverse curl
Pelvis Tilter

DPESS pages 342–346
Scattered within boundaries set by cones.
Direct students to run throughout area. On signal, student stops and performs a designated stretch/strengthening exercise. Can ask to call out muscles being worked.
Music can be used to cue the running and during the silence you can either call out the exercise or cue it on the CD/tape.

LESSON FOCUS (15–20 MINUTES)

Rules and Etiquette

Rally and Play Tennis

DPESS page 492
Discuss rules and etiquette of game.
Give handout for homework.
Use Whistle Mixer to create groups of 4 per court.
Direct students to rally the ball to each other practicing all strokes.

GAME (5 MINUTES)

Four Player Figure 8 Rally

Assign two players to hit all forehands and the other two all backhands. Right-handed players should be assigned forehands when they are stationed in the deuce court (right side when facing the net) and backhands when in the ad court. Left-handed players are given opposite directions.
Forehands DOWN THE LINE, Backhands CROSSCOURT, Backhands DOWN THE LINE, and Forehands CROSSCOURT.

Direct students to play.
Partners should stand close together. Length of court can be increased gradually as players' skills improve.
Each of the four players is practicing a different shot.
Rotate them through all four positions so that they will try all shots.

EVALUATION/REVIEW AND CHEER
Review important rules of tennis.
Cheer: 2, 4, 6, 8, Playing tennis is so great!

Tennis Lesson Plan 12

EQUIPMENT:

1 tennis racquet per student
2 tennis balls per student

CD/cassette player
Music CD/tape for Continuity Exercise Routine

INSTRUCTIONAL ACTIVITIES	TEACHING HINTS

INTRODUCTORY ACTIVITY (2–3 MINUTES)

Eliminate today to allow more time for Doubles Tennis.

FITNESS DEVELOPMENT (8–12 MINUTES)

Continuity Exercises

These exercises are a type of interval training. Create a CD/cassette tape with 30–35 seconds of music and 20 seconds of silence. Students jump rope during music. During silence, instruct students to perform an exercise, i.e., push-ups, curl-ups, reverse push-ups, side leg lifts, arm circling, crab walks, coffee grinder, etc. When the music resumes, the students will jump rope.

DPESS page 349

See Lesson 2 this unit for complete details.

LESSON FOCUS AND GAME (20 MINUTES)

Play Tennis Doubles Games

Use elbow-to-elbow technique to create partners. Then, have those partners join with another group to create doubles groups. Assign groups to courts.

EVALUATION/REVIEW AND CHEER

Discuss how games went. Ask if any rules questions came up during game play that need clarification.
Review rules and etiquette for exam.
Cheer: 3, 2, 1 Tennis is really fun!

Tennis Lesson Plan 13

EQUIPMENT:

1 tennis racquet per student
2 tennis balls per student

CD/cassette player
Music CD/tape for exercise routine

INSTRUCTIONAL ACTIVITIES	TEACHING HINTS

INTRODUCTORY ACTIVITY (2–3 MINUTES)

Eliminate today to allow time for exam.

FITNESS DEVELOPMENT (8–12 MINUTES)

Exercise Routine

Intersperse jogging, stretching and strengthening activities.

Stretches

Lower leg stretch (with partner, or wall)
Balance beam stretch
Sit and reach
Side leg stretch
Groin stretch
Body twist
Ankle hold, or hand down
Squat stretch
Standing hip stretch
Elbow grab stretch

Strengthening

Push-ups; Curl-ups; Rocking Chair; Reverse curl; Pelvis Tilter

DPESS pages 342–347

Scattered within boundaries set by cones
Direct students to run throughout the area. On signal, they will stop and perform a designated stretch/strengthening exercise.
The student will name the muscle being stretched/strengthened when asked to call it out.
Music can be used to cue the running and during the silence you can either call out the exercise or cue it on the CD/tape.

LESSON FOCUS AND GAME (20 MINUTES)

Distribute written exam to one half of the class.
Distribute skills exam to other half of the class.

Use a management game to divide class in half. When students complete skill exam, have them take written exam. Rotate written exam students to skills exam.

TENNIS WRITTEN EXAM

NAME: _____

True/False: Please mark a true state with a "+" and if the statement is false mark it with an "O."

_____ 1. If you leave the ground with both feet while serving, it is illegal.

_____ 2. Is it legal to step on the base line while serving?

_____ 3. The serving grip is pure eastern grip.

_____ 4. The slide service is less accurate than the flat serve.

_____ 5. The ball should be contacted by the racquet on "its" downward flight.

_____ 6. In preparing to serve, stand with your right side toward the net.

Multiple Choice: Please put the correct letter in the silence.

_____ 1. In the set position, the feet are:
   a. together, weight is even
   b. comfortable apart, weight on balls of feet
   c. apart, weight is even

_____ 2. In the grip, the racquet is:
   a. perpendicular to ground, palm of hand down
   b. parallel to ground, racquet face standing on edge
   c. parallel, racquet face at a slant

_____ 3. Most of the time your knees should be:
   a. stiff, and bend when ball reaches the racquet
   b. bent and flexible
   c. any way that is comfortable

_____ 4. The tennis swing should be:
   a. in definite steps
   b. smooth, slow and continuous motion
   c. hurried swing, not too loose

_____ 5. In the serve the set position is:
   a. facing net, feet together, weight even on both feet
   b. side toward net, feet shoulder width apart, weight on back foot
   c. body and racquet in a comfortable position

Fill in the Silence:

1. In the back swing shift your weight to the (right/left) _____ foot.

2. In the forward swing the racquet should be at the (highest/lowest)_____ point.

3. For a slice serve, the ball is on the (right/left)_____ side.

3. When serving on the right side of the court, the ball should land in the opponent's (right/left)_____ court.

4. In the follow through, the racquet _____.

Tennis Lesson Plan 14

EQUIPMENT:

1 tennis racquet per student	CD/cassette player
2 tennis balls per student	Music CD/tape for aerobic workout

INSTRUCTIONAL ACTIVITIES	TEACHING HINTS

INTRODUCTORY ACTIVITY (2–3 MINUTES)

Eliminate to allow time to play tennis.

FITNESS DEVELOPMENT (8–12 MINUTES)

Aerobic Workout

DPESS pages 358–359

Create an Aerobic Exercise Routine lasting 8–10 minutes. The CD/tape you make should be 120 to 150 beats per minute. A pre-recorded Aerobic Dance Exercise CD/tape allowing the last 2 minutes to be used for a short cool down activity and approximately 5 minutes for abdominal and upper body strengthening, as well as stretching.

You don't have to be a dancer to create an enjoyable, high-energy routine. An example of 4 phrases of movement identified as A, B, C, D, that you could combine into a routine is:

A: Hop on the left foot 8 times while pointing and tapping the right foot forward and then to the side (e.g., forward, side, forward, side, forward, side). Repeat the entire phrase while hopping (bouncing) on the right foot 8 times and tapping the left foot forward and to the side as described.

B: Run in place 8 times and clap on each run.

C: 8 jumping jacks using full arm movements.

D: Slide to the right 8 times and clap on the 8th slide. Repeat to the left.

The suggested phrases can be first performed in the A, B, C, D format and then combined in any order to feel works well with the movement and the music. A simple way to add variety to the routine you have created is to add different arm movements each time you repeat the phrase. Then the original 4 phrases of movement can be repeated as originally choreographed.

LESSON FOCUS AND GAME (15–25 MINUTES)

Round Robin Tennis Tournament

Assign students to tournament court by explaining Round Robin Chart.

Students not interested in tournament play could be assigned a singles/doubles game.

EVALUATION/REVIEW AND CHEER

Review tournament rules.

Establish which team plays, which team for the final tournament day.

Cheer: Yeah, the tournament is here!

Tennis Lesson Plan 15

EQUIPMENT:
1 tennis racquet per student
2 tennis balls per student

CD/cassette player
Music CD/tape for exercise routine

INSTRUCTIONAL ACTIVITIES	TEACHING HINTS

INTRODUCTORY ACTIVITY AND FITNESS DEVELOPMENT (8–12 MINUTES)

Exercise Routine
Intersperse jogging, stretching and strengthening activities.

DPESS pages 342–347
Scattered within boundaries set by cones
Direct students to run throughout the area. On signal, they will stop and perform a designated stretch/strengthening exercise.

Stretches
  Lower leg stretch (with partner, or wall)
  Balance beam stretch
  Sit and reach
  Side leg stretch
  Groin stretch
  Body twist
  Ankle hold, or hand down
  Squat stretch
  Standing hip stretch
  Elbow grab stretch

The student will name the muscle being stretched/strengthened when asked to call it out.

Music can be used to cue the running, and during the silence you can either call out the exercise or cue it on the CD/tape.

Strengthening
  Push-ups
  Curl-ups
  Rocking Chair
  Reverse curl
  Pelvis Tilter

LESSON FOCUS AND GAME (15–25 MINUTES)

Round Robin Tennis Tournament

Continue tournament.
Assign students to court area using chart.

EVALUATION/REVIEW AND CHEER

Conclude unit.
Cheer: Tennis, yes!

SERVE: SKILL TEST CHECK LIST

Name: _____

Directions: Perform four serves in a row. Observer look at 2 check points on each serve.

CHECK LIST RATING SCALE:
3–Outstanding
2–Average
1–Below Average

		Record Rating			
I.	**SET POSITION**				
A.	Grip				
	1. Continental Grip				
	2. Fingers spread				
B.	Stance				
	1. Side toward net				
	2. Weight on rear feet; feet spread				
C.	Racquet				
	1. Pointing to serve area				
	2. Standing on edge				
	3. Left hand cradling				
II.	**BACKSWING (Ball Toss)**				
A.	Ball Toss				
	1. Ball thrown to correct height				
	2. Ball thrown above left foot				
B.	Racquet Arm				
	1. Both arms work smoothly together				
	2. Racquet raises almost to shoulder level				
	3. Racquet head drops well behind back (wrist touches shoulder)				
C.	Weight Transfer				
	1. Weight shifts to front foot				
	2. Balance maintained by front knee bend				
III.	**FORWARD SWING**				
A.	Throwing Motion				
	1. Smooth, continuous motion				
	2. Elbow leads wrist and racquet forward and up				
B.	Contact				
	1. Highest point above left foot				
	2. Adequate wrist action				
	3. Adequate Spin				
C.	Follow Through				
	1. Racquet head leads through line of shot				
	2. Racquet finishes on left side of body				
	3. Right foot comes through to help regain balance				
Total Points					

FOREHAND AND BACKHAND SKILL: SKILL TEST CHECK LIST

Name: _____

Directions: Observe only one section at a time. Mark rating in column following each practice. Practice 4 forehand drive strokes and 4 backhands before changing roles.

CHECK LIST RATING SCALE:
3–Outstanding
2–Average
1–Below Average

	Record Rating			
I. SET POSITION				

A. Grip
   1. Shaking hands (forehand)
      Palm on top (backhand)
   2. Fingers spread				

B. Stance
   1. Feet spread; knees bent
   2. Weight on balls of feet				

C. Racquet
   1. Parallel to ground
   2. Standing on edge
   3. Left hand, cradling racquet				

II. BACKSWING				

A. Pivot
   1. Step promptly toward ball with nearest foot
   2. Side turned completely				

B. Racquet
   1. Backswing; begun early
   2. Racquet head back first, with firm wrists (left hand helps backhand)				

C. Run to Ball
   1. Move quickly to ball
   2. Sets on rear foot				

III. FORWARD SWING				

A. Ready position
   1. Racquet head drops below point of contact
   2. Racquet nearly parallel to ground, extends toward back fence				

B. Weight Transfer
   1. Front foot steps into line of shot
   2. All weight on ball of front foot
   3. Knees bent; good balance				

C. Point of Contact
   1. Ball contacted well in front of body
   2. Wrist firm; racquet parallel				

D. Follow Through
   1. Racquet head continues out through line of shot
   2. Racquet standing on edge
   3. Forehand: wrist eye level; looking over elbow
   4. Backhand: wrist above head; racquet nearly vertical to ground
   5. Pose				

Observer's Signature: _____ Date: _____

Volleyball

OBJECTIVES:

The student will:

1. Demonstrate teamwork by communicating with classmates to move in same direction during the Loose Caboose.
2. Perform various cardiovascular, strength building and stretching activities as demonstrated in class.
3. Increase his eye hand coordination when throwing and catching a bean bag.
4. Decrease his reaction time and increase quickness by performing various movement activities in the Wave Drill.
5. Demonstrate visual skills and creativity by leading and following movements during the Shadow Partner activity.
6. Run smoothly and rhythmically while performing locomotor movements to the beat of the music.
7. Dodge/elude classmate quickly without falling or colliding with another student during the Tag Introductory Activity.
8. Demonstrate teamwork by staying connected to their teammates during the Capture the Flag Introductory Activity.
9. Demonstrate agility and ability to change directions while avoiding other students in the Diving Under Freeze Tag game.
10. Perform various fitness activities at different stations, as demonstrated in class to improve her fitness levels.
11. Demonstrate good listening skills by matching movements to the sound of the drum.
12. Demonstrate proper stretching and cardiovascular activities as demonstrated in class.
13. Perform various jump rope activities and strength building activities as demonstrated in class.
14. Name the changes in body functions that occur when one exercises, e.g., increased heart rate, breathing rate.
15. Perform various jump rope, stretching and strength building activities during the Continuity Exercises.
16. Perform proper arm swing techniques while hitting the ball against the wall as demonstrated in class.
17. Demonstrate proper volleyball approach jumps to the net as demonstrated in class.
18. Execute proper technique when setting the volleyball as demonstrated in class.
19. Perform proper footwork and ball control when setting the volleyball, as demonstrated in class.
20. Improve her eye-hand coordination by hitting and catching a volleyball to herself.
21. Perform the underhand serve as demonstrated in class.
22. Perform the overhand serve using technique demonstrated in class.
23. Perform the forearm pass while using techniques demonstrated in class.
24. Communicate with his teammates calling for the ball as demonstrated in class, e.g., "mine," "yours."
25. Demonstrate eye hand coordination by performing the bump pass for 1 minute as demonstrated in class.
26. Set the ball back and forth with his partner 10 times in a row, using the technique demonstrated in class.
27. Back set to a partner 10 times using the technique demonstrated in class. Execute the spiking approach at the appropriate station using techniques demonstrated in class.
28. Self-evaluate her spiking skills while trying to spike the ball into a target at the designated station practice.
29. Practice two-handed blocks and perform two-man blocks during the lesson focus activities.
30. Perform one and two arms forearm passes using skills demonstrated by the instructor.
31. Execute the side roll 5 times while reaching and forearm passing the ball.
32. Perform various volleyball skills correctly during the partner Task Sheet Evaluation activities.
33. Volley the ball in groups of 6 and complete 5 consecutive volleys during the Keep It Up game.
34. Demonstrate an understanding of the Overhand Serve and Forearm Pass by evaluating classmates using Task Sheets.
35. Participate in a game that requires three touches per side before the ball goes over the net using skills demonstrated in class by the instructor.
36. Practice improving communication skills by working with teammates in the game Three-and-Over.
37. Demonstrate his understanding of the game of volleyball by playing a modified game.
38. Demonstrate knowledge and understanding of basic volleyball rules and terminology by scoring a minimum of 75% on a written exam.
39. Demonstrate knowledge and understanding of volleyball skills by playing in the tournament and using techniques demonstrated in class.

VOLLEYBALL BLOCK PLAN
3 WEEK UNIT

Week #1	Monday	Tuesday	Wednesday	Thursday	Friday
Introductory Activity	Loose Caboose	Bean Bag Toss	Wave Drill	Weave Drill	Formation Rhythmic Running
Fitness	Astronaut Drills	Continuity Exercises	Jump Rope Activities to Music	Four Corners to Music	Circuit Training to Music
Focus	Underhand Serve	Forearm Bump Pass	Overhand Serve	Overhand Set Serves	Forearm Bump Pass
Game	Scooter Cageball Soccer	Wheel Barrow Relay	Tug-of-War	Push-Up Tag	3 Hit Volleyball

Week #2	Monday	Tuesday	Wednesday	Thursday	Friday
Introductory Activity	Bean Bag Touch and Go	Seat Roll	Fastest Tag	Addition Tag	Capture the Flag
Fitness	Mini Challenge Course	Parachute Fitness	Continuity Exercises	Squad Leader Exercises	Stations
Focus	Spiking	Setting	Spiking and Dinking	Blocking	Forearm Bump
Game	King & Queen of the Court	Mini Pyramids	Keep it Up or Hula Hoop Targets	Modified Volleyball Game	Dig It

Week #3	Monday	Tuesday	Wednesday	Thursday	Friday
Introductory Activity	Octopus Tag	Following Activity	Diving Under Freeze Tag	Eliminate to allow time for other sections	Eliminate to allow time for other sections
Fitness	Mirror Drills in Place	Fitness Challenge	Walk–Jog–Sprint	Continuity Exercises	Written Volleyball Exam
Focus	Task Sheets	Task Sheets	Volleyball Round Robin Tournament	Volleyball Round Robin Tournament	Continue Tournament after exam
Game	Keep It Afloat	Three-and-Over	Volleyball Round Robin Tournament	Volleyball Round Robin Tournament	Continue Tournament

Volleyball Lesson Plan 1

EQUIPMENT:

1 volleyball per student
CD/cassette player
1 scooter per person

Continuity Exercise Music CD/tape
1 cageball
Colored pinnies for 1/2 of class

INSTRUCTIONAL ACTIVITIES	TEACHING HINTS

INTRODUCTORY ACTIVITY (2–3 MINUTES)

Loose Caboose

One child is designated as the "loose caboose." He tries to hook onto a train. Trains are formed by 3 or 4 children standing in column formation with each child placing their hands on the waist of the child in front of them.

The trains, by twisting and turning, try to keep caboose from hooking on to the back. If the caboose hooks on, the front child becomes new caboose.

DPESS page 313

Using Whistle Mixer, create groups of 3–4.
Select several "its" and designate them as the "loose caboose."

FITNESS DEVELOPMENT (8-12 MINUTES)

Astronaut Drills

Use intervals of music and silence to signal duration of exercise. Music segments indicate aerobic activity while intervals of silence announce flexibility and strength development activities.

Arm Circles; Jump or Hop back & forth, side to side; Crab Alternate Leg Extensions; Skip; Twist; Slide; Lunge; Jumping Jack Variations; Flying Angel Sit-ups.

Hop to Center and Back; Push-ups; Gallop.

Arm Stretch–across body; Trot; Arm Stretch–over head; Power Taped Jumper; Shoulder Rolls; Ankle Circles.

Head Circles in frontal plane; Stretch & Touch Toes.

DPESS pages 348–349

Circle or scattered formation with space between students

Children should be in constant movement except when stopped to do strength and flexibility activities.

LESSON FOCUS (15-20 MINUTES)

Underhand Serve

Demonstrate:

- Against wall
- Serving to partner over net or posted rope

Serve and Catch

Start with a ball on each side of the net.

Several balls are served at same time from serving area.

All balls must be caught on the other side of net. Once the ball is caught, it can be served from the opposing serving area. The object is to catch the ball and quickly serve so that the opponent cannot catch the ball.

A point is scored when the ball is served underhand, goes over the net, and hits the ground in-bounds.

DPESS 452–453.

Student practices alone.
Use elbow-to-elbow technique to create pairs.
Assign pairs to practice area.
Divide class into even numbers of groups.
Create groups using Back-to-Back technique.
Direct: Hands on hips–one group
              Hands on head–other group
1 scorekeeper is needed for each group.
Assign groups to courts.

GAME (3-5 MINUTES)

Scooter Cageball Soccer

While sitting on scooter, advance Cageball with feet only to score goals.

DPESS page 403

Use a management technique to create teams.
Give pinnies to teams and assign teams to courts.

EVALUATION/REVIEW AND CHEER

Students huddle close together so you can ask review questions. What were some of the key points to remember about an underhand serve? Answer: Eyes on the ball, dominant foot back, heel of the hand makes contact with the ball, follow through, stand with dominate foot back.

Cheer: We love volleyball!

Volleyball Lesson Plan 2

EQUIPMENT:

1 bean bag per person
Volleyball courts and nets

1 volleyball per person
Continuity Exercise Music CD/tape
CD/cassette player

INSTRUCTIONAL ACTIVITIES	TEACHING HINTS

INTRODUCTORY ACTIVITY (2–3 MINUTES)

Bean Bag Toss

On signal, students pick up a bean bag and throw and catch the bean bag as directed in place and while jogging around the room.

DPESS page 309
Scattered formation
On signal students will return bean bags and scatter themselves on the mat.

FITNESS DEVELOPMENT (8–12 MINUTES)

Continuity Exercises

These exercises are a type of interval training.

Create a CD/cassette tape with 30–35 seconds of music and 20 seconds of silence. Alternate music and silence.

Students jump rope during music and execute exercises as directed during silence. Sample exercises:

Leg Kicks R/L; Standing Bend & Stretch; Jumping Jacks; Arm Circles; Arm Thrusts; Stretch Arms Overhead; Sitting Stretch–touch toes; Push-ups; Stretch in out-reach; Curl-ups; Sitting Body Twist; Leg Lunges; Standing Stretch and Touch Toes; Shoulder Circles.

DPESS pages 349–350

LESSON FOCUS (15–20 MINUTES)

Forearm bump pass

Demonstrate passing skill

- Stance: shoulder width and square with the ball; hips and knees flexed.
- Arm position.
- When contact is made, bump the ball
- Off of the lower forearms above the wrist.

Review serving skills

DPESS pages 452–453
Use management technique of: Toe-to-Toe with 3 people:
- 1 places hands on hips   =DOER
- 1 places hands on knees =TOSSER/retriever
- 1 kneels on ground   = OBSERVER

OBSERVER will observe the doer and give verbal feedback.
Repeat practice activity of yesterday.

GAME (5 MINUTES)

Wheelbarrow Relay

DPESS page 405
See Lesson 13, Weight Training Unit for details.

EVALUATION/REVIEW AND CHEER

Students huddle together for review.
Teacher will review by asking students pertinent questions regarding elements of the lesson.
Cheer: 1, 2, 3, 4, Forearm passes help us score!

Volleyball Lesson Plan 3

EQUIPMENT:

Cones
1 volleyball per student
CD/cassette tape for rope jumping

Tug-of-War rope(s)
Volleyball courts
1 individual jump rope per person
CD/cassette player

INSTRUCTIONAL ACTIVITIES	TEACHING HINTS

INTRODUCTORY ACTIVITY (2–3 MINUTES)

Wave Drill

Students are in ready position (knees bent). Students
  shuffle left, right, backward or forward on whistle or
  hand signal.
- 1–whistle = Forward
- 2–whistles = Backward
- 3–whistles = Left
- 4–whistles = Right

DPESS page 305

FITNESS DEVELOPMENT (8–12 MINUTES)

Rope Jumping Activities

Jump Rope interspersed with the following:
Leg Lunges
Stretch Arms across body
Sit-Ups
Push-Ups
Shoulder Rolls
Ankle Rolls
Stretch Arms overhead
Stretch-touch toes
Sitting-Twist Body

DPESS page 309
Scattered formation
Jump rope to the music. When music stops place rope
  on the ground and do the instructed activity.

LESSON FOCUS (15–20 MINUTES)

Overhand Serves

Demonstrate serve.
Review Underhand Serve.

Review Bump Pass

DPESS pages 452–453
Use Back-to-Back management technique.
Assign students to courts with partner to practice 10
  types of serves each.
Review drill in Lesson 2.
Repeat drill of Lesson 2 today.

GAME (5 MINUTES)

Tug-of-War

Traditional; pull rope over head; pull with backs to
  opponents; pull with one hand on ground or in air; pull
  from seated position.

DPESS page 407
Review drill in Lesson 2.
Repeat today.

EVALUATION/REVIEW AND CHEER

Students huddle close together to answer review questions presented by instructor.
Cheer: 2, 4, 6, 8, Teamwork is really great!

Volleyball Lesson Plan 4

EQUIPMENT:

1 volleyball per student
Cones for markers

CD/cassette player
Music tape for fitness activities

INSTRUCTIONAL ACTIVITIES	TEACHING HINTS

INTRODUCTORY ACTIVITY (2–3 MINUTES)

Weave Drill
The weave drill is similar to the wave drill except that students shuffle in and out of a series of obstacles such as cones. A shuffling step is used rather than a crossover step.

DPESS page 306
Cones are spread out in rows. Each student should stand next to a cone. Everyone is facing the same direction. Wait for signal to go left or right.

FITNESS DEVELOPMENT (8–12 MINUTES)

Four Corners
Movement to music.

Skipping	Jumping
Hopping	Galloping

DPESS page 347
Cones mark a square.
Scattered formation around the perimeter of the 4 cones. When music starts they move in a clockwise direction. As they pass a corner they change locomotor movement.

Stretching:
Legs
Arms (across body, over head)
Roll: Shoulders, Ankles, Wrists
Twist Body

DPESS pages 342–344
Teacher or student can direct these activities.

LESSON FOCUS (15- 20 MINUTES)

3 Station Practice:
1. Front overhand pass
Demonstrate practice drill:
Partners stand 8 ft. apart and pass back and forth using the technique.

DPESS pages 452–453
Use Back-to-Back technique to make pairs.
1 person puts hands on hips. That person gets 1 ball for partners. 2 lines facing partner:

x   x   x   x

x   x   x   x

2. Over the net set
Drill demonstration: Set the ball once to self, then over the net partner.

Partners stand on opposite sides of the net.
2 to 3 partner sets to a court.
Variation: 2 people to a side, set to each other and then set over the net.
As skills are mastered, groups can be larger.
Assign 1/3 of the class to this with partner station.

3. Serving Review
Demonstrate drill.

GAME (5 MINUTES)

Push-Up Tag
"its" try to tag. Safe position = push-up position and activity. Can only perform 3.

DPESS page 312
Select several "its" to be taggers.
Students must stay active throughout game.

EVALUATION/REVIEW AND CHEER

Students huddle close together. Questions: What did you learn today? Name the two types of serves you've practiced.
Cheer: Roses are red, violets are blue, P.E. is great, volleyball rules.

Volleyball Lesson Plan 5

EQUIPMENT:

1 individual jump rope per person	Pre-recorded music CD/tape for exercise
1 volleyball per student	CD/cassette player
Whistle	Drum and beater

INSTRUCTIONAL ACTIVITIES	TEACHING HINTS

INTRODUCTORY ACTIVITY (2–3 MINUTES)

Formation Rhythmic Running

On signal (drum, clap)

- Runners freeze in place. They resume running when the regular beat begins again.
- Runners make a full turn in four running steps, lifting the knees high while turning.
- Runners go backward, changing the direction of the circle.

DPESS page 313

Circle formation: Follow the back of somebody's neck to create a circle.

The tone of the drum controls the quality of the movement, light sound light run, heavy sound heavy run.

When the drum stops students run in scattered formation; when it resumes, they return to circular formation and follow rhythm.

FITNESS DEVELOPMENT (8–12 MINUTES)

Circuit Training to music

7 Circuits: Push-Ups, Bend & Stretch, Sit-Ups, Arm Circles, Windmills, Rope Jumping, Sit & Stretch

Record a CD/tape with 60 seconds of music and 5 seconds of silence for rotating to the next station.

DPESS 348.

Divide class up into 7 groups.

Assign each group to begin at a given circuit.

Students active while music is playing, when music stops, rotate clockwise to the next station.

LESSON FOCUS (15- 20 MINUTES)

Forearm Bump Pass

Demonstrate drills:

- Pass the ball 2–3 feet off the wall to yourself.
- Partner underhand tosses ball to you. You forearm pass back to your partner. 10 times then switch. Repeat.
- Partner bounces ball to you. You forearm pass back to your partner. 10 times then switch. Repeat.

DPESS pages 452–453

Use management game to create groups of two.

Scattered formation throughout gym.

GAME (5–7 MINUTES)

3 Hit Volleyball

6 players per team. Use as many courts as needed. Need to have an even number of teams so everyone is playing.

DPESS page 354

Use Whistle Mixer to form teams.

Use regulation rules, but must have 3 hits per side. Can also allow 2 serves without penalty if desire.

EVALUATION/REVIEW AND CHEER

Review daily activities. Teacher will ask lead up questions for self-discovery. Talk about teamwork.

Cheer: Fun for all, we enjoyed volleyball!

Volleyball Lesson Plan 6

EQUIPMENT:

1 volleyball per student
Volleyball courts
1 bean bag (different colors) per student

20 cones for markers
Tug-of-War rope
Several mats

INSTRUCTIONAL ACTIVITIES	TEACHING HINTS

INTRODUCTORY ACTIVITY (2–3 MINUTES)

Bean Bag Touch and Go

Spread different colored bean bags throughout the area. On signal, students run to a bean bag, touch it, and resume running. The touch must be made with a designated body part. E.g., "Touch 6 yellow bean bags with your right hand."

DPESS page 309

Scattered formation

To increase the challenge, the color of the bean bag can be specified.

Students can also move to a bean bag, perform a pivot, and resume running.

FITNESS DEVELOPMENT (8–12 MINUTES)

Mini Challenge Course (4 courses)

Course #1: Do crouch jumps, pull or scoot movements down a bench; put body through two hoops; and skip to a cone.

Course #2: Weave in and out of four wands held upright by cones; Crab Walk to cone; hang from a climbing rope for 5 seconds; gallop to a cone.

Course #3: Do a tumbling activity the length of the mat; agility run through hoops; Frog Jump to cone; slide to cone.

Course #4: Move over and under six obstacles; Log roll length of mat; while jumping, circle around three cones; run to next cone.

DPESS page 351

Whistle Mixer–blow whistle 4 times, groups of 4.

1 person hand on head	(course #1)
1 person hand on knees	(course #2)
1 person hand on hips	(course #3)
1 person knee on ground	(course #4)

Rotation: Tosser–Retriever–Hitter–Tosser

LESSON FOCUS (15–20 MINUTES)

Station Practice

Spiking Station #1: **Spike** ball against wall using the arm swing form taught in class. Repeat.

Station #2: **Toss and hit.** The tosser tosses ball like a set partner who spikes ball back using the arm swing motion. No foot approach. Switch roles and repeat.

Station #3: **Approach and Tip Ball**. At the net. Tosser tosses ball up, hitter makes approach and tips the ball into other court. Tosser becomes hitter. Hitter shags ball.

DPESS pages 453–454

Toe-to-Toe 1 other person. Pairs combine with another pair to make a group of 4.

Everyone gets a ball.

Assign groups to stations.

Explain rotation.

Two shaggers needed in this activity

GAME (5–7 MINUTES)

King/Queen of the Court

3 on 3 game using the spike and tip. Winning team stays on court, other team goes to sideline and new team comes on. Repeat.

DPESS page 354

Toe-to-Toe with 3 people. Four groups of 3 to each court. Depending on # of courts, may vary.

EVALUATION/REVIEW AND CHEER

Students huddled close together.

Questions: Which station was the most challenging. Why?

How was the game?

Cheer: 1, 2, 3, Fit is the way to be!

Volleyball Lesson Plan 7

EQUIPMENT:

1 volleyball per student   Volleyball courts/nets
Parachute

INSTRUCTIONAL ACTIVITIES	TEACHING HINTS

INTRODUCTORY ACTIVITY (2–3 MINUTES)

Seat Roll

Students are on all fours with head up, looking at the instructor. When instructor gives a left or a right hand signal, students respond quickly by rolling that direction on their seat.

DPESS page 304
Scattered formation
Example for signals could be:
1 whistle = left
2 whistles = right

FITNESS DEVELOPMENT (8–12 MINUTES)

Parachute Fitness

1. Jog in a circle with chute held in left hand. Reverse.
2. Standing, raise the chute overhead, lower to waist.
3. Slide to the right; return slide to the left.
4. Sit and perform Abdominal Challenges–30 sec.
5. Skip.
6. Freeze; face the center, and stretch the chute tightly with bent arms. Hold for 8–12 seconds. Repeat 5 X.
7. Run in place, hold the chute at waist level.
8. Sit with legs under the chute. Do a seat walk toward the center. Return to the perimeter. Repeat.
9. Place chute on the ground. Jog away from the chute and return on signal. Repeat.
10. On side, perform side leg flex (lift chute with legs).
11. Lie on back with legs under the chute. Shake the chute with the feet.
12. Hop to the center of the chute and return. Repeat.
13. Assume the push-up position with the legs aligned away from the center of the chute. Shake the chute with one arm while the other arm supports the body.
14. Sit with feet under the chute. Stretch by touching the toes with the chute. Relax with other stretches while sitting.
15. Perform parachute stunts like the Dome or Mushroom to end.

DPESS page 352
Evenly space students around the parachute.
Use different grips to add variation to the activities.
Encourage students to move together.
Use music to motivate students.

LESSON FOCUS (15–20 MINUTES)

Setting
Demonstrate drills:
- Stand across from partner and set back and forth.
- Set to self and then to your partner.

Back Set
Demonstrate.
- Set once to yourself then back set to your partner.

Set Spike Review at net

DPESS pages 452–453
Back-to-Back with someone
Setter, you must time your push-up with the toss.
Knees bent in ready position, hands always above head

GAME (5–7 MINUTES)

Mini Pyramids
Partners work together to create pyramids.

DPESS pages 399–400
Can combine groups

EVALUATION/REVIEW AND CHEER

Students huddle close together. Any questions? What did you learn today? What did you like best?
Cheer: You bet, we love to set!

Volleyball Lesson Plan 8

EQUIPMENT:

1 volleyball per student
Volleyball courts/nets
Continuity Music CD/tape

1 jump rope per student
1 hula hoop per student
CD/cassette player

INSTRUCTIONAL ACTIVITIES	TEACHING HINTS

INTRODUCTORY ACTIVITY (2–3 MINUTES)

Fastest Tag

DPESS page 312
See Lesson 8, Badminton unit for instructional details.

FITNESS DEVELOPMENT (8–12 MINUTES)

Continuity Exercises
Students alternate jump rope activity with exercises done
  in two-count fashion. Teacher/student can lead.
Movement examples alternated with rope jumping:
  Double Crab Kick; Knee Touch Curl-up;
  Push-up Challenges; Bend–touch toes.
Rope Jumping: Swing-Step Forward while jumping;
  Side Flex; Stretch Arms–over head
  Stretch Arms–across body; Curl–ups
Rope Jumping: Hot Peppers;
Sit and Twist body

DPESS pages 349–350
Scattered formation
Each student gets a jump rope.
Recorded intervals of music alternated with silences
  should be used to signal rope jumping (with music)
  and performing exercises (without music).
Allow each student to adjust the workload to his or her
  fitness level. This implies resting or walking if the
  rope jumping is too strenuous.

LESSON FOCUS (15–20 MINUTES)

Station #1: Spiking.
  Approach without using the ball. Repeat 5 times.
  Approach, spike ball out of partner's hand. Partner
  stands on ladder or jumping box. Repeat 5–10 times.
  Rotate positions.
Station #2: **Toss, approach, catch.** Person at net tosses
  up ball as if a set. Partner approaches and catches ball
  in the air. Repeat 3 times, and then change roles.
  Repeat.
Station #3: **Spiking.** Each group has a tosser, a hitter and
  two retrievers. The hitter approaches and hits the ball,
  trying to keep the ball inside the court. Rotate. Repeat
  until each hits 5–10 times.
Station #4: **Dinking.** Same activity as Station 3 but
  execute a dink shot instead of a spike.

DPESS pages 452–453
Use management technique to create partners.
Assign groups to area in gym.

Combine 2 sets of partners to create groups of 4 when
  rotate or begin at this station.
Assign students to a court.

Use the same groups as in Station 4.

GAME (5–7 MINUTES)

Keep it Afloat
Set ball to each other and count how many in a certain
  time period.

DPESS page 454
Work in partners.

Hula Hoop Targets
Serve or spike balls into targets. A team scores a point if
  ball lands in hula hoop when it touches the ground.
Game begins when teacher gives signal.

EVALUATION/REVIEW AND CHEER

Huddled around teacher. Any questions? Ask students questions about spiking. How many steps are in the approach?
  What was the hardest part? The easiest?
Cheer: You bet, we love to set!

Volleyball Lesson Plan 9

EQUIPMENT:

1 volleyball per 4 students	4 cones
Squad Leader Instructions	

INSTRUCTIONAL ACTIVITIES	TEACHING HINTS

INTRODUCTORY ACTIVITY (2–3 MINUTES)

Addition Tag	DPESS page 312
Two couples are it. "Its" stand with inside hands joined trying to tag with free hands. All tagged join couple. The three then chase until they catch a fourth. Once a fourth person is caught, the four divide and form two couples, adding another set of taggers to the game.	Scattered formation; designate boundaries. A tag is legal only when the couple or group of three keep their hands joined.

FITNESS DEVELOPMENT (8–12 MINUTES)

Squad Leader Exercise	DPESS page 346
Choose 4 squad leaders. Give each squad leader a card with planned routines on it and a designated area. Play music for 3 minutes and then stop so squads can rotate clockwise. Squad leaders stay where they are; when music begins, squad leader leads the new group.	Use Whistle Mixer to make 4 Squads. Identify Squad Leader. SQUAD #1 Leads Upper Body Exercises SQUAD #2 Leads Abdominal Exercises SQUAD #3 Leads Lower Body Exercises SQUAD #4 Leads Stretching Exercises

LESSON FOCUS (10–12 MINUTES)

Blocking	DPESS pages 452–453
Demonstrate skills and drills:	Use a management technique to create groups of 3.
• Blocking position	Assign students to courts and sides of courts.
• Blocking with person opposite net simulating spiking	Everyone should repeat each drill 5 times.
Two-person blocks.	
Repeat above drills with a setter, a ball, and a spiker.	

GAME (5–7 MINUTES)

Modified game	DPESS pages 353–354
Play 4 minutes then rotate courts. 6 players per team.	When whistle blows, rotate clockwise.

EVALUATION/REVIEW AND CHEER

Students are huddled close to teacher. Ask for questions.
Cheer: 3, 5, 7, 9, P.E. is so fine!

Volleyball Lesson Plan 10

EQUIPMENT:

8 jump ropes	20 tennis balls	8 10" playground balls	8 basketballs
8 hula hoops	1 flag belt/scarf per student	1 volleyball per student	

INSTRUCTIONAL ACTIVITIES	TEACHING HINTS

INTRODUCTORY ACTIVITY (2–3 MINUTES)

Capture the Flag (Variation of Flag Grab). Single file line. Person at end of the line tucks flag into waistband. At whistle, teams connect with their teammates with hands on shoulders in front of them. Teams run around trying to pull flag out of the other teams pants without having flag stolen.	DPESS page 314 Scattered formation Use a management game to create teams of equal size (5–6) Identify the boundaries. Make sure that the area is clear/safe to run.

FITNESS DEVELOPMENT (8–12 MINUTES)

Circuit Training Stations	DPESS page 348
#1: Sit-Ups; #2: Juggle 3 tennis balls; #3: Run in place; #4: Dribble basketball/switch hands; #5: Push-Ups; #6: Jump Rope; #7: Balance a Ball; #8: Hula Hoops; Cool down walking for 30 seconds.	8 stations–2 minutes at each station Use music to indicate activity time, no music time to rotate counter clockwise to the next station. Divide class up evenly for stations.
Stretch areas worked in the station fitness activities.	Lay out equipment so that each person will have his or her own.

INSTRUCTIONAL ACTIVITIES	TEACHING HINTS

LESSON FOCUS (10–12 MINUTES)

Forearm Passes
Drill #1: Two arm pass; Drill #2: One arm pass/bump;
  Drill #3: Bump and side roll; Drill #4: Back rolls. Start
  with drill #1, one partner tosses or hits the ball to the
  other who performs the drill 10 times.

DPESS pages 452–453
Elbow-to-Elbow with another person
1 person put your hands on your hips.
Person with hands on your hips, go and get 2 balls.

GAME (5–7 MINUTES)

Dig It: Regulation volleyball, except there has to be at
least one dig before the ball goes over the net.

Toe-to-Toe with 6 people
Any 1 handed, underhand hit will qualify for a dig.

EVALUATION/REVIEW AND CHEER

Students huddled close together. Review elements of forearm pass and roll.
Cheer: 3, 5, 7, 9, P.E. is so fine!

Volleyball Lesson Plan 11

EQUIPMENT:

1 volleyball per student	Volleyball courts/nets	10 cones
CD/cassette player	Music CD/tape for exercise	Task Sheets, clipboard, pencils

---

INSTRUCTIONAL ACTIVITIES	TEACHING HINTS

INTRODUCTORY ACTIVITY (2–3 MINUTES)

Octopus Tag (similar to Addition Tag)
Start off with two "its." Each time someone is tagged
  they join onto one of the ends. Students stay hooked
  together by either holding hands or interlocking arms.
  Only person on the end can tag. For tag to be valid,
  students must remain hooked. Play until all are tagged.

DPESS page 312
Scattered formation
Designate boundaries.
Work on teamwork. Communicate with each other.

FITNESS DEVELOPMENT (8–12 MINUTES)

Mirror Drill in Place
Mirror/Shadow exercises partner executes.
1. Do an aerobic type exercise to music.
2. Do a stretching activity when the music stops.
Each partner does 1 and 2 above and then switch roles.
REPEAT until signal is given.

DPESS page 313
Back-to-Back with someone
1 person put your hands on your hips–LEADER FIRST.

LESSON FOCUS (15–20 MINUTES)

Task Sheets Skill Evaluation
Develop a Task Sheet covering all skills taught.
List specific areas students are to observe.
Rotation:
  DOER-RETRIEVER-OBSERVER-DOER

Toe-to-Toe with 3 people
DOER = 1 person hands on hips
  get 3 Task Sheets/1 pencil/1 clipboard
RETRIEVER = 1 person hand on knee
OBSERVER = 1 person hand on shoulder

GAME (5–7 MINUTES)

Keep it Afloat
Each team forms a circle of no more than 6 students. The
  object of the game is to see which team can make the
  greater number of volleys in a specified time or which
  team can keep the ball in the air for the greater number
  of consecutive volleys without error.

DPESS page 454
Use management game to create 5–6 to a group/team
Circle formation
On teacher's signal, the game is started with a volley by
  one of the players.

EVALUATION/REVIEW AND CHEER

Students are huddled close together. Discuss the Task Sheets
Cheer: 6, 4, 2, Teamwork's for me and you!

Volleyball Lesson Plan 12

EQUIPMENT:

Individual mats
1 volleyball per person

Continuity Exercise CD/tape
Volleyball courts/nets

1 Task Sheet per person, clipboard, pencil
CD/cassette player

INSTRUCTIONAL ACTIVITIES	TEACHING HINTS

INTRODUCTORY ACTIVITY (2–3 MINUTES)

Follow the Leader Activity
Leader performs aerobic type activity when the music is playing and a stretching activity when there is no music, then that leader drops to end of line, next person in line is new leader. REPEAT.
EVERYONE IN LINE FOLLOWS THE LEADER AND DOES WHAT THE LEADER IS DOING.

DPESS page 313
Toe-to-Toe with 4-6 people. 1 person put your hands on your hips, YOU'RE THE LEADER FIRST.
Scattered Squad Formation with Leaders

Δ   L   L\   Δ
Δ L   L / L   Δ

Within a designated area
The leader can stay in one place or move around designated area.

FITNESS DEVELOPMENT (8–12 MINUTES)

Fitness Challenge
Alternate locomotor movements with strength challenges. Repeat the challenges as necessary. Challenge movement suggestions follow:
Flexibility and Trunk Development Challenges
1. Bend in different directions; 2. Stretch down slowly and back up; 3. Combine bending and stretching movements; 4. Sway back and forth; 5. Twist one body part; add body parts; 6. Make your body move in a large circle; 7. In a sitting position, wave your legs at a friend; 8. Make circles with your legs.
Shoulder Girdle Challenges
In a push-up position, do the following challenges:
1. Lift one foot; the other foot; 2. Wave at a friend; wave with the other arm; 3. Scratch your back with one hand; reverse; 4. Walk your feet to your hands; 5. Turn over; shake a leg; crab walk.
Abdominal Development
From a supine position:
1. Lift your head and look at your toes; 2. Lift your knees to your chest; 3. Wave your legs at a friend.
From a sitting position: 1. Slowly lay down with hands on tummy; 2. Lift legs and touch toes.

Scattered formation.
Music can be used, e.g. locomotor movement to music, other movements when there is no music.
Individual mats can be used as a "home" to keep students spaced properly.
Repeat the various trunk challenges as necessary.
Use different qualities of movement such as giant skips, tiny and quick gallops, or slow giant steps during locomotor activities to motivate students.
As students become more fit, repeat the entire sequence.

LESSON FOCUS (15–20 MINUTES)

Task Sheet: Overhand Serve, Forearm Pass
Explain Task Sheet.
Rotation:
DOER → RETRIEVER →OBSERVER →DOER

DPESS pages 452–453
Toe-to-Toe with 2 other people
1 person hands on hips =   DOER
1 person hand on knees = RETRIEVER
1 person hand on shoulder = OBSERVER
Direct Doer and Retriever to bring equipment to group: Clipboard, pencil and 3 Task Sheets, and 2 balls.

GAME (5–7 MINUTES)

Three Hit Volleyball
This game emphasizes the basic offensive strategy of volleyball. The game follows regular volleyball rules with the exception that the ball must be hit three times before going over the net.

DPESS page 454
Use as many courts as possible.
Combine 2 practice groups to make a team. Encourage the students to count out loud the number of times the ball has been or is being played. The team loses the serve or the point if the ball is not played three times.

Volleyball Lesson Plan 13

EQUIPMENT:

8 cones
Continuity Exercise Music CD/tape

CD/cassette player
1 volleyball per student
Volleyball courts and nets

INSTRUCTIONAL ACTIVITIES	TEACHING HINTS

INTRODUCTORY ACTIVITY (2–3 MINUTES)

Frozen Tag with variation
Students move in a designated area, when tagged they freeze. They can be unfrozen when someone crawls or dives under and between their legs.

DPESS page 312
Scattered formation
Select 1–3 "its."
When player goes outside the area, it's equivalent to being tagged.

FITNESS DEVELOPMENT (8–12 MINUTES)

Walk-Jog-Sprint
When the music is playing, walk, jog, or sprint. When there is no music, students will follow exercise led by the teacher. Exercises are to increase strength and flexibility.

DPESS page 354
Scattered formation
Designate the running perimeter.
Faster students may pass on the outside only.

LESSON FOCUS (15–20 MINUTES)

Round Robin Volleyball Tournament

Explain Round Robin Chart.

GAME (5–7 MINUTES)

Volleyball Tournament continues

EVALUATION/REVIEW AND CHEER

Students are huddled close together. What were some of the skills that you used today? Which skill did you use the most? Explain rotation for tomorrow.
Cheer: 2, 4, 6, 8, Volleyball is really great!

Volleyball Lesson Plan 14

EQUIPMENT:

2 volleyballs per court
Tournament Chart

Volleyball courts/nets (5–6 players per team)

INSTRUCTIONAL ACTIVITIES	TEACHING HINTS

INTRODUCTORY ACTIVITY (2–3 MINUTES)

Eliminate today to allow time for tournament.

FITNESS DEVELOPMENT (8–12 MINUTES)

Continuity Exercises

DPESS pages 349–350
See Lesson 2, this unit for details.

LESSON FOCUS (15–20 MINUTES)

Volleyball Tournament Continued

GAME (5–7 MINUTES)

Volleyball Tournament Continued

EVALUATION/REVIEW AND CHEER

Ask how tournament is going. Are there any questions on rules, or the Round Robin Tournament?
Cheer: 6, 4, 2, We enjoyed playing you!

Volleyball Lesson Plan 15

EQUIPMENT:

2 volleyballs per court
1 Volleyball Written Exam per student

Volleyball courts and nets
Pencils

INSTRUCTIONAL ACTIVITIES	TEACHING HINTS

INTRODUCTORY ACTIVITY (2–3 MINUTES)

Eliminate today to allow exam and tournament time.

FITNESS DEVELOPMENT (8–12 MINUTES)

Stretch and Jog upon completion of exam

LESSON FOCUS (15–20 MINUTES)

WRITTEN EXAM

GAME (5–7 MINUTES)

Continue Tournament Play

Be sure to direct students to stretch and jog before playing volleyball.

EVALUATION/REVIEW AND CHEER

Teams huddle together. Are there any questions regarding the exam?
Introduce the next unit.
Cheer: 3, 5, 7, 9, P.E. is so fine!

VOLLEYBALL EXAM

MATCHING
Directions: Write the letter of the choice that gives the best definition or best matches the term on your answer sheet.

_____ 1. defense system
_____ 2. save
_____ 3. offensive system
_____ 4. "roof"
_____ 5. off-hand spike
_____ 6. kill
_____ 7. dink
_____ 8. strong side right-hander
_____ 9. strong side left-hander
_____ 10. topspin
_____ 11. W-formation
_____ 12. back set
_____ 13. bump
_____ 14. off-speed hit
_____ 15. free ball
_____ 16. opening up
_____ 17. side out
_____ 18. crosscourt hit
_____ 19. double hit
_____ 20. floater
_____ 21. wrist snap
_____ 22. heel plant
_____ 23. open hand
_____ 24. ace
_____ 25. turn outside hand in

a. 4-2
b. the setter is on the side opposite the hitter's hitting hand
c. offensive drop shot
d. left front position
e. 2-1-3
f. blockers have their hands over the net
g. one-arm desperation play to save a hard-driven ball
h. the setter is on the hitter's strong-arm side
i. no spin
j. a spiked ball that isn't returned
k. ball will float
l. puts topspin on the ball
m. ball will drop
n. right front position
o. transfers forward momentum into upward momentum
p. setter sets the ball over a head to the player behind the setter.
q. an easy return from the opponent
r. a serve that is not returned
s. serve reception
t. turning to face the player who is playing the ball
u. a spike directed diagonally to the longest part of the court.
v. the serve changes hands
w. hand position of the blocker closest to sideline
x. a player plays the ball twice in succession
y. a spike that is hit after the speed of the striking arm is greatly reduced
z. forearm pass
aa. correct hand position for spike and serve

MULTIPLE CHOICE
Directions: Select the **best** answer and mark it on your answer sheet.

26. The main difference in execution between the floater and the topspin serve is
    a. how you stand in relation to the net in the ready position
    b. where you contact the ball and how you follow through
    c. in how you swing your hitting arm
    d. how high you release the ball on the toss

27. The reason for a player being unsuccessful in serving accurately with an overhand serve is
    a. no weight shift   b. poor ball toss   c. no backswing   d. no arm extension   e. All of the above

28. An on-hand spike is
    a. always performed by the right forward
    b. hit on the opposite side of your body as the approaching set
    c. hit without an approach
    d. hit on the same side of your body as the approaching set

29. Once the serve is passed to the setter, the setter should make every effort to play the ball using
    a. an overhead pass or set   c. a block
    b. an underhand pass   d. a spike

30. A ball that is served to the opponent and hits the court in bounds without anyone hitting it is called
  a. a kill   b. a perfect serve   c. an ace   d. a spike

31. A ball not spiked by your opponent but returned to you high and easy is called
  a. a block   b. a free ball   c. a cake   d. a base defense

32. When your opponent plays the ball and you are waiting to see what they will do, you should be in
  a. serve reception formation   c. base defensive formation
  b. free ball formation   d. block + 2-1-3 defensive formation

33. When spiking a ball, the ball is contacted with
  a. the heel of an open hand   c. the side of a closed fist
  b. the fingertips   d. the front of a closed fist

34. The most accurate method of playing the ball is
  a. the block   b. the overhead pass   c. the spike   d. the forearm pass

35. The reason the floater serve moves during flight is because
  a. the ball has no spin on it   c. the ball has backspin
  b. the ball has topspin on it   d. the ball is hit with a closed fist

36. When performing a forearm pass, the arms generally
  a. swing upward with force   c. remain almost stationary
  b. make contact at shoulder level   d. follow through above the shoulders

37. The term used to describe one team's losing the serve is
  a. Hand out   b. Side out   c. Point   d. Rotation

38. When the right back has called for the ball, indicating to his/her teammates that he/she will receive the serve, all of his teammates should
  a. open up to the right back   c. get ready for the 2-1-3 formation
  b. run toward the right back to help out   d. call the lines for him/her

39. The serve is approaching the left back of the receiving team. The person who has the prime responsibility of calling the ball out over the end line is the (see diagram ⇓⇓)

  a. LF   b. LB   c. RB   d. CB

Net→		RF
LF	CF	RB
	LB	CB

40. The following are all defensive plays, **except for**
  a. a spike   b. a block   c. a dig   d. a save

41. All the following terms are associated with the spike, **except**
  a. Off-hand   b. Cushioning   c. Off-speed   d. Step-close takeoff

42. The primary responsibility of the center back in the 2-1-3 defensive alignments is
  a. to dig the spike   c. to pick up all dinks that come over the block
  b. to block the spike   d. not to play the ball, if at all possible

43. The purpose of the heel plant in the spike is to
  a.   Avoid too much force on the toes
  b.   Change forward momentum into upward momentum
  c.   Prevent wear and tear on the soles of your sneakers
  d.   Help you get greater arm swing

Weight Training

OBJECTIVES:

The student will:

1. Execute given locomotor movements when called out by the instructor during the High Five activity.
2. Demonstrate starting, stopping, dodging, tagging and cooperation during the Tag Game Introductory activity.
3. Participate in parachute aerobic activities and weight training to improve their fitness.
4. Participate in the Weave Drill demonstrating agility and the ability to follow directions during movements.
5. Participate in the PACER running activity to improve their cardiovascular endurance.
6. Participate in Aerobic Workout to improve his cardiovascular endurance and muscle strength and tone.
7. Participate in Continuity Exercises to improve her cardiovascular endurance fitness level.
8. On a self-check test, write six of the nine benefits of weight training covered in the lesson.
9. Identify all of the equipment available for use in the weight room by passing a self-check test.
10. Demonstrate an understanding of acceptable conduct while using the weight room by passing an objective exam with a score of 100%.
11. Demonstrate an understanding of general safety procedures while using the weight room by passing an objective exam with a score of 100%.
12. Complete the Warm-Up/Cool-Down and Overload and Specify Principles lessons to the satisfaction of the instructor.
13. Execute an overhand grip using the techniques demonstrated in the videotape in class.
14. Execute an underhand grip using the technique demonstrated on the videotape in class.
15. Demonstrate an understanding of repetition, set and cadence by completing lesson 10 with 100% accuracy.
16. Execute the proper procedure for adding and removing weights from a bar while it is resting on the rack and floor.
17. Demonstrate proficiency in spotting to the satisfaction of the instructor.
18. Demonstrate an understanding of the principle of progression by passing a self-check test with a score of 100%.
19. Perform two sets of ten repetitions of bench press using the maximum amount of weight and proper form.
20. Execute two sets of ten repetitions of lat pull downs using the maximum amount of weight and proper form.
21. Perform two sets of ten repetitions of shoulder press using the maximum amount of weight and proper form.
22. Identify the major muscle groups of the body by passing an objective exam with a score of 90%.
23. Execute two sets of ten repetitions of barbell curls using the maximum amount of weight and proper form.
24. Execute two sets of ten repetitions of Triceps extensions using the maximum amount of weight and proper form.
25. Perform two sets of abdominal crunches while performing the maximum number of repetitions in each of the sets and using proper form.
26. Complete two sets of ten repetitions of leg press using maximum weight and proper form.
27. Perform two sets of ten repetitions of leg extensions using the maximum amount of weight and proper form.
28. Execute two sets of ten repetitions of leg curls using the maximum amount of weight and proper form.
29. Complete 2 sets of heel lifts using the maximum number of repetitions in each of the sets and proper form.
30. List the exercises in the proper sequence beginning with exercises for the larger muscles to the smaller muscles for each major muscle group in the upper body by passing a self-check test with a score of 90%.
31. List the exercises in the proper sequence beginning with exercises for the larger muscles to the smaller muscles for each major muscle group in the lower body by passing a self-check test with a score of 100%.
32. Demonstrate an understanding of the elements in a program designed to increase muscular strength and size by passing a self-check test with a score of 100%.
33. Demonstrate an understanding of the elements in a program designed to increase muscular endurance and tone by passing a self-check test with a score of 100%.
34. By completing a written assignment, develop, write, practice, and modify a personal weight-training program demonstrating an understanding of the scientific principles and practical theories covered in this class.
35. Play Crab Cage ball demonstrating cooperative and teamwork skills.
36. Play Butt Tug demonstrating agility, and cooperative skills.
37. Juggle scarves during the Game portion of class using techniques demonstrated in class.
38. Play Long Team Cage ball demonstrating teamwork and using skills demonstrated in class.
39. Demonstrate teamwork and cooperation during the Mass Stand Up Game and Wheelbarrow Relay Games.
40. Demonstrate cooperation and agility during the Spider Tag Game.
41. Demonstrate cooperation and teamwork during the Parachute Team Ball Game.
42. The student will pass a comprehensive written exam covering material from the preceding lessons with a score of 75% or better.
43. The student will demonstrate an understanding of the basic physiological and theoretical concepts of weight training by passing an objective exam with a score of 75%.

```
┌──────────────────────────────────────┐
│   WEIGHT TRAINING BLOCK PLAN          │
│          3 WEEK UNIT                   │
└──────────────────────────────────────┘
```

Week #1	Monday	Tuesday	Wednesday	Thursday	Friday
Introductory Activity	Move and Perform Stretch	Weave Drill	Rooster Hop Drill	Coffee Grinder Square	Flash Drill
Fitness	Aerobic Workout	Continuity Exercises	Running	Rope Jumping to Music	Aerobic Workout
Focus	Introduce Weight Room: Safety, Conduct, Format	Upper Body Lifts	Demonstrate Safe Equipment	Anatomy and Progression	Upper and Lower Body Weight Exercises
Game	Frisbee 21	Juggling Scarves	Frisbee Tennis	Juggling Scarves	Frisbee Around 9

Week #2	Monday	Tuesday	Wednesday	Thursday	Friday
Introductory Activity	Burpee Drill	Eliminate	Move and Stretch	Over, Under, and Around	Move and Change Directions
Fitness	PACER Running	Continuity Exercises	PACER Running	Jog, Walk, Jog	Jog, Walk, Jog
Focus	Heel Lift Shoulder Press Program Design Sequencing	Create Individual Weight Training Programs	Individual Weight Training Program	Individual Weight Training Program	Individual Weight Training Program
Game	Team Tug-of-War	Bowling Pin Relay	Crab Cage ball	Butt Tug	Mass Stand Up

Week #3	Monday	Tuesday	Wednesday	Thursday	Friday
Introductory Activity	Fastest Tag	Throwing and Catching Bean Bags on the Move	Aerobic Workout	Running High Fives	Eliminate today
Fitness	Parachute Aerobic Activities	Walk-Jog-Sprint	Individual Weight Training Program	Partner Fitnessgram Testing	Rhythmic Aerobic Exercise
Focus	Individual Weight Training Program	Individual Weight Training Program	Individual Weight Training Program	Partner Fitnessgram Testing	Individual Weight Training Program
Game	Long Team Cage ball	Addition Tag	Wheelbarrow Relay	Spider Tag	Parachute Activities

Weight Training Lesson Plan 1

EQUIPMENT:

Task Sheets 1–4 for each student
1 frisbee per 2 students

CD/cassette player
Rhythmic Aerobic Fitness CD/tape

INSTRUCTIONAL ACTIVITIES	TEACHING HINTS

INTRODUCTORY ACTIVITY (2–3 MINUTES)

Move and Perform a Stretch

Move and perform a stretching activity on the sound of the whistle. Move and stretch to the sound of music. Skip, hop, shuffle, jog and walk.

DPESS pages 308–309

Scattered formation

Direct starting and stopping locomotor movements to selected stretches using a whistle or a timed music CD/tape.

FITNESS DEVELOPMENT (8–12 MINUTES)

Aerobics Workout

Create a music CD/tape or purchase a pre-recorded Aerobic Exercise CD/tape with 120–150 BPM.

DPESS pages 358–359

Scattered formation

See Lesson Plan 7 in Racquetball for details

LESSON FOCUS (15–20 MINUTES)

Introduce Weight Room:

1. Equipment
2. Safety
3. Conduct
4. Lesson formats

Demonstrate Lunges and Bench Step Ups

Explain benefits.

DPESS pages 484–488

Explain safety rules.

Explain use of Task Sheets.

Explain and distribute Lessons 1, 2, 3, & 4.

Divide class up into 3 groups.

Assign each group to begin on a different lesson.

Describe rotation procedures.

When a group has completed one lesson and the group has not rotated, assign Lesson 1.

GAME (5 MINUTES)

Frisbee 21

Game Rules:

- Players stand 10 yards apart
- Throw disc back and forth. Throws must be catchable.
  1 point = 1 hand catch
  2 points = 2 hand catch

DPESS page 465

Create partners using "elbow-to-elbow" technique.

Have 1 person kneel. The standing partner gets a Frisbee from perimeter of area and brings to partner.

Player must get 21 points to win and win by 2 points.

TASK SHEET 1: THE BENEFITS OF WEIGHT TRAINING

Name: _____

Objectives:

Upon completion of the lesson you will:

1. Demonstrate an understanding of the benefits of weight training by writing six of the nine benefits described in the lesson.
2. Demonstrate a positive attitude while participating in weight training activities as a means toward achieving a positive attitude toward lifetime fitness.

Instructions:

This lesson consists of a list of nine benefits of weight training. Each of the benefits is followed by a brief description of the benefit. After carefully studying the list, go to the instructor for your self-check test on this lesson. On the self-check test, you will be asked to write six of the nine benefits of weight training. If you are unable to write six benefits, you must retake the test until you are able to do so.

The Benefits of Weight Training

Through your enthusiastic and dedicated participation in a quality weight-training program you may experience one or more of the following benefits:

1. **Improve strength**: In the course of this class, you may experience measurable gains in muscular strength. Your body will respond to the workload placed upon it (weights) by increasing the strength of the working muscles.
2. **Improved muscular endurance**: You will be able to lift a specific amount of weight more times after participating in weight training activities.
3. **Increased muscle size**: Some gains in the size of the muscle may accompany any gains in strength or endurance.
4. **Decreased body fat**: Excessive calories result in fat storage. Exercise burns calories. You will burn calories FASTER both DURING exercise and AFTER exercise. Calories are burned in the muscles. By increasing the size of your muscles, you are increasing your body's ability to burn calories.
5. **Improved appearance**: By reducing visible body fat and increasing the size or tone of your muscles, you can improve your physical appearance.
6. **Improved self-concept**: By improving your muscular strength, size, or endurance, you may also experience an increase in self-esteem, pride, and confidence. Also, you may experience positive feelings from reducing body fat and weight.
7. **Decreased fatigue**: After participating in a weight-training program, you will experience more energy and less fatigue in performing your everyday activities.
8. **Reduce chance of injury**: By strengthening the muscles and joints in your body, you may decrease both the frequency and degree of any possible injuries.
9. **Increased physical efficiency and productivity**: All of your bodily functions may appear to work better and require less energy. You will have more energy during and at the end of your day for enjoyable experiences.

REVIEW THE LESSON CAREFULLY AND PROCEED TO TAKE THE SELF-CHECK TEST.

SELF-CHECK TEST FOR: THE BENEFITS OF WEIGHT TRAINING

Name: _____

Date: _____   **Period** _____

Directions: Write six of the nine benefits of weight training covered in the previous lesson. When you have finished, get an answer key from the instructor and correct your test. If you miss any answers, go back and review the previous lesson and retake the test. Continue this procedure until you can write six of the nine benefits of weight training. Write six of the nine benefits of weight training:

1. _____
2. _____
3. _____
4. _____
5. _____
6. _____

(OPTIONAL): Write the other three benefits if you can:

7. _____
8. _____
9. _____

(ANSWER KEY)
SELF-CHECK TEST FOR:

THE BENEFITS OF WEIGHT TRAINING

Write six of the nine benefits of weight training:

1.   IMPROVE STRENGTH
2.   IMPROVE MUSCULAR ENDURANCE
3.   INCREASE MUSCLE SIZE
4.   DECREASE BODY FAT
5.   IMPROVE APPEARANCE
6.   IMPROVE SELF-CONCEPT

(OPTIONAL): Write the other three benefits if you can:

7.   DECREASE FATIGUE
8.   REDUCE CHANCE OF INJURY
9.   INCREASE PHYSICAL EFFICIENCY AND PRODUCTIVITY

TASK SHEET 2: EQUIPMENT IDENTIFICATION

Name: _____

Date: _____   **Period** _____

Objectives:

Upon completion of this lesson you will:

1.   Identify all of the equipment available for your use in the weight room.

Instructions:

A display of the various equipment is arranged for you to walk by and identify. Each piece of equipment will have a folded card attached to it. On the outside of the card you will find a number. The name of that particular piece of equipment will be written on the inside of the card. As you walk by the equipment, carefully open the cards to learn the names of the equipment. Mark a check on this sheet next to the number of each piece of equipment that you studied. After you have studied the equipment, ask your instructor for a self-check test.

1. _____ Universal machine	11. _____ weight training belt
2. _____ barbell	12. _____ Olympic curl bar
3. _____ barbell rack	13. _____ Olympic bench
4. _____ dumbbell	14. _____ squat rack
5. _____ dumbbell rack	15. _____ adjustable standard bench
6. _____ standard plate	16. _____ adjustable slate board
7. _____ standard collar	17. _____ abductor/adductor machine
8. _____ Olympic bar	18. _____ heel lift board
9. _____ Olympic plate	19. _____ lat pull down
10. _____ leg extension/leg curl	20. _____ Olympic collar

SELF-CHECK TEST FOR: EQUIPMENT IDENTIFICATION

Name: _____

Date: _____ **Period** _____

Directions: A display of the various equipment will be arranged for you to walk by and identify. Each piece of equipment will have a number attached to it. You are to identify the equipment by writing the number next to the appropriate piece of equipment listed below. After completing the test, get an answer key from your instructor and correct your own test. If you missed any answer, go back to the display and correctly identify the items missed.

1. _____ Universal machine
2. _____ barbell
3. _____ barbell rack
4. _____ dumbbell
5. _____ dumbbell rack
6. _____ standard plate
7. _____ standard collar
8. _____ Olympic bar
9. _____ Olympic plate
10. _____ leg extension/leg curl

11. _____ weight training belt
12. _____ Olympic curl bar
13. _____ Olympic bench
14. _____ squat rack
15. _____ adjustable standard bench
16. _____ adjustable slate board
17. _____ abductor/adductor machine
18. _____ heel lift board
19. _____ lat pull down
20. _____ Olympic collar

TASK SHEET 3: ACCEPTABLE CONDUCT

Name: _____

Date: _____ **Period** _____

Objectives:

Upon completion of this lesson you will:

1. Demonstrate an understanding of acceptable conduct while utilizing the weight room by passing an objective exam with a score of 100%.

Instructions:

This lesson consists of a list of guidelines for acceptable conduct. You will find the behavior or rule listed and followed by the reason for the rule. After carefully studying the lesson, you will take a test covering acceptable conduct. You must pass with a score of 100%. You must understand and adhere to the safety rules if you are to participate in this class. If you score less than 100% on the test, your instructor will have you review the lesson and retake the test.

Acceptable Conduct

While using the weight room, you will display acceptable conduct by:

RULE: Not touching any equipment until directed to do so by your instructor.

REASON: If you are occupied with the equipment, you cannot listen for any important information or directions from your instructor. Also, you may be making noise and keeping others from hearing directions.

RULE: Dressing appropriately for activity.

REASON: You must have freedom of movement. Your clothes cannot inhibit your ability to exercise through the full range of motion. Street clothes are unacceptable.

RULE: Refraining from making excessive noise or engaging in horseplay.

REASON: Noise and horseplay disturb other students and make it difficult to communicate and concentrate. It is unsafe.

RULE: Not eating or drinking in the weight room.

REASON: You can easily choke on food if you eat while exercising. You cannot adequately digest food while you are exercising. You may spill your food or drink in the weight room.

RULE: Not banging or dropping the weights.

REASON: You can damage the equipment or floor or drop a weight on yourself or a classmate. Banging weights creates annoying noises and disturbs others. You are not exercising properly when you allow the weights to drop quickly.

RULE: Returning all equipment to the proper place.

REASON: Other students may be looking for that piece of equipment. It is not safe to leave weights or equipment on the floor.

RULE: Using a towel when appropriate to keep equipment clean and free from sweat, grease, and dirt.

REASON: It is highly undesirable to sit or lay in someone else's sweat or grease. All forms of dirt can corrode the equipment and keep it from working properly.

* If necessary, review the lesson again prior to taking your test.

SELF-CHECK TEST FOR: WEIGHT ROOM ACCEPTABLE CONDUCT TEST

Name: _____

Date: _____ **Period** _____

Directions: (TRUE/FALSE) Write the entire word TRUE or FALSE in the space provided. Any other symbol or mark will be scored as incorrect.

1. _____ Students should not touch any equipment until directed to do so by the instructor.
2. _____ Students may drop or bang the weights as long as it doesn't bother anybody.
3. _____ Students should return all equipment to the proper place.
4. _____ Students should use a towel to keep equipment clean and free from sweat, grease, and dirt.
5. _____ Students may eat or drink in the weight room as long as they are neat and clean up after themselves.
6. _____ Screaming and yelling in the weight room is acceptable because it helps you to lift more weight.
7. _____ Physical education uniforms are permitted in the weight room since they will not restrict your movement. Street clothes are not permitted for working out.

TASK SHEET 4: GENERAL SAFETY PROCEDURES

Name: _____

Date: _____ **Period** _____

Objectives:

Upon completion of the lesson you will:

1. Demonstrate an understanding of general safety procedures while using the weight room by passing an objective exam with a score of 100%.

Instructions:

This lesson consists of a list of guidelines for general safety procedures. You will find the behavior or rule listed followed by the reason for the rule. After carefully studying the lesson, you will take a test on the general safety procedures and pass with a score of 100%. You must understand and adhere to the rules if you are to safely and successfully participate in this class. If you score less than 100% on the test, your instructor will have you review the lesson and retake the test.

General Safety Procedures

While using the weight room, you will demonstrate an understanding of general safety procedures by:

RULE: Always following the rules of acceptable conduct.

REASON: By doing so, you are contributing to a safe environment for all students.

RULE: Performing only the lifts taught in this class.

REASON: The lifts for this class were carefully analyzed and explained. You might not perform another lift properly or safely. Someone else may see you do it and try to imitate you unsuccessfully.

RULE: Utilizing proper exercise techniques.

REASON: Any deviation may be dangerous to your health and safety or to the health and safety of others. You may not receive the full benefit of the exercise if you change the technique.

RULE: Using spotters on all required lifts and whenever desired.

REASON: Spotters ensure safety and can provide motivation.

RULE: Using weight training belts on all required lifts and whenever desired.

REASON: The belts will help support your back and reduce the chance of injury.

RULE: Inspecting the cables/collars prior to each exercise and notify the instructor if they need repair.

REASON: The weights may fall off the bar and injure you or another student.

RULE: Reporting any broken or damaged equipment to the instructor.

REASON: The instructor may not be aware of it. The instructor can inform other students of the situation. The instructor may be able to fix it.

GENERAL SAFETY PROCEDURES TEST

Name: _____

Date: _____ **Period** _____

Directions: (TRUE/FALSE) Write the entire word TRUE or FALSE in the space provided. Any other symbol or mark will be scored as incorrect.

1. _____ Students are demonstrating safe behavior when following the guidelines for acceptable conduct.
2. _____ Students may perform exercises that were learned from a magazine or book.
3. _____ Students may change an exercise technique as long as it makes it easier for them to lift the weight and they are careful.
4. _____ Students must use spotters on all required lifts.
5. _____ Students must use weight belts on all required lifts.
6. _____ Students may not use spotters whenever they desire because spotters are scarce in the weight room.
7. _____ Students do not need to inspect the collars prior to each exercise because the instructor does it before class.
8. _____ Students should notify the instructor if a collar needs tightening.
9. _____ When students discover broken equipment, they should remain silent because they may be blamed for damaging it.

Weight Training Lesson Plan 2

EQUIPMENT:

Task Sheets 5–9	CD/cassette player
3 juggling scarves per student	Continuity Exercise CD/tape

INSTRUCTIONAL ACTIVITIES	TEACHING HINTS

INTRODUCTORY ACTIVITY (2–3 MINUTES)

Weave Drill

Use locomotor movements: carioca, skip, slide, jog, etc.
Give directions with whistle signal and arm movements.

DPESS page 306
Scattered formation
Have cones set up so that students can weave in and around.

FITNESS DEVELOPMENT (8–12 MINUTES)

Continuity Exercises

Jump Rope
Sit ups
Jump Rope
Push-ups
Jump Rope
Double Crab Kick (20)
Side Leg Flex (12 each side)
Jump Rope
Reclining Partner Pull-up (10 times each)
Jump Rope
Curl-ups
Jump Rope
Reverse Curl-ups
Jump Rope
Stretch all body parts

DPESS page 349
Scattered formation; alternate jumping rope and performing two count exercises. Rope jumping is done to pre-recorded music (40 seconds) and exercise done on silence pre-recorded to 30 seconds.

DPESS pages 342–344

LESSON FOCUS (15–20 MINUTES)

Demonstrate Upper Body Equipment, Lifts, and Grips

DPESS pages 484–487
Divide the class in half.
Distribute Lessons 5 and 6 to 1/2 of class.
Distribute Lessons 7–9 to the other 1/2 of class.
Describe rotation procedures.
Task Sheets can be completed outside of class.

GAME (5 MINUTES)

Juggling Scarves: 2–3 scarves cascading

DPESS pages 392–394 Add challenges listed.

TASK SHEET 5: WARM-UP AND COOL-DOWN

Name: _____

Objectives:
Upon completion of this lesson you will:
1.   Understand the importance of the warm-up.
2.   Understand the importance of cool-down.

Instructions:
This lesson is presented with a paragraph of information followed by questions pertaining to the paragraph. The answers to the questions are found beside the three asterisks (***) that follow each question. By folding a piece of paper and sliding it down the page, you keep the answers covered until you have made a response to the question. After you respond, slide the paper down and compare your answer with the answer given beside the asterisks. If your answer is correct, then go to the next question. If your answer is incorrect, then review the preceding paragraph and find out why your answer was wrong. Be sure to write the correct answer on your lesson.

Warm-Up

Prior to any vigorous exercise, including weight training, you should engage in an appropriate warm-up activity. Your body is very much like a car in that it performs much better after a few minutes of warming up prior to driving it in the morning. Much of the wear and tear on a car occurs during the first few minutes of driving after an inadequate warm-up.

Appropriate warm-up activities for weight training consist of performing exercises that are intense enough to cause perspiration and increase body temperature. By increasing the temperature of the body and muscles, you make it easier for the muscles to contract and they are less prone to injury. The warm-up exercises you choose should come from the exercises you are going to perform in your workout. Prior to beginning your workout set, you should perform the exercise with a very light weight that you can lift ten times very easily. This will get your muscles accustomed to performing the movement with a light weight so they are better prepared for the heavier workout weight.

1.   Prior to any vigorous physical activity you should engage in an appropriate _____ activity.
      *** warm-up
2.   Your body can suffer extra wear and tear and possibly _____ from an inadequate warm-up.
      *** injury
3.   An appropriate warm-up activity should be intense enough to cause _____ and increase body temperature.
      *** perspiration
4.   Increasing the temperature of the muscles makes it easier for them to _____.
      *** contract
5.   Your warm-up set should be performed with a light weight that you can easily lift _____ times.
      *** ten

Cool-Down

You have already learned the importance of an adequate warm-up prior to vigorous exercise. An adequate cool-down after exercise is equally important. It is not good for the human body to exercise hard for a period of time and then to stop abruptly. It needs to be cooled down gradually.

The blood in your body will go to the place that it is needed the most. After eating a meal, a great deal of blood will go to the digestive system to help digest the food. This means that there would be less blood available for the working muscles if you were to engage in physical activity immediately after eating. For this reason, it is recommended that you do not eat for approximately thirty minutes prior to or after exercising. During vigorous exercise, the blood in your body goes to the working muscles to supply them with the necessary oxygen and nutrients and to carry off the waste products produced by exercise. When you stop exercising, the blood is still in the muscles and needs time to circulate back to the heart and brain. If you stop suddenly and sit down, blood may pool in your muscles and prevent an adequate supply of blood from reaching the brain. This may cause you to be become a little light headed or dizzy. By walking or moving around for a few minutes after exercise, your muscles will help to pump the blood out of the muscles and back to the heart. This will also reduce the amount of post-exercise soreness.

1. The cool-down is _____ important as the warm-up.
    a. more   b. less   c. just as
    *** c
2. It is not good for you to exercise hard and then to _____ abruptly.
    *** stop
3. The blood in your body will go to the place that it is _____ the most.
    *** needed
4. It is recommended that you do not eat for approximately _____ minutes prior to or after exercising.
    a. ten   b. thirty   c. five   d. fifteen
    *** thirty
5. During exercise, the blood goes to the working muscles to supply them with the necessary nutrients and _____.
    *** oxygen
6. Sitting down immediately after exercising may cause the blood to _____ in the muscles.
    *** pool
7. Walking or moving around after exercise will help to reduce the amount of _____ in working muscles.
    *** soreness

TASK SHEET 6:
THE OVERLOAD PRINCIPLE AND THE PRINCIPLE OF SPECIFICITY

Name: _____

Objectives:
Upon completion of this lesson you will:
1.   Identify the overload principle on a written exam.
2.   Identify the principle of specificity on a written exam.

Instructions:
This lesson is presented with a paragraph of information followed by questions pertaining to the paragraph. The answers to the questions are found beside the three asterisks (***) that follow each question. By folding a piece of paper and sliding it down the page, you keep the answers covered until you have made a response to the question. After respond, slide the paper down and compare our answer with the answer given beside the asterisks. If your answer is correct, then go to the next question. If your answer is incorrect, then review the preceding paragraph and find out why your answer was wrong. Be sure to write the correct answer on your lesson.

Overload Principle
In order to improve in any area of physical fitness, you must constantly work your body at levels that it normally doesn't encounter. For example, to improve flexibility you must stretch your muscles beyond the point that they are normally stretched in your everyday activities. To improve your muscular strength or endurance through weight training, you must lift an amount of weight beyond what is normal for you. In order to increase the size and strength of your biceps (upper arm), you would need to curl a barbell or dumbbell of adequate weight. You would not "overload" your muscles or benefit from simply flexing your arm a few times. Moving the weight of your arm is an activity that is encountered everyday.

1.   The overload principle states that you must work your body at levels that it (does/doesn't) _____ normally encounter in your everyday activities.
    *** doesn't
2.   To improve flexibility you must _____ your muscles beyond the point that they are in your everyday activities.
    *** stretch
3.   To improve your muscular _____ or endurance you must lift an amount of weight that is beyond what is normal for you.
    *** strength

Principle of Specificity
The principle of specificity states that you must exercise a particular component of fitness in order to improve that particular component. For example, in order to improve cardiovascular fitness, you would run between fifteen and thirty minutes several times per week. To increase your flexibility, you would do a variety of stretching exercises. Therefore, if it is gains in muscular size, strength, endurance, or tone that you are seeking, you should engage in a quality weight training program.

1.   The principle of specificity states that you must _____ a particular component of fitness in order to improve that particular component.
    *** exercise
2.   In order to improve flexibility, you would perform _____ exercises.
    a.   running   c.   stretching
    b.   lifting   d.   no
    *** c
3.   In order to improve muscular strength, size, endurance, or tone, you would engage in a _____ program.
    *** weight training

TASK SHEET 7: THE BASIC LIFTING TECHNIQUE

Name: _____   **Date**: _____

Partner's Name: _____   **Period** _____

Student Information: You will be working with a partner in this lesson. In this lesson you will learn how to perform the basic lifting technique. This technique includes both lifting the weight from the floor as well as returning it. The two parts are equally important in weight training. Mastery of the basic lifting technique will greatly reduce your chances of back injury.

Objectives: Using a barbell weighing 20 pounds or less, you will perform ten repetitions of the basic lifting technique demonstrating proper form.

Directions:
1. Choose a partner that you would like to work with while completing this lesson.
2. Go to the appropriate viewing station with your partner and view the videotape on the basic lifting technique.
3. Go to the practice area with your partner and decide who will be the doer (lifter) and who will be the observer.
4. The doer will practice performing the basic lifting technique while the observer records and gives feedback.
5. The observer will mark the appropriate response (YES/NO) for each checkpoint and give verbal feedback for each "no" response.
6. The observer should check only one check point at a time.
7. Be sure to switch roles with your partner.
8. You will repeat this lesson until you receive a "yes" response on all of the checkpoints.

BASIC LIFTING TECHNIQUE

LIFTING THE WEIGHT FROM THE FLOOR	Yes	No
1. Assume a stance with the feet shoulder width apart and the toes slightly pointed out and directly underneath the bar.		
2. Keep the back straight throughout the task.		
3. Keep the arms straight throughout the task, keeping them shoulder width apart along the outside of legs.		
4. Bend at the hips and knees until the hands reach the bar.		
5. Grasp the bar firmly, keeping the back and arms straight.		
6. Keep the head in a vertical position with the eyes looking forward.		
7. Inhale prior to lifting the bar.		
8. Stand slowly, extending the hips and legs until the body is in a vertical position.		
9. Exhale approximately two-thirds of the way up.		
RETURNING THE WEIGHT TO THE FLOOR	**Yes**	**No**
10. Keep the head in a vertical position with the eyes looking forward.		
11. Keep the back and arms straight at all times.		
12. Slowly bend at the hips and knees until the bar touches the floor.		
13. Repeat for a total of ten repetitions.		

TASK SHEET 8: OVERHAND GRIP

Name: _____

Student Information: In this lesson you will learn how to perform an overhand grip. Use of the proper grip is very important in performing any lift with proper form. You will use the overhand grip in performing the bench press, lat pull down, shoulder press, and Triceps press down.

Objectives: You will perform ten repetitions of the overhand grip on a barbell using the proper form.

Directions:

1. Go to any area with an unused barbell. Leaving the barbell on the floor, practice the correct form for an overhand grip.
2. Mark the appropriate response (YES/NO) for each checkpoint for the overhand grip.
3. Repeat this lesson until you have responded "yes" to all of the checkpoints.

OVERHAND GRIP		Yes	No
1.	Assume a position close to the barbell with your toes directly underneath the bar.		
2.	Perform the basic technique for lifting a weight from the floor while keeping the arms shoulder width apart along the outside of the legs. Pause at the grip stage.		
3.	Assume a position with the hands where the thumbs are pointed toward each other.		
4.	Place the palms of the hands on the bar making sure they are an equal distance from the weights on the ends.		
5.	Firmly wrap the fingers around the bar.		
6.	Wrap the thumbs firmly around the opposite side of the bar.		
7.	Complete the basic technique for lifting a weight from the floor while using an overhand grip.		
8.	Perform the basic technique for returning the weight to the floor.		
9.	Repeat for a total of ten repetitions.		

Does your grip look like the one below?

TASK SHEET 9: UNDERHAND GRIP

Name: _____

Student Information: In this lesson you will learn how to perform an underhand grip. Use of the proper grip is very important in performing any lift with proper form. You will use the underhand grip in performing the Biceps curl.

Objectives: You will perform ten repetitions of the underhand grip on a barbell using the proper form.

Directions:

1. Go to any area with an unused barbell. Leaving the barbell on the floor, practice the correct form for an underhand grip.
2. Mark the appropriate response (YES/NO) for each checkpoint for the underhand grip.
3. Repeat this lesson until you have responded "yes" to all of the checkpoints.

UNDERHAND GRIP		Yes	No
1.	Assume a position close to the barbell with your toes directly underneath the bar.		
2.	Perform the basic technique for lifting a weight from the floor while keeping the arms shoulder width apart along the outside of the legs. Pause at the grip stage.		
3.	Assume a position with the hands where the thumbs are pointed out away from each other.		
4.	Place the palms of the hands on the bar making sure they are an equal distance from the weights on the ends.		
5.	Firmly wrap the fingers around the bar.		
6.	Wrap the thumbs firmly around the opposite side of the bar.		
7.	Complete the basic technique for lifting a weight from the floor while using an underhand grip.		
8.	Perform the basic technique for returning the weight to the floor.		
9.	Repeat for a total of ten repetitions.		

Does your grip look like the one below?

Weight Training Lesson Plan 3

EQUIPMENT:

PACER Running CD/tape
CD/cassette player

Written Task Sheets 10–15
1 frisbee per 2 students

INSTRUCTIONAL ACTIVITIES	TEACHING HINTS

INTRODUCTORY ACTIVITY (2–3 MINUTES)

Rooster Hop Drill

Students hop 10 yards on one leg in the following
  sequence:

1. Left hand touching the right toe, which is on the
  ground
2. Right hand touching the left toe on the ground
3. Right hand
4. Bend the knees, hands on the floor or ground
5. Legs kick back into an all fours position, head up

DPESS pages 305–306
Scattered formation
Direct students through a variety of movements.

FITNESS DEVELOPMENT (8–12 MINUTES)

PACER Running

Progressive aerobic cardiovascular endurance run

DPESS page 42
Use a timed CD/tape.
Scattered formation

LESSON FOCUS (15–20 MINUTES)

**Demonstrate Spotting and Adding Weight to
Equipment**

Scattered formation
Divide class into two groups.
Distribute and explain Task Sheets 7–9 to Group 1 and
  14–16 to Group 2.
Explain rotation procedures.

GAME (5 MINUTES)

Frisbee Tennis

The same game as regular tennis, but the player must
  catch the Frisbee and throw from that spot. The serve
  starts to the right of the center mark and must go to the
  opposite backcourt, not into the serve box.

DPESS page 465

EVALUATION/REVIEW AND CHEER

Review elements of spotting and Frisbee Tennis.
Cheer: Weight training, yeah!

TASK SHEET 10: REPETITION, SET, AND CADENCE

Name: _____

Objectives:

Upon completion of this lesson you will:

1. Demonstrate the meaning of the term "repetition" as it applies to weight training.
2. Demonstrate the meaning of the term "set" as it applies to weight training.
3. Demonstrate the meaning of the term "cadence" as it applies to weight training

Instructions:

This lesson is presented with a paragraph of information followed by questions pertaining to the paragraph. The answers to the questions are found below the three asterisks (***) that follow each question. By folding a piece of paper and sliding it down the page, you keep the answers covered until you have made a response to the question. After you respond, slide the paper down and compare our answer with the answer given below the asterisks. If your answer is correct, then go to the next question. If your answer is incorrect, then review the preceding paragraph and find out why your answer was wrong. Be sure to write the correct answer on your lesson.

Repetition, Set, and Cadence

The term "repetition" refers to repeated practice of a complete skill or act. In weight training a repetition refers to the number of times an exercise is to be performed. If only one complete cycle (from beginning to end) of the exercise was performed, then we say that one repetition was performed. A person who performs eight complete cycles of Biceps curls has performed eight repetitions of the exercise. The term "rep" is used when describing repetitions.

The term "set" refers to a collection or group of similar items. In weight training a set consists of a group of repetitions. A person who performs ten repetitions of bench press is said to have performed one set of ten repetitions. If a second set of ten repetitions is performed, then two sets of ten repetitions were performed.

The term "cadence" refers to rhythm, beat or time. In weight training, cadence refers to the rate or speed at which a repetition is performed. All exercises should be performed in a smooth and controlled fashion. You should never exercise in a speedy or jerky manner as this may increase the change of injury.

1. In weight training a (repetition/set) _____ refers to the number of times an exercise is to be performed.
   ***
   repetition

2. Exercises should be performed in a _____ manner.
   a. speedy   d. jerky
   b. smooth   e. both b and c
   c. controlled
   ***
   e

3. A _____ consists of a group of repetitions.
   ***
   set

4. Cadence refers to the (number/rate) _____ at which an exercise is performed.
   ***
   rate

5. A person who performed two groups of ten repetitions of leg curls is said to have completed _____ sets.
   a. two   b. ten   c. twenty
      ***
      two

TASK SHEET 11: RANGE OF MOTION AND BREATHING

Name: _____

Objectives:
Upon completion of this lesson you will:
1.   Identify the term of full range of motion and apply it to your work-outs.
2.   State the importance of breathing during exercise.

Instructions:
This lesson is presented with a paragraph of information followed by questions pertaining to the paragraph. The answers to the questions are found below the three asterisks (***) that follow each question. By folding a piece of paper and sliding it down the page, you keep the answers covered until you have made a response to the question. After you respond, slide the paper down and compare your answer with the answer given below the asterisks. If your answer is correct, then go to the next question. If your answer is incorrect, then review the preceding paragraph and find out why your answer was wrong. Be sure to write the correct answer on your lesson.

Range of Motion
In order to achieve maximal benefits from your weight training program, you must perform your exercises through the full range of motion. Range of motion refers to the area covered from the beginning of a movement to the end of a movement. The full range of motion is the greatest amount of movement possible in either direction. For example, in performing a push-up, a person who touches his chest to the ground and then fully extends his arms is considered to have performed the exercise through the full range of motion. However, if a person were to lower his body so his chest was six inches from the ground and only partially extended his arms, then he did not exercise through the full range of motion. When you perform an exercise through the full range of motion you are strengthening your muscles through the full range. If you perform an exercise through less than the full range of motion, then you are limiting your strength development to that particular range.

1.   Range of motion refers to the area covered from the _____ of a movement to the _____ of a movement.
     ***
     beginning and end

2.   If you perform an exercise through less than the full range of motion, then you are _____ your strength development to that particular range.
     ***
     limiting

3.   Full range of motion is the _____ amount of movement possible in either direction.
     ***
     greatest

4.   If you perform an exercise through the full range of motion, then you will _____ your muscles through the full range.
     ***
     strengthen

5.   In performing a push-up, if you touch your chest to the ground and fully extend your arms, you are exercising through _____.
     ***
     the full range of motion

Breathing

Your muscles must have an adequate supply of oxygen in order to function properly. This is especially true in the case of exercise and weight training. Breathing is an important part of exercising since you must breathe air into the lungs in order for your body to transport the much-needed oxygen to the working muscles. In addition, your muscles produce waste products from exercising and some of these waste products can be emitted through the air you exhale from your lungs.

In weight training you must be very careful not to hold your breath during a lift. By doing so you may temporarily raise the pressure in your chest cavity, as well as your blood pressure, to abnormal levels. This may cause you to black out and possibly injure yourself.

There are different and sometimes conflicting theories concerning the method of breathing during weight training. For the purposes of this class and for simplicity, you will exhale during the last third of the positive phase of a lift and inhale during the last third of the negative phase.

For example:
Bench Press:
(positive/exhale):   After two-thirds (during the last one-third) of the movement of pushing the bar off of the chest.
(negative/inhale):   After two-thirds (during the last third) of the movement of returning the bar to the chest.

1. Your muscles must have an adequate supply of _____ in order to function properly during exercise.
    ***
    oxygen

2. Your muscles produce _____ from exercising.
    a.   oxygen
    b.   waste products
    c.   pressure
    ***
    b

3. You must be very careful not to _____ your breath during a lift.
    ***
    hold

4. You will _____ during the last third of the positive phase of a lift.
    ***
    exhale

5. You will _____ during the last third of the negative phase of a lift.
    ***
    inhale

TASK SHEET 12: REST BETWEEN SETS, EXERCISES, AND WORKOUTS

Name: _____

Objectives:
Upon completion of this lesson you will:
1. State the importance and time of rest between sets.
2. State the importance and time of rest between exercises.
3. Identify the importance and time of rest between workouts.

Instructions:
This lesson is presented with a paragraph of information followed by questions pertaining to the paragraph. The answers to the questions are found below the three asterisks (***) that follow each question. By folding a piece of paper and sliding it down the page, you keep the answers covered until you have made a response to the question. After you respond, slide the paper down and compare your answer with the answer given below the asterisks. If your answer is correct, then go to the next question. If your answer is incorrect, then review the preceding paragraph and find out why your answer was wrong. Be sure to write the correct answer on your lesson.

Rest Between Sets
Rest plays a vital role in the success of any weight-training program. Your muscles must have sufficient rest in order to perform effectively. You should rest from 1 to 1 1/2 minutes between sets. After this time your muscles have recovered adequately (about 75% recovered) and are ready to perform another set of the same exercise. If you rest than one minute you may not be working hard enough. Rest of more than 1 1/2 minutes is too much and will also reduce the intensity of your workout.

1. You should rest from _____ to _____ minutes between sets.
   ***
   1 to 1 1/2
2. Rest of more than 1 1/2 minutes will reduce the _____ of your workout.
   ***
   intensity
3. After 1 1/2 minutes your muscles are about _____ recovered and ready to perform another set.
   ***
   75%

Rest Between Exercises
The amount of rest you take between different exercises can also affect the quality of your workout. The time of rest between your last set and the start of a new exercise should be between three and five minutes. After three minutes the energy in your muscles will have been restored to 100%. During this time you may be able to get a drink of water perform a stretch, work in with another person, or take care of some other needs.

1. The time of rest between your last set and the start of a new exercise should be between _____ and _____ minutes.
   ***
   three and five
2. After three minutes the energy in your muscles will have been restored to _____.
   ***
   100%

Rest Between Workouts

The time of rest between workouts is considered by some people to be the most important. During a very hard workout, you break your muscles down. Your body's response to this hard workload placed upon it is to rebuild the muscles to a level even greater than before the workout. Your body will adjust to meet the demands placed upon it. The greater the demands, the greater the adjustments or gains. If there are no demands placed upon the body, then there will be no gains made. This is true with ALL of the components of physical fitness including flexibility and cardiovascular fitness. Therefore, you should rest between one and two days between workouts exercising the same muscle group; you will not be giving your muscles a chance to rebuild and you may find that you actually LOSE strength.

1. During a hard weight training workout you _____ your muscles down.
    ***

    break
2. Your body will adjust to meet the _____ placed upon it.
    ***

    demands
3. You should rest between _____ and _____ days between workouts exercising the same muscle group.
    ***

    one and two

TASK SHEET 13: ADDING AND REMOVING WEIGHTS FROM A BAR RESTING ON THE FLOOR

Name: _____

Student Information: In this lesson you will learn the proper procedure for adding and removing weights from a bar while it is resting on the floor. The weights must be added properly and secured tightly on the bar with the collars in order to ensure safety.

Objectives: You will perform the proper procedure for adding and removing weights from a bar while it is resting on the floor.

Directions:
1. Go to any area with an unused barbell. Practice the proper procedure for adding and removing weights from the bar while it is resting on the ground.
2. Mark the appropriate response (YES/NO) for each checkpoint for the proper procedure.
3. Check only one checkpoint at a time.
4. Repeat this lesson until you have responded "yes" to all of the checkpoints.

ADDING AND REMOVING WEIGHTS

ADDING WEIGHTS TO THE BAR	Yes	No
1. Slide one of the heaviest plates on one end of the bar until it makes contact with the inside collar.		
2. Slide a plate of similar weight on the opposite end of the bar until it makes contact with the inside collar.		
3. Slide the next heaviest plate on one end of the bar until it makes contact with the first plate.		
4. Slide a plate of similar weight on the opposite end of the bar until it makes contact with the first plate.		
5. Repeat the procedure for every plate to be added until reaching the desired amount of weight.		
6. Slide the collars on the bar, pressing all of the weights tightly together against the inside collar.		
7. Tighten the collar by turning the bolt in the appropriate manner until it stops turning.		
8. Slide the remaining collar on the opposite end of the bar, pressing all of the weights tightly together against the inside collar.		
REMOVING WEIGHTS FROM THE BAR	**Yes**	**No**
1. Loosen the collar bolt until able to slide the collar easily off the end of the bar.		
2. On the opposite collar, loosen the collar bolt until able to slide the collar easily off the end of the bar.		
3. Remove one plate from one end of the bar.		
4. Remove one plate from the opposite end of the bar.		
5. Continue to alternate removing one plate at a time from each end of bar until the desired amount of weight remains.		
6. Replace and tighten the collars if leaving plates on the bar.		

TASK SHEET 14: ADDING AND REMOVING WEIGHTS FROM A BAR RESTING ON A RACK

Name: _____   **Date:**_____

Student Information: In this lesson you will be working with a partner in practicing the proper procedure for adding and removing weights from a bar while it is resting on a rack. The weights must be added and removed simultaneously to ensure safety. Also, be sure to secure the weights tightly with the collars.

Objectives: With the use of a partner, you will perform the proper procedure for adding and removing weights from a bar while it is resting on a rack.

Directions:
1. Go to any rack with an unused barbell. With your partner, practice the proper procedure for adding and removing weights from the bar while it is resting on the rack.
2. Mark the appropriate response (YES/NO) for each checkpoint for the proper procedure.
3. Check only one checkpoint at a time.
4. Repeat this lesson until you have responded "yes" to all of the checkpoints.

ADDING AND REMOVING WEIGHTS

ADDING WEIGHTS TO THE BAR	Yes	No
1. Simultaneously slide the heaviest plates on the ends of the bar until they make contact with the inside collar.		
2. Simultaneously slide the next heaviest plates on the ends of the bar until they make contact with the first plate.		
3. Repeat the procedure for every plate to be added until reaching the desired amount of weight.		
4. Slide the collars on the bar, pressing all of the weights tightly together against the inside collar.		
5. Tighten the collar by turning the bolt in the appropriate manner until it stops turning.		
REMOVING WEIGHTS FROM THE BAR	**Yes**	**No**
1. Loosen the collar bolts until you are able to slide the collars easily off the ends of the bar.		
2. Simultaneously remove one plate from the bar.		
3. Simultaneously remove one plate at a time from the bar until the desired amount of weight remains.		
4. Replace and tighten the collars if leaving plates on the bar.		

TASK SHEET 15: SPOTTING

Name: _____

Objectives:

Upon completion of this lesson you will:

1. Demonstrate an understanding of the responsibilities involved in spotting another lifter to the satisfaction of the instructor.

Instructions:

This lesson contains the responsibilities and skills required of a competent spotter. Carefully review and follow the guidelines in the following lessons. Good spotting skills are essential to success and safety in the weight room. After reviewing the lesson, ask your instructor to observe you while you spot another student.

Components of Spotting

1. Focus your full attention on the lifter. Do not look around the room or talk to other students while spotting.
2. Listen for any pre-lift instructions from the lifter concerning the number or type of exercises to be performed.
3. Verbally communicate and coordinate actions with any assisting spotters.
4. Assist the lifter in receiving the weight in the proper starting position for the exercise.
5. Verbally encourage the lifter during the exercise.
6. Give any necessary physical assistance to enable the lifter to complete the desired number of repetitions.
7. Assist the lifter in returning the weight to "its" resting place.

SELF-CHECK TEST FOR: THE COMPONENTS OF SPOTTING

Directions: (TRUE/FALSE) Write the entire word TRUE or FALSE in the space provided. Any other symbol or mark will be scored as incorrect. After taking the test, use the answer key to correct your exam. If you do not score 100%, you must review the lesson and retake the test.

1. _____ The spotter at the lifter's head is the head spotter.
2. _____ The head spotter does not have to listen to anybody, including the lifter.
3. _____ The spotter should give the lifter more than enough assistance than is necessary so the lifter doesn't get tired.
4. _____ The head spotter is the only one who really needs to pay attention. The other spotters may look around the room to see what they would like to do next.
5. _____ The pre-lift instructions given to a spotter by a lifter should include the number of repetitions to be attempted.

ANSWER KEY

1. True
2. False
3. False
4. False
5. True

Weight Training Lesson Plan 4

EQUIPMENT:

Task Sheets 16–20
Individual jump ropes
CD/cassette player

CD/tape for rope jumping
3 juggling scarves per student
Bases/bean bag markers

INSTRUCTIONAL ACTIVITIES	TEACHING HINTS

INTRODUCTORY ACTIVITY (2–3 MINUTES)

Coffee Grinder Square
Identify a locomotor activity to move from one corner to the next. Student performs "Coffee Grinder" on alternate arms at each corner.

DPESS page 307
Use Whistle Mixer to create 4 groups.
Direct starting corner for each group.
Set up square in area using bean bags or bases.

FITNESS DEVELOPMENT (8–12 MINUTES)

Rope Jumping
- Single jump
- Double jump
- Hot Peppers
- Challenges

DPESS pages 480–482
Scattered formation
Use music CD/tape to motivate movement
Can direct or allow student to alternate activities.

LESSON FOCUS (15–20 MINUTES)

Muscle Anatomy Principle of Progression
- Bench Press, Lat Pull down, Shoulder Press

DPESS pages 484–488
Explain Task Sheets.
Divide class into 2 groups.
Assign **Group 1**: Task Sheets 16–17
       Group 2: Task Sheets 18-20
Describe rotation.

GAME (5 MINUTES)

Juggling Scarves
2–3 Scarves Cascading

DPESS pages 392–394
Add challenges, i.e., under leg, behind back.

EVALUATION/REVIEW AND CHEER

Review the Muscle Anatomy Principle of Progressions
Cheer: Weight training, yes!

TASK SHEET 16: MUSCLE GROUPS OF THE BODY

Name: _____

Objectives:

Upon completion of this lesson you will:

1. Identify the major muscle groups of the body on a chart.

Instructions:

In this lesson you will study the major muscle groups of the body. It is important for you to know the location of the muscles in your body in order to improve your understanding of how they work and how to exercise them. Study the diagram that follows until you feel that you are ready to be tested on the muscle locations. When you are ready, see your instructor for the exam. You must pass the exam with a score of 80% before you go on to the next lesson. If you do not score 80% on the exam, study the diagram again and retake the test.

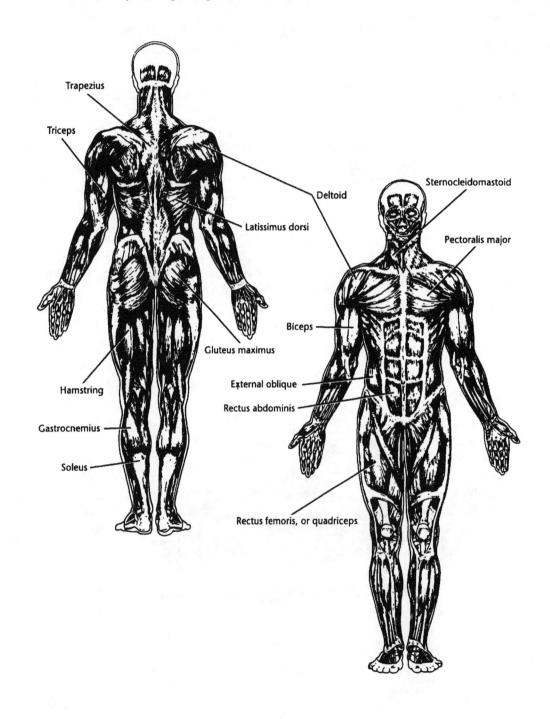

TASK SHEET 17: THE PRINCIPLE OF PROGRESSION

Name: _____

Date: _____ **Period** _____

Objectives:

Upon completion of this lesson you will:

1.   Demonstrate an understanding of the principle of progression by passing a self-check test with a score of 100%.

Instructions:

This lesson consists of information and guidelines for applying the principle of progression. It is very important that you fully understand and apply the principle of progression if you are to successfully overload your muscles. Study the steps carefully to prepare yourself for the self-check test at the end of the lesson. You must pass the self-check test with a score of 100%. If you do not score 100%, review the lesson and retake the test.

Principle of Progression

STEPS:

1.   Decide on the number of sets and repetitions to be performed.
2.   Select a reasonable amount of weight that might be lifted to complete the desired amount of repetitions successfully.
3.   Perform the exercise with proper form until muscular failure or until unable to maintain correct form.
4.   On the following sets, slightly increase the weight used when able to perform one additional repetition above the desired amount. Continue to do so until you are able to perform only the desired number of repetitions.
5.   On the following sets, slightly decrease the weight used when unable to perform the desired number of repetitions with proper form. Continue to do so until you are able to perform the desired number of repetitions.

* Carefully review the steps if necessary prior to taking the self-check test.

SELF-CHECK TEST FOR: THE PRINCIPLE OF PROGRESSION

Directions: Fill in the silence with the correct word. After completing the test, get an answer key from the instructor and correct your test. If you miss any questions, review the previous lesson and retake the test. Continue this procedure until you score 100% on this test.

1.   You should perform the exercise with proper form until muscular _____ or until unable to maintain correct form.
2.   You should slightly _____ the weight used when you can perform one additional repetition above the desired amount while maintaining proper form.
3.   You should slightly _____ the weight used when you are unable to perform the desired amount of repetitions with proper form.
4.   Kim's goal is to perform ten repetitions of bench press using the maximum amount of weight. She did 12 reps easily on her last set. On her next set Kim should _____ the amount of weight she uses.
5.   Jim's goal is to perform ten repetitions of lat pull downs using the maximum amount of weight. On his last set he was only able to perform seven repetitions. On his next set Jim should _____ the amount of weight he uses.

ANSWER KEY

1.   Failure
2.   Increase
3.   Decrease

4.   Increase
5.   Decrease

TASK SHEET 18: BENCH PRESS

Student's Name: _____   **Date**: _____
Observer's Name: _____   **Period**: _____
Spotter's Name: _____

Student Information: In this lesson you will learn the proper form for performing the bench press. You will be working with two partners in this lesson. One person will act as the lifter (doer), one as the observer (recorder), and the other person will be the spotter. You will rotate until all students have acted in all three roles. All weight training exercises must be performed slowly and with the proper form in order to gain the maximum benefits and to ensure safety. The bench press exercises the pectoral muscles in the chest and the triceps in the upper arm.

Objectives: You will perform one set of ten repetitions of bench press while using your maximum amount of weight and proper form.

Directions:
1. Choose two partners that you would like to work with while completing this lesson.
2. Go to the appropriate viewing station with your partners and view the videotape on performing the bench press.
3. Go to the bench press area with your partners and decide who will act first as the doer, observer, and spotter.
4. The doer will practice performing the bench press while the observer records and gives feedback to the doer. You will repeat this lesson until you have received "yes" responses on all of the checkpoints.
5. The observer will check the appropriate response (YES/NO) for each checkpoint for the bench press. The observer should check only one checkpoint at a time and give verbal feedback to the lifter on each checkpoint marked "no."
6. You will always use at least one spotter when performing the bench press. The spotter's only responsibility is that of spotting the lifter (doer). The observer is <u>not</u> to act as a spotter.

BENCH PRESS		Yes	No
1.	Select a weight that might be performed for a total of only ten repetitions.		
2.	While on your back, assume a position on the bench with the eyes directly under the bar.		
3.	Spread the feet and legs wide for good balance and support.		
4.	Keep the feet flat on the floor at all times.		
5.	Keep the head, shoulders, and hips on the bench throughout the lift.		
6.	Using an overhand grip, grasp the bar between one and two handgrips out from a shoulder width grip. Make sure the grip is evenly centered on the bar.		
7.	Lift the bar off the rack until the arms are fully extended.		
8.	Position the bar directly over the shoulders.		
9.	Slowly lower the bar to the center of the chest while keeping the elbows out.		
10.	Inhale approximately two-thirds of the way down.		
11.	Touch the bar lightly on the center of the chest.		
12.	While keeping the elbows out, straighten the arms and press the bar back to the starting position above the shoulders.		
13.	Exhale approximately two-thirds of the way up.		
14.	Perform one set of as many repetitions as possible using proper form.		
15.	Apply the principle of progression to find the maximum weight for ten repetitions.		
16.	Perform one set of ten repetitions using maximum weight and proper form.		

TASK SHEET 19: LAT PULLDOWN

Student's Name: _____   **Date**: _____

Student Information: In this lesson you will learn the proper form for performing the lat pull down. You will be working with two partners in this lesson. One person will act as the lifter (doer), one as the observer/recorder. You will rotate with your partner after completing the lesson. All weight training exercises must be performed slowly and with the proper form in order to gain the maximum benefits and to ensure safety. The lat pull down exercises the latissimus dorsi muscles in the back and the biceps in the upper arm.

Objectives: You will perform one set of ten repetitions of lat pull downs while using your maximum amount of weight and proper form.

Directions:
1. Choose two partners that you would like to work with while completing this lesson.
2. Go to the appropriate viewing station with your partner and view the videotape on performing the lat pull down.
3. Go to the lat pull down machine with your partner and decide who will be the doer and the observer.
4. The doer will practice performing the lat pull down while the observer records and gives feedback. You will repeat this lesson until you have received "yes" responses at all of the checkpoints.
5. The observer will check the appropriate response (YES/NO) for each checkpoint for the lat pull down. The observer should check only one checkpoint at a time and give verbal feedback to the lifter on each checkpoint marked "no."

LAT PULLMAN		Yes	No
1.	Select a weight that might be performed for a total of only ten repetitions.		
2.	Face the machine and assume as wide an overhand grip as possible on the bar.		
3.	Slowly lower the body until the arms are fully extended.		
4.	Allow the body's weight to pull the bar down until reaching a sitting or kneeling position.		
5.	Keep the back perpendicular to the ground.		
6.	Tuck the chin slightly.		
7.	Inhale.		
8.	Smoothly pull the bar down behind the head to the base of the neck.		
9.	Exhale approximately two-thirds of the way down.		
10.	Allow the bar to slowly raise to the starting position.		
11.	Inhale approximately two-thirds of the way up.		
12.	Perform one set of as many repetitions as possible using proper form.		
13.	Apply the principle of progression to find your maximum weight for ten repetitions.		
14.	Perform one set of ten repetitions using your maximum weight and proper form.		

TASK SHEET 20: SHOULDER PRESS

Student's Name: _____   **Date**: _____

Observer's Name: _____   **Period** _____

Spotter's Name: _____ **Spotter's Name**: _____

Student Information: In this lesson you will learn the proper form for performing the shoulder press. You will be working with three partners in this lesson. One person will act as the lifter (doer), and one as the observer/recorder. You will rotate with your partner after completing the lesson until all students have had an opportunity to act in each role. All weight training exercises must be performed slowly and with the proper form in order to gain the maximum benefits and to ensure safety. The shoulder press exercises the deltoid muscles in the shoulders and the triceps in the upper arm.

Objectives: You will perform one set of ten repetitions of shoulder press while using your maximum amount of weight and proper form.

Directions:
1. Choose three partners that you would like to work with while completing this lesson.
2. Go to the appropriate viewing station with your partner and view the videotape on performing the shoulder press.
3. The doer will practice performing the shoulder press while the observer records and gives feedback. You will repeat this lesson until you have received "yes" responses at all of the checkpoints.
4. The observer will check the appropriate response (YES/NO) for each checkpoint for the shoulder press. The observer should check only one checkpoint at a time and give verbal feedback to the lifter on each checkpoint marked "no."
5. The two spotters will give the bar to the lifter at the beginning of the lift and take it from the lifter at the end of the lift.
6. You will always use two spotters when performing the shoulder press. The spotters' only responsibility is that of spotting the doer (lifter). The observer is <u>not</u> to act as a spotter.

SHOULDER PRESS	Yes	No
1. Select a weight that might be performed for a total of only ten repetitions.		
2. Stand erect with the feet slightly wider than shoulder width apart.		
3. Receive the bar from the spotters with the bar resting on the upper chest just below the collarbone.		
4. Assume an overhand grip at shoulder width.		
5. Inhale.		
6. Keep the legs and back straight throughout the lift.		
7. Extend the arms and press the bar overhead until the arms are straight with the bar directly over the shoulders and hips.		
8. Exhale approximately two-thirds of the way up.		
9. Lower the bar slowly to the starting position.		
10. Inhale approximately two-thirds of the way down.		
11. Perform one set of as many repetitions as possible using proper form.		
12. Apply the principle of progression to find your maximum weight for ten repetitions.		
13. Perform one set of ten repetitions using your maximum weight and proper form.		

Weight Training Lesson Plan 5

EQUIPMENT:

Aerobic Exercise CD/tape
CD/cassette player

1 frisbee per 2 students
Task Sheets 21–26

INSTRUCTIONAL ACTIVITIES	TEACHING HINTS

INTRODUCTORY ACTIVITY (2–3 MINUTES)

Flash Drill

Students stand in a ready position facing the teacher. The teacher exclaims "feet," and students stutter the feet quickly.

DPESS pages 307–308

Scattered formation
See Lesson 3, Tennis Unit for complete details

FITNESS DEVELOPMENT (8–12 MINUTES)

Aerobic Workout

Create a music CD/tape or purchase a pre-recorded Aerobic Exercise CD/tape with 120–150 BPM.

DPESS pages 358–359

Scattered formation.
See Lesson Plan 7, Racquetball Unit for details.

LESSON FOCUS (15–20 MINUTES)

Biceps Curl Task Sheet
Triceps Extension Task Sheet
Abdominal Exercise Task Sheet
Leg Press Task Sheet
Leg Extension Task Sheet
Leg Curl Task Sheet

DPESS pages 484–488

Divide class into 5 groups.
Assign students exercises to complete previously learned materials while waiting for equipment.
Assign each group to a Task Sheet and a station.
Describe rotation.

GAME (5 MINUTES)

Frisbee Around 9

A target is set up with 9 different throwing positions around it, each 2 feet farther away. The throwing positions can be clockwise or counterclockwise around the target. They can also be in a straight line from the target. Points are awarded based on the throwing position number (for example, number 7 means 7 points for hitting the target). The game can be played indoors or out.

DPESS page 467

Create partners using Elbow-to-Elbow technique.

TASK SHEET 21: BICEPS CURL

Student's Name: _____   **Date**: _____

Student Information: In this lesson you will learn the proper form for performing the biceps curl. You will be working with a partner in this lesson. One person will act as the lifter (doer), and one as the observer/recorder. You will rotate with your partner after completing the lesson. All weight training exercises must be performed slowly and with the proper form in order to gain the maximum benefits and to ensure safety. The biceps curl exercises the biceps in the upper arm.

Objectives: You will perform one set of ten repetitions of biceps curls while using your maximum amount of weight and proper form.

Directions:

1. Choose three partners that you would like to work with while completing this lesson.
2. Go to the appropriate viewing station with your partner and view the videotape on performing the biceps curl.
3. Go to any unused barbell with your partner and decide who will be the doer and the observer.
4. The doer will practice performing the biceps curl while the observer records and gives feedback. You will repeat this lesson until you have received "yes" responses at all of the checkpoints.
5. The observer will check the appropriate response (YES/NO) for each checkpoint for the biceps curl. The observer should check only one checkpoint at a time and give verbal feedback to the lifter on each checkpoint marked "no."

BICEPS CURL		Yes	No
1.	Select a weight that might be performed for a total of only ten repetitions.		
2.	Lift the barbell from the floor using the basic lifting technique with an underhand grip at shoulder width.		
3.	Keep the head in a vertical position throughout the lift.		
4.	Keep the back and legs straight at all times.		
5.	Keep the upper arms perpendicular to the floor throughout the lift.		
6.	Keep the elbows and upper arms in contact with the sides of the body throughout the lift.		
7.	Inhale.		
8.	Flex the arms fully, curling the bar to a position toward the upper chest.		
9.	Exhale approximately two-thirds of the way up.		
10.	Slowly lower the bar until the arms are fully extended		
11.	Inhale approximately two-thirds of the way down.		
12.	Perform one set of as many repetitions as possible using proper form.		
13.	Apply the principle of progression to find your maximum weight for ten repetitions.		
14.	Perform one set of ten repetitions using your maximum weight and proper form.		

TASK SHEET 22: TRICEPS EXTENSION

Student's Name: _____   **Date**: _____

Student Information: In this lesson you will learn the proper form for performing the triceps extension. You will be working with a partner in this lesson. One person will act as the lifter (doer), and one as the observer/recorder. You will rotate with your partner after completing the lesson. All weight training exercises must be performed slowly and with the proper form in order to gain the maximum benefits and to ensure safety. The triceps extension exercises the triceps muscles in the upper arm.

Objectives: You will perform one set of ten repetitions of triceps extensions while using your maximum amount of weight and proper form.

Directions:
1. Choose three partners that you would like to work with while completing this lesson.
2. Go to the appropriate viewing station with your partner and view the videotape on performing the triceps extension.
3. Go to any unused barbell with your partner and decide who will be the doer and the observer.
4. The doer will practice performing the triceps extension while the observer records and gives feedback. You will repeat this lesson until you have received "yes" responses at all of the checkpoints.
5. The observer will check the appropriate response (YES/NO) for each checkpoint for the triceps extension. The observer should check only one checkpoint at a time and give verbal feedback to the lifter on each checkpoint marked "no."

TRICEPS EXTENSION		Yes	No
1.	Select a weight that might be performed for a total of only ten repetitions.		
2.	Face the machine and stand erect with the feet shoulder width apart.		
3.	Assume a narrow overhand grip approximately four inches wide.		
4.	Pull the bar to the chest until the elbows and upper arms point straight down.		
5.	Keep the upper arms stable and elbows pointed straight down throughout the exercise.		
6.	Keep the upper arms and elbows in contact with the sides of the body throughout the lift.		
7.	Inhale.		
8.	Keep the back and legs straight.		
9.	Press the bar down until the arms are fully extended.		
10.	Exhale approximately two-thirds of the way down.		
11.	Control the bar slowly back to the starting position.		
12.	Inhale approximately two-thirds of the way up.		
13.	Perform one set of as many repetitions as possible using proper form.		
14.	Apply the principle of progression to find your maximum weight for ten repetitions.		
15.	Perform one set of ten repetitions using your maximum weight and proper form.		

TASK SHEET 23: ABDOMINAL CRUNCH

Student's Name: _____ **Date:** _____

Student Information: In this lesson you will learn the proper form for performing the abdominal crunch. Stronger abdominal muscles will help support your upper body and take the burden off of your weaker lower back muscles. By strengthening your abdominal muscles you can help reduce your chance of lower back injury.

Objectives: While using proper form, you will perform two sets of abdominal crunches, performing the maximum number of repetitions in each of the sets.

Directions:
1. Go to the abdominal exercise area and practice performing the abdominal crunch.
2. Mark the appropriate response (YES/NO) for each checkpoint for the abdominal crunch.
3. Repeat this lesson until you have responded "yes" to all of the checkpoints.
4. After successfully completing this lesson, go to your instructor for your skills test on the lesson.

ABDOMINAL CRUNCH		Yes	No
1.	Assume a supine position (on your back) on the floor with your knees bent and your feet flat on the floor.		
2.	Cross your arms over your chest with your hands touching the opposite shoulders.		
3.	Tuck your chin to your chest.		
4.	Keep your lower back in contact with the floor at all times.		
5.	Inhale.		
6.	Curl-up, lifting only the shoulder blades off of the ground.		
7.	Exhale in the "up" position.		
8.	Return to the starting position.		
9.	Inhale in the "down" position.		
10.	Perform one set of as many repetitions as possible using proper form.		
11.	Perform a second set of as many repetitions as possible using proper form.		

TASK SHEET 24: LEG PRESS

Student's Name: _____   **Date**: _____

Student Information: In this lesson you will learn the proper form for performing the leg press. You will be working with a partner in this lesson. One person will be the lifter (doer), and one will be the observer/recorder. Change roles with your partner after completing the lesson. Avoid "locking" the knee joints when performing the leg press as this places excessive stress on the joints and may increase your chance of injury. The leg press exercises the quadriceps muscles.

Objectives: You will perform one set of ten repetitions of leg presses while using your maximum amount of weight and proper form.

Directions:

1. Choose a partner that you would like to work with while completing this lesson.
2. Go to the appropriate viewing station with your partner and view the videotape on performing the leg press.
3. Go to the leg press machine with your partner and decide who will be the doer and the observer.
4. The doer will practice performing the leg press while the observer records and gives feedback. You will repeat this lesson until you have received "yes" responses at all of the checkpoints.
5. The observer will check the appropriate response (YES/NO) for each checkpoint for the leg press. The observer should check only one checkpoint at a time and give verbal feedback to the lifter on each checkpoint marked "no."

LEG PRESS		Yes	No
1.	Select a weight that might be performed for a total of only ten repetitions.		
2.	Assume a position in the seat with your back resting against the backrest.		
3.	Place the balls of your feet against the pedals with the toes pointed straight up.		
4.	If possible, adjust the seat to a position where your legs are bent at or slightly less than right angles.		
5.	Grasp the handles if provided, or fold your arms in front of your body.		
6.	Maintain body contact with the bottom and back of the seat throughout the lift.		
7.	Inhale.		
8.	Extend your legs completely and avoid "locking" the knees.		
9.	Exhale when your legs are extended approximately two-thirds of the distance.		
10.	Slowly control the weight back to the starting position.		
11.	Inhale approximately two-thirds of the distance back.		
12.	Perform one set of as many repetitions as possible using proper form.		
13.	Apply the principle of progression to find your maximum weight for ten repetitions.		
14.	Perform one set of ten repetitions using your maximum weight and proper form.		

TASK SHEET 25: LEG EXTENSION

Student's Name: _____ **Date**: _____

Student Information: In this lesson you will learn the proper form for performing the leg extension. You will be working with a partner in this lesson. One person will act as the lifter (doer), and one as the observer/recorder. You will rotate with your partner after completing the lesson. All weight training exercises must be performed slowly and with the proper form in order to gain the maximum benefits and to ensure safety. Avoid "locking" the knee joints when performing the leg extension as this places excessive stress on the joints and may increase your chance of injury. The leg extension exercises the quadriceps muscles in the front of the upper leg.

Objectives: You will perform one set of ten repetitions of leg extensions while using your maximum amount of weight and proper form.

Directions:
1. Choose a partner that you would like to work with while completing this lesson.
2. Go to the appropriate viewing station with your partner and view the videotape on performing the leg extension.
3. Go to the leg extension machine with your partner and decide who will be the doer and the observer.
4. The doer will practice performing the leg extension while the observer records and gives feedback. You will repeat this lesson until you have received "yes" responses at all of the checkpoints.
5. The observer will check the appropriate response (YES/NO) for each checkpoint for the leg extension. The observer should check only one checkpoint at a time and give verbal feedback to the lifter on each checkpoint marked "no."

LEG EXTENSION		Yes	No
1.	Select a weight that might be performed for a total of only ten repetitions.		
2.	Sit upright on the bench with your legs hanging over the end at right angles.		
3.	Place the top of your feet under the padded rollers.		
4.	Keep the back straight throughout the lift.		
5.	Support your upper body by gripping the sides of the bench.		
6.	Inhale.		
7.	Extend the legs completely and avoid locking the knees.		
8.	Exhale when the legs are approximately two-thirds extended.		
9.	Slowly return the weight to the starting position.		
10.	Inhale when the legs are approximately two-thirds flexed.		
11.	Perform one set of as many repetitions as possible using proper form.		
12.	Apply the principle of progression to find your maximum weight for ten repetitions.		
13.	Perform one set of ten repetitions using your maximum weight and proper form.		

TASK SHEET 26: LEG CURL

Student's Name: _____ **Date**: _____

Student Information: In this lesson you will learn the proper form for performing the leg curl. You will be working with a partner in this lesson. One person will act as the lifter (doer), and one as the observer/recorder. You will rotate with your partner after completing the lesson. All weight training exercises must be performed slowly and with the proper form in order to gain the maximum benefits and to ensure safety. The leg curl exercises the hamstring muscles in the back of the upper leg.

Objectives: You will perform one set of ten repetitions of leg curls while using your maximum amount of weight and proper form.

Directions:

1. Choose a partner that you would like to work with while completing this lesson.
2. Go to the appropriate viewing station with your partner and view the videotape on performing the leg curl.
3. Go to the leg curl machine with your partner and decide who will be the doer and the observer.
4. The doer will practice performing the leg curl while the observer records and gives feedback. You will repeat this lesson until you have received "yes" responses at all of the checkpoints.
5. The observer will check the appropriate response (YES/NO) for each checkpoint for the leg curl. The observer should check only one checkpoint at a time and give verbal feedback to the lifter on each checkpoint marked "no."

LEG CURL		Yes	No
1.	Select a weight that might be performed for a total of only ten repetitions.		
2.	Assume a prone (on your stomach) position on the bench with your knees over the edge		
3.	Place your heels under the padded rollers.		
4.	Keep your chest, hips, and thighs in contact with the bench at all times.		
5.	Grip the sides of the bench for support.		
6.	Inhale.		
7.	Flex your legs, bringing your heels as close to your buttocks as possible.		
8.	Exhale when the legs are approximately two-thirds extended.		
9.	Slowly return the weight to the starting position.		
10.	Inhale when the legs are approximately two-thirds flexed.		
11.	Perform one set of as many repetitions as possible using proper form.		
12.	Apply the principle of progression to find your maximum weight for ten repetitions.		
13.	Perform one set of ten repetitions using your maximum weight and proper form.		

Weight Training Lesson Plan 6

EQUIPMENT:

Task Sheets 27–30	CD/cassette tape player
PACER Running CD/tape	1–2 long Tug-of-War ropes

INSTRUCTIONAL ACTIVITIES	TEACHING HINTS
INTRODUCTORY ACTIVITY (2–3 MINUTES)	

Burpee-Flip Drill	**DPESS pages 306–307**
Call out a number, and students yell the number while performing the movement. The sequence is as follows:	Scattered formation
1. Standing position	
2. Bend knees, hands on floor	
3. Legs back into an all fours position, head up	Variation: put a push-up in before the flip. Step 4 would
4. Half flip right to a crab position	be the down motion and Step 5 would be the up
5. Half flip right to an all-fours position	motion. Use caution to ensure that students are far
This drill can also be done with a left flip or with two	enough apart in case one student flips the wrong way.
flips, one left and one right, and so forth. Challenge	
students work in unison with a group.	

INSTRUCTIONAL ACTIVITIES	TEACHING HINTS

FITNESS DEVELOPMENT (8–12 MINUTES)

PACER Running	**DPESS page 42**

LESSON FOCUS (15–20 MINUTES)

Heel Lift Task Sheet	**DPESS pages 484–488**
Shoulder Press Task Sheet	Demonstrate skills.
Program Design Task Sheet	Describe Program Design/Task Sheets and Sequencing.
Sequencing Task Sheet	Divide class in half.
	Half given Task Sheets 27–28
	Half given Task Sheets 29–30

GAME (5 MINUTES)

Team Tug-of-War	**DPESS page 401**
Small groups and classes can have contests with the large commercially available tug-of-war ropes.	Divide class into equal groups of 2 or 4 for this game. Explain safety rules before beginning game.

TASK SHEET 27: HEEL LIFT

Student's Name: _____   **Date**: _____

Partner's Name: _____   **Period**: _____

Student Information: In this lesson you will learn the proper form for performing the heel lift. The heel lift exercises the Gastrocnemius muscle in the lower leg.

Objectives: While using proper form, you will perform two sets of heel lifts, performing the maximum number of repetitions in each of the sets.

Directions:
1. Go to the heel lift board and practice performing the heel lift.
2. Mark the appropriate response (YES/NO) for each checkpoint for the heel lift.
3. Repeat this lesson until you have responded "yes" to all of the checkpoints.
4. After successfully completing this lesson, go on to the next Task Sheet.

HEEL LIFT		Yes	No
1.	Assume a position with the balls of your feet on the heel lift board and your heels as low as possible.		
2.	Point your toes straightforward.		
3.	Keep your back and legs straight.		
4.	Extend your arms to the wall or a permanent structure for support and balance.		
5.	Raise up on the toes as far as possible.		
6.	Exhale approximately two-thirds of the way up.		
7.	Slowly return to the starting position, fully stretching the calf muscles.		
8.	Inhale approximately two-thirds of the way down.		
9.	Perform one set of as many repetitions as possible using proper form.		
10.	Perform a second set of as many repetitions as possible using proper form.		

TASK SHEET 28: SHOULDER PRESS

Student's Name: _____   **Date**: _____

Observer's Name: _____   **Period** _____

Spotter's Name: _____

Spotter's Name: _____

Student Information: In this lesson you will learn the proper form for performing the shoulder press. You will be working with three partners in this lesson. One person will act as the lifter (doer), and one as the observer/recorder. The other two partners will act as spotters on each end of the bar. You will rotate with your partner after completing the lesson until all students have had an opportunity to act in each role. All weight training exercises must be performed slowly using the proper form in order to gain the maximum benefits and to ensure safety. The shoulder press exercises the deltoid muscles in the shoulders and the triceps in the upper arm.

Objectives: You will perform one set of ten repetitions of shoulder press while using your maximum amount of weight and proper form.

Directions:
1. Choose three partners that you would like to work with while completing this lesson.
2. Go to unused barbell with your partners and decide who will be the doer, observer, and two spotters.
3. The doer will practice performing the shoulder press while the observer records and gives feedback. You will repeat this lesson until you have received "yes" responses at all of the checkpoints.
4. The observer will check the appropriate response (YES/NO) for each checkpoint for the shoulder press. The observer should check only one checkpoint at a time and give verbal feedback to the lifter on each checkpoint marked "no."
5. The two spotters will give the bar to the lifter at the beginning of the lift and take it from the lifter at the end of the lift.
6. You will always use two spotters when performing the shoulder press. The spotters' only responsibility is that of spotting the doer (lifter). The observer is <u>not</u> to act as a spotter.
7. After successfully completing this lesson, go on to the next activity.

SHOULDER PRESS		Yes	No
1.	Select the maximum weight that you performed for a total of ten repetitions.		
2.	Stand erect with the feet slightly wider than shoulder width apart.		
3.	Receive the bar from the spotters with the bar resting on the upper chest just below the collarbone.		
4.	Assume an overhand grip at shoulder width.		
5.	Inhale.		
6.	Keep the legs and back straight throughout the lift.		
7.	Extend the arms and press the bar overhead until the arms are straight with the bar directly over the shoulders and hips.		
8.	Exhale approximately two-thirds of the way up.		
9.	Lower the bar slowly to the starting position.		
10.	Inhale approximately two-thirds of the way down.		
11.	Perform one set of ten repetitions using your maximum weight and proper form.		
12.	Perform a second set of ten repetitions using your maximum weight and proper form.		

TASK SHEET 29: PROGRAM DESIGNS

Student's Name: _____   **Date**: _____

Objectives:

Upon completion of this lesson you will:

1. Demonstrate an understanding of the elements in a program designed to increase muscular strength and size by passing a self-check test with a score of 100%.
2. Demonstrate an understanding of the elements in a program designed to increase muscular endurance and tone by passing a self-check test with a score of 100%.

Instructions:

This lesson consists of information describing the elements of two program designs. The first description describes a program designed to increase muscular strength and size. The second description concerns a program designed to increase muscular endurance and tone. You will study the elements of both programs prior to taking the self-check tests. You must score 100% on the test. If you fail to score 100%, review the lesson and retake the test until you are able to do so. The answer key for the self-check test is available from your instructor.

PROGRAM DESIGNS

A PROGRAM DESIGNED TO INCREASE MUSCULAR STRENGTH AND SIZE:

1. Consists of a program emphasizing LOW repetitions and HIGH weights.
2. Your overload is in the amount of weight lifted, not the number of repetitions performed.
3. Generally, any number of repetitions under ten can be considered as LOW.

A PROGRAM DESIGNED TO INCREASE MUSCULAR ENDURANCE AND TONE:

1. Consists of a program emphasizing HIGH repetitions and LOW weights.
2. Your overload is in the number of repetitions performed, not weight lifted.
3. Generally, any number of repetitions over ten can be considered as HIGH.

REVIEW THIS LESSON CAREFULLY, THEN TAKE THE SELF-CHECK TEST ON PROGRAM DESIGNS.

SELF-CHECK TEST FOR: PROGRAM DESIGNS

Name: _____

Date: _____   **Period**: _____   **Score**: _____

Directions: Fill in the silence with the correct word. After completing the test, get an answer key from the instructor and correct your test. If you miss any questions, review the previous lesson and retake the test. Continue this procedure until you score 100% on this test.

1. A program design consisting of _____ repetitions and _____ weight will improve muscular strength and size.
2. A program design consisting of _____ repetitions and _____ weight will improve muscular endurance and tone.
3. Nancy's program consists of performing fifteen repetitions of each upper body exercise and twenty repetitions of each lower body exercise. Nancy is trying to improve her muscular _____ and _____.
4. Rich's program consists of performing five repetitions of each upper body exercise and eight repetitions of each lower body exercise. Rich is trying to improve his muscular _____ and _____.

ANSWER KEY

1. A program design consisting of <u>LOW</u> repetitions and <u>HIGH</u> weight will improve muscular strength and size.
2. A program design consisting of <u>HIGH</u> repetitions and <u>LOW</u> weight will improve muscular endurance and tone.
3. Nancy's program consists of performing fifteen repetitions of each upper body exercise and twenty repetitions of each lower body exercise. Nancy is trying to improve her muscular <u>ENDURANCE</u> and <u>TONE.</u>
4. Rich's program consists of performing five repetitions of each upper body exercise and eight repetitions of each lower body exercise. Rich is trying to improve his muscular <u>STRENGTH</u> and <u>SIZE</u>.

TASK SHEET 30: SEQUENCING EXERCISES

Student's Name: _____ **Date**: _____

Objectives:
Upon completion of this lesson you will:
1. Understand the concept of sequencing exercises.
2. Understand the advantages of working large muscle groups before working small muscle groups.
3. List exercises in the proper sequence according to the size of the muscle groups for both the upper and lower body.

Instructions:
This lesson is presented with paragraphs of information followed by questions pertaining to the material. The answers to the questions are found below the three asterisks (***) that follow each question. By folding a piece of paper and sliding it down the page, you keep the answers covered until you have made a response to the question. You are not to write on this lesson. Instead, write your answers on the programmed lessons answer sheets. After responding, slide the paper down and compare your answer with the answer given below the asterisks. If your answer is correct, then go on to the next question. If your answer is incorrect, then review the preceding paragraph and find out why your answer was wrong. Be sure to write the correct answer on your answer sheet. After completing the lesson, you must pass a self-check test with a score of 100%. If you do not score 100%, review the lesson and retake the test. The answer key for the self-check test is available from your instructor.

SEQUENCING EXERCISES
In order to achieve the desired results from a weight-training program, you must perform the exercises in the proper sequence or order. There are different methods of sequencing exercises. The order the exercises are performed will be determined by the desired outcome or goals. For this class, you will utilize one of the simplest and yet effective procedures for sequencing exercises. You will exercise the large muscle groups prior to exercising the small muscle groups. For example, you should work your back muscles before working your arm muscles. If you worked your arms before working your back, you would be limiting your very large back muscles to the limit of the weaker and now fatigued arm muscles.

Questions:
1. Sequencing refers to the (order/number) _____ of exercises to be performed.
   ***
   order
2. The method of sequencing exercises is determined by:
   a. the amount of time a person has to work out
   b. the desired outcome or goals of the individual
   c. the workout partner
   ***
   b
3. For the purpose and goals of this class, you will sequence your exercises working your large muscle groups before your _____ muscle groups.
   ***
   small
4. If you exercise the small muscle groups before the large ones, you are _____ the large muscle groups to the limit of the weaker and now fatigued small muscle groups.
   ***
   limiting
5. While working your upper body, you should exercise you back muscles before your _____ muscle.
   a. neck
   b. chest
   c. arm
   ***
   c

(Sequencing, cont.)

Your arms are used in performing the bench press, lat pull down, and shoulder press, as well as every other upper body exercise. The smaller muscles (arms) will be getting worked very hard while you are working the large muscle groups (chest, back, and shoulders). This same principle of sequencing may be applied to the muscle groups of the lower body.

The suggested order of sequencing exercises for your UPPER BODY is as follows:

1.	BENCH PRESS	AND/OR	INCLINE BENCH PRESS
2.	LAT PULLDOWN	AND/OR	UPRIGHT ROW
3.	SHOULDER PRESS	AND/OR	BEHIND THE NECK PRESS
4.	BICEPS CURL	AND/OR	LOW PULLEY CURL
5.	TRICEPS EXTENSION	AND/OR	LOW PULLEY TRICEPS EXTENSION
6.	ABDOMINAL CRUNCH	AND/OR	ABDOMINAL CURL

The suggested order of sequencing exercises for the LOWER BODY is as follows:

1. LEG PRESS
2. LEG EXTENSION
3. LEG CURL
4. HEEL LIFT

Questions:

6. The bench press should be performed before the _____.
   a. lat pull down
   b. triceps extension
   c. biceps curl
   d. all of the above
   ***
   d

7. The leg curl should be performed after the _____.
   a. abdominal crunch
   b. leg extension
   c. heel lift
   ***
   b

8. The lat pull down should be performed before the _____.
   a. leg press
   b. bench press
   c. shoulder press
   ***
   c

PROCEED TO TAKE THE SELF-CHECK TEST ON SEQUENCING EXERCISES.

SELF-CHECK TEST FOR: THE PRINCIPLE OF SEQUENCING	

Name: _____

Date: _____ **Period:** _____ **Score:** _____

Directions: List the exercises in the proper sequence beginning with exercises for the larger muscles to the smaller muscles for each of the major muscle groups listed below. Write the number representing the order the exercise should be performed in the space provided. When you have completed the test, check the answer key to correct your test. If you miss any questions, review the previous lesson and retake the test. Continue this procedure until you are able to score 100% on this test.

EXERCISES FOR THE UPPER BODY:

GROUP 1:
_____ barbell
_____ bench press
_____ abdominal crunch
_____ lat pull down
_____ triceps extension
_____ should press

GROUP 2:
_____ behind the neck press
_____ low pulley curl
_____ incline bench press
_____ low pulley triceps extension
_____ upright row
_____ abdominal curl

EXERCISES FOR THE LOWER BODY:
_____ leg curl
_____ heel lift
_____ leg press
_____ leg extension

(ANSWER KEY)

EXERCISES FOR THE UPPER BODY:

GROUP 1:
(4) barbell
(1) bench press
(6) abdominal crunch
(2) lat pull down
(5) triceps extension
(3) should press

GROUP 2:
(3) behind the neck press
(4) low pulley curl
(1) incline bench press
(5) low pulley triceps extension
(2) upright row
(6) abdominal curl

EXERCISES FOR THE LOWER BODY:
(3) leg curl
(4) heel lift
(1) leg press
(2) leg extension

Weight Training Lesson Plan 7

EQUIPMENT:
Continuity Exercise music CD/tape

CD/cassette player
4 bowling pins per 5 students

INSTRUCTIONAL ACTIVITIES	TEACHING HINTS

INTRODUCTORY ACTIVITY (2–3 MINUTES)
Eliminate to allow more time for Lesson Focus.

FITNESS DEVELOPMENT (8–12 MINUTES)

Continuity Exercises

These exercises are a type of interval training. Create a CD/cassette tape with 30–35 seconds of music and 20 seconds of silence. During the music, the students will jump rope.

During the silence, instruct the students to do an exercise, i.e., push-ups; curl-ups; reverse push-ups; side leg lifts on each side; coffee grinder, arm circling, crab walks forward and backward, etc.

DPESS page 349
Scattered formation
When the music resumes, the students jump rope. During each silence direct a different exercise.

LESSON FOCUS (15–20 MINUTES)

Discuss creating own program
- Setting fitness goals
- Weight Training record chart

Divide class in half.
- Half given Task Sheet 31 & 32
- Half given Task Sheet 33 to create Weight Training Chart. This group will need to make sure their goals match their chart.

Distribute Task Sheet 32.
- Look at chart.
- Direct students to go to stations and evaluate weights to create own chart.

Review sequencing, progression, and safe workouts.

Describe daily procedures.

GAME (5 MINUTES)

Bowling Pin Relay

Four bowling pins per squad are used. They are evenly spaced in front of each squad in a fashion similar to the potato relay. The first person in line lays all of the pins down, and the next person stands them up. Only 1 hand can be used.

DPESS page 405
Use Whistle Mixer to create equal groups of 5.
Assign each group to a relay line.

REVIEW/EVALUATION AND CHEER

Review elements of personal goal setting.
Discuss personal progress in goals to date.
Students create cheer.

TASK SHEET 31: FITNESS GOALS

Student's Name: _____   **Date**: _____

Objectives:

Upon completion of this lesson you will:

1. Have read the lesson covering the benefits of weight training.
2. Evaluate personal fitness needs by completing a check list.
3. State your personal fitness goals pertaining to weight training.

Instructions:

This lesson will help you to evaluate your fitness needs, thus enabling you to state your personal fitness goals. First, go back and review lesson #1 on the benefits of weight training. Then complete this lesson. When stating your goals you may want to refer to the benefits listed. Complete the checklist below.

PERSONAL FITNESS NEEDS & GOALS CHECK LIST

I. Place a check next to the benefits that you would like to gain.

_____   IMPROVE STRENGTH
_____   IMPROVE MUSCULAR ENDURANCE
_____   INCREASE MUSCLE SIZE
_____   DECREASE BODY FAT
_____   IMPROVE APPEARANCE
_____   IMPROVE SELF-CONCEPT
_____   DECREASE FATIGUE
_____   REDUCE CHANCE OF INJURY
_____   INCREASE PHYSICAL EFFICIENCY AND PRODUCTIVITY

II. Place a check next to the general areas that you would like to concentrate on and improve.

_____   STRENGTH AND SIZE
_____   ENDURANCE AND TONE
_____   UPPER BODY
_____   LOWER BODY
_____   OVERALL (UPPER & LOWER) BODY DEVELOPMENT

III. Place a check next to the specific areas that you would like to concentrate on and improve.

Gain strength and size in the: Firm and tone the:

_____   arms   _____   arms
_____   back   _____   back
_____   shoulders   _____   shoulders
_____   chest   _____   chest
_____   waist   _____   waist
_____   thighs   _____   thighs
_____   hips   _____   hips
_____   calves   _____   calves

IV. Study the items that you have checked. Review the preceding lessons for any information concerning the attainment of these goals.

TASK SHEET 32: WRITTEN ASSIGNMENT

Student's Name: _____   **Date**: _____

Objectives:
Upon completion of this lesson you will:
1. Develop, write, practice, and modify a personal weight-training program demonstrating an understanding of the scientific principles and practical theories covered in this class.

Instructions:
This lesson will help you to learn the steps in developing, writing, and modifying a personal fitness and weight training program. Write an outline of a daily workout to include cardiovascular endurance, flexibility, strength and muscular endurance. You may want to refer to some of the previous lessons for assistance.

TASK SHEET 33: WEIGHT TRAINING CHART

Objectives:
Upon completion of this lesson you will:
1. Understand the usefulness of a weight-training chart for monitoring your workouts.
2. Use a weight-training chart to record your exercises.

Instructions:
The weight-training chart on the following two pages is an example you can follow to properly sequence exercises and use the principle of progression. Look at the charts. Notice how Kimbie has ordered her exercises beginning with the larger muscles then working the smaller muscles. Also, if you will look at the dates of her workouts and the exercises she performed, you will notice that Kimbie has broken her workouts into upper body days and lower body days. This philosophy is just one of many that is supported in the field of weight training. Basically, any workout that you develop based on the previously explained concepts and principles will be sound. Do you see that Kimbie is constantly striving for improvement as evidenced by her small yet consistent increases in the weight she attempts? Study the chart carefully. You will be required to make a weight-training chart while participating in this class. When you are finished analyzing the chart, go to your instructor and ask for a chart for yourself. Fill in all of the required information at the top of your chart. The "% FAT" and "IDEAL WEIGHT" are optional items. However, you may fill them in if you have access to the information and want to keep a record of it. Keep your chart with you in class. When you have filled one chart completely, keep it in your notebook for your records. Then, get another silence form from your instructor to continue keeping a record of your progress.

*** WORK HARD AND HAVE FUN!

NAME Kimbie Casten   AGE 17   SEX F   HEIGHT 5'2"   WEIGHT 110 lbs.

DATE STARTED PROGRAM September 1, 2005   % FAT 22%   TARGET % FAT 22%   IDEAL WEIGHT 110 lbs.

EXERCISE	EQUIPMENT	Reps	9/1 WT.	9/2 WT.	9/3 WT.	9/4 WT.	9/5 QT.	WT.	WT.	WT.	WT.	WT.	WT.	WT.	WT.	WT.
WARM-UP:	CYCLE:	1	5 min	5 min	5 min	10 min	10 min									
Incline Bench Press	Olympic Incline Bench	10	45	45	45	50	50									
		8	50	50	50	55	55									
		6	55	55	55	60	60									
		4	60	60	60	65	65									
		4	60	60	60	65	65									
Lat Pull down	Universal	10	30	30	30	30	40									
		10	30	30	30	30	40									
		10	30	30	30	30	40									
Shoulder Press	Olympic	10	45	45	45	45	50									
		10	45	45	45	45	50									
		10	45	45	45	45	50									
Biceps Curls	Olympic	10	20	20	20	20	30									
		10	20	20	20	20	30									
		10	20	20	20	20	30									
Triceps Extension	Universal	10	20	20	20	20	30									
		10	20	20	20	20	30									
		10	20	20	20	20	30									
Abdominal Curls	Slant Board	20	20	20	20	25	25									
		20	20	20	20	25	25									
		20	20	20	20	25	25									

NAME Kimbie Casten

DATE STARTED PROGRAM September 1, 2005   AGE 17   SEX F   HEIGHT 5'2"   WEIGHT 110 lbs.

% FAT 22%   TARGET % FAT 22%   IDEAL WEIGHT 110 lbs.

EXERCISE	EQUIPMENT	Reps	9/1 WT.	9/2 WT.	9/3 WT.	9/4 WT.	9/5 QT.	WT.	WT.	WT.	WT.	WT.	WT.	WT.
WARM-UP:	CYCLE:													
Leg Press	Universal	10	100	100	100	100	110							
		8	120	120	120	120	130							
		8	120	120	120	120	130							
		8	120	120	120	120	130							
Leg Extension	Universal	10	50	50	50	50	60							
		10	50	50	50	50	60							
		10	50	50	50	50	60							
Leg Curls	Universal	10	30	30	30	30	40							
		10	30	30	30	30	40							
		10	30	30	30	30	40							
Heel Lift	Heel Lift Machine	10	60	60	60	60	70							
		10	60	60	60	60	70							
		10	60	60	60	60	70							

Weight Training Lesson Plan 8

EQUIPMENT:
PACER Running CD/tape
CD/cassette Player
Cage ball

INSTRUCTIONAL ACTIVITIES	TEACHING HINTS

INTRODUCTORY ACTIVITY (2–3 MINUTES)

Move and Perform a Stretch
Move and perform a stretching activity on the sound of
   the whistle. Move and stretch to the sound of music.
   Skip, hop, shuffle, jog and walk.

DPESS pages 308–309
Scattered formation
Direct starting and stopping locomotor movements to
   selected stretches using a whistle or a timed music
   CD/tape.

FITNESS DEVELOPMENT (8–12 MINUTES)

PACER Running
Progressive aerobic cardiovascular endurance run.

DPESS page 42
Use a timed CD/tape.
Scattered formation

LESSON FOCUS (15–20 MINUTES)

Individual Weight Training Programs

GAME (5 MINUTES)

Crab Cage ball

DPESS pages 402–403
See Lesson Plan 7, Racquetball Unit for details.

Weight Training Lesson Plan 9

EQUIPMENT:
Whistle

INSTRUCTIONAL ACTIVITIES	TEACHING HINTS

INTRODUCTORY ACTIVITY (2–3 MINUTES)

Over, Under, and Around

DPESS pages 310–311
See Lesson Plan 5 from Racquetball Unit for details.

FITNESS DEVELOPMENT (8–12 MINUTES)

Jog, Walk, Jog
Direct students to jog as far as they can. When tired, they
   can walk, and resume jogging when able.

DPESS page 347

LESSON FOCUS (15–20 MINUTES)

Individual Weight Training Program

GAME (5 MINUTES)

Butt Tug
One line moves to the left 1 step. Bend over, cross the
   arms between the legs, and grasp the hand of 2
   different people from the other team. Now begin
   tugging. Try forming 2 teams in the described position
   and have a race while maintaining the handgrips.

DPESS page 406
Divide class into even lines.
Each line stands Back-to-Back with another line.

Weight Training Lesson Plan 10

EQUIPMENT:
Whistle

INSTRUCTIONAL ACTIVITIES	TEACHING HINTS
INTRODUCTORY ACTIVITY (2–3 MINUTES)	

Move and Change Direction
Indicate direction change with whistle.

DPESS page 308
Scattered formation

FITNESS DEVELOPMENT (8–12 MINUTES)

Jog, Walk, Jog
Direct students to jog as far as they can. When tired, they can walk, and resume jogging when able.

DPESS page 347

LESSON FOCUS (15–20 MINUTES)

Individual Weight Training Program

GAME (5 MINUTES)

Mass Stand Up
Start with 2 people sitting Back-to-Back. Lock elbows and try to stand up. Increase the number to 3 people, then 4, and so forth. See how many people can stand up simultaneously.

DPESS page 406
Using Back-to-Back, create partners.

Weight Training Lesson Plan 11

EQUIPMENT:
Parachute
CD/cassette player

Music CD/tape
Cage ball

INSTRUCTIONAL ACTIVITIES	TEACHING HINTS
INTRODUCTORY ACTIVITY (2–3 MINUTES)	

Fastest Tag: Every player is a tagger. Object is to tag other players without being tagged. Players that get tagged must sit where they are and wait till only one person or 2 or 3 is left. If two people tag each other at the same time both are out.

DPESS page 312
Create boundaries with cones/lines.
Establish number left that indicates that game complete.

FITNESS DEVELOPMENT (8–12 MINUTES)

Parachute Rhythmic Aerobic Activities

DPESS page 312
See Lesson Plan 11, Badminton Unit for details

LESSON FOCUS (15–20 MINUTES)

Individual Weight Training Program

GAME (5 MINUTES)

Long Team Cage ball
The teams move into sitting position in 2 lines facing each other 10 to 15 feet apart. The teacher rolls or throws a cage ball between the 2 lines. The object is for 1 team to kick the ball over the other team. A point is scored against a team when the ball goes over or through a line. The team with the fewer points wins. Again, a point is awarded if a player stands or touches the ball with the hands. More than 1 cage ball can be used simultaneously.

DPESS page 403
Use a management game to create 2 teams.

Weight Training Lesson Plan 12

EQUIPMENT:
1 bean bag per 2 students
Whistle

INSTRUCTIONAL ACTIVITIES	TEACHING HINTS
INTRODUCTORY ACTIVITY (2–3 MINUTES)	
Throwing and Catching Bean Bags on the Run	DPESS pages 389–390
Toss, move, and catch. Cover as much ground as possible between the toss and catch. Move forward, backward, and sideways, using different steps such as running, the carioca, shuffle, and slide.	Scattered formation Use Elbow-to-Elbow to create partners. 1 bean bag per group Direct running activity and tossing challenges.
FITNESS DEVELOPMENT (8–12 MINUTES)	
Walk-Jog-Sprint	DPESS page 354

Direct movements with whistle signals:
  1 whistle = walk
  2 whistles = jog
  3 whistles = sprint
Alternate jogging, walking, sprinting.
	Scattered formation
	Students begin by walking around the area.

LESSON FOCUS (15–20 MINUTES)	
Individual Weight Training Program	
GAME (5 MINUTES)	
Addition Tag	DPESS page 312
The "its" must hold hands and can tag only with their outside hands. When they tag someone, that person must hook on. This continues and the tagging line becomes longer and longer. Regardless of the length of the line, only the hand of the line is eligible to tag.	Select 2–4 "its." Set boundaries.

Weight Training Lesson Plan 13

EQUIPMENT:
Whistle
Music

CD/cassette player

INSTRUCTIONAL ACTIVITIES	TEACHING HINTS
INTRODUCTORY ACTIVITY (2–3 MINUTES)	
Eliminate to allow more time for Individual Program.	
FITNESS DEVELOPMENT (8–12 MINUTES)	
Aerobic Workout	DPESS pages 358–359
	See Lesson Plan 7, Racquetball Unit for details.
LESSON FOCUS (15–20 MINUTES)	
Individual Weight Training Program	
GAME (5 MINUTES)	
Wheelbarrow Relay	DPESS page 405
Use the wheelbarrow position as the means of locomotion. All members of each squad must participate in both the carrying position and the down formation.	Create squads of 6 people. Assign squad to a space. Explain rules and boundaries.

Weight Training Lesson Plan 14

EQUIPMENT:
Fitnessgram Testing Cards
Sit and reach boxes
Equipment described in manual for test.

INSTRUCTIONAL ACTIVITIES	TEACHING HINTS

INTRODUCTORY ACTIVITY (2–3 MINUTES)

Running High Fives
Students jog/skip around, when whistle is blown student runs to find a partner, jumps in air, gives the new partner a "high five", and then continues moving until whistle is blown again.

DPESS page 314
Scattered formation.
Explain rules.
High 5 at peak of jump

FITNESS DEVELOPMENT (8–12 MINUTES)

Combine with Lesson Focus today.

LESSON FOCUS (15–20 MINUTES)

Fitnessgram Testing

DPESS page 42
Allow students to select a partner to work with.
If complete test, work on Weight Training.

GAME (5 MINUTES)

Spider Tag
A pair is "it" and they chase until they tag another pair. The new pair becomes "it."

DPESS page 312
Use Back-to-Back to make pairs.
Stand Back-to-Back with partner with elbows locked.
Variation: Each group tagged can join the original "its" until a selected number are "its" and begin game again.

Weight Training Lesson Plan 15

EQUIPMENT:
CD/cassette player
Aerobic exercise CD/tape

Parachute
4–6 rubber balls/volleyballs

INSTRUCTIONAL ACTIVITIES	TEACHING HINTS

INTRODUCTORY ACTIVITY (2–3 MINUTES)

Eliminate today.

FITNESS DEVELOPMENT (8–12 MINUTES)

Aerobic Workout

DPESS pages 358–359
See Lesson Plan 7, Racquetball Unit for details.

LESSON FOCUS (15–20 MINUTES)

Individual Weight Training Program

GAME (5 MINUTES)

Parachute Team Ball
Use two to six balls. Try to bounce the balls off the opponents' side, scoring one point for each ball.

Create teams around taut parachute.
Each team defends half of the chute.

Note:
Written exam could be administered.

MUSCLE IDENTIFICATION EXAM

Name: _____

Date: _____ **Period** _____ **Score**: _____

Directions: Write the name of the muscle on the silence line pointing to the muscle.

EXAM PAGE 2

Directions: (TRUE/FALSE) Write the entire word TRUE or FALSE in the space provided. Any other symbol or mark will be scored as incorrect.

1. _____ You should not scream or yell in the weight room because it makes it difficult for others to concentrate.
2. _____ Weight training will help to improve your flexibility.
3. _____ The cool-down is not as important as the warm-up and should only be performed if time permits.
4. _____ You should use the proper lifting technique even when lifting a light object from the floor.
5. _____ Barbell curls should be performed before lat pull downs because the biceps are more important then the latissimus dorsi.
6. _____ When performing the bench press, you should lift your hips off of the bench to produce more power.
7. _____ You must "overload" your muscles in order to improve their size and endurance.
8. _____ Leg presses should be performed before leg curls.
9. _____ "Cadence" refers to the rate or speed at which a repetition is performed.
10. _____ You should lock your knee joints when performing the leg press because "its" easier and gives your muscles a chance to relax.
11. _____ You must use a spotter on all of the required lifts.
12. _____ Sally should decrease the amount of weight she uses if she can perform one additional repetition above the amount desired while using proper form.
13. _____ You perform an exercise through the full range of motion if you move as far as possible in both directions.
14. _____ Triceps extensions should be performed after bench press.
15. _____ When performing triceps extensions, your elbows should be pointed straight down and remain in contact with the sides of your body.

Directions: (FILL IN THE SILENCE) Fill in the silence with the correct word or phrase.

1. You should rest one to _____ minutes between sets.
2. You should inhale during the last _____ of the negative phase of a lift.
3. In applying the principle of progression, you should perform an exercise with proper form until muscular _____ or until unable to maintain correct form.
4. A program consisting of high repetitions and low weight will help to improve muscular _____ and _____.
5. A _____ should always be worn when performing shoulder presses.
6. A proper warm-up can help reduce the chance of _____.
7. You should slightly _____ the weight used when you can perform one additional repetition above the desired amount while maintaining proper form.
8. A _____ consists of a group of repetitions.
9. The _____ muscle group is located on the back of the upper leg.
10. Consistent participation in a good weight-training program may help you to _____ your body fat.

Directions: (MULTIPLE CHOICE) Choose the best answer to complete each statement and write the letter in the space provided at the beginning of each question.

1. _____ The principle of _____ states that you must exercise a particular component of fitness in order to improve in that particular component.
   a. progression   c. overload
   b. order   d. specificity
2. _____ A program consisting of low repetitions and high weight will help to improve muscular _____ and size.
   a. flexibility   c. strength
   b. endurance   d. coordination
3. _____ The _____ principle states that a person must work at a level above that normally encountered in everyday activities in order to improve a component of physical fitness.
   a. overload   c. overtime
   b. sequencing   d. strength
4. _____ The time between your last set and the start of a new exercise should be no less than three minutes and no more than _____ minutes.
   a. ten   c. three and one-half
   b. five   d. seven
5. _____ The _____ muscle is located at the back of the upper arm.
   a. triceps   c. biceps
   b. back arms   d. quadriceps

Flag Football

OBJECTIVES:

The student will:
1. Run, change directions, pivot, evade other students, and assume poses during Introductory Activities.
2. Demonstrate cooperation and cooperation in the High Five's, Blob Tag, Triangle Tag, and Mini Pyramids activities.
3. Participate in continuity Exercises, Parachute Fitness, Partner Racetrack Fitness, Challenge Courses, Circuit and Aerobic Workout activities to improve their fitness.
4. Demonstrate a variety of passes, catches, and stances during the lesson focus portion of class.
5. Demonstrate hand-offs, blocks, and punting skills during the lesson focus portion of class.
6. Practice a variety of Flag Football Plays as demonstrated in class to the satisfaction of the instructor.
7. Practice offensive and defensive plays as demonstrated in class to the satisfaction of the instructor.
8. Participate in a Flag Football Tournament during class.
9. Pass a skill exam scoring 70% of better.
10. Pass a written exam scoring 70% or better.

FLAG FOOTBALL BLOCK PLAN
2 WEEK UNIT

Week #1	Monday	Tuesday	Wednesday	Thursday	Friday
Introductory Activity	Run and Change Direction	Weave Drill	Vanishing Bean Bags	Blob Tag	Run and Assume a Pose
Fitness	Parachute Fitness	Partner Racetrack Fitness	Continuity Exercises	Fitness Scavenger Hunt	Circuit Training
Lesson Focus	Passing and Lateral Pass	Passing/ Catching	Stances Centering the Ball	Shoulder & Pass Blocks/ Spinning Drill	Hand-Offs Punting
Game	Triangle plus 1 Tag	Leapfrog	Mad Scramble	Hoops and Plyometrics	Foot Tag

Week #2	Monday	Tuesday	Wednesday	Thursday	Friday
Introductory Activity	Rubber Band	Triangle Tag	Move, Stop, Pivot	Mini Pyramids	Mass Stand Up
Fitness	Jump and Jog Fitness	Partner Racetrack	Mini Challenge Course	Aerobic Workout	Random Running
Lesson Focus	Rules, Strategies, Plays	Flag Football Skills Test	Flag Football Written Exam	Flag Football Tournament	Flag Football Tournament
Game	Sitting Wrestle	Spider Tag	Flag Football		

Flag Football Lesson Plan 1

EQUIPMENT:

1 football per student
40 small cones
1 Task Sheet per student
1 pencil and clipboard per 3 Students

10 flags
1 exercise CD/tape
1 CD/cassette player
1 large parachute

INSTRUCTIONAL ACTIVITIES	TEACHING HINTS

INTRODUCTORY ACTIVITY (2–3 MINUTES)

Run and Change Direction
Students run in any direction, changing directions on signal.

Scattered formation
Specify type of angle (i.e., right, obtuse, 45-degree).

FITNESS DEVELOPMENT (8–12 MINUTES)

Parachute Fitness
Jog: hold chute in right hand. Change directions, switch hands. Slide, hold chute with both hands.
Skip: hold chute with right hand. Change directions, switch hands. Freeze and shake chute.
Sit with bent legs under chute for curl-ups. Lay on right side, lift left leg up. Reverse. Stand up and shake chute. Jog and lift chute up and down. Repeat.

DPESS page 352
Use music to make fitness fun and exciting.
Use signal to change task.
Keep all movements under control.

LESSON FOCUS (15–20 MINUTES)

Reciprocal Task Sheet: Passing and Lateral Passing
Practice: Assign groups to coned areas.
Explain Task Sheets. Demonstrate skills on the Task Sheets. When complete one, take the second one.

DPESS page 427
Use Whistle Mixer to make groups of 3.
Have equipment and Task Sheets at assigned stations.
Cones set up 15 feet apart, opposite each other.

GAME (5 MINUTES)

Triangle plus 1 Tag
Triangle moves around to avoid getting leader tagged.
Tagger tries to tag leader.

DPESS page 312
Use Whistle Mixer to make groups of 4.
Identify leader and tagger.
3 make triangle and hold hands.

EVALUATION/REVIEW AND CHEER

Review elements of passing and lateral skills practiced.
Cheer: 2, 4, 6, 8, Flag football is great!

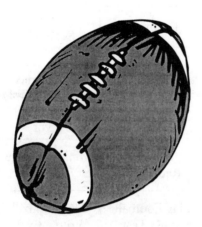

Reciprocal Task Sheet: Flag Football Passing

Doer: _____   **"Shagger"**: _____

Observer: _____

Directions: Student will work in groups of three. Place first and last name on lines provided above. One person performs the task while partner shags the ball. Observer checks "yes" or "no" after each performance. Observer will also provide feedback on the performance. Perform task 10 times and rotate positions. Each student will turn in a Task Sheet.

Objective: The student will perform a flag football pass 10 times using technique demonstrated by the instructor.

Check "Yes" (Y) or "No" (N)

	Y/N	Y/N	Y/N	Y/N	Y/N	Y/N	Y/N	Y/N	Y/N	Y/N
Point shoulder opposite of the throwing arm towards receiver.										
Bring ball up to the throwing shoulder with both hands.										
Throwing hand fingers are placed on laces of the ball.										
Weight on rear leg										
On throw, step forward with front foot in the direction of the receiver.										
Throwing arm is extended and wrist is flicked upon release.										
Follow through										

Reciprocal Task Sheet: Flag Football Lateral Pass

Doer: _____   **"Shagger"**: _____

Observer: _____

Directions: Student will work in groups of three. Place first and last name on lines provided above. One person performs the task while partner shags the ball. Observer checks "yes" or "no" after each performance. Observer will also provide feedback on the performance. Perform task 10 times and rotate positions. Each student will turn in a Task Sheet.

Objective: The student will perform a lateral pass 10 times using technique demonstrated by the instructor.

Check "Yes" (Y) or "No" (N)

	Y/N	Y/N	Y/N	Y/N	Y/N	Y/N	Y/N	Y/N	Y/N	Y/N
Hold ball in both hands.										
Side to target before pass.										
Pass ball to partner.										
Ball passed sideways or behind.										
Ball aimed at chest area.										
Follow-through with both hands.										
Ball "floats" during pass.										
Ball spirals (That's not what you are trying to do in this pass).										

Flag Football Lesson Plan 2

EQUIPMENT:

1 football per 3 students
5 jump ropes
40 small cones

1 Task Sheet per student
1 pencil and clipboard per 3 students
Music exercise CD/tape & CD/cassette player

INSTRUCTIONAL ACTIVITIES	TEACHING HINTS

INTRODUCTORY ACTIVITY (2–3 MINUTES)

Weave Drill
Students are in ready position. They will shuffle left, right, forward, backward, over, and around obstacles on signal by the teacher's hand motion.

DPESS page 306

Scattered formation in front of teacher. Mark area with cones.

FITNESS DEVELOPMENT (8–12 MINUTES)

Partner Racetrack Fitness
Set up 10 stations in a circle track formation. Students have Task Card with exercise to perform. 2 students perform task while other 2 partners run around the track.

DPESS pages 356–367

Use Whistle Mixer to create groups of 4. Use Toe-to-Toe to make partners in the group. Use music for motivation.

LESSON FOCUS (15–20 MINUTES)

Task Sheet: Catching
Demonstrate skills on Task Sheet.
Partners stand 10' apart and across from each other. Observer on side of doer.
Passing: Review Passing Skills from day before.

DPESS page 427

Use Whistle Mixer to make groups of 3.
Have equipment and Task Sheets at assigned areas with cones marking 10'.

GAME (5 MINUTES)

Leap Frog
Rotate positions.

DPESS page 398

Use Whistle Mixer to make groups of 2–3.

EVALUATION/REVIEW AND CHEER

Review elements and difficulties of skills practiced.
Cheer: 1, 2, 3, Catch the ball thrown to me!

Reciprocal Task Sheet: Catching

Doer: _____   **"Shagger":** _____

Observer: _____

Directions: Student will work in groups of three. Place first and last name on lines provided above. One person performs the task while partner throws the ball to the catcher. Observer checks "yes" or "no" after each performance while providing feedback. Perform task 10 times then rotate positions. Each student will turn in a Task Sheet.

Objective: The student will catch the football 10 times using form demonstrated by the instructor.

	Y/N	Y/N	Y/N	Y/N	Y/N	Y/N	Y/N	Y/N	Y/N	Y/N
Begin in stationary position facing the thrower.										
Feet shoulder width apart										
Hands held at chest anticipating the throw										
Catch ball with fingers spread apart and										
Absorb force when ball comes into hands.										
Bring ball into chest upon catch.										

Check "Yes" (Y) or "No" (N)

Flag Football Lesson Plan 3

EQUIPMENT:

40 small cones	Continuity exercise CD/tape & player
1 Task Sheet per student	1 football per 3 students
1 pencil and clipboard per 3 students	1 jump rope per student

INSTRUCTIONAL ACTIVITIES	TEACHING HINTS

INTRODUCTORY ACTIVITY (2–3 MINUTES)

Vanishing Bean Bags	DPESS page 309
Take away bean bags after each episode	Scattered formation

FITNESS DEVELOPMENT (8–12 MINUTES)

Continuity Exercises	DPESS pages 349–350
Students jump rope during music. Pause during music; students perform exercises, i.e., push-ups, crab walk, curl-ups, arm circles, stretches, etc.	Scattered formation Use music to make fitness fun.

LESSON FOCUS (15–20 MINUTES)

Stances: Demonstrate the following stances.	DPESS pages 427–428
2-point stance; 3-point stance; 4-point stance	Have students demonstrate when you call out 2, 3 or 4. Use Whistle Mixer to make groups of 3 for Task Sheet.
Centering the Ball Task Sheet	
Model Task Sheet activities.	Have equipment and Task Sheets in designated areas.

GAME (5 MINUTES)

Mad Scramble	Scattered formation
Student tries to pull the flags on others while protecting own flag from being pulled off.	Use Whistle Mixer to make groups of 7 with assigned color flags.

EVALUATION/REVIEW AND CHEER

Review types of Stances and elements of Centering the Ball.
Cheer: 5, 3,1, Flag football is really fun!

Reciprocal Task Sheet: Centering the Ball

Doer: _____   **"Shagger":** _____

Observer: _____

Directions: Work in groups of three. Place your first and last name on lines provided. One person performs the task while the other acts as a quarterback; the third person is the observer. The observer will check "yes" or "no" in the appropriate box after the task is performed while providing feedback to the doer. Rotate roles after 10 attempts. Each student will turn in a Task Sheet.

Objective: The student will demonstrate the 2, 3, 4-Point Stance using technique demonstrated by the instructor.

Check "Yes" (Y) or "No" (N)

	Y/N	Y/N	Y/N	Y/N	Y/N	Y/N	Y/N	Y/N	Y/N	Y/N
Position yourself so that you reach for the ball.										
Bend over and grasp the ball over the laces.										
Left hand on top of ball with fingers parallel to the seams										
Ball tilts slightly upwards.										
Head between the legs										
Eyes on the receiver										
Throw ball between legs.										
Both arms pull backward and upward.										
Ball spirals in air on "its" way to the quarterback.										

Flag Football Lesson Plan 4

EQUIPMENT:
30 small cones
20 Scavenger Hunt Direction cards
1 Task Sheet per student
1 pencil and clipboard per 3 students

1 hoop per student
1 exercise CD/tape
1 CD/cassette player
30 footballs

INSTRUCTIONAL ACTIVITIES	TEACHING HINTS

INTRODUCTORY ACTIVITY (2–3 MINUTES)

Blob Tag
Last person in the chain tags.

DPESS page 312
Scattered formation
Select first taggers.

FITNESS DEVELOPMENT (8–12 MINUTES)

Fitness Scavenger Hunt
Set up 10 stations. Each group has cards giving hints to each station where exercise directions are given.

DPESS page 356
Scattered formation
Use Whistle Mixer to create groups of 4.

LESSON FOCUS (15–20 MINUTES)

Shoulder and Pass Blocks and Spinning Drill Task Sheet

DPESS page 428
Use Whistle Mixer to make groups of 3. Have equipment and Task Sheets at designated areas.

GAME (5 MINUTES)

Hoops and Plyometrics
With whistle blows, that number of students must get inside a hoop within 5 seconds or less.

DPESS pages 309–310
Scattered formation. Students locomote until directions given on how many students end up in each hoop.

EVALUATION/REVIEW AND CHEER

Discuss skills worked on in the lesson: Passing, Catching, Centering, Stances
Cheer: Flag football is the game to play!

Reciprocal Task Sheet: Shoulder and Pass Blocks; Spinning

Doer: _____   **Defensive Player/Blocker**: _____

Observer: _____

Directions: You will work in groups of three. Place first and last name on lines provided above. One person performs the task while the other acts as a defensive player or blocker. The third person will be the observer and check "yes" or "no" after each performance while providing feedback to the doer. Perform the task ten times and rotate positions. Each student will turn in a Task Sheet.

Objectives:
1. The student will execute the shoulder and block pass 10 times using technique demonstrated by the instructor.
2. The student will demonstrate the proper spinning technique 10 times using technique demonstrated by the teacher.

Check "Yes" (Y) or "No" (N)

	Y/N	Y/N	Y/N	Y/N	Y/N	Y/N	Y/N	Y/N	Y/N	Y/N
Shoulder Block										
Begin in a 3- or 4-point stance.										
Move forward making shoulder contact with defensive player at chest level.										
Head between opponent and the ball carrier										
Elbows are out.										
Hands held near the chest										
Pass Block										
Begin in a 2-, 3- or 4-point stance.										
Move backward slightly with your rear foot as the opponent charges.										
Stay between the quarterback and the rusher.										
Spinning										
Jog toward defensive player.										
As defensive player approaches, turn 360 degrees (full circle) in a spinning motion.										
Fast Footwork										
Defensive player stays square in front of the ball carrier.										

Flag Football Lesson Plan 5

EQUIPMENT:

1 Task Sheet per student
1 football per 3 students
40 small cones

1 pencil and clipboard per 3 students
1 exercise CD/tape
1 CD/cassette player

INSTRUCTIONAL ACTIVITIES	TEACHING HINTS

INTRODUCTORY ACTIVITY (2–3 MINUTES)

Run and Assume Pose

DPESS pages 308–309
Scattered formation

FITNESS DEVELOPMENT (8–12 MINUTES)

Circuit Training: Rotate stations at music intervals.
Jogging; Sit-ups; Jumping jacks; Push-ups; Hop in place;
Stretch; Reverse push-ups; Jump rope; Arm circles

DPESS page 348
Use Whistle Mixer to create groups of 4. Continuity
CD/tape to signal time at each station.

LESSON FOCUS (15–20 MINUTES)

Hand-Off and Punting Task Sheet
Explain Task Sheets and demonstrate as written.
Have each group go to designated areas.

DPESS page 428
Use Whistle Mixer to make groups of 4. Have
Equipment and Task Sheets at designated areas.

GAME (5 MINUTES)

Foot Tag
Students face a partner with hands on shoulders. On
signal, students try to touch each other's toes.

DPESS page 312
Use Toe-to-Toe to create groups of 2. Use whistle for
signal. Do not stomp toes.

EVALUATION/REVIEW AND CHEER

Review elements of the Hand-Off and Punting Skills
Cheer: We love football!

Reciprocal Task Sheet: Hand-Off Pass

Doer: _____

Center: _____

Receiver: _____

Observer: _____

Directions: You will work in groups of four. Place first and last name on Task Sheet. One person performs the task, one is the center and the other a receiver. The fourth person is the observer who marks "yes" or "no" in the box after each attempt while providing feedback. Perform the task ten times and rotate positions. Each student will turn in a Task Sheet.

Rotation: Passer =>   Center=>   Receiver=>   Observer=>

Objective: The student will execute the proper hand-off pass 10 times as demonstrated by the instructor.

Check "Yes" (Y) or "No" (N)

	Y/N	Y/N	Y/N	Y/N	Y/N	Y/N	Y/N	Y/N	Y/N	Y/N
Ball is held with both hands.										
When receiver is 6 feet away, switch ball to hand nearest to receiver.										
Elbow bent and partially away from the body										
Receiver approaches quarterback with the near arm bent and in front of the chest.										
Other arm is about waist high, with the palm up.										
As ball is exchanged, receiver clamps down on the ball to secure it.										

Reciprocal Task Sheet: Punting

Doer: _____   Center: _____
Receiver: _____   Observer:_____

Directions: Students will remain in groups of four. Place first and last name on lines provided above. One person performs the task, a second person acts as center and the third person shags the ball. The fourth person is the observer who marks "yes" or "no" after each attempt while providing feedback. Perform the task 10 times and rotate positions. Each student will turn in a Task Sheet.

Rotation: **Punter** =>   **Center** =>   **Shagger** =>   **Observer**=>

Objective: The student will execute a punt 10 times using technique as demonstrated by the instructor.

Check "Yes" (Y) or "No" (N)

	Y/N	Y/N	Y/N	Y/N	Y/N	Y/N	Y/N	Y/N	Y/N	Y/N
Begin in a standing position with arms extended to receive the ball.										
Kicking foot is placed slightly forward.										
Center passes ball to you.										
After receiving the ball, take two steps forward beginning with your dominant foot.										
Ball is slightly turned in and held waist high.										
Kicking leg is swung forward, as impact knee is straightened to provide maximum force on kick.										
Toes are pointed.										
The long axis of the ball makes contact on instep.										
Ball is dropped rather than tossed into the air.										

Flag Football Lesson Plan 6

EQUIPMENT:

Flag Football Rules and Strategy handouts   Continuity Music CD/cassette & player

INSTRUCTIONAL ACTIVITIES	TEACHING HINTS

INTRODUCTORY ACTIVITY (2–3 MINUTES)

Rubber Band
Students move away from instructor performing a locomotor movement (jump, hop, slide, etc.). On signal, students run back to instructor.

DPESS page 309
Scattered formation. Use whistle for signals.

FITNESS DEVELOPMENT (8–12 MINUTES)

Jump and Jog Fitness
One partner jumps rope at the cone, other jogs around the circle. Change roles.
Variations in moving around circle:
- Slide
- Carioca
- Power Skip

DPESS page 357
Use continuity music CD/tape to signal activity change.
Set up 5–6 cones in a circle in gym or on the field.
3 Jump ropes at each cone

LESSON FOCUS (15–20 MINUTES)

Flag Football Rules, Strategies and Plays
Prepare handouts for home studying.

DPESS pages 429–430
Explain rules, positions, plays, and game strategies.

GAME (5 MINUTES)

Sitting Wrestle
Sit on floor facing partner. Bend legs, feet flat on floor, toes touching, and hands grasped.

Use Toe-to-Toe to create groups of 2.
Try to pull partner's buttocks off floor.

EVALUATION/REVIEW AND CHEER

Review rules of Flag Football.
Cheer: 1, 2, 3, Football helps me!

Flag Football Lesson Plan 7

EQUIPMENT:

20 footballs
10 jump ropes
1 Task Sheet per student

1 pencil and clipboard per 3 students
1 exercise CD/tape & 1 CD/cassette player

INSTRUCTIONAL ACTIVITIES	TEACHING HINTS

INTRODUCTORY ACTIVITY (2–3 MINUTES)

Triangle Tag
Form a triangle by holding hands. One person puts flag in pocket. Person with flag is leader. Group tries to keep leader from getting flags pulled. When flag pulled, leader becomes tagger and tagger becomes leader.

DPESS page 312
Use Whistle Mixer, make groups of 3
Choose 3 people to be the taggers.

FITNESS DEVELOPMENT (8–12 MINUTES)

Partner Racetrack Fitness
10 stations in circular track formation. Each station has task card with exercise to perform. 2 students perform task while other 2 run around track.

DPESS pages 356–357
Use Whistle Mixer, create groups of 4. Use Toe-to-Toe to make partners. Use music for motivation.

LESSON FOCUS (15–20 MINUTES)

Flag Football Skills Test
Explain reciprocal Task Sheet for self-testing.

Assign students to groups and testing areas.
Distribute clipboards, pencils, and Task Sheets.

GAME (5 MINUTES)

Spider Tag
Students work in partners. One pair of students are "it," and chase other pairs. When tagged, they become "it."

DPESS page 312
Scattered formation in pairs
Back-to-Back, elbows locked

EVALUATION/REVIEW AND CHEER

Review rules of Flag Football for Written Exam.
Cheer: Let's play football!!

Reciprocal Task Sheet: Flag Football Skills Test

Doer: _____   **Catcher/Defender**: _____
Observer: _____

Directions: Work with 2 other students. Place all names on your Task Sheet. One person is the "doer," one-person catches, throws, defends, while the third person is the observer. Observer checks "yes" or "no" and provides feedback and completes Task Sheet. Rotate positions upon completion of Task Sheet. Each person turns in a Task Sheet.

Check "Yes" (Y) or "No" (N)

	Y/N	Y/N	Y/N	Y/N	Y/N	Y/N	Y/N	Y/N	Y/N	Y/N
Passing										
Pass ball 10 yards.										
Catching										
Catch ball 5 times in a row from a 10-yard pass.										
Centering Ball										
Center ball and "hike" 5 times.										
Blocks										
Perform shoulder block on partner.										
Perform pass block with partner.										
Hand Off										
Hand off to the right.										
Hand off to the left.										
Punting										
Punt ball 5 times.										

Flag Football Lesson Plan 8

EQUIPMENT:

1 exam per student
1 pencil per student
1 flag set per student

2 tumbling mats
3 benches; high jump bar; jumping box
2 footballs

INSTRUCTIONAL ACTIVITIES	TEACHING HINTS
INTRODUCTORY ACTIVITY (2–3 MINUTES)	
Move, Stop and Pivot	DPESS page 308
Students use locomotor movement; on signal they stop then pivot and resume movement.	Scattered formation Teacher directs movements.
FITNESS DEVELOPMENT (8–12 MINUTES)	
Mini-Challenge Course	DPESS page 351
Start lying face down; Run around 2 chairs; Run; Hurdle over 3 benches; High jump over bar; Crab walk length of mat feet first; Agility run around 3 chairs; Forward roll length of mat; Vault 36 over a jumping box.	Set up course with space between stations.
LESSON FOCUS (15 MINUTES)	
Written Exam	Every student will take the written exam.
GAME (10 MINUTES)	
Flag Football	Use management game to divide the class into teams.
EVALUATION/REVIEW AND CHEER	

Review game play and questions from written exam.
Cheer: 1, 4, 6, 8, The game was great!

Flag Football Lesson Plan 9

EQUIPMENT:

2 footballs
Fitness CD/tape

1 flag set per student
CD/cassette player

INSTRUCTIONAL ACTIVITIES	TEACHING HINTS
INTRODUCTORY ACTIVITY (2–3 MINUTES)	
Mini Pyramids	DPESS pages 398–399
Perform locomotor movement. On signal students find a partner and build pyramid or partner stand.	Scattered formation. Find new partner each time. Stand on proper points of support.
FITNESS DEVELOPMENT (8–12 MINUTES)	
Aerobic Workout	DPESS page 352
See Racquetball, Lesson 7 for complete details.	Scattered formation Use CD/tape to direct exercise.
LESSON FOCUS AND GAME (20 MINUTES)	
Flag Football Tournament	Create teams using management game.
EVALUATION/REVIEW AND CHEER	

Discuss tournament play and review any rules necessary.
Cheer: 3, 2, 1, Football is fun!

Flag Football Lesson Plan 10

EQUIPMENT:
2 footballs   1 flag set per student

INSTRUCTIONAL ACTIVITIES	TEACHING HINTS

INTRODUCTORY ACTIVITY (2–3 MINUTES)

Mass Stand Up
Students sitting Back-to-Back. Lock elbows and try to stand up.

DPESS page 406
Scattered formation

FITNESS DEVELOPMENT (8–12 MINUTES)

Random Running
Students run around at own pace. On signal, students will perform assigned exercise

DPESS page 354
Continuous movement
Motivate students with music.

LESSON FOCUS AND GAME (20 MINUTES)

Flag Football Tournament

Continue with teams from yesterday.

EVALUATION/REVIEW AND CHEER

Discuss tournament play and introduce next unit.
Cheer: Teamwork wins games!

Orienteering

OBJECTIVES:

The student will:
1. Move and set up or knock down cones as demonstrated by the instructor.
2. Demonstrate balance and coordination in the Triangle Plus One Tag while following the safety rules as explained by the instructor.
3. Demonstrate agility and coordination in the Weave Drill One Tag while following the safety rules as explained by the instructor.
4. Participate in the Partner Fitness Racetrack to improve his/her personal fitness.
5. Participate in parachute fitness as demonstrated by the instructor.
6. Participate in the fitness obstacle courses using a Task Sheet as explained by the instructor.
7. Study the use and operation of a compass.
8. Read class safety rules and obtain signature to demonstrate understanding as discussed by the instructor.
9. Complete Task Sheets covering orienteering activities.
10. Complete a mini-orienteering course as explained by the instructor.
11. Participate in the Orienteering Course Challenge in squads demonstrating the rules and skills learned during the unit.
12. Pass a knowledge test covering the elements of orienteering with a score of 70% or better.

ORIENTEERING BLOCK PLAN
2 WEEK UNIT

Week #1	Monday	Tuesday	Wednesday	Thursday	Friday
Introductory Activity	Combination Movements	Cone Up, Cone Down	Blob Tag	Follow the Leader	Hoops on the Ground
Fitness	Parachute Fitness Activity	Partner Racetrack Fitness	Circuit Training	Continuity Exercises	Partner Racetrack Fitness
Lesson Focus	Class Rules & Orienteering	Compassing Introductory Activity	Compassing and Bearings	Bearings and Landmarks	Numbers and Numerals
Game	Hula Hoop Pass	Stream Crossing	Boardwalk	Faith Fall and Trust Dive	Snowball Tag Relay

Week #2	Monday	Tuesday	Wednesday	Thursday	Friday
Introductory Activity	Triangle Plus 1 Tag	Weave Drill	Square Drill	Back-to-Back	Push-up Tag
Fitness	Challenge Course	Partner Racetrack Fitness	Challenge Course	Circuit Training	Walk-Jog-Sprint
Lesson Focus	Mt. Robson I	Quiz	Orienteering Course	Orienteering Challenge	Point-to-Point Orienteering
Game	Knots	Bowling Pin Relay	Snowball Tag Relay	Grass in the Wind	Hula Hoop Pass

Orienteering Lesson Plan 1

EQUIPMENT:

Whistle	2 parachutes
Class safety rules handout	CD/tape player
7 hula hoops	Pre-recorded continuity CD/tape

INSTRUCTIONAL ACTIVITIES	TEACHING HINTS

INTRODUCTORY ACTIVITY (2–3 MINUTES)

Combination Movements (Similar to Move and Change the Type of Locomotion)	DPESS page 308
Examples:	Scattered formation. Direct students to skip.
Hop and turn around; Skip and freeze; Jump turn 180 degrees; Hop and make a pose; Create own moves; Jump, roll, jump up	Students will move in space until signal is given to change movements.

FITNESS DEVELOPMENT (8–12 MINUTES)

Parachute Fitness Activities	DPESS pages 351–352
Use fitness music CD/tape with 45 sec. for locomotor movements followed by a 20 second music silence for strengthening and stretching.	Around parachute

LESSON FOCUS (15–20 MINUTES)

Class Safety Rules Handout	DPESS pages 507–513
Introduction to Orienteering	Scattered formation
History; standard course; types of courses; describe the differences between feet and meters; pacing activity	Pacing activity: students walk the area and find a landmark to pace their steps.

GAME (5 MINUTES)

Hula Hoop Pass	DPESS page 390
Students will pass the hoop around the circle until it returns to the start without breaking hands.	Circle formation. Joined hands. Approximately 5 people per circle. Use Whistle Mixer to create groups.

EVALUATION/REVIEW

Review safety rules, pacing, and types of orienteering courses.

RECIPROCAL TASK SHEET 1: PACING YOUR STEPS

Doer:_____   **Observer:**_____

Timer:_____

Directions: Work in groups of three. Doer: Find a landmark in the area and pace your steps to that point. Observer: Watch the posture of doer and give feedback. Timer: Write down the time it takes the doer to get to the landmark. Rotate roles.

List the landmark:_____

Steps needed to reach landmark:_____ Time to travel to landmark:_____

Posture evaluation	Yes	No
Head up facing forward		
Shoulders straight (back as sometimes stated)		
Back upright and in good alignment		
Knees extended to 70 degrees on each stride		
Foot strikes ground in heel toe motion		
Medium size steps used to get to landmark		

High five your partner on completion of the task.

Orienteering Lesson Plan 2

EQUIPMENT:

CD/tape player

25 cones; 25 carpet squares; 6 padded mats

Pre-recorded continuity CD/tape

36 Task Sheets; 36 clipboards w/pencils

INSTRUCTIONAL ACTIVITIES	ORGANIZATION TEACHING HINTS

INTRODUCTORY ACTIVITY (2–3 MINUTES)

Cone Up, Cone Down

On signal, students will move in the space provided and place the cones into their opposite positions.

Place cones, half upright and half on their sides.

2 teams of students designated "up" or "down" teams.

FITNESS (8–12 MINUTES)

Partner Racetrack Fitness

DPESS pages 356–357

LESSON FOCUS (15–20 MINUTES)

Introduction to the Compass

DPESS pages 507–509

Students will follow the directions on the Task Sheet.

GAME (5 MINUTES)

Stream Crossing

The first team to move all members across the stream is the winner.

DPESS page 506

Students will have to cooperate with each other in order to get their entire team across.

EVALUATION/REVIEW

Review elements of reading the compass and cooperative skills developed in this lesson.

TASK SHEET 2: COMPASSING INTRODUCTION

Name:_____   **Date:**_____

Directions: You will complete this Task Sheet working on your own. Pick up a compass from your teacher. Read and answer the questions below. Upon completion, turn your compass and this Task Sheet into your teacher.

1. Place the safety cord on the compass around your wrist. Place the compass in the palm of your hand looking at the dial. Which direction is the needle pointing?

2. Turn the dial on the compass so the arrow lines up when the needle is pointing North. Which direction are you facing now? (Be sure you use the "direction-of-travel arrow").

    Turn yourself around 180 degrees. Which direction is the needle facing now?

3. Once you have established which direction is North, write down the buildings that are to the East.

4. Write down the buildings that are to the West.

5. Look around. Identify an object and write it down._____ Identify the direction to which you are facing:_____
    List which direction that object is in relation to you:_____

Return the compass and this paper to your instructor.

Orienteering Lesson Plan 3

EQUIPMENT:

CD/cassette player

8 buddy boards

36 compasses

8 hula hoops

Pre-recorded continuity CD/tape

8 padded mats

36 Task Sheets; 36 clipboards w/pencils

8 jump ropes

INSTRUCTIONAL ACTIVITIES	ORGANIZATION TEACHING HINTS
INTRODUCTORY ACTIVITY (2–3 MINUTES)	
Blob Tag	DPESS page 312
	Scattered formation
FITNESS DEVELOPMENT (8–12 MINUTES)	
Circuit Training	DPESS page 348
Students will execute fitness drills at different stations moving to Continuity Exercise CD/tape.	When the music ends, students rotate to next station and perform exercise listed.
LESSON FOCUS (15–20 MINUTES)	
Compassing and Bearings	DPESS pages 507–509
	Task Sheet provided that gives directions and degrees to follow
GAME (5 MINUTES)	
Boardwalk	DPESS pages 503–504
Students will use buddy walkers and work together in walking from a beginning point to a finish point.	
EVALUATION/REVIEW	
Review activities on Task Sheet.	

TASK SHEET 3: COMPASSING AND BEARINGS

Name:_____**Date:**_____

Directions: You will complete this Task Sheet working on your own. Pick up a compass from your teacher.

1. Complete the Compass Check List Below.
2. Complete the Bearings Section Below.

Compass Check List: For each item listed in the Record Bearing Section Below, answer these questions:

	Yes	No
Is the compass lying flat on a surface?		
Is the magnetic needle lined up with the North index line?		
Select a target and line up the direction-of-travel arrow with the object you have selected.		
Record the bearing that is lined up with the Index line and the direction-of-travel line.		

Bearings Section

Object	Bearings	Object	Bearings
Gym		Swimming Pool	
School Library		Tennis Courts	
Garden		Cafeteria	
Parking Lot		Write in:	

Congratulations on completing this Task Sheet. Turn this Task Sheet and your equipment in to your instructor.

Orienteering Lesson Plan 4

EQUIPMENT:

CD/cassette player
36 compasses
2–4 jumping boxes or elevated platforms

Pre-recorded continuity CD/tape
36 Task Sheets; 36 clipboards w/pencils

INSTRUCTIONAL ACTIVITIES	TEACHING HINTS

INTRODUCTORY ACTIVITY (2–3 MINUTES)

Follow the Leader
Students will alternate leading in a single file line
   performing an imaginative locomotor skill.

DPESS page 313
Single file line
Alternate leaders

FITNESS DEVELOPMENT (8–12 MINUTES)

Continuity Exercises
When the music changes the instructor will demonstrate a
   new skill for the class to perform.

DPESS pages 349–350
The CD/tape should have 30 seconds of music followed
   by a 20 second silence; repeat the pattern for 8
   minutes.

LESSON FOCUS (15–20 MINUTES)

Bearings and Landmarks

DPESS pages 507–509
See Task Sheet listing bearings and topographical items.
Make groups of 3 students for Task Sheet completion.

GAME (5 MINUTES)

Faith Fall and Trust Dive

DPESS pages 504–505
Stress safety and trust during this activity.

EVALUATION/REVIEW

Review what was needed to help "Faith and Fall" be successful.
Discuss elements covered on Bearings and Landmarks Task Sheet.

TASK SHEET 4: BEARINGS AND LANDMARKS

Doer:_____   **Observer:**_____

Timer:_____

<u>**Directions:**</u> Work in groups of three. Doer: Find a landmark in the area and pace your steps to that point. Observer: Read the map and guide the doer to the landmark. Timer: Write down the time it takes the doer to get to the landmark. There are six landmarks on this map, so everyone should perform each skill twice. Rotate roles.

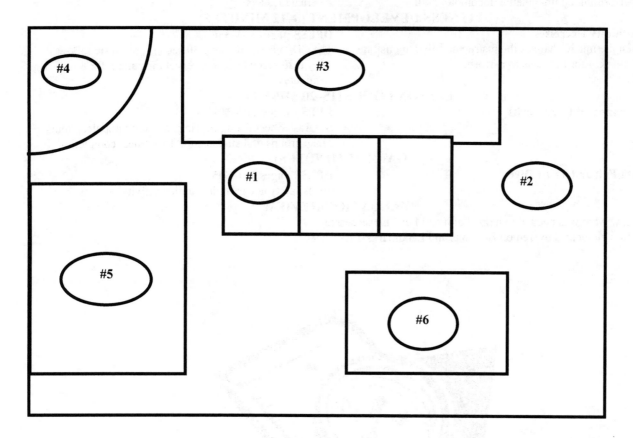

Bearings for Checkpoints/Time and Paces (ex: 120°/2:35/215)	
#1	#4
#2	#5
#3	#6

Orienteering Lesson Plan 5

EQUIPMENT:

CD/cassette player
36 compasses
8 hula hoops

Pre-recorded continuity CD/tape
36 Task Sheets; 36 clipboards w/pencils

INSTRUCTIONAL ACTIVITIES	ORGANIZATION TEACHING HINTS

INTRODUCTORY ACTIVITY (2–3 MINUTES)

Hoops on the Ground

Students will perform an instructor selected locomotor movement run around a group of hula hoops on the floor.

DPESS page 313

Scattered formation

When the teacher blows the whistle a given number of times, that number of students should go into a hoop.

FITNESS DEVELOPMENT (8–12 MINUTES)

Partner Racetrack Fitness

Modify activities with a variety of options such as arm curls, fist pull apart, back builder, etc.

DPESS pages 356–357

Allow students to work in groups to encourage fun with fitness.

LESSON FOCUS (15–20 MINUTES)

Numbers and Numerals

Students will use their compasses and stand on a number on the floor. They will then find the bearings for the corresponding numeral on the walls around them.

DPESS page 508

GAME (5 MINUTES)

More than one person will be "it" to begin the game and the team with the most people at the end wins.

Snowball Tag Relay

Modify the game with the introduction of two separate teams. The team that catches the most people, or has more people in their line at the end, wins the relays.

DPESS page 406

EVALUATION/REVIEW

Review elements of compass reading that students may still need to work on.

TASK SHEET 5: NUMBERS AND NUMERALS

Name:_____ **Date:**_____

Directions: You will complete this Task Sheet working on your own. Pick up a compass from your teacher. Look for a number on the ground. Then look for the corresponding Roman numeral on the wall. Write down the bearing for each number.

NUMBERS AND NUMERALS

NUMBER/NUMERAL	BEARING	NUMBER/NUMERAL	BEARING
1/I		6/VI	
2/II		7/VII	
3/III		8/VIII	
4/IV		9/IX	
5/V		10/X	

Orienteering Lesson Plan 6

EQUIPMENT:

12 jump ropes
CD/tape player
36 compasses
8 hula hoops

6 jumping blocks
Pre-recorded continuity CD/tape
36 Task Sheets; 36 clipboards w/pencils

INSTRUCTIONAL ACTIVITIES	ORGANIZATION TEACHING HINTS

INTRODUCTORY ACTIVITY (2–3 MINUTES)

Triangle Plus One Tag   DPESS page 312
Students must cooperate with peers to accomplish task.

FITNESS DEVELOPMENT (8–12 MINUTES)

Challenge Course   DPESS page 351
Jump over blocks, hop through hops, rope jump, jog, run
   around cones, etc.

LESSON FOCUS (15–20 MINUTES)

Students are in squads to receive the orienteering
assignment. Briefly explain the Task Sheet and have
the students move onto the track.

Hiking the Mountains Task Sheet #6

This activity is for pacing as well as improving target
   heart rate during the activity.

DPESS page 510
Students walk the track at their pace. Concentrate on
   personal stride and answering questions on the sheet.

GAME (5 MINUTES)

"Knots" (Entanglement)   DPESS page 407
Group leader moves the hands of his/her squad until
   everyone has someone else's hands and are in "knots."

Students proceed to work cooperatively with peers to
   "untangle" themselves.

EVALUATION/REVIEW

Review elements included in Task Sheet.

TASK SHEET 6: HOW MANY STEPS TO HIKE THE MOUNTAINS?

Name:_____ **Date:**_____

Description: The mountains surrounding Los Angeles extend approximately 30 miles. One of the largest peaks is Mount Wilson. Your task is to find out how many steps it takes to reach Mount Wilson.

1. How many steps will it take?
    Walk one lap around a ¼ mile track. Count every right footstep and keep track of the amount of time it takes to complete the lap. Record your results. Repeat three times. Calculate the average.
    ½ steps:_____   Time:_____
    ½ steps:_____   Time:_____
    ½ steps:_____   Time:_____
    Average:_____   Average:_____
2. How many half steps per ¼ mile?_____
3. How many half steps per mile? _____
4. How many full steps per mile? _____
5. How many steps for the entire mountain range?_____
6. It would take me _____ steps to hike the mountains around Los Angeles.

Orienteering Lesson Plan 7

EQUIPMENT:

4 bowling pins per 5–6 students   CD/tape player
Continuity CD/tape   12 mats
9 jump ropes

INSTRUCTIONAL ACTIVITIES	TEACHING HINTS
INTRODUCTORY ACTIVITY (2–3 MINUTES)	
Weave Drill	DPESS page 306
Students shuffle at the signal of the instructor.	Scattered formation
FITNESS DEVELOPMENT (8–12 MINUTES)	
Modify activities with new options: push-ups, jump rope, stretching, sit-ups, back bends, jumping jacks.	
Work in groups to encourage each other in having fun with fitness.	
Partner Racetrack Fitness	DPESS pages 356–357
	Students participate at their own fitness level.
LESSON FOCUS (15–20 MINUTES)	
Written Quiz	
GAME (5 MINUTES)	
Bowling Pin Relay	DPESS page 405
EVALUATION/REVIEW	
Discuss elements of difficulty on the quiz.	

Orienteering Lesson Plan 8

EQUIPMENT:

CD/tape player & CD/tape   18 cones
Hula hoops   12 jump ropes
6 jumping blocks

INSTRUCTIONAL ACTIVITIES	TEACHING HINTS
INTRODUCTORY ACTIVITY (2–3 MINUTES)	
Square Drill	DPESS page 305
	Students need to be aware of peers while moving around the perimeter.
FITNESS DEVELOPMENT (8–12 MINUTES)	
Challenge Course	DPESS page 351
LESSON FOCUS (15–20 MINUTES)	
Orienteering Course	DPESS pages 507–510
Students will incorporate the compassing and mapping skills learned in the previous lessons.	Squad formation
	Students will work in groups of 5–9 and record start and finish times.
GAME (5 MINUTES)	
Snowball Tag Relay	DPESS page 406
EVALUATION/REVIEW	
Discuss any elements on the course that were difficult.	

ORIENTEERING COURSE

Directions: Work with 3–5 other people. Record your start and finish times:

Start time:_____   **Finish time:** _____

From the gym, go SW until you reach a building. Write the name of the building:_____. Retrace your steps back to the starting point. Enter the gym and walk to the center of the basketball court. Name three other sports played in the gym:_____, _____, _____.
Exit the building. Head E 25 steps. Go N 25 steps. Write the name(s) of the edifices you have passed:_____. Count the steps it takes you to go to the school library.
What direction did you walk to get there?____
List any types of technology that you see inside the library:_____. List the names of the people you see in the library:_____. Count the steps it takes you to go to the cafeteria:_____. What direction(s) did you walk to get there?_____
Return to the gym in the most straightforward path. Count your steps to get there. Record the directions you walked:_____. How many steps did you walk to get there?_____.

Congratulations! You finished the Orienteering Course!!!

Orienteering Lesson Plan 9

EQUIPMENT:
12 jump ropes   CD/tape player
Continuity CD/tape   12 mats
36 Task Sheets w/clipboards and pencils

INSTRUCTIONAL ACTIVITIES	TEACHING HINTS
INTRODUCTORY ACTIVITY (2–3 MINUTES)	
Back-to-Back	DPESS page 150
	Scattered formation.
Students jog around in the space provided. When the music stops, the student partners with another Back-to-Back as soon as possible.	
FITNESS DEVELOPMENT (8–12 MINUTES)	
Circuit Training	DPESS page 348
LESSON FOCUS (15–20 MINUTES)	
Challenge Course	DPESS pages 509–510
You need to create a challenge course appropriate to your school and teaching facility. Give the students directions requiring them to use the compass and count their steps.	Groups of 3–7 work together. Leave rewards at specific points to make the challenge really fun and memorable for the students.
GAME (5 MINUTES)	
Grass in the Wind (Similar to Human Circle Pass)	DPESS page 505
Students cooperate in their squads to perform "grass in the wind" (human circle pass.)	The student in the middle learns trust for his/her squad. Rotate.
EVALUATION/REVIEW AND CHEER	

Discuss elements of the Challenge Course that proved to be difficult.
Cheer: Orienteering if really fine!

Orienteering Lesson Plan 10

EQUIPMENT:
Whistle
36 compasses
8 hula hoops

INSTRUCTIONAL ACTIVITIES	TEACHING HINTS

INTRODUCTORY ACTIVITY (2–3 MINUTES)

Push-Up Tag
To avoid being tagged student assumes a push-up
   position.

DPESS page 312
Scattered formation
Rules the same as any other tag game.

FITNESS DEVELOPMENT (8–12 MINUTES)

Walk-Jog-Sprint
When teacher blows the whistle, one = walk; two = jog;
   and three whistles = sprint.

DPESS page 354
Scattered formation within boundaries

LESSON FOCUS (15–20 MINUTES)

Point-to-Point Orienteering

DPESS pages 510–512

GAME (5 MINUTES)

Hula Hoop Pass
Students will try to pass the hoop around without
   breaking the chain.

DPESS page 390
Circle formation
See lesson #1 for more details.

EVALUATION/REVIEW AND CHEER

Discuss elements of the Point-to-Point Orienteering that may have been difficult.
Discuss what is necessary to make the Hula Hoop Pass game successful.
Cheer: Orienteering!

Rhythmic Gymnastics

OBJECTIVES:

The student will:
1. Participate in Blob Tag, Fugitive Tag, Push-Up Tag, Vanishing Bean Bags, and Flag Grab demonstrating agility, quick changes in direction and sportsmanship.
2. Participate in Parachute Fitness Activities to improve arm strength and overall fitness.
3. Participate in Circuit Training, Continuity Exercises, Fitness Scavenger, and Aerobic workout to improve fitness.
4. Perform Rhythmic Gymnastics Ball, Rope, Hoop, and Ribbon skills using form demonstrated in class.
5. Create and perform alone or with a partner a routine demonstrating skills learned in class to the music provided by the instructor.

RHYTHMIC GYMNASTICS BLOCK PLAN
2 WEEK UNIT

Week #1	Monday	Tuesday	Wednesday	Thursday	Friday
Introductory Activity	Blob Tag	Whistle March	Vanishing Bean bags	Parachute Locomotor Activity	New Leader Activity
Fitness	Continuity Exercises	Parachute Fitness Activities	Fitness Scavenger Hunt	Fitness Scavenger Hunt	Circuit Training with Jog
Lesson Focus	Ball	Ball Routine	Ribbon	Ribbon Exchanges	Hoop
Game	Frisbee Catch	Push-Up Tag	Hula Hoop Pass	Pentabridge Hustle	Musical Hoops

Week #2	Monday	Tuesday	Wednesday	Thursday	Friday
Introductory Activity	Mirror Drill	New Leader Activity with Music	Frozen Tag	Formation Rhythmic Running	Juggling Scarves
Fitness	Aerobic Workout	Walk, Jog, Sprint	Fitness Challenge Course	Circuit Training with Jog	Aerobic workout
Lesson Focus	Rope	Rope Routine	Review All Apparatus	Develop Routine	Perform Routine
Game	Frisbee 21	Fugitive Tag	Flag Grab and Chase		

Rhythmic Gymnastics Lesson Plan 1

EQUIPMENT:

Continuity music CD/tape for fitness   Music player

Frisbee per 2 students

1 volleyball/rubber ball/team handball/rhythmic gymnastics ball per student

INSTRUCTIONAL ACTIVITIES	TEACHING HINTS

INTRODUCTORY ACTIVITY (2–3 MINUTES)

Blob Tag

Select 2–3 "its."

DPESS page 312

Change "its" 1 or 2 times during activity.

FITNESS DEVELOPMENT (8–12 MINUTES)

Continuity Exercises

These exercises are a type of interval training. Create a CD/cassette tape with 30–35 seconds of music and 20 seconds of silence. During music the students jump rope. During pause, lead floor exercises.

DPESS pages 349–350

When the silence begins, instruct the students to do an exercise, i.e., push-ups; curl-ups; reverse push-ups; etc.

When the music resumes, the students jump rope. During each silence direct a different exercise.

Stretching

During the last silence, conduct stretching exercises to stretch the areas worked, i.e., calves; quadriceps; etc.

DPESS pages 342–344

Slower and lower volume music should be added to this portion of the CD/tape for enjoyable stretching.

Bear Hug

Lunge Forward: Achilles and calf stretch

Lunge forward and extend rear leg straight back.

DPESS page 342

Attempt to place the rear foot flat on the floor. Hands on front thigh for support. Back flat and on upward diagonal.

Hamstring Stretch-Reverse Lunge: From the lunge position, shift lunge and weight to rear leg, extend front leg. Keep heel on ground, toe flexed, pointing to sky.

Hold stretch for 30 seconds. Change legs.

Hands on front thigh for support, back flat but on upward diagonal.

Standing Hip Bend (Both sides)

Hold the position for 20–30 seconds.

DPESS page 343

Elbow Puller and Pusher (Both sides)

DPESS page 344

LESSON FOCUS (15–20 MINUTES)

Rhythmic Gymnastics Ball Activities

Rolling: In a sitting position: Roll ball under the legs, around the back; around the body; down the legs; down the arms; down the legs, lift legs and toss the ball off the toes into the air and catch.

DPESS page 431

In handling the ball, the fingers should be closed slightly bent, with the ball resting in the palm. In wing, the ball can roll from the fingertips

Bouncing: Combine basketball-dribbling drills with graceful body movements; execute locomotor dance-type movements while bouncing.

Locomotor suggestions: Chase, slides, run and leap, skip, walk on toes, etc.

Toss and catch the ball while sitting/kneeling on floor, walking, skipping, galloping, leaping, and running.

Use one hand only while tossing and catching the ball.

Try each hand. Perform body waves with the ball.

Swinging: Swing ball in front of body from side to side. Circle ball around body, neck, legs and around palm. Let ball rest on palm of hand as you turn around.

The ball must rest lightly in the palm while the movements are performed. No gripping of ball with fingers is permitted.

GAME (5 MINUTES)

Frisbee Catch

Partners can keep score or just free throwing and catching.

1 hand catch = 2 points

2 hand catch = 1 point

Keep score to 20 points and then start over.

DPESS pages 463–465

Demonstrate throwing and catching a Frisbee.

Use Back-to-Back with a new person to create partners. One person puts a hand on their head. The person with his hand on his head is to go and get a Frisbee for the pair and return to the partner.

EVALUATION/REVIEW AND CHEER

Were there any fitness activities you did today that were particularly difficult and need more work?

Which of the Rhythmic Gymnastics ball activities that you did today were the best? Were any of them hard to do?

Cheer: Frisbee, yeah!

Rhythmic Gymnastics Lesson Plan 2

EQUIPMENT:

Music for Whistle March
Parachute
1 ball per student

CD/tape player
Music for fitness

INSTRUCTIONAL ACTIVITIES	TEACHING HINTS

INTRODUCTORY ACTIVITY (2–3 MINUTES)

Whistle March: Clap dominant beat. Clap and march in place to beat. March around room in time to music played while moving around room. When blow whistle a given number, students make groups that size by linking elbows. Blow whistle once to signal solo marching.

Direct students to create new groups each time.
Students without group go to center to find others.

Play music tape with dominant beat.

FITNESS DEVELOPMENT (8–12 MINUTES)

Parachute Fitness Activities

DPESS page 336
See Golf, Lesson Plan 2 for complete details.

LESSON FOCUS (15–20 MINUTES)

Review ball activities taught in Lesson 1

Balancing movements plus ball skills

Balance on 1 foot with 1 arm extended out while tossing ball with other hand. Hold a balance while kneeling on the floor and circle or swing ball, etc.

Ball Routine:

Bounce the ball in place while extending opposite arm out horizontally; Bounce the ball while moving forward slowly walking or sliding using an arm movement; Run forward while making swing tosses from side to side; Bounce the ball while making a full turn; Run low to the ground in a figure-eight pattern; Toss the ball up and catch it with one hand; repeat on other side; Finish with a toss and catch the ball blindly behind the back.

All students have their own ball to practice skills.
Direct various balances combined with circling, tossing, swinging ball movements practiced in Lesson 1.

You can draw the floor pattern on a poster board for students to follow or you can allow them to draw a floor pattern.
First practice routine without any music, and then add music.

GAME (5 MINUTES)

Push-Up Tag

Select several "its." Rotate roles frequently.

DPESS page 312
Perform push-ups or push-up position to be "safe."

EVALUATION/REVIEW AND CHEER

Were you able to perform the routine? What areas caused difficulty? Were there any fitness activities that were particularly challenging?

Cheer: Rhythmic gymnastics rocks!

Rhythmic Gymnastics Lesson Plan 3

EQUIPMENT:
1 bean bag per student
Cones for station markers
1 hula hoop per student

Fitness Scavenger Hunt cards
1 rhythmic gymnastics ribbon per student

INSTRUCTIONAL ACTIVITIES	TEACHING HINTS

INTRODUCTORY ACTIVITY (2–3 MINUTES)

Vanishing Bean Bags

DPESS page 309
Spread bean bags out in area. Begin with 1 bag/student. Have students begin by moving around the area until you give a signal.

FITNESS DEVELOPMENT (8–12 MINUTES)

Fitness Scavenger Hunt
Each group is given a card indicating where to go. Once at the station another card will be there indicating the exercise/activity to perform and how.

DPESS page 356
Scattered formation
Use Whistle Mixer to create groups of four.
10 stations

LESSON FOCUS (15–20 MINUTES)

Swinging the Ribbon: The entire body should coordinate with these large, swinging motions:
Swing the ribbon forward and backward in the sagittal plane on the side of the body.
Swing the ribbon across and in front of the body in the frontal plane. Swing the ribbon overhead from side to side; Swing the ribbon upward and catch the end of it.
While holding both ends of the ribbon, swing it upward, around, and over the body. Jump through it.

Spread students out so ribbons won't tie up with other students' ribbons.
Step forward and backward as the ribbon is swung.
Follow-through very high with the working arm.
This can be done while still or while sliding to the side.
Overhead swings coordinate well with a balance movement.

Circling Movements: Large circles are made in front, on the side and around the body. Use the whole arm to create the circular movements; smaller circles involve the wrist. Circles are made in different planes: frontal, sagittal, and horizontal.
Circle the ribbon horizontally, vertically, or diagonally.
Circle the ribbon in front of the body, around the body, and overhead and behind the body.
Run while circling the ribbon overhead; leap as the ribbon is circled downward and under the legs.

Body can circle in place or through space.
Student can run and leap through the large circles being made with the ribbon.
Circle the ribbon at different levels.

Small movements on the toes coordinate with this action.
Coordinate body movements with the ribbon movements.

Add dance steps and turns while circling the ribbon.

Figure-Eight Movements. Figure eights are made in the three planes. The two halves of the figure eight should be the same size and on the same plane level. The figure can be made with long arm movements or with movements of the lower arm or wrist. Practice both types.

While performing a figure eight, hop through the loop when the ribbon passes the side of the body.

Zigzag Movements: Zigzag movements are made in the air or on the floor. These are done with continuous up-and-down hand movements, using primarily wrist action.
Run backward while zigzagging the ribbon in front of the body. Run forward while zigzagging ribbon behind the body at different levels.

Execute the zigzag in the air in front, around, and behind the body.

Perform zigzagging of ribbon at different levels in front, side, and back of body.

Spiraling movements: The circles making up the spiraling action can be the same size or of an increasing or decreasing progression.
Perform forward and backward rolls while spiraling.

Spirals can be made from left to right or the reverse.
Execute spirals around, in front of, on the side of the body while performing locomotor dance steps.

INSTRUCTIONAL ACTIVITIES	TEACHING HINTS

GAME (5 MINUTES)

Hula Hoop Pass
Place a hula hoop over the clasped hands of two
members of each squad. On signal–pass the hoop
around the circle without releasing handgrips.

DPESS page 390
Scattered–in groups
Approximately 5 per group. Members of each group
hold hands.

EVALUATION/REVIEW AND CHEER

Was there any difficulty with any particular ribbon movement? What was needed to make the Hula Hoop Pass
successful?
Cheer: Ribbon is cool!

Rhythmic Gymnastics Lesson Plan 4

EQUIPMENT:
1 parachute   1 rhythmic gymnastics ribbon per student
Fitness Scavenger Hunt cards

INSTRUCTIONAL ACTIVITIES	TEACHING HINTS

INTRODUCTORY ACTIVITY (2–3 MINUTES)

Parachute Locomotor Routine: Use popular music 16
runs CW; 16 runs CCW; 8 jumps in place; 16 skips
forward; 8 count lift overhead; 8 count lower to toes; 4
count lift; 4 count lower to toes; Repeat all
Face chute and hold with 2 hands: Slide CW; Slide CCW

DPESS pages 351–352
Whistle to change action.
"Tighten 'chute!"
Hold parachute overhead on CW run.
Whistle to signal direction change.

FITNESS DEVELOPMENT (8–12 MINUTES)

Fitness Scavenger Hunt
Each group is given a list directing them to designated
areas to find directions for exercise/activity at that
location.

DPESS page 356
Use Whistle Mixer to create groups of 3.
Each group is assigned a different starting point.
Each station lists exercises that work the entire body.

LESSON FOCUS (15–20 MINUTES)

**Review Ribbon Swinging, Circling, Spiraling, Figure
8, and Zig Zag movements from yesterday's lesson.**
Throwing and Catching: These skills are usually
combined with swinging, circling, or figure-8
movements.
Exchanges: During group routines, the ribbon is handed
or tossed to a partner. The wand is usually exchanged
although both ribbon and wand can be handed off.
Students create a routine using movements learned
Direct students to create a 30 second to 1 minute routine.

The ribbon is tossed with one hand and is caught with the
same hand or with the other hand. Throwing and
catching is a difficult maneuver.
Practice with a partner.
Create partners using Elbow-to-Elbow technique.

Allow students a given amount of time to create routine.
Play music for the routine. Have several groups "show"
their created routines at once.

GAME (5 MINUTES)

Pentabridge Hustle

DPESS page 310
See Golf Lesson Plan 5 for complete details.

EVALUATION/REVIEW AND CHEER

Were any parts of the Fitness Scavenger Hunt particularly difficult? Review positive elements of the routines created
during the class period.
Cheer: Ribbon figure 8s, yes!

Rhythmic Gymnastics Lesson Plan 5

EQUIPMENT:

Music for fitness and introductory activity
1 hoop per student

Music player
Circuit Training cones and signs

INSTRUCTIONAL ACTIVITIES	TEACHING HINTS
INTRODUCTORY ACTIVITY (2–3 MINUTES)	
New Leader Activity moving to music	DPESS page 311
Leader begins moving to beat/style of music. Others follow until you signal for a leader change.	Use management game to create groups of 3–5 Use management technique to identify first leader
FITNESS DEVELOPMENT (8–12 MINUTES)	
Circuit Training Fitness with Jog	DPESS page 357
Explain each station.	Using Whistle Mixer, create groups to go to Stations
LESSON FOCUS (15–20 MINUTES)	
Hoop: Swing the hoop—across the body; around the body with same hand, then a hand change; overhead same hand, then change hands; swing down and up on side of body; in figure-eight pattern in front of the body.	The swinging movement should be very large. Good alignment between body and the hoop is important. Hoops can be swung in frontal, sagittal, or horizontal plane. Add locomotor movements, i.e., slide, chase, gallop, etc.
Spin the hoop: Spin in front of the body; Spin on the floor; Spin and kick one leg over the hoop; Reverse; Add a full turn after the kick over; Reverse.	One or both hands can be used when spinning the hoop. Locomotor movements can be performed around the spinning hoop.
Circling Movements: Hoops can be circled on the hand, wrist, arm, leg, or body. Changes from one hand to the other can be performed.	Extend the arm in front of the body, to the side or overhead. Circle the hoop on the hand between the thumb and first finger.
Circle the hoop while swaying or sliding from side to side. Hold onto both sides of the hoop circle it in front of the body.	Add locomotor movements such as: gallop, slide, skip, run, leaps while circling the hoop in all planes.
GAME (5 MINUTES)	
Musical Hoops	Scattered formation
Hoops, one fewer than the number of students, placed on the floor. Players are given a locomotor movement to do around the hoops while the music is played.	When the music stops, the students step inside and empty hoop. One student per hoop. Repeat with another locomotor movement. Examples are: slide, gallop, run, skip, leap, and carioca.
EVALUATION/REVIEW AND CHEER	

Were any hoop activities particularly difficult? Which activity did you enjoy the most?
Cheer: Hoops are cool!

Rhythmic Gymnastics Lesson Plan 6

EQUIPMENT:

1 woven rope per student
Aerobic exercise tape/CD

Tape or CD player

INSTRUCTIONAL ACTIVITIES	TEACHING HINTS
INTRODUCTORY ACTIVITY (2–3 MINUTES)	
Mirror Drill in Place	DPESS page 313
	Use a management game to make pairs. Identify first leader/follower. Signal time for leader and follower to change roles after approximately 30-40 seconds.

INSTRUCTIONAL ACTIVITIES	TEACHING HINTS

FITNESS DEVELOPMENT (8–12 MINUTES)

Aerobic Workout to Music

Create a music CD/tape 120–150 beats per minute or use Aerobic Exercise CD/tape.

DPESS 358.

Scattered formation within a coned area on the athletic field.

DPESS pages 358–359

Standing Hip Bend	40 seconds
Trunk Twist	30 seconds
Slides each direction	30 seconds
Skip around cones	30 seconds
Jumping Jacks	30 seconds
Triceps Push-Ups	30 seconds
Curl-Ups	30 seconds
Knee Touch Curl-Ups	30 seconds
Push-Ups	30 seconds
Gallop around cones	30 seconds
Jump Rope	1 minutes
Lower Leg Stretch	30 seconds
Balance Beam Stretch	30 seconds
Rocking Chair	30 seconds
Carioca around cones	1 minutes
Jog in place	
Calf Stretch	

LESSON FOCUS (15–20 MINUTES)

Rope: Circle the rope on each side of the body while holding both ends of the rope.

Rope size is determined by standing on the center of the rope with both feet and extending the rope ends to the hands held at the "armpit" level. There should not be handles on the ends of the rope.

Allow students plenty of time to practice these skills.

Make **figure 8 swings**: Holding both ends of the rope, or, holding the center of the rope and swinging the ends.

Pendulum swing rope in front of body and jump it.

Hold one hand near midline of body, the other parallel and approximately 12" in front of body.

Run or skip over rope turned forward and backward.

Schottische step over a turning rope.

Direct students to be safe and watch out for others.

Spread students out for safety.

Jump over a backward turning rope, and then **toss** the rope into the air. Catch both ends of rope.

Holding the ends and center of the rope, kneel and horizontally circle the rope close to the floor.

Variation: Stand and circle the rope horizontally overhead.

Perform a body wrap with the rope.

Hold one end on the hip; wrap the rope around the body with the other hand.

GAME (5 MINUTES)

"Frisbee 21"

Game Rules:

- Players stand 10 yards apart
- Throw disc back and forth. Throws must be catchable.
- 1 point = 1 hand catch
  2 points = 2 hand catch

DPESS page 465

Create partners using "elbow-to-elbow" technique.

Have 1 person kneel. The standing partner gets a Frisbee from perimeter of area and brings to partner.

Player must get 21 points to win and win by 2 points.

EVALUATION/REVIEW AND CHEER

Were there any rope activities that were really challenging yet fun? Which ones?

What was challenging about Frisbee 21?

Cheer: Fun, fun, Frisbee 21!

Rhythmic Gymnastics Lesson Plan 7

EQUIPMENT:

Music for introductory activity

1 rhythmic rope per student

Music player

1 flag belt per person

INSTRUCTIONAL ACTIVITIES	TEACHING HINTS

INTRODUCTORY ACTIVITY (2–3 MINUTES)

New Leader

Play music and leader must create movements to music.

DPESS page 311

Create pairs by playing "Back-to-Back."

FITNESS DEVELOPMENT (8–12 MINUTES)

Walk-Jog-Sprint

1 Whistle = Sprint

2 Whistle = Walk

3 Whistle = Jog

DPESS page 354

Scattered formation within boundaries

Teacher directs length of time for each activity by monitoring class. Progressively increase the time of each activity.

Stretch: Achilles Tendon; Lower Leg; Balance Beam; Bear Hug; Leg Pick-Up; Side Leg; Hurdler's; Groin Stretch; Sitting Toe Touch; Body Twist

Strength: Crab Walk; Push-ups; Reclining Partner Pull-ups; Curl-ups; Reverse curls; Curl-ups with twist

DPESS pages 342–344

Scattered formation

DPESS pages 344–345

LESSON FOCUS (15–20 MINUTES)

Review rope skills taught yesterday.

Single and double **jump forward and backward.**

While holding both ends of the rope in one hand, **circle the rope sagittally backward** at the side of the body and run forward.

Perform a locomotor dance step and simultaneously toss and catch the rope.

Hold both ends of the rope and swing it around the body like a cape.

Perform leaps while circling the rope sagittally at one side of the body.

Hold the rope around the foot and make shapes with the body and foot-rope connection. Utilize different balancing movements while stretching the rope.

Allow students to explore and combine activities previously taught.

Spread students out for safety.

Variation: Toss the rope and catch it while running.

Chase, run and leap, waltz step, slide, triplet, etc. are examples of locomotor steps to use.

Variation: Turn the body around simultaneously.

Leaps can be forward or sideward. Rope can circle in front of body as well as on side.

These involve held body positions, with the rope underneath the foot or hooked around a foot.

Suggest movements that could be combined while students are exploring.

GAME (5 MINUTES)

Fugitive Tag

Identify leader in group. They are first fugitive. Rotate.

DPESS page 312

Use Back-to-Back to create partners. Both wear belts.

EVALUATION/REVIEW AND CHEER

Were any rope activities particularly challenging? Which one do you enjoy most and why?

Cheer: Rhythmic rope rates!

Rhythmic Gymnastics Lesson Plan 8

EQUIPMENT:

Challenge Course instructions and cones
Balance beam for Challenge Course
Ropes, balls, ribbons, hoops: 1 per student

Ladder for fitness course
Music for fitness
Music player

INSTRUCTIONAL ACTIVITIES	TEACHING HINTS

INTRODUCTORY ACTIVITY (2–3 MINUTES)

Frozen Tag
Select 2 "its"

DPESS page 312
Scattered formation.

FITNESS DEVELOPMENT (8–12 MINUTES)

Fitness Challenge Course
Design a course using the following components:

- Agility run through hoops
- Log rolls
- Run and weave through a coned course
- Leap over a taut rope
- Cross a horizontal ladder (or hang for 5–10 seconds)
- Power jump onto and off of three jumping boxes
- Walk the length of a balance beam
- Run high knees for 50 yards
- Curl-ups
- Crab Walks from one cone to another
- Stretching exercises

DPESS page 351

Divide class into groups of 4–5. Assign each group a starting point on the Challenge Course. Use music to motivate.

Course should be created to exercise all parts of the body
Allow students to run the Challenge Course 3 times
Allow students to develop new challenges for the course
Music can be used for fun and to motivate students
Students will travel the course at their own pace. Have a passing lane to the right.

LESSON FOCUS (15–20 MINUTES)

Review rope, ball, ribbon, hoop skills previously taught.

Guide students through review of each apparatus.

GAME (5 MINUTES)

Flag Grab and Chase
One team wears flags positioned in the back of the belt. On signal, the chase team captures as many flags as possible within a designated amount of time. The captured flags are counted. The teams switch positions and the team that captures the most flags wins.

DPESS page 314
Scattered formation inside large boundary area.
Split class into using a management game such as Back-to-Back; Toe-to-Toe; or elbow-to-elbow to make two groups by then directing one in the group to put hand on hips. Then separate the two groups into teams.
Direct one team to pick up belts with flags attached.

EVALUATION/REVIEW AND CHEER

Identify which apparatus you enjoy most and explain why. What was challenging in the Challenge Course?
Students create cheer today.

Rhythmic Gymnastics Lesson Plan 9

EQUIPMENT:

Circuit training station signs and cones
Music for Rhythmic Gymnastics routines

Ribbons, balls, hoops, ropes for whole class
Music player

INSTRUCTIONAL ACTIVITIES	TEACHING HINTS
INTRODUCTORY ACTIVITY (2–3 MINUTES)	
Formation Rhythmic Running	DPESS page 313
Run 3 times	Give instructions to "fall in" to a circle or lines.
Run in a small circle 4 times	Play drum or tambourine to set rhythm.
Jump in place 8 times	Increase tempo when you repeat.
Run 8 times and clap on counts 1, 4, 5, 7, and 8	
Repeat above	
FITNESS DEVELOPMENT (8–12 MINUTES)	
Circuit Training Fitness with Jog	DPESS page 357
Explain each station.	Using Whistle Mixer, create groups to go to stations
LESSON FOCUS AND GAME COMBINED (20 MINUTES)	
Students create a routine using apparatus of their choice. Routine can be done in 2's or solo.	Play music that can be used for the routine.
EVALUATION/REVIEW AND CHEER	

Discuss creative presentations due the next day.
Students create cheer.

Rhythmic Gymnastics Lesson Plan 10

EQUIPMENT:

3 juggling scarves per student
CD/tape for aerobic workout

Music player
Ropes, hoops, ribbons, balls: 1 per student

INSTRUCTIONAL ACTIVITIES	TEACHING HINTS
INTRODUCTORY ACTIVITY (2–3 MINUTES)	
Juggling Scarves	DPESS page 392
Column juggling; Cascading	Scattered formation; 3 scarves per student
FITNESS DEVELOPMENT (8–12 MINUTES)	
Aerobic Workout	DPESS pages 358–359
	See Lesson 7, Racquetball Unit for details.
LESSON FOCUS AND GAME COMBINED (20 MINUTES)	
Several groups perform routines for class simultaneously.	Do not have anyone perform alone as it can cause embarrassment. Set etiquette/behavior rules before presentations begin. Clap for all students.
Play appropriate music for the routines.	
EVALUATION/REVIEW AND CHEER	

Make a general comment praising student creativity.
Cheer: Rhythmic gymnastics, yeah!

Rhythms and Dance

OBJECTIVES:

The student will:
1. Identify rhythm and move to the beat played on the drum by the instructor.
2. Demonstrate rhythmical awareness while participating in Whistle March to music.
3. Demonstrate respect for classmates while participating in Standing and Running High Five's.
4. Participate in the Parachute Rhythmic Aerobic Activity, Fitness Scavenger Hunt, Challenge Course, and Aerobic workout to improve fitness.
5. Perform Cotton Eyed Joe, Sweetheart Schottische, 8-Count Polka, Swing, Foxtrot and Waltz demonstrating rhythmical awareness and using form demonstrated in class by the instructor.
6. Demonstrate eye-hand coordination, cooperative skills, and agility while participating in the Wand and Tag activities presented by the instructor.
7. Demonstrate teamwork and cooperative skills while participating in Relay races, Long Rope Routines, Tag and Cageball Games.

RHYTHMS AND DANCE BLOCK PLAN
2 WEEK UNIT

Week #1	Monday	Tuesday	Wednesday	Thursday	Friday
Introductory Activities	Rhythm Identification	Whistle March	Balance Tag	Whistle March Schottische	Hoops and Plyometrics
Fitness	Parachute Rhythmic Aerobic Activity	Fitness Scavenger Hunt	Aerobic workout	Continuity Exercises	Circuit Training Fitness with Jog
Lesson Focus	California Strut Cotton Eyed Joe Line Sweetheart Schottische	Cotton Eyed Joe Partners Sweetheart Schottische	8-Count Polka	East Coast Swing and Turns	California Strut, Cotton Eyed Joe, Sweetheart Schottische, 8-Count Polka, Swing
Game	Wands: Reaction Time & Broomstick Balance	Blob Tag	Long Team Cageball	Long Jump Rope Routines	Scooter Cageball Soccer

Week #2	Monday	Tuesday	Wednesday	Thursday	Friday
Introductory Activities	New Leader Activity to Music	Standing High Five's	Mirror Drill in Place to Music	Running High Five's	Whistle March to Music
Fitness	12 Ways of fitness	Aerobic workout	Fitness Cookie Jar Exchange	Challenge Course	Long Jump Rope Fitness Routine
Lesson Focus	Cha-Cha, Swing & Pretzel Steps	Waltz Swing	Waltz Cha Cha	Waltz Foxtrot	Review all Dances
Game	Spider Tag	Clothespin Tag	Loose Caboose	Pass and Squat Relays	

Rhythms and Dance Lesson Plan 1

EQUIPMENT:

Drum and beater

Tape/CD music CD/tape player

Tape/CD for fitness, Cotton Eyed Joe, Sweetheart Schottische

1 wand per student

Parachute

INSTRUCTIONAL ACTIVITIES	TEACHING HINTS

INTRODUCTORY ACTIVITY (2–3 MINUTES)

Rhythm Identification

Play simple rhythmical patterns on drum. Students pat the rhythm on their thighs. Change rhythm and tempo.

Play simple music and have students tap beat on thighs with eyes closed and then open.

Play music. Students clap the beat. Then, march in place to beat while clapping, then walk around and clap.

Students march to beat of music and High Five students.

Students sit or lay on ground with eyes closed. Repeat with student's eyes open.

Demonstrate sitting and leaning back on hands enabling tapping toes lightly on ground to beat.

Students stand and move around room.

Use several pieces of music with easily identifiable beats.

FITNESS DEVELOPMENT (8–12 MINUTES)

Parachute Rhythmic Aerobic Activity

Direct a variety of locomotor movements holding the chute with one hand or both. Activities include: sliding; skipping; galloping; jogging; etc. Then add stretching and strengthening exercises while standing, seated, or lying down on side, back, or stomach.

DPESS page 352

Use a lively piece of music with a bold beat.

LESSON FOCUS (15–20 MINUTES)

California Strut

Cotton Eyed Joe as a line dance

First, students tap beat on thigh by listening to music.

Demonstrate dance using Whole-Part-Whole teaching method.

Sweetheart Schottische line dance or couples dance

Have students move forward to new partner every other schottische pattern.

Weikart, P., *Rhythmically Moving*, 4.

Music and instructions for <u>all dances</u> available from: *Wagon Wheel Books and Records; 16812 Pembrook Lane; Huntington Beach, CA 92649; (714) 846-8169*

Use Elbow-to-Elbow to make couples.

Couples follow the back of another couple's neck while walking to create a circle and "fall-in."

GAME (5 MINUTES)

Wands: Reaction Time

Broomstick Balance

DPESS page 402

DPESS page 402

Use same partners students ended with during dance.

EVALUATION/REVIEW AND CHEER

Were there any dance steps you learned today that you need to practice more?

Cheer: Hear the beat!

Rhythms and Dance Lesson Plan 2

EQUIPMENT:
Fitness Scavenger Hunt instruction cards
Tape/CD music CD/tape player
Music for Whistle March, Cotton Eyed Joe, Sweetheart Schottische, 8-Count Polka

INSTRUCTIONAL ACTIVITIES	TEACHING HINTS

INTRODUCTORY ACTIVITY (2–3 MINUTES)

Whistle March: Clap dominant beat. Clap and march in place to beat. March in time to music played while moving around room. When blow whistle a given number, students make groups that size by linking elbows. Blow whistle once to signal solo marching.

Direct students to create new groups each time.
Students without group go to center to find others.

Play music with a dominant beat.

FITNESS DEVELOPMENT (8–12 MINUTES)

Fitness Scavenger Hunt
Each group is given a card indicating where to go. Once at the station another card will be there indicating the exercise/activity to perform and how.

DPESS page 356
Scattered formation
Use Whistle Mixer to create groups of four.
10 stations

LESSON FOCUS (15–20 MINUTES)

Review Cotton Eyed Joe and Sweetheart Schottische.
Teach both dances as a couples dance following each review in a double circle. Partners face counter clockwise (CCW).

Scattered formation.
Use Elbow-to-Elbow to create partners. Once have partner, they follow the back of the necks of another couple and "fall-in" to make a circle.

GAME (5 MINUTES)

Blob Tag
Select 2 "its." Only the person at the end of the line tags.

DPESS page 312

EVALUATION/REVIEW AND CHEER

Which dance steps are used in both 8-Count Polka and Cotton-Eyed Joe?
What is the main dance step in Sweetheart Schottische?
Cheer: Country Western Dance, yeah!

Rhythms and Dance Lesson Plan 3

EQUIPMENT:

Music for aerobic exercise
Music for Swing, 8-Count Polka

Music CD/tape player
Cage ball

INSTRUCTIONAL ACTIVITIES	TEACHING HINTS

INTRODUCTORY ACTIVITY (2–3 MINUTES)

Balance Tag
Select 2–3 "its."

DPESS page 312
Designate how many seconds one must balance if tagged.

FITNESS DEVELOPMENT (8–12 MINUTES)

Aerobic workout

- Walk in place with knees high to the beat.
- Jump in place 8 x hitting the sides of thighs with hands and straight arms.
- Walk in place on toes performing 16 steps moving arms down and up on the sides/front of body
- Run in place 8 x while lifting feet high in the rear.
- Run in place 8 x while lifting knees high in front.
- 8 jumping jacks full arm movements
- 8 jumping jacks moving arms down and only half way up (to the shoulder level)
- Mountain Climber 8 x alternating feet
- Pony: "Hop, step, step." Repeat on the other side.
- Heel, toe, slide, and slide 4 x each direction
- Hop on one foot and lift up the opposite knee. Reverse.
- Hop on one foot, and swing kick the opposite foot forward. Reverse.
- Charleston Bounce Step: Step R, kick the L foot forward, step back on the L foot, and touch the R toe back. Repeat 8 x. Reverse.
- Can-Can Kick: Hop, kick opposite leg high.
- Perform full body stretches
- Strengthening exercises

Casten, C. and Jordan, P. *Aerobics Today, 2ⁿᵈ Ed.* Wadsworth, 2002.

Use music appropriate for Aerobic Exercise, 120–170 beats per minute.

DPESS pages 358–359

DPESS pages 342–345

Mountain Climber: Jump and land forward and backward a distance of about one foot. Alternate feet. Arms swing in opposition to leg movements.

Heel, toe, slide, and slide: Hop on the left foot while tapping the right heel to the right side. While hopping again on the left foot, swing the right foot to the front and touch the toe on the floor. Perform 2 slides to the right. Repeat the entire phrase by hopping on the right foot and sliding to the left.

LESSON FOCUS (15–20 MINUTES)

Introduce 8-Count Polka without partners.

Practice with partners and in a double circle CCW.

Instructions on record/tape/CD
Scattered formation
Scattered formation with partner
Use management games in Lesson 2 to make circle with partners.

GAME (5 MINUTES)

Long Team Cage Ball
Create two teams using management game.

DPESS page 403
Use Back-to-Back to make pairs. Identify each person by placing a hand on a different body part. People with hand on "head" go to one side to become a team. Other person goes to other side to become the other team.

EVALUATION/REVIEW AND CHEER

What steps in 8-Count Polka and Swing are similar? Were there any steps used in Aerobics that were challenging? Tomorrow, we will review all the dances you have learned so far.
Cheer: Dance, yeah!

Rhythms and Dance Lesson Plan 4

EQUIPMENT:

Continuity music CD/tape	CD/tape player
Schottische music CD/tape	1 jump rope per student
Swing music	1 long jump rope per 5 students

INSTRUCTIONAL ACTIVITIES	TEACHING HINTS

INTRODUCTORY ACTIVITY (2–3 MINUTES)

Whistle March Schottische Identify beat by saying steps out loud first.	Just like Whistle March except use Schottische music. Sound whistle to make group sizes. Change frequently.

FITNESS DEVELOPMENT (8–12 MINUTES)

Continuity Exercises Use a variety of floor strengthening exercises.	DPESS page Jump on music, floor work on 20 sec. pause in music.

LESSON FOCUS (15–20 MINUTES)

Teach East Coast Swing basic steps without partners	Scattered formation
Use whole-part-whole teaching method.	Music tape/CD has instructions listed. *
East Coast Swing with Partners	Use management, Lesson 2 to make partners. Scattered formation
Introduce turns for each partner in Swing Practice.	Demonstrate with a student partner. Demonstrate both leader (male) and follower (female) parts.

GAME (5 MINUTES)

Long Rope Routines 1 whistle = rope up and over 2 whistles = run to end of line Practice trotting and responding to whistles.	Use Whistle Mixer to create groups of 4–5. Stretch long rope out on L side of students. Add music for fun and interest.

EVALUATION/REVIEW AND CHEER

Which dance learned so far is your favorite? Why?
Was there any part of learning the Swing with turns that presented difficulty?
Cheer: 2, 4, 8, swing is great!

Rhythms and Dance Lesson Plan 5

EQUIPMENT:

Music for Cotton Eyed Joe, Sweetheart Schottische, 8 Count Polka

Music CD/tape player	1 hoop per student
Cageball	1 scooter per student

INSTRUCTIONAL ACTIVITIES	TEACHING HINTS

INTRODUCTORY ACTIVITY (2–3 MINUTES)

Hoops and Plyometrics Sound whistle to signal movement challenges.	DPESS pages 309–310

FITNESS DEVELOPMENT (8–12 MINUTES)

Circuit Training Fitness with Jog Explain each station.	DPESS page 357 Using Whistle Mixer, create groups to go to stations.

LESSON FOCUS (15–20 MINUTES)

Review Swing with turns; Cotton Eyed Joe, Sweetheart Schottische, and 8-Count Polka	Change partners frequently using management games.

GAME (5 MINUTES)

Scooter Cageball Soccer Must remain on scooter to earn goal point	DPESS page 403 Using management games, create two teams.

EVALUATION/REVIEW AND CHEER

Was there one station on the Circuit Training that was particularly challenging? Why?
Which dance is your favorite and why?
Use name of the favorite dance for today's cheer.

Rhythms and Dance Lesson Plan 6

EQUIPMENT:

Music for Leader Activity
Music for Cha Cha

Music CD/tape player

INSTRUCTIONAL ACTIVITIES	TEACHING HINTS
INTRODUCTORY ACTIVITY (2–3 MINUTES)	
New Leader Activity moving to music	DPESS 311.
Leader begins moving to beat/style of music. Others follow until you signal for a leader change.	Use management game to create groups of 3–5. Use management technique to identify first leader.
FITNESS DEVELOPMENT (8–12 MINUTES)	
12 Ways of Fitness	DPESS page 357
	Select 12 leaders.
LESSON FOCUS (15–20 MINUTES)	
Demonstrate Cha-Cha basic steps	DPESS page 480
Explain history. Show video clip of Cha-Cha.	Wright, J. *Social Dance*. Human Kinetics, 2003.
Review Swing and add the Pretzel step	Use management game to create partners. Change often.
GAME (5 MINUTES)	
Spider Tag	DPESS page 312
Select "its" and change them frequently.	Use Back-to-Back to create pairs.
EVALUATION/REVIEW AND CHEER	

Review history of Cha-cha and basic steps taught.
What was the most difficult aspect of Spider Tag?
Cheer: Cha, cha, cha, yeah!

Rhythms and Dance Lesson Plan 7

EQUIPMENT:

Music for Waltz and Swing
3 clothes pins

Music CD/tape player
Music for aerobic exercises

INSTRUCTIONAL ACTIVITIES	TEACHING HINTS
INTRODUCTORY ACTIVITY (2–3 MINUTES)	
Standing High Fives	DPESS page 314
	Use Toe-to-Toe to create partners about the same height
FITNESS DEVELOPMENT (8–12 MINUTES)	
Aerobic Workout	See Lesson 3 for details
	Scattered formation
LESSON FOCUS (15–20 MINUTES)	
Demonstrate Waltz basic steps	DPESS page 480
Explain history. Show video clip of Waltz.	Wright, J. *Social Dance*. Human Kinetics, 2003.
Teach in scattered formation, then as couples.	Use management game to create partners.
Practice Swing	Use management game to change partners.
GAME (5 MINUTES)	
Clothespin Tag	DPESS page 312
Select 2–3 "its" to begin. Change often.	
EVALUATION/REVIEW AND CHEER	

What was the hardest activity worked on today and why?
Which dance taught so far is the favorite and why?
Cheer: We love to swing!

Rhythms and Dance Lesson Plan 8

EQUIPMENT:

Music for Mirror Drill

Music for Waltz and Cha Cha

Cones to mark Fitness area

Music CD/tape player

Fitness Cookie Jar & instructions

INSTRUCTIONAL ACTIVITIES	TEACHING HINTS

INTRODUCTORY ACTIVITY (2–3 MINUTES)

Mirror Drill in Place to Music

Leader makes movements motivated by the style music.

DPESS page 313

Use Back-to-Back to create partners.

FITNESS DEVELOPMENT (8–12 MINUTES)

Fitness Cookie Jar Exchange

Play music for motivation and fun.

DPESS page 356

Place Cookie Jar in center of gym/space.

LESSON FOCUS (15–20 MINUTES)

Review Waltz steps in square and balance pattern

Practice with a partner.

Review Cha-Cha and practice

Teach the Cha-Cha chase step

Scattered formation

Use management game to create partners.

Change partners with management game.

Change partners with management game.

GAME (5 MINUTES)

Loose Caboose

Select 2 "its."

DPESS pages 313–314

Use Toe-to-Toe to make pairs of students.

EVALUATION/REVIEW AND CHEER

Were there any exercises in the Fitness Cookie Jar that were particularly difficult? Why?

Do you like the chase step? Why?

Cheer: Waltz rules!

Rhythms and Dance Lesson Plan 9

EQUIPMENT:

Cones for station markers
Challenge Course signs
Hoops, ropes, jumping boxes for Challenge activities

Music for Challenge Course, Waltz, Foxtrot
Music CD/tape player
1 basketball per relay squad

INSTRUCTIONAL ACTIVITIES	TEACHING HINTS

INTRODUCTORY ACTIVITY (2–3 MINUTES)

Running High-Fives
Create interval music CD/tape: 15 sec. on, 15 sec. off

DPESS page 314
Alternate with high and low five's.

FITNESS DEVELOPMENT (8–12 MINUTES)

Challenge Course
Have cones at each station with instructions.
Use music for fitness fun.

DPESS page 351
Using Whistle Mixer create equal groups for the stations you have created.

LESSON FOCUS (15–20 MINUTES)

Teach Waltz turns and practice Waltz patterns
Box pattern 4x, balance 4x, box 4x, 6 count turn, repeat

DPESS page 480

Teach Foxtrot basic step without partners
Teach Foxtrot with partners

Wright, J. *Social Dance.* Human Kinetics, 2003.
Use management game to create partners.

GAME (5 MINUTES)

Pass and Squat Relays
Direct relay and repeat the challenge.

DPESS pages 405–406
Using Whistle Mixer, create 5–7 equal teams.

EVALUATION/REVIEW AND CHEER

What was the most challenging activity on the Challenge Course?
What are the similarities between the Waltz and Foxtrot?
Who is the Foxtrot named after?
Cheer: Foxtrot is hot!

Rhythms and Dance Lesson Plan 10

EQUIPMENT:

Music CD/tape player
1 long jump rope per 3 students
Music for: Whistle March, Long Rope Fitness, Foxtrot, Cotton Eyed Joe, 8 Count Polka, Sweetheart Schottische, Swing, and Waltz

INSTRUCTIONAL ACTIVITIES	TEACHING HINTS

INTRODUCTORY ACTIVITY (2–3 MINUTES)

Whistle March
Sound whistle to make group sizes and return to 1 sound.

See Lesson 2 for details.

FITNESS DEVELOPMENT (8–12 MINUTES)

Long Jump Rope Fitness Routine

DPESS page 357
Use Whistle Mixer to make groups of 3.

LESSON FOCUS AND GAME (20 MINUTES)

Foxtrot patterns: Box 4x, progressive 4x, hesitation L turn; repeat with hesitation turn to R.

DPESS page 480

Review and practice all dances taught during the unit: Cotton Eyed Joe, 8-Count Polka, Sweetheart Schottische, Swing, Waltz, Foxtrot

Use management games to continually change partners.

Other dances that can be taught in unit: Miserlou, Mayim, Mayim, Polka, popular line dances.

DPESS page 480

EVALUATION/REVIEW AND CHEER

Out of all the dances learned which were the hardest? Why? Which were the most fun? Why?
Cheer: 2, 4, 6, 8, Dancing is really great!

Team Handball

OBJECTIVES:

The student will:

1. Participate in Medic Tag demonstrating knowledge of rules and good sportsmanship.
2. Demonstrate agility in Bean Bag Touch and Go.
3. Demonstrate awareness and respect for classmates during the High Fives game.
4. Participate in Circuit training, Four Corners, Astronaut Drills and Aerobics Workouts to improve overall fitness.
5. Demonstrate dribbling skills using the team handball.
6. Demonstrate the following passes: chest, bounce, overhead, one-handed shoulder/baseball, side arm, hand-off, roller, hook, jump, and the behind-the-back pass.
7. Demonstrate goal shooting using the following passes: chest, bounce, overhead, one-handed shoulder/baseball, side arm, hand-off, roller, hook, jump, and the behind-the-back pass.
8. Demonstrate goal shooting using the following techniques: Jump shot, dive shot, lob shot, penalty shot, and behind-the-back.
9. Participate in the following games demonstrating cooperation with classmates and good sportsmanship: Frisbee 21, Over and Under Ball Relay, Octopus, Chain Tag, and Over the Wall.
10. Perform the No Bounce, No Steps, and No Contact game technique demonstrated by the instructor.
11. Demonstrate passing, shooting skills when playing Sideline Team Handball.
12. Demonstrate good sportsmanship in all games.
13. Demonstrate knowledge of the rules of Team Handball while playing the game.
14. Pass a skills test demonstrating skills taught during the unit and to the satisfaction of the instructor.
15. Pass a written exam with a score of 70% or better.

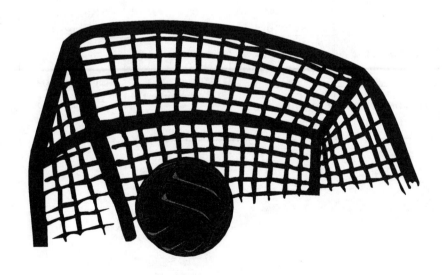

TEAM HANDBALL BLOCK PLAN
2 WEEK UNIT

Week #1	Monday	Tuesday	Wednesday	Thursday	Friday
Introductory Activity	Medic Tag	Back-to-Back Takedown	Fetch Relay	Bean Bag Touch and Go	Flash Drill
Fitness	Circuit Training	Continuity Exercises	Four Corners Fitness	Aerobics Workout	Astronaut Drills
Lesson Focus	Passing Skills	Passing Skills and Goal Shooting	Goal Shooting and Dribbling	Task Sheet Skill Review	Three Bounces, Three Steps, and No Contact
Game	Frisbee 21	Over and Under Ball Relay	No Bounce, No Step, and No Contact	Balance Tag	Octopus

Week #2	Monday	Tuesday	Wednesday	Thursday	Friday
Introductory Activity	Addition Tag	Mirror Drill in Place	Running High Fives	Mass Stand-Up	Wave Drill
Fitness	Astronaut Drills	Parachute Fitness Activities	Fitness Scavenger Hunt	Partner Racetrack Fitness	Fitness Cookie Jar Exchange
Lesson Focus	Rules of the Game	Skill and Written Test	Team Handball Tournament	Team Handball Tournament	Team Handball Tournament
Game	Sideline Team Handball	Sideline Team Handball			

Team Handball Lesson Plan 1

EQUIPMENT:

Circuit training signs for each station	1 Frisbee per 2 students
1 team handball per 2 students	CD/cassette player
	Fitness CD/tape for circuit training

INSTRUCTIONAL ACTIVITIES	TEACHING HINTS

INTRODUCTORY ACTIVITY (2–3 MINUTES)

Medic Tag

DPESS page 312
Different types of rehabilitation can be used, i.e., touch a body part or run a circle around the person.

FITNESS DEVELOPMENT (8–12 MINUTES)

Circuit Training

DPESS page 348
See Golf Unit, Lesson Plan 10 for details.

LESSON FOCUS (15–20 MINUTES)

Passing skills:
Demonstrate the following skills: chest, bounce, overhead, one-handed shoulder/baseball, side arm, hand-off and roller pass.

DPESS pages 448–450
Students work in pairs practicing each skill.

GAME (5 MINUTES)

Frisbee 21

DPESS page 465
Use a management game to create pairs of students.

EVALUATION/REVIEW AND CHEER

Discuss each pass taught and any problems students may have encountered in the learning process.
Cheer: 2, 4, 6, 8, Team handball is GREAT!

Team Handball Lesson Plan 2

EQUIPMENT:

1 rubber ball per 5–7 students for relay	CD/tape for Continuity Exercises
5 cones for station markers	CD/tape player
Station signs	Goals

INSTRUCTIONAL ACTIVITIES	TEACHING HINTS

INTRODUCTORY ACTIVITY (2–3 MINUTES)

Back-to-Back Takedown

DPESS page 401
Use Back-to-Back game to create pairs.

FITNESS DEVELOPMENT (8–12 MINUTES)

Continuity Exercises
Direct the exercises students should complete during the silence on the CD/tape: push-ups, side leg lifts, etc.

DPESS pages 349–350
Create music CD/tape to guide the continuity exercises.

LESSON FOCUS (15–20 MINUTES)

Review passing skills taught yesterday.
Teach: Hook pass, jump pass, behind-the-back pass
Demonstrate use of all passes for goal shooting.
Practice all skills in stations:
Station 1: chest, bounce, overhead, one-handed shoulder/baseball; **Station 2:** side arm, hand-off and roller pass; **Station 3:** Hook pass, jump pass, behind-the-back pass; **Stations 4 & 5:** Goal shooting using passes learned.

DPESS pages 448–450

GAME (5 MINUTES)

Over and Under Ball Relay

DPESS page 405
Use management game to make groups of 5–7 for relay.

EVALUATION/REVIEW AND CHEER

Discuss the challenges of each pass and style of goal shooting.
Cheer: Goal shooting, that's for me!

Team Handball Lesson Plan 3

EQUIPMENT:

2 foam balls per student for goal shooting	Goals
4 cones	CD/cassette player
Fitness station signs	Fitness tape/CD

INSTRUCTIONAL ACTIVITIES	TEACHING HINTS

INTRODUCTORY ACTIVITY (2–3 MINUTES)

Fetch Relay

DPESS page 406

Three students are designated as "taggers."

FITNESS DEVELOPMENT (8–12 MINUTES)

Four Corners Fitness

Post signs on cones to direct activities at each station.

DPESS page 347

Using Whistle Mixer, divide class into groups of 4.

Use music CD/tape with short silences to indicate rotation.

LESSON FOCUS (15–20 MINUTES)

Demonstrate and practice Goal Shooting Skills: jump shot, dive shot, lob shot, penalty shot, behind the back shot.

DPESS pages 448–450

No Bounce, No Steps, and No Contact Game

Use passing skills practiced in previous lessons.

Scattered formation

Use 3–5 balls in the playing area.

GAME (5 MINUTES)

Entanglement

DPESS page 407

Players may not hold both hands of the same player.

EVALUATION/REVIEW AND CHEER

Discuss the Goal Shooting skills taught.

Ask what was challenging about the No Bounce, No Steps, No Contact Game

Cheer: 1,2,3, Teamwork is G-R-E-A-T!!

Team Handball Lesson Plan 4

EQUIPMENT:

1 team handball ball per student	1 Task Sheet per person
1 bean bag per student	One clipboard and pencil per 3 students
Cassette tape/CD for fitness	CD/cassette player

INSTRUCTIONAL ACTIVITIES	TEACHING HINTS

INTRODUCTORY ACTIVITY (2–3 MINUTES)

Bean Bag Touch & Go

On signal, students move and touch as many bean bags as possible.

DPESS page 309

Scattered formation

Spread bean bags throughout the area.

Direct various locomotor movements.

FITNESS DEVELOPMENT (8–12 MINUTES)

Rhythmic Aerobic Exercise

Model the exercises to music.

DPESS page 358

Use a tape or CD for the exercises.

LESSON FOCUS (15–20 MINUTES)

Task Sheet practice reviewing skills

DPESS pages 448–450

Demonstrate skills and activities on Task Sheet.

Use Whistle Mixer to make groups of 3 for Task Sheet.

GAME (5 MINUTES)

Balance Tag

DPESS page 312

Select several "its."

EVALUATION/REVIEW AND CHEER

Review elements of skills practiced on Task Sheet.

Cheer: 1, 2, 3 we love P.E.!!

RECIPROCAL TASK SHEET: PASSING AND GOAL SHOOTING

Doer's Name: _____

Observer's Name: _____

Shagger's Name: _____

Directions: Work with a partner. Record the dates and check the appropriate response for each checkpoint for each skill listed. Have your partner check you a minimum of 4 times per skill. See your instructor for additional Task Sheets. Partner (observer)–try to observe no more than two checkpoints at one time. Shagger: retrieve the ball and return to doer. On Penalty Shot, you become the "goalie." Rotate positions after each person completes one type of shot.

(Record date of practice)	DATES							
OVERHEAD PASS TEAM HANDBALL TO TARGET 10 FEET AWAY	Yes	No	Yes	No	Yes	No	Yes	No
1. Eyes on target								
2. Steps into pass								
3. Hits target area								
4. Short of target								
OVERHEAD PASS TEAM HANDBALL TO TARGET 15 FEET AWAY								
1. Eyes on target								
2. Steps into pass								
3. Hits target area								
4. Short of target								
JUMP PASS TEAM HANDBALL TO TARGET 5 FEET AWAY								
1. Eyes on target								
2. Jumps and then passes								
3. Hits target area								
4. Short of target								
JUMP PASS TEAM HANDBALL TO TARGET 10 FEET AWAY								
1. Eyes on target								
2. Jumps and then passes								
3. Hits target area								
4. Short of target								
PENALTY SHOOTING								
1. Stand 7 meters from goal with "goalie" 3 meters ahead of you, between you and the goal								
2. Keeps foot stationary until ball thrown								
3. Releases ball in 3 seconds or less								
4. Uses side-arm throw								
5. Uses shoulder throw								

Team Handball Lesson Plan 5

EQUIPMENT:

1 double disk Frisbee per 3–4 students	4–5 team handballs
Goals	Music and player for Astronaut Drills (optional)

INSTRUCTIONAL ACTIVITIES	TEACHING HINTS

INTRODUCTORY ACTIVITY (2–3 MINUTES)

Flash Drill	DPESS pages 307–308
Teacher/leader directs movements.	Scattered formation

FITNESS DEVELOPMENT (8–12 MINUTES)

Astronaut Drills: Direct locomotor, stretching, strengthening, and aerobic exercises.	DPESS pages 348–349

LESSON FOCUS (15–20 MINUTES)

Three Bounces, Three Steps, and No Contact	DPESS pages 448–450
Behind-the-back, chess pass, and catching skills reinforced.	Scattered formation
	Students will practice all the passing techniques.
Students pass the ball rather than dribble. Five balls being tossed at the same time.	

GAME (5 MINUTES)

Double Disc Frisbees	DPESS page 469
	Create groups of 3–4 students using Whistle Mixer.

EVALUATION/REVIEW AND CHEER

Discuss the day's activities.
Cheer: 1,2,3, Teamwork is G-R-E-A-T!!

Team Handball Lesson Plan 6

EQUIPMENT:

Music CD/tape for fitness	Music player
Goals	3–5 team handballs
Rules Handout	

INSTRUCTIONAL ACTIVITIES	TEACHING HINTS

INTRODUCTORY ACTIVITY (2–3 MINUTES)

Addition Tag	DPESS page 312
	Rotate "its" several times.

FITNESS DEVELOPMENT (8–12 MINUTES)

Astronaut Drills	DPESS pages 348–349
Timed music CDs/tapes for the Grass Drills adds fun.	

LESSON FOCUS (15–20 MINUTES)

Teach the Rules of Team Handball	DPESS pages 448–450
	Instructor can create written handout for studying rules.

GAME (5 MINUTES)

Sideline Team Handball	DPESS pages 448–450
Create 2–3 games depending on class size.	Place opposite team members on each sideline.

EVALUATION/REVIEW AND CHEER

Review rules of Team Handball.
Review outcome of the Sideline Team Handball Game.
Cheer: Team handball, yeah!

Team Handball Lesson Plan 7

EQUIPMENT:

1 Written Exam per student	4–5 team handballs
1 Skill Checklist per student	Parachute

INSTRUCTIONAL ACTIVITIES	TEACHING HINTS
INTRODUCTORY ACTIVITY (2–3 MINUTES)	
Mirror Drill in Place	DPESS page 313
Identify first leader and follower. Rotate.	Use Back-to-Back to make partners.
FITNESS DEVELOPMENT (8–12 MINUTES)	
Parachute Fitness Activities	DPESS page 352
Direct locomotor movements around parachute: slide, gallop, trot, skip, etc.	Direct stretching and strengthening activities between locomotor activities: Curl-up, Toe Toucher, Sitting Leg Lifts, Sitting Pulls, Isometric exercises, etc.
LESSON FOCUS (15–20 MINUTES)	
Skill and Written Test on rules and skill techniques	Divide class in half. Half of class skill tests/other half written tests. Switch.
GAME (5 MINUTES)	
Sideline Team Handball	DPESS pages 449–450
Create different teams than used the day before.	
EVALUATION/REVIEW AND CHEER	

Review elements of exams that caused difficulty.

Students create cheer

Team Handball Lesson Plan 8

EQUIPMENT:

Interval music tape/CD	CD/cassette tape player
Team handballs for game	Laminated scavenger hunt cards

INSTRUCTIONAL ACTIVITIES	TEACHING HINTS
INTRODUCTORY ACTIVITY (2–3 MINUTES)	
Running High Fives	DPESS page 314
	Create interval music CD/tape.
FITNESS DEVELOPMENT (8–12 MINUTES)	
Fitness Scavenger Hunt	DPESS page 356
	Create small groups using Whistle Mixer.
LESSON FOCUS AND GAME COMBINED (15–20 MINUTES)	
Play Team Handball	Create Round Robin Tournament Set-Up.
EVALUATION/REVIEW AND CHEER	

Review rules of Team Handball and skills that you observed need to be worked on.

Cheer: Team handball teams rule!

Team Handball Lesson Plan 9

EQUIPMENT:

Cones for station signs

Station signs for Partner Racetrack Fitness Instructions

Music and player for fitness

Goals

Team handballs for tournament

INSTRUCTIONAL ACTIVITIES	TEACHING HINTS
INTRODUCTORY ACTIVITY (2–3 MINUTES)	
Mass Stand Up	DPESS page 406
	Create pairs using Back-to-Back technique.
FITNESS DEVELOPMENT (8–12 MINUTES)	
Partner Racetrack Fitness	DPESS pages 356–357
	Create new pairs using Elbow-to-Elbow technique.
LESSON FOCUS AND GAME COMBINED FOR TOURNAMENT (15–20 MINUTES)	
Play Team Handball	Continue Round Robin Tournament.
EVALUATION/REVIEW AND CHEER	

Review rules of Team Handball and skills that you observed need to be worked on.

Cheer: Team handball, yes!

Team Handball Lesson Plan 10

EQUIPMENT:

Cones for marking Wave Drill

Fitness Cookie Jar and instruction cards

Goals

Music for fitness

Team handballs for tournament

CD/cassette tape player

INSTRUCTIONAL ACTIVITIES	TEACHING HINTS
INTRODUCTORY ACTIVITY (2–3 MINUTES)	
Wave Drill	DPESS page 305
FITNESS DEVELOPMENT (8–12 MINUTES)	
Fitness Cookie Jar Exchange	DPESS page 356
	Students can work in pairs or alone.
LESSON FOCUS AND GAME COMBINED (20 MINUTES)	
Play Team Handball	Continue Round Robin Tournament.
EVALUATION/REVIEW AND CHEER	

Discuss results of tournament and make all students feel comfortable with the outcome. Everybody is a winner!

Students create final cheer for the unit.

Track and Field

OBJECTIVES:

The student will:
1. Participate in Spider Tag demonstrating agility and sportsmanship.
2. Demonstrate proper tagging skills and safety rules explained by the instructor during tag games.
3. Participate in the Four Corners Fitness Activities to improve her overall fitness levels.
4. Demonstrate changing from walking to sprinting quickly when given a signal by the instructor.
5. Demonstrate the ability to perform locomotor movements and change directions on command.
6. Rapidly change movements and count the number of repetitions performed during the Magic Number Challenge.
7. Participate in Continuity Exercise Activities to increase cardiovascular endurance, strength, and flexibility.
8. Participate in Circuit Training activities to improve fitness.
9. Participate in Sprinting, Running Long Jump, High Jump, Hurdling, Shot Put, Discus, Relays, and Long Distance running events using form demonstrated in class.
10. Demonstrate starting, stopping, running skills in Bean Bag Touch and Go.
11. Play "Frisbee 21" with a partner demonstrating one- and two-hand catching and throwing accuracy.
12. Demonstrate good sportsmanship and cooperation during partner and team Tug-of-War activities.

> ## TRACK AND FIELD BLOCK PLAN
> ## 2 WEEK UNIT

Week #1	Monday	Tuesday	Wednesday	Thursday	Friday
Introductory Activity	Spider Tag	Move and Change Directions	Leaping Lena with a Forward Roll	Coffee Grinder Square	Burpee Flip Drill
Fitness	Walk, Jog, Sprint	Circuit Training	Fitness Scavenger Hunt	Rope Jumping Partner Resistance Exercises	Parachute Fitness
Lesson Focus	Videotape Introduction Starts	Running Long Jump	Relays Long Jump 50 meter run	Shot Put Review other skills	High Jump Review other skills
Game	Team Tug-of-War	Triangle Plus One Tag	Frisbee 21	Mini Pyramids	Hula Hoop Pass

Week #2	Monday	Tuesday	Wednesday	Thursday	Friday
Introductory Activity	Gauntlet Run	Running High 5's	Partner Tug-of-War	Pentabridge Hustle	
Fitness	Fitness Scavenger Hunt	Continuity Exercises	Circuit Training	Four Corners & Stretching Exercises	Parachute Fitness
Lesson Focus	Discus Long Distance Running	Hurdling 7 Station Activities	Continue 7 Station Activities	Review all events for Track Meet	Class Track Meet
Game	Bean Bag Touch and Go		Frisbee Catch		

Track and Field Lesson Plan 1

EQUIPMENT:

Videotape on Track and Field   Starting blocks
Tug-of-War Rope

INSTRUCTIONAL ACTIVITIES	TEACHING HINTS

INTRODUCTORY ACTIVITY (2–3 MINUTES)

Spider Tag

DPESS page 312
Use Toe-to-Toe to make groups of 2.
Select one pair to be it.

FITNESS DEVELOPMENT (8–12 MINUTES)

Walk, Jog, Sprint
1st whistle = WALK; 2nd whistle = JOG;
3rd whistle = SPRINT
Strength Exercises: Push-ups, curl-ups, reverse push-ups, coffee grinder, etc.

DPESS page 354
Explain directions for this activity. Keep continuous movement going for good aerobic exercise.
DPESS pages 344–346

LESSON FOCUS (15–20 MINUTES)

Introduce all Track and Field events with a video.
Demonstrate starts with and without blocks.
Demonstrate techniques for crossing finish line.
High knee running
Practice starts and finishes in a 50 yard/meter race

DPESS pages 451–452
Scattered formation around demonstrator

Practice various distances running with high knees.

GAME (5 MINUTES)

Team Tug-of-War
2 teams; each team on half of the rope. On signal, teams pull rope. First team to pull others over the line wins.

DPESS page 401
Use a "Back-to-Back" to create two groups.

EVALUATION/REVIEW AND CHEER

What are the important points to remember when using starting blocks in a race?
What are some tricks you learned today about crossing the finish line?
Cheer: 1, 2, 3, I love P.E.!

Track and Field Lesson Plan 2

EQUIPMENT:

Music for Circuit Training   Music player
Station cones and instructional signs for fitness Rake for long jump
Cones to mark 50 yard/meter start and finish lines

INSTRUCTIONAL ACTIVITIES	TEACHING HINTS

INTRODUCTORY ACTIVITY (2–3 MINUTES)

Move and Change Direction
Students will jog toward each other and give high fives to the other group. Then, skip the other direction, and return giving high fives as the students meet the other group again.

DPESS page 308
Divide the students into two groups using Toe-to-Toe and then separating into two halves.

FITNESS DEVELOPMENT (8–12 MINUTES)

Circuit Training
When the music starts, each group will perform the exercise described on each labeled cone. When the music stops, students walk counter-clockwise to the next station performing arm circles.
Exercises listed at **stations**: Push-ups, knee-lifts, jumping jacks, trunk twisters, sit-ups, arm extensions, single crab kicks, arms up and down, jog in place, triceps push-ups.

DPESS page 348
Using Whistle Mixer, make groups of 5–6 to begin at each station.

Place instructions for each station on cones set-up to identify location of station. Use illustrations to assist in understanding of the activities.

INSTRUCTIONAL ACTIVITIES	TEACHING HINTS

LESSON FOCUS (15–20 MINUTES)

Running Long Jump: Demonstrate taking off board and deciding on distance to run.

Stations: 1) Running Long Jump
        2) 50 yard/meter run

DPESS pages 451–452

Use Toe-to-Toe to make partners; separate class into 2 groups, then assign to particular stations. Repeat.

GAME (5 MINUTES)

Triangle Plus 1 Tag
Person outside triangle tries to tag leader. Leader and tagger change places when tagged.

DPESS page 312
Create groups of 4 using management game. 3 make triangle formation holding hands. Select leader in group.

EVALUATION/REVIEW AND CHEER

How did you feel after running a sprinting event? What is fun about running long jump?
Who can tell us how one decides where to begin the run for the Running Long Jump Event?
Cheer: P.E., P.E., yeah, P.E.!

Track and Field Lesson Plan 3

EQUIPMENT:

Fitness Scavenger Hunt instructional cards
Batons
Cones to mark finish line
VCR player

Videotape on Relays
Rake for long jump
1 frisbee per 2 students

INSTRUCTIONAL ACTIVITIES	TEACHING HINTS

INTRODUCTORY ACTIVITY (2–3 MINUTES)

Leaping Lena with a Forward Roll
Practice forward rolls before beginning this drill.

DPESS page 306
Scattered formation

FITNESS DEVELOPMENT (8–12 MINUTES)

Fitness Scavenger Hunt
Exercises listed on scavenger cards at stations

DPESS page 356
Use Whistle Mixer to create groups of 3. Assign each group to a starting point.

LESSON FOCUS (15–20 MINUTES)

Introduce Relay Races with a videotape
Relays: Demonstrate baton hand-offs.

DPESS pages 451–452
Using batons or paper towel cardboard interior rolls, have students work in pairs practicing the hand-off.

3 Stations: Relay practice; Running Long Jump; 50 yard/meter run.
Assign students to station.

Use Whistle Mixer to create groups of 3. Then identify each person in the group differently, i.e., hand on head, hand on stomach, hand on knees. Like positions join.

GAME (5 MINUTES)

Frisbee 21
Game Rules: Throw disk back and forth; 1 point = 1 hand catch; 2 points = 2 hand catch

DPESS page 465
Use Elbow-to-Elbow to create partners. Identify student to bring Frisbee to partner.

EVALUATION/REVIEW AND CHEER

Explain the cues used when passing a baton to a teammate in a relay race.
Ask if any fitness challenges were difficult and why?
Cheer: Relays, OK!

Track and Field Lesson Plan 4

EQUIPMENT:

Cones to mark square for Coffee Grinder Square	1 individual rope per person
Tape/CD for rope jumping	Tape/CD player
Shot put	Rake for long jump
Batons	Tennis balls to use as shots

INSTRUCTIONAL ACTIVITIES	TEACHING HINTS

INTRODUCTORY ACTIVITY (2–3 MINUTES)

Coffee Grinder Square
Demonstrate Coffee Grinder activity.

DPESS page 307
Have cones set up to delineate square for activity.

FITNESS DEVELOPMENT (8–12 MINUTES)

Rope Jumping

DPESS page 309
Use music to make rope jumping more enjoyable.

Partner Resistance Exercises
Demonstrate the exercises focusing on the upper body
listed in this section of the textbook.

DPESS pages 350–351
Use Back-to-Back to create partners. Best to find partner
of equal height (and girth).

LESSON FOCUS (15–20 MINUTES)

Shot Put: Demonstrate shot put throw.
All students practice by using a tennis ball.
**4 Stations: Shot Put; Running Long Jump; 50
yard/meter run; Relay racing. Rotate.**

DPESS pages 451–452
Create safe throwing situation.
Teacher supervises Shot Put station since newest activity.
Use management game to create groups for stations.

GAME (5 MINUTES)

Mini Pyramids
On signal, student finds group and builds a group
stunt/pyramid. On next signal, pyramids safely
dismantled and students move around again until
signal.

DPESS page 399
Use Whistle Mixer to make groups of 3–5.

EVALUATION/REVIEW AND CHEER

Were any of the partner resistance exercises particularly difficult? Which ones and why?
Which Track and Field event is your favorite and why?
Cheer: 2, 4, 6, 8, Track and Field is really great!

Track and Field Lesson Plan 5

EQUIPMENT:

High Jump videotape
Station markers and instructions
Shot put
Batons
1 hula hoop per 5 students for game(s)

VCR player
High jump equipment
Rake
Parachute

INSTRUCTIONAL ACTIVITIES	TEACHING HINTS

INTRODUCTORY ACTIVITY (2–3 MINUTES)

Burpee-Flip-Drill

DPESS pages 306–307

FITNESS DEVELOPMENT (8–12 MINUTES)

Parachute Fitness Activities
Toe Touches
Explain isometrics. Lift chute taut to chin. Bend forward and touch grip to toes. Hold taut to chin.
Curl-ups: Curl-up, bend knees, lie back, extend legs. Repeat 16 times.
Dorsal Lifts

Sitting leg lift: Sit–legs under chute, on signal lift a leg off ground for 6 to 10 seconds. Try to keep leg straight. Alternate legs.
Run while holding L hand on parachute. Reverse.
Skip while holding L hand on parachute. Reverse.
Slide while holding both hands on parachute. Reverse directions.
Trot while holding L hand on parachute. Reverse.

DPESS pages 351–352
Hold parachute sitting while in extended leg position around the parachute.
16 repetitions
Hold parachute sitting position in a circle. Curl-up, bent knees. Extended legs under chute and lie on back.
Lying prone—head toward chute, arms straight, chest taut—lift arms and chest, then lower. Repeat 8 times.
When blow whistle: Freeze.
Try variation: Side leg lefts. Lie on side. Lift top leg and lower.
Stress safety.
Move around carefully.
Review good technique for each locomotor movement.

LESSON FOCUS (15–20 MINUTES)

High Jump Introduction with a videotape
Demonstrate high jump take-offs and landings.
Use a student to demonstrate if you are unable to.
5 Stations: High jump; Shot Put; Running Long Jump; 50 yard/meter run; Relay racing. Rotate.

DPESS pages 451–452
Supervise the High Jump station since that is the newest skill introduced.
Use management game to create the five groups for the stations. Assign groups to stations.

GAME (5 MINUTES)

Hula Hoop Pass
Place a hula hoop over the clasped hands of two members of each squad. On signal–pass the hoop around the circle without releasing handgrips.

DPESS page 390
Scattered–in groups
Approximately 5 per group. Members of each group hold hands.

EVALUATION/REVIEW AND CHEER

What are the important elements to remember in high jumping? Which style worked best for you and why?
What did you need to do to make the Hula Hoop pass successful?
Cheer: P.E....The BEST!

Track and Field Lesson Plan 6

EQUIPMENT:

Challenge items for Gauntlet Run: 5 hoops, 10 cones to jump over and run around, 4 long jump ropes to leap across, as if a waterbed.

Long Distance Race videotape

High jump standards, pole, landing mat

VCR player

1 bean bag per student

Shot put(s)

Discus(es)

Fitness Scavenger Hunt instructional cards

Rake for running long jump pit

INSTRUCTIONAL ACTIVITIES	TEACHING HINTS

INTRODUCTORY ACTIVITY (2–3 MINUTES)

Gauntlet Run

DPESS page 309

FITNESS DEVELOPMENT (8–12 MINUTES)

Fitness Scavenger Hunt

Exercises listed on scavenger cards at stations

DPESS page 356

Use Whistle Mixer to create groups of 3. Assign each group to a starting point.

LESSON FOCUS (15–20 MINUTES)

Introduce Long Distance races with a videotape.

Introduce Discus Throw with a videotape.

5 Stations: Discus Throw; Shot Put; Relays; Running Long Jump; High Jump. Rotate.

DPESS pages 451–452

Use management game to divide students into 5 groups.

Assign groups to stations.

Stay with Discus Throw, since that is the newest activity.

GAME (5 MINUTES)

Bean Bag Touch and Go

Indicate how many bean bags must be touched and the locomotor activity to perform.

DPESS page 309

Scattered formation with bean bags scattered on floor.

EVALUATION/REVIEW AND CHEER

Introduce upcoming class Track meet.

Cheer: We run for fun!

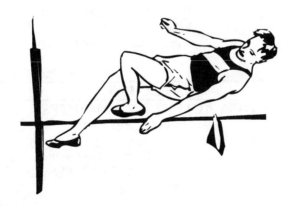

Track and Field Lesson Plan 7

EQUIPMENT:

Hurdles	Batons
Shot put	Discus
High jump equipment	Cones and signs to mark stations
Music tape/CD for Continuity Exercises	Music player

INSTRUCTIONAL ACTIVITIES	TEACHING HINTS

INTRODUCTORY ACTIVITY (2–3 MINUTES)

Running High Five's
Direct the locomotor movement to be performed.
High Five partner on signal.

DPESS page 314
Scattered formation

FITNESS DEVELOPMENT (8–12 MINUTES)

Continuity Exercises
Play CD/tape to direct activities. Have exercises to use
  during music silence well in mind.

DPESS page 349
See Golf, Lesson 1 for complete details.

LESSON FOCUS AND GAME (20 MINUTES)

Demonstrate hurdling techniques.
7 Stations: Hurdles; High jump; Shot Put; Running Long
  Jump; 50 yard/meter run; Relay racing; Discus Throw;
  Rotate.

DPESS page 451
Stay with Hurdles, since that is the newest activity.
Use management game to divide students into 7 stations.
    Rotate allowing equal time at each station today.
    Tomorrow complete rotation.

EVALUATION/REVIEW AND CHEER

Were there any fitness activities that were particularly challenging today and why?
What are the important points to remember when hurdling?
Cheer: Hurdling, we like it!

Track and Field Lesson Plan 8

EQUIPMENT:

Cones	Circuit Training Signs
Music CD/tape for fitness	Music player
Hurdles	High jump equipment
Shot put	Rake
Cones to mark start and finish lines	Batons/cardboard rolls
Discus	

INSTRUCTIONAL ACTIVITIES	TEACHING HINTS

INTRODUCTORY ACTIVITY (2–3 MINUTES)

Partner Tug-of-War Activities
Partner pulls: Side to side; Facing; Crab position hooked
  on foot; Back-to-Back

DPESS page 401

Use elbow-to-elbow to make pairs.

FITNESS DEVELOPMENT (8–12 MINUTES)

Circuit Training

DPESS page 348
See Golf, Lesson 10 for complete details.

LESSON FOCUS (15–20 MINUTES)

Continue rotations where left off yesterday.
7 Stations: Hurdles; High jump; Shot Put; Running Long
  Jump; 50 yard/meter run; Relay racing; Discus Throw;
  Rotate.

Review rotation with students from yesterday.
Stay with Hurdles, since that is the newest activity.
Use management game to divide students into 7 stations.
    Rotate allowing equal time at each station today.

INSTRUCTIONAL ACTIVITIES	TEACHING HINTS

GAME (5 MINUTES)

Frisbee Catch
Partners can keep score or just free throwing and
   catching.
1-hand catch = 2 points
2-hand catch = 1 point
Keep score to 20 points and then start over.

DPESS pages 463–465
Demonstrate throwing and catching a Frisbee.
Use Back-to-Back with a new person to create partners.
   One person puts a hand on their head. The person with
   his hand on his head is to go and get a Frisbee for the
   pair and return to the partner.

EVALUATION/REVIEW AND CHEER

What do you need to work on before the track meet?
Cheer: Track, "its" for me!

Track and Field Lesson Plan 9

EQUIPMENT:

Cones for Four Corners fitness	Signs for cones
Hurdles	Rake
High jump equipment	Shot
Discus	Music CD/tape for fitness
Music CD/cassette player	

INSTRUCTIONAL ACTIVITIES	TEACHING HINTS

INTRODUCTORY ACTIVITY (2–3 MINUTES)

Pentabridge Hustle
Demonstrate bridges and locomotor activities to be used.

DPESS page 310
Use Whistle Mixer to create groups of 5.

FITNESS DEVELOPMENT (8–12 MINUTES)

Stretching
   Lower Leg Stretch
   Achilles Tendon Stretch
   Balance Beam Stretch
   Side Leg Stretch
   Groin Stretch
   Cross-Legged Stretch
   Body Twist
   Standing Hip Bend
   Elbow Grab Stretch

DPESS pages 342–346
Place arms on wall or fence for support.

Aerobic Activity
Four Corners
   Skipping
   Jogging
   Sliding
   Running backwards
   Jumping
   Leaping
   Hopping
   Galloping

DPESS pages 347–348
Set up 4 cones creating a square. Each cone should list
   two locomotor activities.

Student executes the movement on the cone until she gets
   to next cone.

Music CD/tape directs length of aerobic exercising.

Stretch Activities
Partner Resistance Exercises

DPESS pages 343–346

LESSON FOCUS AND GAME (20 MINUTES)

Review events in tomorrows class Track Meet.
Practice events for tomorrows class Track Meet.

DPESS page 451
Allow students to pick their event(s) in which to
   participate during the meet.

EVALUATION/REVIEW AND CHEER

Are there any events you need clarified before the meet?
Cheer: I'm ready to run!

Track and Field Lesson Plan 10

EQUIPMENT:

Parachute

Music CD/cassette player

High jump equipment

Rake

Batons

Discus

Music for fitness

Magic Number Cards

3 measuring tapes for field events

Clipboards, pencils, and score sheets

Shot put

Hurdles

INSTRUCTIONAL ACTIVITIES	TEACHING HINTS

INTRODUCTORY ACTIVITY (2–3 MINUTES)

Magic Number Challenge

Hold up a card with 3 numbers on it (i.e., 8, 10, 5). The students must then perform 3 selected movements the specified number of times.

DPESS page 309

Scattered formation

Students put together a series of movements based on the magic numbers given.

Suggest movements or ask for student suggestions.

FITNESS DEVELOPMENT (8 MINUTES)

Parachute Fitness Activities

DPESS pages 351–352

See Lesson 4, Golf Unit for details.

LESSON FOCUS AND GAME (20 MINUTES)

Class Track Meet

Allow students to select the events in which to race.

Locate assistants to help with each event.

Hold several events simultaneously.

EVALUATION/REVIEW AND CHEER

Discuss results of track meet.

Introduce next unit of study.

Cheer: 2, 4, 6, 8, Track's great!

Name:_____   **Class period:**_____

TRACK AND FIELD QUIZ

1. What are the most important techniques for efficient running?
    - a. Speed
    - b. Long strides
    - c. Arm control
    - d. a & b
    - e. b & c

2. Where is the shot-put placed before the throw?
    - a. In the hand, at the neck?
    - b. Under the arm?
    - c. At waist level?
    - d. Anywhere will work

3. When handing off a baton in a relay race, the runner is responsible for telling the receiver when to begin running and place their hand out for receipt of the baton.
    - a. True/False

4. In the Running Long Jump, the jump is measured:
    - a. From their hands when landing hands are put down behind the feet
    - b. When the runner lands and puts hands down in front of their feet it is still measure from the hands
    - c. From wherever the runner requests

5. It is important to have a count or a rhythm and take-off on the correct foot when hurdling.
    - a. True/False

6. How many people participate in the 400-meter relay?
    - a. 2
    - b. 3
    - c. 4
    - d. 5

7. In a track meet, how many chances does one have in Shot Put?
    - a. 1
    - b. 2
    - c. 3

8. Name the types of jumps/landings you learned in class for High Jump:

9. In a track meet, how many chances does one have in Discus?
    - a. 1
    - b. 2
    - c. 3

10. Describe the long distance events you learned about in class.

Archery

OBJECTIVES:

The student will:

1. Eagle demonstrate agility, leg strength, and listening skills participating in the Introductory activities of Seated Rolls, Quarter, Wave Drill, Lateral Shuffle, and the Rooster Hop Drill while following the instructor's directions.
2. Increase her aerobic fitness, strength, and endurance by participating in Continuity Exercises, Four Corners, Astronaut Drill, and Circuit Training using form demonstrated by the instructor.
3. Demonstrate bracing the bow using form demonstrated by the instructor.
4. Demonstrate Nocking the Arrow, Extend and Draw, and Anchor Hold using form demonstrated by the instructor.
5. Describe the methods of aiming at the target when asked by the instructor.
6. Demonstrate Nocking the Arrow, Extend and Draw, Anchor Hold, and Release and Afterhold in a continuous manner using form demonstrated by the instructor.
7. Participate in Partner Bean Bag Challenges, Hoop Challenges demonstrating throwing and catching skills, eye-hand coordination and cooperation following the rules set by the instructor.
8. Participate in Potato Relays, Addition Tag, and Team Paper, Scissors, and Rock games demonstrating cooperation and running speed following the rules of the games.

```
┌─────────────────────────────┐
│  ARCHERY BLOCK PLAN         │
│  1 WEEK UNIT                │
└─────────────────────────────┘
```

Week #1	Monday	Tuesday	Wednesday	Thursday	Friday
Introductory Activity	Seat rolls alternated with jogging in place	Quarter Eagle	Wave Drill	Lateral Shuffle	Rooster Hop Drill
Fitness	Continuity Exercises	Four Corners	Astronaut Drills	Continuity Exercises	Circuit Training
Lesson Focus	Brace Bow Stance Nock Arrow Extend and Draw Anchor Hold Release and Afterhold	Safety Rules Review Skills Shoot 1 arrow Review skills Shoot 6 arrows at target	Review Aiming Shoot for points	Shoot for points	Shoot for points Team Shoot for points
Game	Partner Bean Bag Challenges	Hoop Challenges	Potato Relays	Addition Tag	Team Paper, Scissors, and Rock

Archery Lesson Plan 1

EQUIPMENT:

Continuity Music CD/tape	Boom box/CD player
1 bean bag per two students	1 bow per person
6 arrows per person	Targets
Cones to mark teaching areas	

INSTRUCTIONAL ACTIVITIES	TEACHING HINTS

INTRODUCTORY ACTIVITY (2–3 MINUTES)

Seat rolls alternated with jogging in place

DPESS page 304
Teacher directs movement activities.
Be sure students have safe distance between them.

FITNESS DEVELOPMENT (8–12 MINUTES)

Continuity Exercises
* Curl-ups
* Push-ups
* Reverse push-ups
* Coffee grinder
* Side leg lifts
* Stretches

DPESS pages 341–359
Student jumps rope during music. When music stops,
   teacher directs strengthening, stretching exercises.

LESSON FOCUS (15–20 MINUTES)

Brace Bow
Stance
Extend and Draw
Anchor Hold
Nock Arrow
Aiming
Release and Afterhold

DPESS pages 409–410
Step Through Method demonstrated by teacher.

Each skill demonstrated one at a time by teacher, student
   practices.

Allow student to shoot one arrow on command. Retrieve
   on command.

Safety rules must be emphasized and followed.

GAME (5 MINUTES)

Partner Bean Bag Challenges with partner
* Catch with hands.
* Catch on top of hand, palm face down.
* Catch on top of foot.
* Toss under leg.
* Toss behind back.

DPESS page 389
Bean bags spread around perimeter
Students put in groups of 2 using Toe-to-Toe
1 person picks up bean bag on command.
Offer partner tossing and catching challenges.

EVALUATION/REVIEW AND CHEER

Review procedures for Bracing Bow.
Ask student to explain aiming techniques.
What was the most challenging part of Fitness?
What were the most challenging Bean Bag challenges?
Cheer: Archery is fun!

Archery Lesson Plan 2

EQUIPMENT:

1 bow per person	6 arrows per person
Cones to mark teaching area	Four Corners signs
1 hoop per person	6 individual jump ropes for Four Corners

INSTRUCTIONAL ACTIVITIES	TEACHING HINTS

INTRODUCTORY ACTIVITY (2–3 MINUTES)

Quarter Eagle

DPESS page 304
Students in scattered formation
Teacher indicates directions for activity.

FITNESS DEVELOPMENT (8–12 MINUTES)

Four Corners
- Jump rope at one cone
- Signs indicating exercises at the other
  3 cones: Curl-ups, Sit-ups, Push-ups,
  Jumping Jacks, Reverse Push-ups

DPESS page 347
Use Whistle Mixer to divide class into 4 groups.
Assign one group per corner cone.
Alternate locomotor movement to travel to each corner:
running, leaping, sliding, and galloping.

LESSON FOCUS (15–20 MINUTES)

Safety rules
Review Skills
Shoot 1 arrow
Review skills
Shoot 6 arrows at target

DPESS pages 409–410
Practice safety instructions without arrows.
After shooting 1 arrow, retrieve the arrow and review
skills observed needing improvement.
Direct students to shoot 6 arrows and wait for retrieval
signal.
Repeat

GAME (5 MINUTES)

Hoop Challenges
- Spin hoop on end.
- Jump over spinning hoop.
- Roll hoop and go through rolling hoop.
- Circle hoop on: hand, leg, neck.
- Jump through as if rope jumping.
- Boomerang hoop
- Toss hoop in air and catch.
- Toss hoop in air, let it bounce, then catch.
- In partners, roll hoop to partner using simultaneous
  rolls.
- Toss and catch hoop with partner.

DPESS page 390
One hoop per person gotten from perimeter of room

Use Back-to-Back to make partners.

EVALUATION/REVIEW AND CHEER

How many arrows hit the target?
What do you need to work on to improve in archery?
Cheer: Archery and hoops,…. Fun!

Archery Lesson Plan 3

EQUIPMENT:

Cones to mark teaching area	1 cone/spot per person for Wave Drill
1 bow per person	6 arrows per person
Targets	Bean bags for Potato Relays

INSTRUCTIONAL ACTIVITIES	TEACHING HINTS

INTRODUCTORY ACTIVITY (2–3 MINUTES)

Wave Drill

DPESS page 305
Teacher directs the movements.
Scattered formation

FITNESS DEVELOPMENT (8–12 MINUTES)

Astronaut Drills
- Create a pattern of various locomotor movements such as hopping, running, jumping, leaping, skipping, and running on the toes.
- Perform exercises, such as arm circles, body twists, and trunk and upper-body stretches, while moving around the area.

DPESS page 341
Scattered formation

LESSON FOCUS (15–20 MINUTES)

Review aiming
Shoot for points
Archery Relay

DPESS pages 409–410
Spread out in a line double arms distance apart.
Each team has one target; each person has one arrow. The first person in line shoots and goes to end of line. All team members shoot one arrow and then the team score is tallied. The team with the highest score is the winner.

GAME (5 MINUTES)

Potato Relays
Direct student to pick up bean bag, run to other hoop and drop bean bag. Run to end of line.
Continue until all bean bags are in starting hoop.

DPESS page 405
Using Whistle Mixer, create teams of 5.
Place empty hoops 15' from each lined up team.
Place 5 bean bags in each hoop in front of each team.

EVALUATION/REVIEW AND CHEER

What is challenging about aiming for the target in archery?
What is enjoyable about archery?
Cheer: 2, 4, 6, 8, Archery is great!

Archery Lesson Plan 4

EQUIPMENT:

1 individual jump rope per person
Cones to mark teaching area
6 arrows per person
Tic-tac-toe covers for targets

Continuity exercise music CD/tape
1 bow per person
Targets

INSTRUCTIONAL ACTIVITIES	TEACHING HINTS

INTRODUCTORY ACTIVITY (2–3 MINUTES)

Lateral Shuffle

DPESS page 305
Scattered formation
Teacher directs shuffling.

FITNESS DEVELOPMENT (8–12 MINUTES)

Continuity Exercises
- Curl-ups
- Push-ups
- Reverse push-ups
- Coffee grinder
- Side leg lifts
- Stretches

DPESS page 349
Scattered formation
Ropes around perimeter of teaching area
Direct each student to pick up rope and begin jumping.
Jump when music playing.
Direct the exercises when music stops.

LESSON FOCUS (15–20 MINUTES)

Archery Aiming Review
Tic-Tac-Toe Archery game

DPESS pages 409–410
Allow student to practice shooting 2 rounds of 6 arrows.
   Retrieve arrows.
Place tic-tac-toe covers on each target.
Each student shoots 1 arrow at tic-tac-toe target.
First team to get tic-tac-toe wins.

GAME (5 MINUTES)

Addition Tag

DPESS page 407
Pick several "its" to begin the game.
Explain rules.
Repeat with new "its" when lines are long.

EVALUATION/REVIEW AND CHEER

What was the most challenging aspect of the Tic-Tac-Toe Archery Game?
What muscles were worked during Continuity Exercises?
What types of fitness were being developed during the Continuity Exercises?
Cheer: Tic-Tac-Toe, yeah!

Archery Lesson Plan 5

EQUIPMENT:

1 bow per person	6 arrows per person
1 target per 4 people	Cones to mark teaching area and 8 for Circuit Training
Circuit Training signs to attach to cones	6–7 jump ropes

INSTRUCTIONAL ACTIVITIES	TEACHING HINTS

INTRODUCTORY ACTIVITY (2–3 MINUTES)

Rooster Hop Drill

Hop 10 yards on one leg with:

(1) left hand touching the right toe, which is on the ground;

(2) right hand touching left toe on the ground;

(3) right hand touching the right toe on the ground;

(4) left hand touching the left toe on the ground.

DPESS page 305

Call out the variations for students to complete.

Ask for another suggestion from students.

FITNESS DEVELOPMENT (8–12 MINUTES)

Circuit Training

Station 1: Jump Rope

Station 2: Curl-ups

Station 3: Run in place

Station 4: Push-ups

Station 5: Reverse push-ups

Station 6: Treadmills

Station 7: Jumping Jacks

Station 8: Side leg lifts

DPESS page 349

Use Whistle Mixer to create 6 even groups.

Create a music CD/tape with 30–40 seconds for each station and 5 seconds to rotate to the next station.

Run to each new station.

Make signs for each circuit training station.

Allow enough time for students to go through circuit at least 2 times.

LESSON FOCUS (15–20 MINUTES)

Archery skill review warm-up

4 students or less per target

Allow each student to shoot 6 arrows.

Team Maximum Point Game

Each team tries to accumulate the most points

On 3 rounds of shooting.

Teacher says go.

Each person in team shoots 6 arrows.

Count points using points in textbook.

Team remembers points.

Shoot two more rounds.

Team with most points is team winner.

GAME (5 MINUTES)

Team Paper, Scissors, and Rock

Two teams huddle on their half of the field. Each team decides which of the three choices (paper, scissors, or rock) they will reveal when the game begins. The teams come out to midfield line and face each other with one foot on the line. The teacher counts: "one, two, three, show." The teams reveal their group decision on the word "show" with the appropriate hand signal and the winning team chases the losing team and tries to tag them before they reach a safe zone. If tagged, they must switch teams.

DPESS page 407

Use Toe-to-Toe technique; then split class into 2 teams.

Set boundaries with cones. Safe zone is about 10–20 yards from the starting line.

The teacher counts: "one, two, three, show."

EVALUATION/REVIEW AND CHEER

What have you enjoyed the most about this Archery Unit?

What muscle groups were worked during fitness today?

Cheer: 2, 4, 6, 8 Archery is great!

Bowling

OBJECTIVES:

The student will:
1. Participate in the Rubber Band Introductory Activity demonstrating agility, locomotor movements and the ability to follow instructions given by the instructor.
2. Demonstrate agility and follow the movements and instructions of the leader during the Introductory Activities: Wave Drill and Square Drill.
3. Demonstrate fitness activities including sit-ups, push-ups, crab-kicks, etc. during the 12 Ways of Fitness.
4. Participate in Continuity Exercises demonstrating basic jump roping skills, strength, agility, rhythm and flexibility while following the directions given by the instructor.
5. Follow the directions while participating in Circuit Training Fitness activities as directed by the instructor.
6. Demonstrate the grip, stance, approach and delivery of the bowling ball as demonstrated by the instructor.
7. Demonstrate the 4-Step Approach and Delivery of the bowling ball using the form modeled by the instructor.
8. Practice bowling skills directed by the instructor on the indoor carpet using form demonstrated by the instructor.
9. Illustrate proper etiquette and scoring skills by completing a scoring worksheet and participating in etiquette discussions.
10. Demonstrate proper etiquette while on the field trip to the Bowling Center.
11. Participate in the Bowling Pin Relay demonstrating agility and teamwork while following the rules of the game.
12. Participate in the Over and Under Ball Relay using form demonstrated and following the rules established by the instructor.
13. Participate in the Fetch Relay demonstrating agility and teamwork while following the rules of the game.
14. Participate in the game of Addition Tag and True or False Partner Tag demonstrating teamwork and cooperation while following the rules of the game.
15. Play a game of Red Pin Bowling using form and rules demonstrated by the instructor.
16. Play a game of Bowling at the Bowling Center using appropriate game rules, etiquette, courtesy, and appropriate behavior for a field trip as established by the instructor.

BOWLING BLOCK PLAN
1 WEEK UNIT

Week #1	Monday	Tuesday	Wednesday	Thursday	Friday
Introductory Activity	Rubber Band	Wave Drill	Square Drill	All Fours Circle	Trip to Bowling Center for Bowling
Fitness	The 12 Ways of Fitness	Continuity Exercises	Circuit Training Fitness with a Jog	Continuity Exercises	
Lesson Focus	Grip, Stance, Approach, 1-Step Delivery of Ball	Aim 4-Step Approach and Delivery of ball	Rules Etiquette Scoring Practice Bowling	Practice Bowling and Scoring Play Red Pin	
Game	Bowling Pin Relay	Over and Under Ball Relay	True or False Partner Tag	Addition Tag	

Bowling Lesson Plan 1

EQUIPMENT:

Fitness Station signs

Carpet for bowling lane

1 bowling ball per station. No more than 4–5 students per station.

Bowling demonstration instructional CD/tape

Bowling pins: 4 per group of 4–5 students

INSTRUCTIONAL ACTIVITIES	TEACHING HINTS
INTRODUCTORY ACTIVITY (2–3 MINUTES)	
Rubber Band	DPESS page 309
FITNESS DEVELOPMENT (8–12 MINUTES)	
The 12 Ways of Fitness	DPESS page 357
	Create groups of 12 students.
	Have station descriptions printed for each station.
LESSON FOCUS (15–20 MINUTES)	
Play an instructional videotape of Bowling.	
Demonstrate the grip and stance.	DPESS page 460
Demonstrate a one-step plus delivery of ball.	Students practice following each demonstration.
	Using Whistle Mixer, divide students into appropriate sized groups.
	Divide students so half are at one end of the carpet facing the rest of their group.
	Students practice and rotate roles: Bowler, retriever/bowler, people on the sides of the gutters to retrieve balls.
GAME (5 MINUTES)	
Bowling Pin Relay	DPESS page 462
EVALUATION/REVIEW AND CHEER	
Review techniques of grip, stance, and delivery by asking questions such as: Describe the one-step delivery of the bowling ball. Show me the proper grip and stance of a bowling ball.	
Discuss fitness challenge stations and ask what needs to be worked on in the future.	
Cheer: 2, 4, 6, 8, Bowling makes me feel great!	

Bowling Lesson Plan 2

EQUIPMENT:

Perimeter cones

Continuity Music CD/tape

One bowling ball per carpet

Rubber ball per group of 6–10 students for relay game

Obstacle boundary cone for students to shuffle over

One individual jump rope per person

Bowling pins per carpet

INSTRUCTIONAL ACTIVITIES	TEACHING HINTS
INTRODUCTORY ACTIVITY (2–3 MINUTES)	
Wave Drill	DPESS page 305
	Give hand signals for the direction students will shuffle

INSTRUCTIONAL ACTIVITIES	TEACHING HINTS

FITNESS DEVELOPMENT (8–12 MINUTES)

Continuity Exercises

Include during music silence: curl-ups, reverse push-ups, coffee grinder, stretches, leg-lifts, etc.

DPESS page 349
Set jump ropes around perimeter of teaching area. One rope per student.
Directions: When music is on, student jumps rope; when there is a sound silence, follow the instructor through a variety of strength, agility, and stretching activities.

LESSON FOCUS (15–20 MINUTES)

Demonstrate:
- Aiming the ball
- 4-Step Approach and Delivery of bowling ball

DPESS page 461
Student practices Aiming.
Student practices the 4-Step Approach without a ball.
Student practices the 4-Step Approach and delivery of the bowling ball on the carpeted alley.

GAME (5 MINUTES)

Over and Under Ball Relay

DPESS page 368
Create teams using Whistle Mixer.
Place teams on spots 10–15' apart.
Ball begins at the front of the line.
Pass ball overhead and under legs.
Last person runs to front.

EVALUATION/REVIEW AND CHEER

Tell me the cues I explained about aiming a ball.
Show me the 4-Step Approach in Bowling.
Show me the 4-Step Approach and delivery of the ball.
Where should the thumb be facing when the ball is released?
What was the most challenging part of the fitness today?
Cheer: Bowling makes me feel great!

Bowling Lesson Plan 3

EQUIPMENT:

4 perimeter cones
Music CD/tape
Rules handout
Bowling carpets, 10 pins and 2 balls for each station

Cones to put Circuit Training Signs onto
Boom box
Scoring forms

INSTRUCTIONAL ACTIVITIES	TEACHING HINTS

INTRODUCTORY ACTIVITY (2–3 MINUTES)

Square Drill

DPESS page 305
Mark square off with cones.
Students spread out in center and watch for teacher to indicate direction to shuffle around the square.

FITNESS DEVELOPMENT (8–12 MINUTES)

Circuit Training Fitness with a Jog

DPESS page 359
Create music CD/tape to direct the changing of fitness activities. CD/tape should have 30 seconds of music and 10 seconds of silence.
Direct changing stations during the silence. Students can also jog around the area before progressing to the next station.

INSTRUCTIONAL ACTIVITIES	TEACHING HINTS

LESSON FOCUS (15–20 MINUTES)

DPESS, page 463

Explain rules of the game.
Etiquette to use at a bowling center
Scoring: Manual and electronic
Practice Bowling on carpets

Create rules of the game Handout. While some students bowl, go over the Handout with the others. Reverse activities.
Go over scoring with a small group of the class while others practice bowling skills. Reverse the activities.
Obtain copies of score sheets from a Bowling Center for students to practice on while playing.

GAME (5 MINUTES)

True or False Partner Tag

DPESS, page 312

EVALUATION/REVIEW AND CHEER

Can you explain how a strike is scored?
How many times can a person roll the ball when it is her turn?
How is a strike marked on the score sheet?
What part of fitness was the most challenging today?
Cheer: Strikes and spares win the game, yeah!

Bowling Lesson Plan 4

EQUIPMENT:

Music tape/CD for Continuity Exercises	CD/cassette player
1 set of bowling pins per group of 4 students	1 red pin per group

INSTRUCTIONAL ACTIVITIES	TEACHING HINTS

INTRODUCTORY ACTIVITY (2–3 MINUTES)

All Fours Circle

DPESS page 307

FITNESS DEVELOPMENT (8–12 MINUTES)

Continuity Exercises

During music silence, direct: curl-ups, reverse push-ups, coffee grinder, stretches, leg-lifts, etc.

DPESS page 349

Set jump ropes around perimeter of teaching area. One rope per student.
Directions: When music is on, student jumps rope; when there is a sound silence, follow the instructor through a variety of strength, agility, and stretching activities.

LESSON FOCUS (15–20 MINUTES)

Practice Bowling and Scoring (review)
Play Red Pin

DPESS pages 462–463

Using Whistle Mixer, divide students into appropriate groups based on your equipment.

GAME (5 MINUTES)

Addition Tag

DPESS page 312

Select 2–3 "its" for the game.
Change after one group has a long line of students.

EVALUATION/REVIEW AND CHEER

What was the most challenging activity during fitness?
What body parts were used today during fitness?
How has your bowling improved?
Are you ready to go to the bowling center tomorrow?
Cheer: Bowling … can't wait!

Bowling Lesson Plan 5

EQUIPMENT:

Transportation   Money for Bowling Center fees
Clean socks

INSTRUCTIONAL ACTIVITIES	TEACHING HINTS
Field Trip to a Bowling Center	Remind students on the bus of proper behavior.
	Divide groups up for Bowling Center lanes before you arrive.
	Demonstrate electronic scoring.
	Supervise all students playing at the Center.
	Have students thank the Bowling Center.

EVALUATION/REVIEW AND CHEER

What was the most fun today?
Will you bowl on your own now that you've come to a
  center?
What skills did you discover you need to work on?
Cheer: Bowling's GREAT!

Frisbee Golf

OBJECTIVES:

The student will:
1. Participate in Vanishing Bean Bags and Blob Tag in a cooperative manner.
2. Form a variety of pyramids and demonstrate the proper points of support while performing them.
3. Participate in Four Corners activities to improve fitness.
4. Participate in Hexagon Hustle to improve fitness.
5. Participate in Aerobic Workouts to improve overall fitness.
6. Demonstrate the proper grip of a Frisbee.
7. Demonstrate the difference between Walk-Jog-Sprint in the fitness activity.
8. Cooperatively work with teammates during the Frisbee activities.
9. Execute Frisbee throwing using form demonstrated by the instructor.
10. Pass the Frisbee into a hoop with the right and left hands.
11. Trap a Frisbee with both hands after it has been tossed from 10 feet.
12. Participate in Potato Relays.
13. Demonstrate respect of a partner while Wand Wrestling.
14. Demonstrate rules of safety while participating in Team Tug-of-War.
15. Play group tag demonstrating sportsmanship.

FRISBEE GOLF BLOCK PLAN
1 WEEK UNIT

Week #1	Monday	Tuesday	Wednesday	Thursday	Friday
Introductory Activity	Vanishing Bean Bags	Move & Assume Pose	Blob Tag	Burpee Flip Drill	Mini Pyramid
Fitness	Aerobic Workouts	Hexagon Hustle	Walk-Jog-Sprint	Fitness Scavenger Hunt	Four Corners
Lesson Focus	Frisbee Passing and Catching	Roller Toss Frisbee Keep Away	Tee Off to Target Putting	Throwing Accuracy Rules of Frisbee Golf	Frisbee Golf
Game	Potato Relays	Wand Wrestling	Team Tug-of-War	Frisbee 21	

Frisbee Golf Lesson Plan 1

EQUIPMENT:

1 bean bag per student
25 hula hoops

Aerobic music & music player
1 frisbee per student

INSTRUCTIONAL ACTIVITIES	TEACHING HINTS

INTRODUCTORY ACTIVITY (2–3 MINUTES)

Vanishing Bean Bags   DPESS page 309

FITNESS DEVELOPMENT (8–12 MINUTES)

Aerobic Workouts

Jump in place 8x; Walk in place 16x; Run in place 8x; Perform 8 jumping jacks; 8 Mountain climbers; Jump Twist 8x. Perform 4 slides each side; Hit side of thighs with straight arms; Run while lifting feet high in the rear; Lift knees high in front while running and clapping 8x; Repeat whole phrase; Hop swing alternate legs 8x; Charleston bounce step (Step L, kick R foot forward, step back R and touch L toe back. Repeat 8 times). Reverse; Schottische 8x; Grapevine both directions 4x; Walk in place 8x; Leg and upper body stretches; Run 3x in place then hop and clap. Alternate 4x; Swing arms overhead while jump-twisting to cool down.

DPESS page 358
Casten, C. and Jordan, P. *Aerobics Today, 2nd Ed.*
Wadsworth, 2002.
Use music appropriate for Aerobic Exercise.

LESSON FOCUS (15–20 MINUTES)

Frisbee Hoops Toss

Demonstrate passing a Frisbee with each hand using sidearm, backhand and across the chest throws.

Teach how to aim a Frisbee using different throws.

DPESS pages 463–465
Direct each student to stand next to a Frisbee.

Create groups of 2 using Back-to-Back for passing practice and the "Tossing into Hoops" activity.

Frisbee Catch

Demonstrate passing and catching methods and styles.

DPESS pages 464–465
Students pass and catch at graduated distances: 5'–10'.

GAME (5 MINUTES)

Potato Relays

Use hoops and bean bags for the relay.

DPESS page 405
Use Whistle Mixer/Squads to create teams.

EVALUATION/REVIEW AND CHEER

Discuss the successes and difficulties with passing and catching the Frisbee.
Cheer: 2, 4, 6, 8, Playing frisbee is really great!

Frisbee Golf Lesson Plan 2

EQUIPMENT:

25 hula hoops for targets
8 cones
1 wand per 2 students

1 frisbee per student
CD/tape for fitness
CD/tape player

INSTRUCTIONAL ACTIVITIES	TEACHING HINTS

INTRODUCTORY ACTIVITY (2–3 MINUTES)

Move and Quickly Stop Assuming Pose

Students perform locomotor movements. Freeze on signal and assume various balancing poses on various body parts.

DPESS page 308
Scattered formation

FITNESS DEVELOPMENT (8–12 MINUTES)

Hexagon Hustle
Use music for activity as students hustle around perimeter cones. During music silence perform flexibility, stretching, and strengthening activities.

DPESS page 348 (a form of Circuit Training)
Make a hexagon with 6 cones. Assign groups to begin at each cone. Place sign with directions on both sides of cone. The signs identify the hustle activity.

LESSON FOCUS (15–20 MINUTES)

Roller Toss: Stance; Arm movement; Aiming.
Demonstrate rolling Frisbee on ground to target.
Demonstrate proper posture.
Demonstrate swing technique.

DPESS pages 463–464
Use Back-to-Back to get students into groups of two.
Create an imaginary line from the position to the target.
Students practice rolling the Frisbee 10 times each, then change roles. Repeat.
Use Whistle Mixer to create groups of 3.

Frisbee Keep Away
Students toss Frisbee to each other trying to keep it away from the player standing in the middle.

Change places when center player catches the Frisbee.

GAME (5 MINUTES)

Wand Wrestling

DPESS page 402
Create pairs using Back-to-Back.

EVALUATION/REVIEW AND CHEER

Discuss elements of Frisbee rolling, passing, catching that may have caused difficulties.
Discuss the challenges of Wand Wrestling.
Cheer: We love to play frisbee!

Frisbee Golf Lesson Plan 3

EQUIPMENT:
1 bean bag per student
25 hula hoops

8 cones, 6 hoops, 6 flags, 4 long ropes
40 frisbees

INSTRUCTIONAL ACTIVITIES	TEACHING HINTS

INTRODUCTORY ACTIVITY (2–3 MINUTES)

Blob Tag
When tagged hold hands. Only those at end of chain are eligible to tag.

DPESS page 312
Select 2 or 3 "its."

FITNESS DEVELOPMENT (8–12 MINUTES)

Walk, Jog, Sprint
1st whistle = WALK; 2nd whistle = JOG;
3rd whistle = SPRINT

DPESS page 354

Strength Exercises: Push-ups, curl-ups, reverse push-ups, coffee grinder, etc.

DPESS pages 344–345

LESSON FOCUS (15–20 MINUTES)

Tee Off Target
Left and right hand throw; Full swing review;
Aiming technique
Putt Throw
Demonstrate and practice skills

DPESS pages 463–466
Create a "Tee" area.
Set up targets to hit towards: hoops; flags; ropes; cones.
DPESS page 467
10 feet from targets

GAME (5 MINUTES)

Team Tug-of-War
2 teams; each team on half of the rope. On signal, teams pull rope. First team to pull others over the line wins.

DPESS page 401
Use a "Back-to-Back" to create two groups.

EVALUATION/REVIEW AND CHEER

Discuss elements of Teeing Off and Putting.
Discuss elements needed for Team Tug-of-War to be successful and safe.
Cheer: Fun, fun, fun … Frisbee's really fun!

Frisbee Golf Lesson Plan 4

EQUIPMENT:

25 hula hoops
10 cones

1 frisbee per student
Fitness Scavenger cards

INSTRUCTIONAL ACTIVITIES	TEACHING HINTS

INTRODUCTORY ACTIVITY (2–3 MINUTES)

Burpee-Flip-Drill — DPESS pages 306–307

FITNESS DEVELOPMENT (8–12 MINUTES)

Fitness Scavenger Hunt
Exercises listed on scavenger cards at stations.

DPESS page 356
Use Whistle Mixer to create groups of 3. Assign each group to a starting point.

LESSON FOCUS (15 MINUTES)

Distance and Accuracy Throwing
Demonstrate proper form for: Thumber throw, overhand wrist flips. Review form for: underhand, side arm, and backhand.

DPESS page 465
Use management skills to divide the class in half. Use Toe-to-Toe to group students.
Direct student to take equipment needed to their area.

Throw into hoops on the ground

Set hoops up at 5', 10', and 20' areas.

Rules of Frisbee Golf

DPESS pages 466–467

GAME (5–10 MINUTES)

Frisbee 21
Game Rules: Throw disk back and forth; 1 point = 1 hand catch; 2 points = 2 hand catch

DPESS page 465
Use Elbow-to-Elbow to create partners. Identify student to bring Frisbee to partner.

EVALUATION/REVIEW AND CHEER

Discuss elements that make throwing, catching, and Frisbee 21 successful.
Cheer: Hoorah! Hoorah! Frisbee is the best!

Frisbee Golf Lesson Plan 5

EQUIPMENT:

15 cones
CD/tape for fitness

30 fleece balls
1 frisbee per student
CD/tape player

INSTRUCTIONAL ACTIVITIES	TEACHING HINTS

INTRODUCTORY ACTIVITY (2–3 MINUTES)

Mini Pyramids
On signal, student finds a group to build a partner stunt/pyramid. On next signal, pyramids safely dismantled and students move around again until signal.

DPESS page 400
Scattered formation.
Using Whistle Mixer, create groups of 3–5.

FITNESS DEVELOPMENT (8–12 MINUTES)

Four Corners
Locomotor aerobic activities to direct: Skipping; Jogging; Sliding; Running backwards; Jumping; Leaping; Hopping; Galloping. Follow aerobic work with stretching activities: Lower leg stretch; Achilles tendon stretch; Balance beam stretch; Groin stretch; Cross-legged stretch; twisting; Standing hip bend; etc.

DPESS page 399
Place arms on wall or fence for support.
Music directs length of exercise activities.
Set up 4 cones creating a square.
Each cone should list 2–3 locomotor activities.
Student executes the movement on the cone until she/he gets to the next cone.

LESSON FOCUS AND GAME (20 MINUTES)

Play Frisbee Golf
Set up Frisbee Golf Course with flags, hoops and cones.

DPESS pages 466–467
Using Whistle Mixer, divide class into several teams.

EVALUATION/REVIEW AND CHEER

Discuss elements and challenges of the Frisbee Golf Game.
Cheer: 2, 4, 6, 8, Frisbee is always fun!

FRISBEE GOLF QUIZ

TRUE/FALSE: Fill in an A on the answer sheet if the answer is **true** and B if the answer is **false.**

1. A Frisbee is said to have "hooked" when it curves off to the right.
2. The throwing hand should be pointing to the target at the end of the follow through.
3. After the drive, the person whose Frisbee is farthest from the hole should play first.
4. One should not play an approach shot to the green until the players ahead have left it.
5. When even a player hits a ball that he feels may hit or come close to another person he should yell "fore."

MULTIPLE CHOICE:
Select the best answer and fill in the letter on your answer sheet.

1. What term is used to refer to the first shot on each hole?
    a. The drive
    b. The pitch and run
    c. The approach

2. In order to best sight the line of a putt, how should a player stand?
    a. With the eyes to the right of the Frisbee
    b. Eyes directly over the Frisbee
    c. With the eyes to the left of the Frisbee

3. What is the last stroke necessary to reach the green called?
    a. Approach shot
    b. The drive
    c. The putt
    d. The bomb

4. Which is common to all stances?
    a. Weight on toes
    b. Weight back toward heels
    c. Weight on whole foot
    d. No weight on feet

5. What term refers to the position of the Frisbee on the ground?
    a. Flat
    b. Lie
    c. Set
    d. Bummer

Jogging

OBJECTIVES:

The student will:

1. Perform Snowball Tag, Bean Bag Touch and Go, Group Tag, Loose Caboose demonstrating jogging skills, agility, cooperation skills, and following the rules established by the instructor.
2. Execute the Mirroring activity following the movement of her partner, cooperation, and the ability to follow the instructions established by the instructor.
3. Perform the following fitness activities using skills demonstrated by the instructor and following the instructions as stated: Parachute Rhythmic Aerobic Activities; Exercise to Music; Continuity Exercises; Challenge Course and Four Corners Movement.
4. Demonstrate walk-jog-sprint skills during the lesson focus using form demonstrated by the instructor.
5. Perform the Orienteering Run during the lesson focus following the rules established by the instructor.
6. Participate during the Game portion of class in Frisbee 21, Musical Hoops, Triangle Plus One Tag, Parachute activities and Wheel Barrow Relay using form and instructions established by the teacher.

$$\boxed{\begin{array}{c} \textbf{JOGGING BLOCK PLAN} \\ \textbf{1 WEEK UNIT} \end{array}}$$

Week #1	Monday	Tuesday	Wednesday	Thursday	Friday
Introductory Activity	Snowball Tag	Bean Bag Touch and Go	Mirroring	Group Tag	Loose Caboose
Fitness	Parachute Rhythmic Aerobic Activities	Exercise to Music	Continuity Exercises	Challenge Course	Four Corners Movement
Lesson Focus	Introduction to running form Walk-jog-walk	Walk-Jog-Sprint	Orienteering Run	Cross Country Jog-Walk	Cross Country Jog-Walk
Game	Frisbee 21	Musical Hoops	Triangle Plus One Tag	Parachute Activities	Wheel Barrow Relay

Jogging Lesson Plan 1

EQUIPMENT:
Music CD/tape for fitness   Boom box
1 frisbee per 2 people

INSTRUCTIONAL ACTIVITIES	TEACHING HINTS

INTRODUCTORY ACTIVITY (2–3 MINUTES)

Snowball Tag

DPESS page 309
Select 2 "its."

FITNESS DEVELOPMENT (8–12 MINUTES)

Parachute Rhythmic Aerobic Activities

DPESS page 351
Create a CD/tape 8 minutes long.
Skip both directions, slide both directions, run both
directions, jump to center, hop backward, lift parachute
overhead, lower parachute to toes, repeat above, run
CW with, chute overhead, make a dome.

LESSON FOCUS (15–20 MINUTES)

Introduction to running form
Walk-jog-walk

DPESS page 474
Identify distance student should walk, jog, walk.
Allow students to talk quietly while active.
Explain that jogging is noncompetitive.
Personal improvement is the goal.

GAME (5 MINUTES)

Frisbee 21

DPESS page 465
Use Back-to-Back to create groups of 2.

EVALUATION/REVIEW AND CHEER

What muscles were worked during fitness?
What are the main points in correct running form?
What is the goal of jogging?
Cheer: 2,4,6, 8, If I jog I'll feel great!

Jogging Lesson Plan 2

EQUIPMENT:
1 bean bag per person
1 hoop per person

Music for musical hoops
Boom box

INSTRUCTIONAL ACTIVITIES	TEACHING HINTS

INTRODUCTORY ACTIVITY (2–3 MINUTES)

Bean Bag Touch and Go

DPESS page 309
Scattered formation
On signal, students run to a bean bag, touch it, and resume running. Variation: specify the color of the bean bag and the body part the touch must be made with.

FITNESS DEVELOPMENT (8–12 MINUTES)

Astronaut Drills
- Walk throughout the area.
- Run and hurdle.
- Stop, perform push-ups.
- Walk and do arm circles.
- Crab-walk
- Walk and stretch.
- Bend and stretch.
- Stop and perform curl-ups.
- Stop, find a friend, and perform partner strength exercises.

DPESS page 349
Scattered formation
Students move throughout the area and perform as many exercises as possible.

LESSON FOCUS (15–20 MINUTES)

Walk-Jog-Sprint

DPESS page 474
.This is a continuous movement activity in which the teacher controls the speed of movement with a whistle signal. Three whistles mean sprint, two mean jog, and one means walk. The students start by walking around a given area. The teacher then alternates the periods of walking, jogging, sprinting, for a number of minutes or for a given distance. It is important to progressively build up the time or distance.

GAME (5 MINUTES)

Musical Hoops

DPESS page 310
1 hoop per student on floor
Players are given a locomotor movement to do around the hoops while the music is played. When the music stops, the students step inside an empty hoop. Remove 1 hoop each round.

EVALUATION/REVIEW AND CHEER

What muscles and body parts were used in Fitness today?
Are you finding it easier today to jog?
Cheer: 1,2,3, Jogging is good for me!

Jogging Lesson Plan 3

EQUIPMENT:

Boom box

Continuity exercise music CD/tape

1 jump rope per person

Orienteering map of school area that you make

INSTRUCTIONAL ACTIVITIES	TEACHING HINTS

INTRODUCTORY ACTIVITY (2–3 MINUTES)

Mirroring

DPESS page 313

Use Toe-to-Toe to make groups of two.

One person is the leader and makes a quick movement with the hands, head, legs, or body. The partner tries to be a mirror and perform the exact movement.

FITNESS DEVELOPMENT (8–12 MINUTES)

Continuity Exercises

These exercises are a type of interval training. Create a CD/cassette tape with 30–35 seconds of music and 20 seconds of silence. During the music, the students will jump rope.

DPESS page 349

Scattered formation

Direct students to pick up a rope and move to their own space.

During each silence instruct the students to do a different exercise, i.e., push-ups; curl-ups; reverse push-ups; side leg lifts on each side; coffee grinder, arm circling, crab walks forward and backward, etc.

1 individual jump rope per student

When the music resumes, the students jump rope again.

LESSON FOCUS (15–20 MINUTES)

Orienteering Run

DPESS page 475

Use Back-to-Back to make groups of 2.

Distribute Orienteering run map of school area.

Draw map with 10 checkpoints.

Emphasize running from point to point on the school grounds. Each checkpoint has a secret clue, such as a letter, word, color, or instructions on where to go next. Students can work with a partner.

GAME (5 MINUTES)

Triangle Plus One Tag

DPESS page 312

Use Whistle Mixer to make groups of 4.

3 in triangle formation holding hands. One on outside of triangle. Person outside triangle tries to tag leader.

Leader and tagger change places when tagged.

Triangle rotates to avoid being tagged.

EVALUATION/REVIEW AND CHEER

What was the focus of the fitness activity today?

What was the most interesting part of the Orienteering Run?

Cheer: Jogging makes me feel so great, yeah!

Jogging Lesson Plan 4

EQUIPMENT:

Music CD/tape for challenge course

Challenge Course signs

Parachute

Cones to delineate teaching area

Cones for challenge course signs

6 foam balls

INSTRUCTIONAL ACTIVITIES	TEACHING HINTS

INTRODUCTORY ACTIVITY (2–3 MINUTES)

Group Tag

DPESS page 407

Scattered formation

Designate 3 students as "it." They try and tag others, if
tagged become a tagger. Last one not tagged wins.

FITNESS DEVELOPMENT (8–12 MINUTES)

Challenge Course

Agility run between and around cones.

Hop through hula hoops.

Hurdle over 3 benches set up with space between them.

Leap/jump over ropes set up on a diagonal.

Crab walk (feet first) length of a mat.

Log roll down the length of a mat.

Jump rope 10 times using "Hot Peppers."

Skip around cones set up.

Crab walk (hands first) between markers/cones.

Curl-ups

Jog around the area.

Push-ups

Stretching activities

DPESS page 351

Use Whistle Mixer to create groups to begin at designated
stations.

Make signs for movement at each station.

Use music to motivate moving through obstacle course.
Make a tape/CD with 30 seconds of music followed by
5 seconds of silence to change stations. Make the
CD/tape for a total of 8–9 minutes of playing time.

LESSON FOCUS (15–20 MINUTES)

Cross Country Jog-Walk

DPESS page 474

Students work at their own pace.

Map out a cross-country course around the school
grounds. Ask the students to time themselves on the
jog-walk.

GAME (5 MINUTES)

Parachute Activities

DPESS page 351

Delineate two teams around the chute.

Use two to six balls. Try to bounce the balls off the
opponents' side, scoring one point for each ball.

EVALUATION/REVIEW AND CHEER

What were the most challenging fitness activities today?

How did you feel about the jog-walk today?

Remember your time for tomorrow.

Cheer: Cross-country jogging is great, yeah!

Jogging Lesson Plan 5

EQUIPMENT:

Four Corners signs

Cones to delineate teaching area

4 cones for fitness

Map of cross-country course

INSTRUCTIONAL ACTIVITIES	TEACHING HINTS

INTRODUCTORY ACTIVITY (2–3 MINUTES)

Loose Caboose

Designate one student as the "loose caboose."

Loose caboose students try to hook onto a train.

DPESS page 313

Use Whistle Mixer to make groups of 3–4.

Create several "trains."

Trains are formed by 3–4 students standing in column formation with each person placing their hands on the waist of the person in front of them.

FITNESS DEVELOPMENT (8–12 MINUTES)

Four Corners

Outline a large rectangle with four cones. Place signs with tasks on both sides of the cones. Students move around the outside of the rectangle and change their movement pattern as they approach a corner sign.

The following movement tasks are suggested:

1. Jogging
2. Skipping/Jumping/Hopping
3. Sliding/Galloping
4. Abdominal strengthening exercises
5. Upper body strengthening exercises
6. Side leg work
7. Full body stretches

DPESS page 347, 309

Use Whistle Mixer to create 4 equal groups.

Assign each group a corner to begin at.

LESSON FOCUS (15–20 MINUTES)

Cross Country Jog-Walk

DPESS page 474

Students work at their own pace.

Use the same map as yesterday.

Ask the students to time themselves on the jog-walk and see if they improved today.

GAME (5 MINUTES)

Wheel Barrow Relay

Use the wheelbarrow position as the means of locomotion.

DPESS page 405

Use Whistle Mixer to create even groups.

Within each group do Back-to-Back.

Identify one as the first wheel barrow.

Line each group up.

Have relay race in wheelbarrow position.

Rotate positions before each team is done.

EVALUATION/REVIEW AND CHEER

How was jogging the course today versus yesterday?

What area of fitness does jogging improve?

Cheer: Wheel barrow relays are great!

Rock Climbing

OBJECTIVES:

The student will:
1. Participate in the Coffee Grinder Square as an Introductory Activity.
2. Participate in Continuity Exercises to improve fitness.
3. Participate in the PACER running activity to improve cardiovascular endurance.
4. Participate in parachute activities for fitness.
5. Participate in a rope jumping fitness activity.
6. Demonstrate how to attach a carabineer to a rope through an ATC.
7. When asked, demonstrate safety procedures for rock climbing.
8. Explain the purpose of a safety harness.
9. Demonstrate tying the following knots used in rock climbing: water knot; bite knot; figure eight; and double figure eight knot.
10. Use the rock climbing equipment safely and properly as demonstrated by the instructor in class.
11. Demonstrate the 5 hand and 5 footholds demonstrated in class.
12. Tie the double figure eight and follow through knot.
13. Tie the double figure eight with a bite knot.
14. Describe aloud why tying knots is important in rock climbing.
15. Demonstrate the skill of belaying using form demonstrated in class.
16. Demonstrate the skill of rappelling using form demonstrated in class.
17. Demonstrate the uses and describe the functions of the safety harness.
18. Participate in partner Tug-of-War activities demonstrating safety and respect for a partner.
19. Participate in the Over and Under Ball Relay.
20. Participate in a Wheelbarrow Relay Race demonstrating cooperation skills.

ROCK CLIMBING BLOCK PLAN 1 WEEK UNIT

Week #1	Monday	Tuesday	Wednesday	Thursday	Friday
Introductory Activity	Move and Perform a Stretch	Weave Drill	Coffee Grinder Square	Flash Drill	Running Weave Drill
Fitness	Aerobic workout	Continuity Exercises	PACER Running	Jog, Walk, Jog	Walk, Jog, Sprint
Lesson Focus	Introduction Rope and Knot Tying	Safety Harness and Knots	Equipment Explanation and Demonstration	Hand and Foot Holds Belaying and Rappelling	Field Trip to Rock Climbing Gym/Wall
Game	Partner Tug-of-War Activities	Spider Tag	Over and Under Ball Relay	Wheelbarrow Relay	

Rock Climbing Lesson Plan 1

EQUIPMENT:

19 cones	1 Continuity music type Fitness CD/tape
1 CD/cassette player	1 individual tug-of-war rope per 2 students

INSTRUCTIONAL ACTIVITIES	TEACHING HINTS

INTRODUCTORY ACTIVITY (2–3 MINUTES)

Move and Perform a Stretch

Students move throughout area in designated manner while the music is playing. When music stops, they stop and perform a stretching activity called out by you.

DPESS pages 308–309

Bring students together in a scattered formation.
Use cones to designate activity area.

FITNESS DEVELOPMENT (8–12 MINUTES)

Aerobics Workout

DPESS page 352

See Lesson 1, Frisbee Golf for routine.

LESSON FOCUS (15–20 MINUTES)

Rock Climbing Introduction Through Videotape Rope and Knot Tying

Discuss safety issues of knot tying on a harness.
Demonstrate tying of:
   Double figure eight and follow through knot;
   Double figure eight with a bite knot;
Explain Task Sheets.

Bring students together in a scattered formation.
Have each student get an equipment package and Task Sheets. Students practice knot tying using the Task Sheet instructions. Check each knot.

GAME (5 MINUTES)

Partner Tug-of-War Activities

Pick-Up and Pull. On signal, the opponents run to the rope, pick it up, and the tug-of-war ensues.

Different Positions: Partners can have contests using some of the following positions and activities: facing; Back-to-Back; side to side; one handed; two handed; crab position with the rope hooked over the foot; push-up position; on all fours, etc.

DPESS page 401

Use management game to create partners.
Use management game to select partner to get rope for the pair.
Change partners occasionally.

EVALUATION/REVIEW AND CHEER

Why is it important to warm up before climbing? Why is it important to be able to properly tie the two knots? When do you use the double figure eight with a bite?

Cheer: We love rock climbing!

TASK SHEET: DOUBLE FIGURE EIGHT WITH A BITE KNOT

Name: _____   Class: _____

Directions: Read the steps listed below and use the illustrations at the bottom of the page to practice tying the bite knot. Keep practicing until you are told to stop.

1. Double up the length of rope and form a loop with the closed end.
2. Come around open ends with closed ends.
3. Bring closed end back through loop.

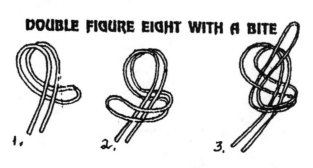

DOUBLE FIGURE EIGHT WITH A BITE

1.   2.   3.

TASK SHEET: DOUBLE FIGURE EIGHT AND FOLLOW THROUGH KNOT

Name: _____ Class: _____

Directions: Read the steps below and use the illustration at the bottom of the page to guide you in tying the knots. Keep practicing the knot tying until you are told to stop.

1. Make a loop near one end of the rope.

2. Bring end of rope behind loop.

3. Bring end of rope around loop and back through between sections of rope.

4. Tighten knot. Figure eight should appear.

5. Extend rope until enough is beyond figure eight to reverse process. Reverse rope between sections.

6. Continue to retrace path of original knot.

7. Complete retracing path and tighten knot.

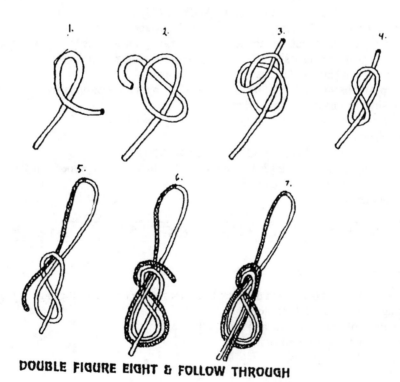

DOUBLE FIGURE EIGHT & FOLLOW THROUGH

Rock Climbing Lesson Plan 2

EQUIPMENT:

10 cones
1 jumprope per student
2 lengths of ¼" nylon rope per student

1 CD/cassette player
1 fitness CD/tape

INSTRUCTIONAL ACTIVITIES	TEACHING HINTS

INTRODUCTORY ACTIVITY (2–3 MINUTES)

Weave Drill
Students around cones using a series of movements i.e., skip, slide, jog, gallop, shuffle, carioca, etc.

DPESS page 306
Bring students together in a scattered formation.
Use whistle to alert to a new movement command.

FITNESS DEVELOPMENT (8–12 MINUTES)

Continuity Exercises
Students rope jump while music is playing, on silence in direct the following exercises: Have students jump rope to music until it stops. Give instructions for exercise, for example: Push-ups; Curl-ups; Reverse push-ups; Side leg lifts (both sides); Coffee grinder; Arm circling; Crab walks (forward, sideways, backward)

DPESS page 349
Have students get a jump rope and spread around the activity area.
Define activity area with cones.
When music resumes, rope jumping resumes.

LESSON FOCUS (15–20 MINUTES)

Harness and Knots
Display and demonstrate use of safety harness.
Demonstrate tying water knot.
Explain reciprocal Task Sheet. Use reciprocal Task Sheet to practice tying the water knot.

Use Toe-to-Toe to create pairs of students. Identify doer and observer. Direct observer to pick up equipment package and reciprocal Task Sheet.

GAME (5 MINUTES)

Spider Tag
Students stand Back-to-Back with a partner with the elbows hooked. A pair of people are "it" and chase the other pairs. If a pair is tagged or becomes unhooked, they are "it."

DPESS page 312
Create pairs.
Keep the game within the activity area.

EVALUATION/REVIEW AND CHEER

Discuss the proper use of safety harness.
Ask questions about tying the "water knot."
Cheer: 3, 2, 1, Rock climbing is fun!

RECIPROCAL TASK SHEET: WATER KNOT

Doer:_____   **Observer:**_____

Directions: Work in teams of two. One person is the "doer" and the other is the "observer." Print your names on the appropriate line above on this Task Sheet. The observer reads the instructions to the doer, offers verbal feedback, and places a check in the "yes" or "no" column recording the performance of the doer. You may show the illustrations at the bottom of the page to the doer to aid her or him in performing the task. Complete the Task Sheet until you are directed to "change roles." Then the doer becomes the observer. Each person has her or his own Task Sheet.

TYING	THE WATER KNOT	1st Try		2nd Try	
Steps	Instructions	Yes	No	Yes	No
1	Tie hitch in piece of webbing.				
2	Bring in second piece of webbing back along first piece through hole in hitch.				
3	Parallel the first piece of webbing with the second piece.				
4	When parallel is completed, tighten the knot and see if it looks correct.				

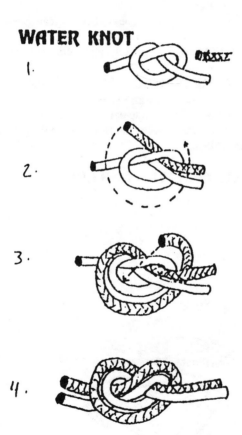

WATER KNOT

1.

2.

3.

4.

Rock Climbing Lesson Plan 3

EQUIPMENT:
4 bean bags
20 cones
1 PACER Running CD/tape
1 CD/cassette player

1 ball per 5 students
4 lengths of 1" tubular webbing per 2 students
1 completed safety harness
1 ball per five students

INSTRUCTIONAL ACTIVITIES	TEACHING HINTS

INTRODUCTORY ACTIVITY (2–3 MINUTES)

Coffee Grinder Square
Students start at one corner of the square, extend the right arm to support the body weight, perform the coffee grinder by having the feet walk 360 degrees around the arm. When a circle is completed, students run to the next corner and reverse arms and do the same motion.

DPESS page 307
Bring students together in a scattered formation.
Use management game to create four groups.
Have one group go to each corner.
Use bean bags to mark corners.

FITNESS DEVELOPMENT (8–12 MINUTES)

PACER Running
Students shuttle run back and forth across a 20-meter distance within a specified time that gradually decreases.

DPESS page 42
Bring students together in a scattered formation.
Mark 20-meter distance with cones.
Move students into one line.
Use PACER CD/tape to time runs.

LESSON FOCUS (15–20 MINUTES)

Equipment Demonstration and Explanation
Demonstrate the use of and show the following: Climbing shoes; Carabiners (Ds, ovals, locking Ds);
Belaying and Rappelling Devices (ATC, Figure 8);
Camming Devices (quad cam); Equipment package per student: 2 lengths of ¼" nylon rope; 1 D karabiner; 1 oval carabiner; 1 locking D carabiner; 1 ATC; and 1 Figure 8.

Bring students together in a scattered formation.
Have students pick up an equipment package and get in scattered formation.
Allow students to assist each other. Have Lesson 2 Task Sheets available for review/instruction.
Have students review the double figure eight and follow through knot and double figure eight with a bite knot followed by properly attaching the carabiners, ATC device, and Figure 8 device to the ropes.

GAME (5 MINUTES)

Over and Under Ball Relay
Pass ball to end of row under legs and over head. Person receiving ball at end runs to front of line.

DPESS page 405
Use Whistle Mixer to create lines of five or six.

EVALUATION/REVIEW AND CHEER

What type of knot is used to make the safety harness? Why is a safety harness necessary?
Cheer: 1, 2, 3, Rock climbing, yes!

Rock Climbing Lesson Plan 4

EQUIPMENT:

10 cones	1 locking D carabiner per student
2 lengths of 1/4" nylon rope per student	1 ATC belaying & rappelling device per student
1 D carabiner per student	1 quad cam per student
1 oval carabiner per student	1 figure 8 belaying and rappelling device per student

INSTRUCTIONAL ACTIVITIES	TEACHING HINTS

INTRODUCTORY ACTIVITY (2–3 MINUTES)

Flash Drill
Stutter feet in place.
Jump up and return to stuttering feet.
Sit on floor and return to stuttering feet.
Shuffle right.
Shuffle left.
Perform a forward roll, stand up stuttering.

DPESS pages 307–308
Bring students together in a scattered formation.
Indicate activity area with cones.

FITNESS DEVELOPMENT (8–12 MINUTES)

Jogging
Students jog as far as they can. When tired, they can walk
   until able to resume jogging.

DPESS page 347
Indicate activity area with cones.

LESSON FOCUS (15–20 MINUTES)

Rock Climbing Hand and Foot Holds
Demonstrate and explain use of:
    Open grip;
    Cling grip;
    Ring grip;
    Pocket grip;
    Pinch grip;
    Foot Holds.
Demonstrate each of the foot holds and explain when to
   use each: Smearing; Edging; Back stepping; Rest step
**Belaying and Rappelling: Discuss use of harness and
   safety when Belaying and Rappelling**
Demonstrate: 1) Tying a double figure eight and a
   follow through knot on harness; 2) Attaching a
   carabiner to a rope through an ATC; 3) Use of guide
   hand and brake hand for slide; 4) Use of guide hand
   and brake hand for stopping; 5) Use of belaying
   commands.
Videotape demonstrating Belaying & Rappelling

Have students practice holds after each demonstration.
Practice each grip after demonstration.

Bring students together in scattered formation.
Have students practice foothold after each demonstration.
   Students can use a fence to practice.
Have each student pick up an equipment package.

Have students practice after each demonstration.
Use management game to make groups of 3.

Show videotape to demonstrate belaying.

GAME (5 MINUTES)

Wheelbarrow Relay
All members of each squad must participate in both the
   carrying position and the floor wheelbarrow position in
   the race.

DPESS page 405
Use management game to create partners.
Combine pairs to create squads of four or six.
Identify race area with cones.

EVALUATION/REVIEW AND CHEER

What is the function of a carabiner? What is the function of a camming device?
Which foot hold is used for a slightly rounded hold? Which foot hold uses the leg like a hand
Cheer: Rock climbing is a cool thing to DO!

Rock Climbing Lesson Plan 5

EQUIPMENT:

50 cones

1 flag for each student

Answer sheets for each group

Station problem solving situation information sheets

INSTRUCTIONAL ACTIVITIES	TEACHING HINTS

INTRODUCTORY ACTIVITY (2–3 MINUTES)

Running Weave Drill

Students run through a maze with a stride determined by the group leader.

DPESS page 306

Make four mazes with pairs of cones.

Use a management game to create four groups.

Use a management game to select a group leader.

FITNESS DEVELOPMENT (8–12 MINUTES)

Walk, Jog, Sprint

Three whistles indicates sprint, two whistles indicates jog, and one whistle indicates walk.

DPESS page 354

Bring students together in scattered formation.

Establish movement area with cones.

LESSON FOCUS AND GAME OR WHOLE PERIOD (15–20 MINUTES)

Field Trip to Climbing Gym or Climbing Wall

Practice all skills by climbing the wall.

GAME (5 MINUTES)

Flag Grab

Students have a flag tucked in belt and attempt to keep others from pulling it out.

DPESS page 401

Scattered formation. Identify play area with cones.

Each student has a flag tucked into her/his shorts.

EVALUATION/REVIEW AND CHEER

Discuss experience putting skills into play on the climbing wall.

Cheer: Rock climbing is really great!

References:

Benge, M. and Raleigh, D. *Climbing Rock*. Carbondale, CO: Elk Mountain Press, 1995.

Long, J. *How to Rock Climb*. Evergren, CO: Chockstone Press, 1993.

ROCK CLIMBING EXAM

1.   Name four good warm-up exercises for rock climbing.

   _____   _____

   _____   _____

2.   Name the three knots covered in this unit.

   _____   _____

   _____

3.   Name the piece of equipment that can be made out of 1" tubular webbing.

   _____

4.   Name two varieties of carabiners.

   _____   _____

5.   Name a type of belaying/rappelling device.

   _____   _____

6.   Name two hand holds.

   _____   _____

7.   Name two foot holds.

   _____   _____

8.   Name the procedure for securing a climber by use of a rope.

   _____   _____

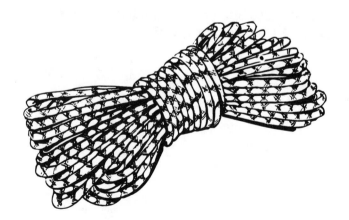

Softball

OBJECTIVES:

The student will:

1. Participate in PACER Running, Rhythmic Parachute Exercises, Jog, Walk, Jog and Continuity Exercises using form demonstrated by the instructor to improve fitness.
2. Participate in the Rooster Hop Drill, Flash Drill, Coffee Grinder Square, Move and Perform a Stretch, and Over, Under and Around to improve agility and demonstrate cooperation with peers.
3. Play Frisbee Softball, Two Pitch Softball, Frisbee Around Nine, and Home Run demonstrating sportsmanship and cooperation.
4. Play Softball following regulation rules and demonstrating skills demonstrated by the instructor during the unit.

> **SOFTBALL BLOCK PLAN**
> **1 WEEK UNIT**

Week #1	Monday	Tuesday	Wednesday	Thursday	Friday
Introductory Activity	Rooster Hop Drill	Flash Drill	Coffee Grinder Square	Move and Perform Stretch	Over, Under, and Around
Fitness	PACER Run	Aerobic Workout	Continuity Exercises	Jog, Walk, Jog	Parachute Rhythmic Exercises
Lesson Focus	Catching Throwing Rules	Batting Throwing Catching	Catching Base Running	Play Softball	Play Softball
Game	Frisbee Around Nine	Frisbee Softball	Two Pitch Softball	Home Run	

Softball Lesson Plan 1

EQUIPMENT:

1 softball per 2 students	1 glove per 2 students
Cones to mark throwing and catching area	CD/tape player
CD/tape for PACER	

INSTRUCTIONAL ACTIVITIES	TEACHING HINTS

INTRODUCTORY ACTIVITY (2–3 MINUTES)

Rooster Hop Drill

Students hop 10 yards on one leg in the following
   sequence:
1. Left hand touching the right toe, which is on the
   ground
2. Right hand touching the left toe on the ground
3. Right hand
4. Bend the knees, hands on the floor or ground
5. Legs kick back into an all fours position, head up

Teaching Hints:
DPESS page 305
Scattered formation
Direct students through a variety of movements.

FITNESS DEVELOPMENT (8–12 MINUTES)

PACER Running

Progressive aerobic cardiovascular endurance run.

Teaching Hints:
DPESS page 42
Use a timed CD/tape.
Scattered formation

LESSON FOCUS (15–20 MINUTES)

Catching skills: Demonstrate catching skills

Ground Balls: Demonstrate drill
   Students roll softball to partner 10x with and without a
   glove. Increase distance between partners.

**Throwing: Demonstrate throwing from standing and
running.**
   Students 10–20' apart to throw and catch from standing

Run and Throw Drill: Demonstrate drill.
   On signal, students will run and throw to another
   student who is directly across from the thrower at
   twenty feet. Repeat. Each student throws 10x.

Teach rules of Softball

Teaching Hints:
DPESS pages 441–445
Use Elbow-to-Elbow to create partners.

Scattered formation where student can view
   demonstration
Use a glove in this drill.
Use same partners.
Can vary distances as needed

GAME (5 MINUTES)

Frisbee Around Nine
   A target is set up with 9 different throwing positions
   around it, each 2 feet farther away. The throwing
   positions can be clockwise or counterclockwise around
   the target. They can also be in a straight line from the
   target. Points are awarded based on the throwing
   position number (for example, number 7 means 7
   points for hitting the target). The game can be played
   indoors or out.

Teaching Hints:
DPESS page 468
Create partners using Elbow-to Elbow technique.

EVALUATION/REVIEW AND CHEER

Is there any similarity between Frisbee Around 9 and Softball?
Name the two drills used in the lesson focus? Where should you be looking during softball?
Cheer: 2, 4, 6, 8, P.E. is really great!

Softball Lesson Plan 2

EQUIPMENT:

Aerobics Workout music CD/tape

8 bats

30 wiffle balls

2 frisbees

Music CD/cassette player

8 gloves

6 batting tees

INSTRUCTIONAL ACTIVITIES	TEACHING HINTS

INTRODUCTORY ACTIVITY (2–3 MINUTES)

Flash Drill

Students stand in a ready position facing the teacher. The teacher exclaims "feet," and students stutter the feet quickly. Teacher moves arms and students move in that direction.

DPESS page 307

Scattered formation

See Lesson 3, Tennis Unit for complete details.

FITNESS DEVELOPMENT (8–12 MINUTES)

Aerobics Workouts

Create a music CD/tape or purchase a pre-recorded Aerobic Exercise CD/tape with 120–150 BPM.

DPESS page 358

Scattered formation.

See Lesson Plan 7, Racquetball Unit for details.

LESSON FOCUS (15–20 MINUTES)

Batting Skills: Demonstrate batting skills.

4 Stations: 1) From a tee; 2) Soft toss; 3) Throwing and Catching Review; 4) Run, Throw and Catch

Hitting from a Tee. Demonstrate skill.

Partners rotate hitting wiffle balls off a tee and into a fence. Each student will hit 5 balls then change rolls.

Demonstrate the **Soft Toss Drill**: Partners will rotate tossing and hitting wiffle balls into a fence. One person tosses a wiffle ball at waist level and the partner hits it into a fence.

Review Run, Throw, Catch drill from yesterday and Throwing and Catching drill from yesterday.

DPESS pages 441–445

Use Toe-to-Toe to create partners. Combine 3–4 sets of partners to create groups for stations.

Scattered formation where student can view demonstration

One student will place a wiffle ball on a tee and the other will hit the ball into a fence. Hitter retrieves balls.

Each student will hit 5 balls and then change roles.

Hitter retrieves balls.

Assign groups to stations.

Signal rotation at equal intervals.

GAME (5 MINUTES)

Frisbee Softball

DPESS pages 466–467

Use Whistle Mixer to create teams.

EVALUATION/REVIEW AND CHEER

Name the drills used in the lesson focus today?

Name the 3 key points for hitting off of the tee?

Cheer: 2, 4, 6, 8, Softball is really great!

Softball Lesson Plan 3

EQUIPMENT:

Music CD/tape for Continuity Exercises

1 glove per 2 students

CD/tape player

1–2 sets of bases

INSTRUCTIONAL ACTIVITIES	TEACHING HINTS

INTRODUCTORY ACTIVITY (2–3 MINUTES)

Coffee Grinder Square

Identify a locomotor activity to move from one corner to next. Student performs "Coffee Grinder" on alternate arms at each corner.

DPESS page 307

Use Whistle Mixer to create 4 groups.

Direct starting corner for each group.

Set up square in area using bean bags or bases.

FITNESS DEVELOPMENT (8–12 MINUTES)

Continuity Exercises

These exercises are a type of interval training. Create a CD/cassette tape with 30–35 seconds of music and 20 seconds of silence. During the music, the students will jump rope.

During the silence, instruct the students to do an exercise, i.e., push-ups; curl-ups; reverse push-ups; side leg lifts on each side; coffee grinder, arm circling, crab walks forward and backward, etc.

DPESS page 348

Scattered formation

When the music resumes, the students jump rope. During each silence direct a different exercise.

LESSON FOCUS (15–20 MINUTES)

Three-Fly Drill: On signal, one partner throws a fly ball directly to the other. The 2nd fly ball should be thrown so the student drop-steps and runs backward without back peddling. The 3rd fly ball should be thrown so the partner has to sprint forward to catch the ball. Switch roles after 5 tries.

DPESS pages 441–445

Demonstrate three-fly drill.

Use Back-to-Back to create partners.

Get Up and Catch

2 students work together. One says "go" and throws a fly ball while the other lies on stomach on the grass and gets up, locates, and catches the fly ball. Repeat 3x. Rotate.

Demonstrate drill.

Be sure you have enough space between groups so students won't run into each other.

Ground ball drills: 2 students work together. First partner throws 3 easy ground balls to the other. One to the left, one directly at student and one to the right. Perform the drills 3 times each. Rotate.

Demonstrate the drills

Increase difficulty with speed of throws, proximity and distance when appropriate.

Base Running Drills: Students run the bases in order Teach sound base running technique.

Use 3 or 4 areas set up with bases.

Students will get tired, so let them run at their own pace.

GAME (5 MINUTES)

Two Pitch Softball

Every team member pitches at least once.

DPESS page 445

Use Whistle Mixer to create teams.

EVALUATION/REVIEW AND CHEER

What is the main difference between catching ground balls and fly balls?

Cheer: Softball's here, yeah!

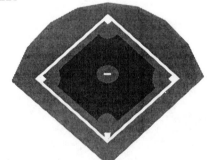

Softball Lesson Plan 4

EQUIPMENT:

Bases for as many fields as you have   Several bats and balls

INSTRUCTIONAL ACTIVITIES	TEACHING HINTS

INTRODUCTORY ACTIVITY (2–3 MINUTES)

Move and Perform a Stretch

Move and perform a stretching activity on the sound of the whistle. Move and stretch to the sound of music. Skip, hop, shuffle, jog and walk.

DPESS page 308

Scattered formation

Direct starting and stopping locomotor movements to selected stretches using a whistle or a timed music CD/tape.

FITNESS DEVELOPMENT (8–12 MINUTES)

Jog, Walk, Jog

Direct students to jog as far as they can. When tired, they can walk, and resume jogging when able.

DPESS page 347, 354

LESSON FOCUS (15–20 MINUTES)

Play Softball

Use Whistle Mixer to create teams. Assign teams to field to play.

GAME (5 MINUTES)

Home Run:

This is a fun drill that allows the students to do a fake homerun swing and jog the bases slowly like they have hit a homerun. Each student should do this 3 times to cool down from 4x4 drill.

DPESS page 445

Use Whistle Mixer to make appropriate groups for the base running set up.

EVALUATION/REVIEW AND CHEER

Are there any rules of softball you need to review?

Cheer: 3,2,1, Softball's really fun!

Softball Lesson Plan 5

EQUIPMENT:

Bases for as many fields as you have   Several bats and balls
Parachute   Music for fitness

INSTRUCTIONAL ACTIVITIES	TEACHING HINTS

INTRODUCTORY ACTIVITY (2–3 MINUTES)

Over, Under, and Around #1

DPESS pages 310–311

See Lesson Plan 5 from Racquetball Unit for details.

Use Back-to-Back to create partners.

FITNESS DEVELOPMENT (8–12 MINUTES)

Parachute Rhythmic Aerobic Activities

DPESS page 352

See Lesson Plan 11, Badminton Unit for details.

LESSON FOCUSAND GAME (20 MINUTES)

Play softball games.

Use teams from yesterday or play Whistle Mixer to create new teams.

EVALUATION/REVIEW AND CHEER

Were there any skills in Softball that you still need to improve?

Cheer: Softball, softball, yeah, softball!

Table Tennis

OBJECTIVES:

The student will:
1. Participate in Move and Change Directions demonstrating quickness and pivoting skills.
2. Practice Juggling 3 Scarves as instructed during the Introductory Activity.
3. Demonstrate agility while participating in Leap Frog, Seat Roll and Jog.
4. Demonstrate the ability to follow instructions and creativity during the Hoops and Plyometrics Introductory activity.
5. Participate in Circuit Training, Continuity Exercises, Fitness Scavenger and Aerobic Workout to improve fitness.
6. Execute the forehand and backhand shots using form demonstrated by the instructor.
7. Execute the forehand and backhand serves using form demonstrated by the instructor.
8. Play Table Tennis following the rules in the class Round Robin Tournament.

TABLE TENNIS BLOCK PLAN
1 WEEK UNIT

Week #1	Monday	Tuesday	Wednesday	Thursday	Friday
Introductory Activity	Move and Change Directions	Juggling Scarves	Seat Roll and Jog	Hoops and Plyometrics	Leap Frog
Fitness	Circuit Training	Aerobic Workout	Fitness Scavenger Hunt	Partner Racetrack Fitness	Continuity Exercises
Lesson Focus	Forehand and Backhand Shots	Forehand and Backhand Serves Rules of the Game	Review all Skills Rally Describe Tournament	Round Robin Tournament	Round Robin Tournament
Game	Triangle Plus One Tag	Spider Tag	Entanglement		

Table Tennis Lesson Plan 1

EQUIPMENT:

Station cones and signs

Music CD/cassette tape player

1 table tennis/ping pong ball per student

Music for Circuit Training

1 ping pong paddle per student

1 table tennis table per 4 students

INSTRUCTIONAL ACTIVITIES	TEACHING HINTS

INTRODUCTORY ACTIVITY (2–3 MINUTES)

Move and Change Direction

Students will jog towards each other and give high fives to the other group. Then, skip the other direction, and return giving high fives as the students meet the other group again.

DPESS page 308

Divide the student into two groups using Toe-to-Toe and then separating into two halves.

FITNESS DEVELOPMENT (8–12 MINUTES)

Circuit Training

When the music starts, each group will perform the exercise described on each labeled cone. When the music stops, students walk counter-clockwise to the next station performing arm circles.

Exercises listed at **stations**: Push-ups, knee-lifts, jumping jacks, trunk twisters, sit-ups, arm extensions, single crab kicks, arms up and down, jog in place, triceps push-ups.

DPESS page 348

Using Whistle Mixer, make groups of 5–6 to begin at each station.

Place instructions for each station on cones set up to identify location of station. Use illustrations to assist in understanding of the activities.

LESSON FOCUS (15–20 MINUTES)

Paddle and Ball Control

Demonstrate different ways of bouncing the ball on the paddle in the air: forehand side of paddle; backhand side; alternating hands; alternating forehand and backhand; bounce ball on table or floor.

Open and Closed Paddle Forehand and Backhand

Student will use open and closed paddle position to hit the ball over the net. Each student will hit five times and rotate counter clockwise.

Scattered formation

1 paddle and ball per student

Demonstrate at Table Tennis table.

Student roles are: ball chasers, catcher, feeder and hitter.

GAME (5 MINUTES)

Triangle Plus 1 Tag

Person outside triangle tries to tag leader. Leader and tagger change places when tagged.

DPESS page 312

Create groups of 4 using management game. 3 make triangle formation holding hands. Select leader in group.

EVALUATION/REVIEW AND CHEER

Were there any activities you learned today that were particularly challenging? Were there any that were very easy for you? Why?

Cheer: P.E. is fun!

Table Tennis Lesson Plan 2

EQUIPMENT:

3 juggling scarves per student
Music CD/cassette tape player
1 table tennis ball per student

Aerobic Workout tape/CD
1 table tennis paddle per student

INSTRUCTIONAL ACTIVITIES	TEACHING HINTS

INTRODUCTORY ACTIVITY (2–3 MINUTES)

Juggling Scarves
Column juggling; Cascading

DPESS page 392- 394.
Scattered formation; 3 scarves per student

FITNESS DEVELOPMENT (8–12 MINUTES)

Aerobic Workout

DPESS page 352
See Lesson 7, Racquetball Unit for details.

LESSON FOCUS (15–20 MINUTES)

Demonstrate the Forehand Drive stance, open and closed paddle position.

Scattered formation

Each student hits ball 5 times using open and closed paddle face position.

Rotate around the table clockwise.

Demonstrate Serves Forehand and Backhand
Each student serves forehand 5 times. Rotate clockwise.
Each student serves backhand 5 times. Rotate clockwise.

Ball placed in palm of hand for serve.
Stand side to target to serve.
5 balls per table
Receivers catch balls for next person.

Describe Table Tennis Rules.

GAME (5 MINUTES)

Spider Tag
Pairs work together to tag other pairs.
When tagged, they become "its."

DPESS page 312
Using a management game, create partners.
Select one pair to be the "its."

EVALUATION/REVIEW AND CHEER

Review Table Tennis Rules.
Are there any questions about the Forehand or Backhand Serve that I taught you today?
Are there any questions about the Forehand or Backhand shot?
Cheer: PE (clap clap), PE (clap clap), PE (clap clap), yeah!

Table Tennis Lesson Plan 3

EQUIPMENT:

Fitness Scavenger Hunt cards
1 table tennis ball per student

Music for fitness (optional)
1 table tennis paddle per student

INSTRUCTIONAL ACTIVITIES	TEACHING HINTS

INTRODUCTORY ACTIVITY (2–3 MINUTES)

Seat Roll and Jog
Direct students to seat roll right/left with hand signal.
   Alternate rolls with jogging in place.

DPESS page 304
Scattered formation
Student begins on "all fours" with head up looking at
   teacher for instructions.

FITNESS DEVELOPMENT (8–12 MINUTES)

Fitness Scavenger Hunt
Exercises listed on scavenger cards at stations.

DPESS page 356
Use Whistle Mixer to create groups of 3. Assign each
   group to a starting point.

LESSON FOCUS (15–20 MINUTES)

Review serves, forehand and backhand drives
Rally using serves, forehand and backhand drives

Scattered around demonstration table
Use Whistle Mixer to create groups of 4. Assign tables.

GAME (5 MINUTES)

Entanglement
Each group makes a tight circle with their arms.

DPESS page 407
Use Whistle Mixer to make several groups.

EVALUATION/REVIEW AND CHEER

What was more difficult? Serves or rallying? Why?
What is the most fun about Table Tennis?
Cheer: P.E. (stomp feet 2x), P.E. (stomp feet 2x), P.E. (stomp feet 2x), yeah!

Table Tennis Lesson Plan 4

EQUIPMENT:

Round Robin Tournament Chart
Station cone markers and station signs for fitness

1 hoop per student

INSTRUCTIONAL ACTIVITIES	TEACHING HINTS

INTRODUCTORY ACTIVITY (2–3 MINUTES)

Hoops and Plyometrics
Each student rolls the hoop while running. On signal, the
   hoops are dropped. Challenge students to move in and
   out of a given number of hoops specified by color.
   State locomotor movement to use. Student then picks
   up the hoop and resumes rolling it.

DPESS pages 309–310
Scattered formation
Each student has a hoop and listens for instructions.

FITNESS DEVELOPMENT (8–12 MINUTES)

Partner Racetrack Fitness
On signal, 1 partner begins the first activity on station
   card while other jogs around perimeter. Switch roles,
   then perform next task alternating positions until they
   complete all tasks at the station. Rotate to next station.
Task suggestions: Strengthening and stretching exercises,
   i.e., sit-ups, push-ups, upper and lower body stretches,
   etc.

DPESS pages 356–357
Use Back-to-Back to create partners.
Assign partners to a station to begin.
Explain station rotation.

LESSON FOCUS AND GAME (20 MINUTES)

Create Round Robin Table Tennis Tournament
Have teams determined ahead of time or use Whistle
   Mixer to determine teams.

DPESS page 294
Assign teams to tables for tournament play.

EVALUATION/REVIEW AND CHEER

What was the most challenging aspect of the Tournament play? Are you ready to continue tomorrow?
Are there any questions about the rules of the game?
Cheer: Table tennis, yes!

Table Tennis Lesson Plan 5

EQUIPMENT:

Continuity exercise music CD/tape
1 paddle per person
Round Robin Tournament Chart

CD/tape player
2 table tennis balls per table

INSTRUCTIONAL ACTIVITIES	TEACHING HINTS

INTRODUCTORY ACTIVITY (2–3 MINUTES)

Leap Frog
See Badminton, Lesson 11 for details.

DPESS page 398
Using Whistle Mixer, create groups of 5.

FITNESS DEVELOPMENT (8–12 MINUTES)

Continuity Exercises

DPESS page 349

LESSON FOCUS AND GAME (20 MINUTES)

Create Round Robin Table Tennis Tournament
Continue play with teams from yesterday.

DPESS page 294

EVALUATION/REVIEW AND CHEER

What was the most challenging aspect of the Tournament play?
Cheer: Table tennis rocks!

NAME:_____   **CLASS PERIOD:**_____

TABLE TENNIS EXAM

1. Select the correct order of techniques for a table tennis serve in a doubles match.
    a. Toss the ball 10 inches in the air, bounce the ball on the table, hit on the opponents side of the table.
    b. Using the palm of the hand toss the ball up 6 inches; hit the ball on the way down. Player must be behind the end of the table; the ball must bounce once on the server's side of the table and go over the net on the diagonal to the opponent's side of the table.
    c. Using the forefinger and the thumb toss the ball in the air, hit the ball on the way down, standing behind the end of the table, the ball must bounce once on the server's side and go over the net on the diagonal to the opponent's side.

Use key below for questions 2 & 3

    a. A netball   b. A let ball

    c. The first fault   d. A good serve

2. If the serve strikes the top of the net and still goes in. This is called

3. If the serve goes into the net and comes back over to the server's side of the table. This is called

4. How many times does a player serve before the other player gets a turn to serve?

    a. One   b. Two

    c. Four   d. Five

5. The server must toss the ball
    a. At least 4 inches in the air   b. At least 5 inches in the air
    c. 6 inches in the air   d. 10 inches in the air

6. A game is played to how many points?
    a. 21   b. 15
    c. 11   d. 13

7. If a game is tied 20-20, by how many points do you need to win?
    a. One point   b. Two points
    c. Three points   d. Five

8. Table Tennis is a high-paying professional sport in some countries. True/False

9. Is it legal to volley in Table Tennis? True/False

10. If the ball hits the edge of the table is it considered good?
    a. Yes   b. No
    c. Sometimes   d. Never

Walking

OBJECTIVES:

The student will:
1. Demonstrate agility, starting, stopping and stretching skills during the Move and Stretch Activity.
2. Demonstrate quickness and teamwork during Run and Lead and Vanishing Bean bags.
3. Demonstrate safety skills explained by the instructor while participating in Individual Stunts.
4. Demonstrate agility and dodging skills during the introductory activities.
5. Participate in strengthening and stretching exercises, jump roping activities, during the Fitness Challenge Course Circuit, Parachute Rhythmic Activities, Four Corners Fitness activities, Continuity Exercises, and Squad Leader Exercises to improve their overall fitness levels.
6. Play Tug-of-War challenges with a partner.
7. Participate in Wand Whirl, Hoops on the Ground, Fetch Relay and Over and Under Relays demonstrating cooperation and good sportsmanship.
8. Follow all instructions in the use of the Pedometers as explained in class by the instructor.
9. Participate in Speed Walking Intervals using full speed as directed.
10. Continuously walk as instructed during the Poker Walk activity.
11. Follow the rules of the Walking "Golf" Tournament during class and demonstrate courtesy to other class members.
12. Complete the "I Spy" Walking Challenge card as directed by the instructor.
13. Play Wand Whirl demonstrating focus and quickness.
14. Play Hoops on the Ground following the instructions described by the instructor.
15. Participate in Individual Tug-of-War activities carefully following the safety rules.
16. Play Fetch Relay running as quickly as possible.
17. Play Over and Under Relay while passing the ball as carefully and quickly and demonstrating agility.

WALKING BLOCK PLAN
1 WEEK UNIT

Week #1	Monday	Tuesday	Wednesday	Thursday	Friday
Introductory Activity	Square Drill	Run and Lead	Individual Stunts	Move and Stretch	Vanishing Bean Bags
Fitness	Squad Leader Exercises	Continuity Exercises	Parachute Rhythmic Activity	Challenge Course Circuit	Four Corners
Lesson Focus	Pedometer Introductory Activities	Speed Walking Intervals	Poker Walk	Walking "Golf" Tournament	"I Spy" Walking Challenge
Game	Wand Whirl	Hoops on the Ground	Partner Tug-of-War	Fetch Relay	Over and Under Relay

Walking Lesson Plan 1

EQUIPMENT:

1 pedometer per student
Cones to mark perimeter
Music for fitness

1 wand per student
Cones on which to put Squad Leader Exercise cards
Boom box

INSTRUCTIONAL ACTIVITIES	TEACHING HINTS

INTRODUCTORY ACTIVITY (2–3 MINUTES)

Square Drill

DPESS page 305

The class forms several 10-yard squares with boundary cones. Students stand in the middle of each side of the square and face the center. On signal, they shuffle around the square to the left or right, depending on the signal of the teacher. A student can be in the center of the square to give a direction signal.

FITNESS DEVELOPMENT (8–12 MINUTES)

Squad Leader Exercises
Exercises for Upper-Body Development

- Push-Ups
- Reclining Partner Pull-Ups
- Rocking Chair
- Crab Walk

Exercises for the Midsection

- Reverse Curl
- Pelvis Tilter
- Knee Touch Curl-Up
- Curl-Up with Twist
- Leg Extension

DPESS page 346

Squad leaders take their squad to a designated area and put the squad through a fitness routine that you have written on a station card.

Background music can be used.

LESSON FOCUS (15–20 MINUTES)

Demonstrate and explain the use of pedometers.
Direct students to:

On signal, students move to their assigned container, pick up a pedometer and put it on while walking. As soon as the pedometer is in place, students should reset the pedometer and keep walking. As soon as they have completed putting on their pedometers on the move, freeze the class and ask them to reset their pedometers.

Walk as fast as possible for 30 seconds.
After 30 seconds, drop down to an easy pace for 30 seconds. Repeat the 30 seconds speed and 30 second rest 8-12 times. Cool down with a 10-minute easy pace walk.

Estimation: How many steps does it take? Measure off a distance that is exactly one-eighth or one-fourth mile in length.

DPESS pages 323–326

Organize class into small groups of 5–6 students using Whistle Mixer.
Pedometers (6) are placed in containers around the area.
Reinforce students who accumulate the most activity time (they will have been the quickest to get their pedometers in place).

Identify the perimeters of a walking course.

Notice how many steps were taken during the 30 seconds.

Reset pedometer at the starting line and walk at a normal pace to the end of the distance. Depending on whether they walked a one-eighth or one-fourth-mile distance, they multiply the number of steps they accumulated by 8 or 4. That is the number of steps it takes them to walk one mile.

Have students record on a Task Sheet how many steps they took during the lesson focus and how many steps a mile will take.

INSTRUCTIONAL ACTIVITIES	**TEACHING HINTS**

GAME (5 MINUTES)

WAND ACTIVITIES
Wand Whirl
Stand wand in front of body. Balance it with 1 finger. Release, turn, and catch the wand.

DPESS page 401
Scattered formation

Wand Balance and Change

Work with a partner.
Each person holds wand in vertical position.
On signal, run across to where partner's wand is and try to catch it before it falls.

Wand Kick over Begin same as Whirl, but leg kick over the wand before turning.

Wand Wrestle
Goal: move the wand to a horizontal plane.

EVALUATION/REVIEW AND CHEER

Have students record how many steps they took in class.
Ask students how many steps they found it takes to walk a mile.
Were there any problems using the pedometer?
What was the most challenging fitness activity?
What muscles were used in fitness?
What was the most challenging Wand activity?
Cheer: Pedometers count my steps, yeah!

Walking Lesson Plan 2

EQUIPMENT:

Cones to mark perimeter of teaching area
Continuity fitness music CD/tape
1 pedometer per student

Boom box
1 hoop per student

INSTRUCTIONAL ACTIVITIES	**TEACHING HINTS**

INTRODUCTORY ACTIVITY (2–3 MINUTES)

Run and Lead (Similar to File Running)
Students jog in formation. Last person sprints to front of line to become leader.

DPESS page 354
Line or circle formation

FITNESS DEVELOPMENT (8–12 MINUTES)

Continuity Exercises
See Badminton Unit, Lesson 3 for complete details.

DPESS page 399
Scattered formation

LESSON FOCUS (15–20 MINUTES)

Checking Pedometer
Show students how to gently move it up and down (ceiling to floor) to see if it is counting correctly. Ask students to reset their pedometer and practice comparing shakes with the pedometer step counts. Ask students to hold the pedometer with the display parallel to the floor. Now shake it up and down. Note that it won't count steps or time when it is in this position.

Have students put pedometer on by taking it from their assigned container. As soon as the pedometer is in place, students should reset the pedometer and keep walking.
Shaking the pedometer too hard will prevent the pedometer from counting accurately. The pedometer measures very small up and down movement.

Speed Walking Intervals
Walk fast for 8 minutes.
Then slow down to an easy pace for 2 minutes.
Repeat this for 2 repetitions. Cool down for 2 minutes at an easy pace.

Have students record how many steps they took during the Speed Walking intervals.
Replace the pedometers in the proper containers after they have been reset.
Record steps on Task Sheet.

INSTRUCTIONAL ACTIVITIES	TEACHING HINTS

GAME (5 MINUTES)

Hoops on the Ground
Spread hoops around the area and give directions to move around using locomotor movements and freeze inside a hoop.

DPESS page 313
Scattered formation

EVALUATION/REVIEW

Did you take more steps during the lesson focus today than yesterday?
What part of the lesson focus was the most enjoyable today?
What muscles did you work during fitness?
What did fitness focus on today?
Turn in pedometers.

Walking Lesson Plan 3

EQUIPMENT:

Several decks of cards for Poker Walk
Cones to mark teaching area
1 individual tug-of-war rope per two students

Parachute
Music CD/tape for fitness

INSTRUCTIONAL ACTIVITIES	TEACHING HINTS

INTRODUCTORY ACTIVITY (2–3 MINUTES)

Individual Stunts
Leg dip; Behind Back Touch; Double Heel Click

DPESS page 398
Scattered formation
Explain stunts and student practices

FITNESS DEVELOPMENT (8–12 MINUTES)

Parachute Rhythmic Aerobic Activity
- Skip both directions.
- Slide both directions.
- Run both directions.
- Jump to center.
- Hop backward.
- Lift parachute overhead.
- Lower parachute to toes.
- Repeat above.
- Run CW with chute overhead.
- Make a dome.
- Strengthening and stretching exercises

DPESS page 352

Direct locomotor movements while holding parachute.

Use music to motivate.

Alternate locomotor movements with seated strength and stretching exercises.

LESSON FOCUS (15–20 MINUTES)

Put pedometer on.
Poker Walk
Students walk to the areas and pick up one card without looking at the card. They walk to as many areas as possible within a time limit and then add up the points.

DPESS pages 323–326
Distribute pedometers.
Page 330
- Pre-arrange several decks of cards at set areas around walking area.
- Have a prize for high- and low-point totals and then change the rules each time. Set it up so anyone can win by just walking to the card areas, picking up the card, and then adding up the points at the end of the time limit.

INSTRUCTIONAL ACTIVITIES	TEACHING HINTS

GAME (5 MINUTES)

Partner Tug-of-War
Pull facing partner.
Pull with backs to partners and between legs.
Pull on foot in crab walk position.
Other foot

DPESS page 401
Use management game to create pairs.
1 rope per 2 students

EVALUATION/REVIEW AND CHEER

Check pedometer steps for the day and compare to previous days.
What was the hardest tug-of-war activity?
Cheer: Walking keeps me fit!

Walking Lesson Plan 4

EQUIPMENT:

1 pedometer per student
Cones to mark perimeters of teaching area
Hoops for Walking Tournament
1 tennis ball per student
Cones to mark fitness Challenge Course Circuit
4 mats for fitness

Signs for Challenge Course
Wands for fitness course
Music for fitness
Boom box for fitness
Balance bench
6 individual jump ropes

INSTRUCTIONAL ACTIVITIES	TEACHING HINTS

INTRODUCTORY ACTIVITY (2–3 MINUTES)

Move and Stretch
- Students run within set perimeter and perform stretches upon designated signal. Use flash cards to signal stretches.
- Both Arms Up: stretch high
- Touch Toes
- Hamstring Stretch: Right leg forward left back with heel on ground. Hold 30 seconds and switch.
- Standing Hip Bend: Both sides. Hold 20 seconds each side.
- Wishbone Stretch: Hands clasped behind back and lean forward.

DPESS page 308

Scattered formation

Teacher calls instructions

FITNESS DEVELOPMENT (8–12 MINUTES)

Challenge Course Circuit
Set up 3–4 parallel (side-by-side) courses in one-half of the area.
Course 1. Crouch jumps; pulls, or scooter movements or balance down a bench; agility hop through two hoops on floor. Skip, slide, or jog to a cone.
Course 2. Weave in and out of four wands held upright by cones; Crab walk between two cones: lead with feet once, hands once. Gallop to a cone.
Course 3. Do a tumbling activity length of mat; agility run through hoops; Leap frog over partner alternating roles between cones.
Course 4. Curl-ups and push-ups on a mat. Sitting stretches. Jump rope in place.

DPESS page 352

Movement should be continuous.

Arrange three or four courses with a group at each course. Students perform the challenges from start to finish and jog back to repeat the course. On signal, groups move to a new course.

Rotate groups to each course after a specified time. Music can be used for motivation and to signal changes.

INSTRUCTIONAL ACTIVITIES	TEACHING HINTS

LESSON FOCUS (15–20 MINUTES)

Walking "golf" tournament

Students throw the ball into a hoop and then walk with their group to a hoop. Students use a scorecard to keep track of the number of throws for each hole.

DPESS page 330

Put on pedometers

Use hula hoops for holes.

Set the course up around your teaching space with cones for the tees.

Each student has an old tennis ball.

Play Whistle Mixer to create even groups.

Provide scorecard.

GAME (5 MINUTES)

Fetch Relay

Squads line up and place 1 member at the other end of the playing area, 10 to 20 yards away. This person runs back to the squad and fetches the next person. The person who has just been fetched in turn runs back and fetches the next person. The pattern continues until all members have been fetched to the opposite end of the playing area.

DPESS page 406

Use Whistle Mixer to create groups of 4–5.

Create lines/squad formation with each group.

Identify first player to go to opposite end of playing area.

EVALUATION/REVIEW AND CHEER

How many steps did you take in class today? How did that compare to previous lessons?

What was challenging about the Walking Tournament?

What areas of the body did fitness work on today?

How many steps did you take today in comparison to the steps you took yesterday?

Collect pedometers

Cheer: We always do our best, and soar above the rest!

Walking Lesson Plan 5

EQUIPMENT:

Challenge cards for "I Spy"
1 bean bag per person
4 cones for Four Corners

1 rubber ball per 4 students for game
Cones to outline teaching area
Signs for each corner

INSTRUCTIONAL ACTIVITIES	TEACHING HINTS

INTRODUCTORY ACTIVITY (2–3 MINUTES)

Vanishing Bean Bags

Spread bean bags throughout the area to allow 1 per
   student. Students move around the area until a signal is
   given. On the signal, they find a bean bag and sit on
   each. Each round, direct a new locomotor movement
   task and take away a bean bag.

DPESS page 309
Scattered formation

FITNESS DEVELOPMENT (8–12 MINUTES)

Four Corners

Outline a large rectangle with four cones. Place signs
   with tasks on both sides of the cones. Students move
   around the outside of the rectangle and change their
   movement pattern as they approach a corner sign.
The following movement tasks are suggested:
   1. Jogging
   2. Skipping/Jumping/Hopping
   3. Sliding/Galloping
   4. Abdominal strengthening exercises
   5. Upper body strengthening exercises
   6. Side leg work
   7. Full body stretches

DPESS page 347
Use Whistle Mixer to create 4 equal groups.

Assign each group a corner to begin at.

LESSON FOCUS (15–20 MINUTES)

"I Spy" Walking Challenge
Challenge Cards:

Identify all of the makes of cars you see on your walk.
Identify all of the colors of the cars you see.
List as many different birds you see on the walk.
List as many different animals you see on the walk.
How many people did you walk by?

DPESS page 330
Distribute pedometers.
Distribute "I Spy" Challenge Cards.
Explain perimeters of walking course.
Use Whistle Mixer to make even groups.

GAME (5 MINUTES)

Over and Under Ball Relay
Distribute 1 ball per group.

DPESS page 368
Use Whistle Mixer to create lines/squads of 5–6.
Assign spaces for lines leaving room between lines.

EVALUATION/REVIEW AND CHEER

Have one student from each group report on what they
   wrote on their challenge cards.
Was there a common car most people saw?
What was the main animal passed on the walk?
How did your steps compare today to the number you
   took yesterday during the lesson focus?
Cheer: 10,000 steps is my goal!

Walking Golf Tournament Score Card

Directions: Work with your group. Place all of your names on the scorecard. Record how many throws it takes each person to make a hole. Do not try more than 3 times. 3 would be the maximum anyone would score. You are striving for a low team score.

Begin the course on the hole number assigned by your teacher and complete the course progressing to each hole. Walk as briskly as possible between holes.

NAME	HOLE NUMBER							
	1	**2**	**3**	**4**	**5**	**6**	**7**	**8**
1.								
2.								
3.								
4.								
5.								
6.								

"I Spy" Walking Scorecard

Directions: Work with your group in the area designated by your teacher. Place all of your names on the scorecard.
Record how many of the following you see on your walk:
Identify all of the makes of cars you see on your walk.
Identify all of the colors of the cars you see.
List as many different birds you see on the walk.
List as many different animals you see on the walk.
How many people did you walk by?

NAME	"I Spy" the items listed below							
	Makes of Cars		Birds		Animals		People	
		color	#	type	#	type	# M	# F
1.								
2.								
3.								
4.								
5.								
6.								

Aerobics

OBJECTIVES:

The student will:

1. Participate in the introductory games of Hospital Tag and Vanishing Bean Bags while demonstrating agility, the ability to follow instructions and cooperation as described by the instructor.
2. Participate in the standing Aerobics routine during the fitness and lesson focus sections of class using form and movements demonstrated by the instructor.
3. Participate in the stretch, isolation and strengthening movements using form and movements demonstrated by the instructor.
4. Play Triangle plus One Tag and Balance Tag using movements described by the instructor and demonstrating cooperation and good sportsmanship with classmates.

**AEROBICS BLOCK PLAN
2 DAY UNIT**

Two Day Unit Plan	Day One	Day Two
Introductory Activity	Hospital Tag	Vanishing Bean Bags
Fitness	Combine fitness and lesson focus today to focus on Aerobics Routine	Combine fitness and lesson focus today on Aerobics Routine
Lesson Focus		
Game	Triangle plus one Tag	Balance Tag

Aerobics Lesson Plan 1

EQUIPMENT:

Aerobic Music CD/cassette tape   CD/cassette tape player

INSTRUCTIONAL ACTIVITIES	TEACHING HINTS
INTRODUCTORY ACTIVITY (2–3 MINUTES)	
Hospital Tag	DPESS pages 312–313
	Select several students to be the "medics."
COMBINE FITNESS AND LESSON FOCUS TODAY (20–25 MINUTES)	
Walk in place while moving arms from hips to overhead.	32 counts
Step to the right and touch your left toe to the right, then step to the left and touch the left toe next to the left foot	8 times
Hop on the left foot 4 times while pointing and tapping the right foot forward and then to the side (for example, forward, side, forward, feet together on count 4, jump/change sides).	Repeat the entire phrase while hopping (bouncing) on the right foot 4 times and tapping the left foot forward and to the side as described. Repeat the phrase again on each side.
Run in place 8 times, clap on each run.	
Do 8 jumping jacks using full arm movements.	
Slide to the right 8 times, clap on the 8th slide.	Repeat to the left.
Jump in place 8 times while hitting the sides of your thighs with straight arms.	
Run in place 8 times while lifting your feet high in the rear.	
Run in place 8 times while lifting your knees high in front.	Repeat the two running in place phrases
Perform 8 jumping jacks, moving your arms down and up in coordination with the leg movements.	
Perform 8 jumping jacks, moving your arms down and only half way up (to the shoulder level) in coordination with each leg movement.	
Mountain Climber	With your feet separated, jump and land forward and backward a distance of about one foot. Alternate feet as you land in front and in back on each jump. Your arms can swing high in opposition to the leg movements.
Pony: "Hop, step, step." Hop on the right foot to the side, and then quickly step with the left foot and then the right foot.	Repeat on the other side.
Heel, toe, slide, slide: Hop on the left foot while tapping the right heel to the right side. While hopping again on the left foot, swing the right foot to the front and touch the toe on the floor. Perform 2 slides to the right.	Repeat the entire phrase by hopping on the right foot and sliding to the left.
Hop on one foot and lift up the opposite knee.	Reverse.
Hop on one foot, and swing kick the opposite foot forward.	Reverse.
Charleston Bounce Step: Use a very bouncy step throughout this phrase. Step right, kick the left foot forward, step back on the left foot, and touch the right toe back.	Repeat 8 times. Reverse with opposite foot leading.
Can-Can Kick: Hop on the right foot, and simultaneously bring the bent left knee up high in front. Hop again on the right foot, lightly touch the left foot on the floor next to the right, and kick the left foot into the air forward and up.	Repeat 4 times and then repeat on the other side. A more advanced version involves alternating sides after each kick.
Walk in place while moving arms from hips to overhead.	32 counts

INSTRUCTIONAL ACTIVITIES	TEACHING HINTS
Walk in place. While staying near the hips, hands are flexed, and move away from the body and back towards the hips.	32 counts
STRETCHES AND ISOLATIONS	
Head isolations	Repeat the set 4 to 8 times.
Lift head up and down. Turn head to the right and then the left.	Caution: All head and neck exercises should be performed smoothly and in a relaxed manner. If the neck is allowed to arch or roll back, unnecessary tension could be placed on the cervical vertebrae.
Shoulder Circles	Reverse the direction of the roll, and repeat it 8 times.
In a slow, smooth manner, circle shoulders forward, up, back, and around 8 times.	
Rib Isolations	Repeat by reversing the direction of the rib isolations.
While standing with good posture, place hands on hips (this helps keep hips from moving). Move ribs forward, back to center, to the side, back to center, to the back, back to center, to the other side, and back to center.	
Rib Circles	Perform them several times in each direction.
Perform rib circles the same way as the rib isolations, but in a continuous manner.	
Hip Isolations	Repeat 8 times.
While standing with good posture, slightly bend the knees. Now smoothly tilt the pelvis forward and then backward.	
Hip Swings	Repeat 8 times. Be sure to execute these movements in a smooth, sustained manner.
Tilt hips and pelvic area to the right and then the left.	
Hip Circles	Reverse the direction and perform the hip circles the same number of times. Keep movements smooth and sustained. Jerking movements should be avoided.
While standing with good posture, slightly bend knees. Smoothly circle hips forward, to the side, to the back, and to the other side. Continue circling hips at least 8 times.	
Deep Lunge	Hold this position for 20 seconds.
Begin in a standing position with good posture. With feet parallel, take a large step forward on one foot. Assume a deep lunge position, place hands on each side of the knee. The heel of the forward foot must remain on the floor, and the knee should be directly above the foot. Keep the extended back leg straight, with the toes of the foot pushing against the floor.	You may want to repeat the entire exercise for each leg.
Now, straighten your forward bent leg and lift the toe up. Gently, without pulling, try to have your head touch your knee. This exercise will stretch your quadriceps, hamstrings, and the Achilles' tendon. Perform the exercise on your other leg.	
Side lunge	Repeat the exercise on each side. This exercise stretches the muscles in the inside of the hip flexor muscles.
Begin in a wide straddle position, with legs and feet turned out. Bend one knee, and keep the other leg straight. Be sure to keep the knee over the toes and the feet flat while in the lunge position. Lift the toes of the straight leg, and let the hips sink as low as possible to get a nice stretch. Keep hands/fingertips on the floor for balance. Hold this position for 15 to 30 seconds, and then perform it on the other side.	

INSTRUCTIONAL ACTIVITIES	TEACHING HINTS

Hamstring Stretch

While lying on back with feet parallel, bend one leg and keep the other foot on the ground for support. Lift the straight leg up and try to keep the knee straight. Place hands under the thigh of the lifted leg. Hold the lifted leg under the thigh for a minimum of 15 seconds, preferably for 30 to 60 seconds.

> This exercise stretches the hamstrings. Repeat on the other side.
>
> Perform another set.

Quadriceps Stretch

Stand up with good posture. Keeping the supporting leg slightly bent, grasp the lower leg near the foot and gently pull foot toward buttocks.

> Proceed carefully, as this exercise can place stress on your knee joint.
>
> Repeat on each leg.

Calf Stretches

Perform either or both of the following calf exercises:

Perform a standing lunge by stepping forward with one foot so that both feet are approximately 1 to 2 feet apart. The front leg is bent, the back leg is straight with the toes facing forward.

> Hold this position for 20 seconds. Repeat on the other leg. Repeat the set again.

Stand facing a wall, approximately 2 feet away from it. Keep the body in a straight line and lunge forward, place both hands on the wall about shoulder level. In the lunge position, the forward leg is bent, and the back leg is straight. There should be a stretch in the calf of the straight leg. If not, adjust the position until a stretch is felt.

> Repeat the exercise on the other leg.

Ankle Circles

While standing or sitting, circle each ankle 10 times in each direction.

> Repeat on other foot.

Ankle Raises

From a standing position in good posture, raise up on the balls of both feet. Hold for 4 counts, and then lower back to the floor in 4 counts.

> Repeat 10 times. Do another set, holding for 2 counts in each position.

Heel Walking

Lift toes up and walk around the room on both heels.

> This strengthens the tibialis muscles.

Sitting Straddle Side Stretch

Sit on the floor in a wide straddle position, with legs straight and toes pointed. Hold arms overhead, and stretch to the side. Hold this position for 10 seconds.

Variation 1: If the knee hurts, bend one leg so the foot faces the body as shown, and stretch over the extended leg.

Variation 2: Instead of holding both arms overhead, stretch one arm overhead and the other one toward the toes.

> Repeat on the other side.
>
> Repeat the total exercise several times.

Sitting Straddle Forward Stretch

Sit on the floor in a wide straddle position. Let gravity pull the torso down, and lean the upper body forward. Be sure to bend from the hips.

> Hold this position for 10 seconds. Sit up, and repeat the exercise.

STRENGTHENING EXERCISES

Push-Up

Perform the maximum number of push-ups.

Reverse Push-Ups

Begin with weight supported on hands and feet with the back parallel to the floor. Fingers must point toward the heels. Shift most weight toward the shoulders. Lower the body halfway to the floor, and then straighten the elbows to return to the starting position.

> Repeat as many times as possible.
>
> This exercise strengthens triceps muscles. Repeat as many times as possible.

Abdominal Curl-Ups

INSTRUCTIONAL ACTIVITIES	TEACHING HINTS
Donkey Leg Lifts Begin on hands and knees, with weight supported on forearms. Keep head looking between hands. Lift a bent leg up to hip level. Lift leg in this position several inches, and then lower it to hip level. Keep hips parallel to the floor, and be sure not to lean to one side.	Repeat this exercise at least 20 times on each leg. This exercise strengthens your gluteal muscles in the buttocks.
Side Leg Lifts Begin lying on side. Have the arm closest to the floor supporting the head and have the top arm bent in front of the chest, with the palm on the floor. Lift the top leg straight up toward the ceiling, keeping it on a forward diagonal between 30°–45° from the body. Point the toe slightly towards the floor. Slowly lower the leg.	This exercise works the abductor muscles located on the upper outside thigh. Repeat this exercise at least 20 times on each leg.
Bent Side Leg Lifts Begin lying on side. Bend both legs. Bring the top leg up toward the chest, and place the knee and lower leg on the floor for support. Lift the top leg up, hold it there, then slowly lower it to the floor.	Repeat this 20 times on each side. This exercise strengthens the abductor muscles.
Pelvic Lifts/Buttocks Exercise Lie on back with knees bent, the soles of the feet on the floor, and hands by the sides. Keeping the lower back close to the floor, contract the abdominal muscles and gluteal muscles to tilt and lift the pelvis approximately 1 to 2 inches toward the ceiling.	Repeat approximately 20 to 30 times. Caution: Do not lift the lower and middle back off the floor.

Stand up and stretch and take deep breathes.

GAME (5 MINUTES)

Triangle plus 1 Tag Triangle moves around to avoid getting leader tagged. Tagger tries to tag leader.	**DPESS page 312** Use Whistle Mixer to make groups of 4. Identify leader and tagger. 3 make triangle and hold hands.

EVALUATION/REVIEW AND CHEER

What muscles were worked today?
What areas need more flexibility work?
What part of the Aerobic Routine did you enjoy the most?
Cheer: Aerobics takes my breath away!

Aerobics Lesson Plan 2

EQUIPMENT:
CD/cassette tape player
One bean bag per student

Aerobics Music CD/cassette tape

INSTRUCTIONAL ACTIVITIES	TEACHING HINTS

INTRODUCTORY ACTIVITY (2–3 MINUTES)

Vanishing Bean Bags
Take away bean bags after each episode.

DPESS page 309
Scattered formation

COMBINE FITNESS DEVELOPMENT AND LESSON FOCUS (20–25 MINUTES)

Walk in place while moving arms from hips to overhead.

Step to the right and touch your left toe to the right, then step to the left and touch the left toe next to the left foot.

Hop on the left foot 4 times while pointing and tapping the right foot forward and then to the side (for example, forward, side, forward, feet together on count 4, jump/change sides).

Run in place 8 times, clap on each run.

Do 8 jumping jacks using full arm movements.

Slide to the right 8 times, clap on the 8th slide.

Jump in place 8 times while hitting the sides of your thighs with straight arms.

Run in place 8 times while lifting your feet high in the rear.

Run in place 8 times while lifting your knees high in front.

Perform 8 jumping jacks, moving your arms down and up in coordination with the leg movements.

Perform 8 jumping jacks, moving your arms down and only half way up (to the shoulder level) in coordination with each leg movement.

Mountain Climber

Pony: "Hop, step, step." Hop on the right foot to the side, and then quickly step with the left foot and then the right foot.

Heel, toe, slide, slide: Hop on the left foot while tapping the right heel to the right side. While hopping again on the left foot, swing the right foot to the front and touch the toe on the floor. Perform 2 slides to the right.

Hop on one foot and lift up the opposite knee.

Hop on one foot, and swing kick the opposite foot forward.

Charleston Bounce Step: Use a very bouncy step throughout this phrase. Step right, kick the left foot forward, step back on the left foot, and touch the right toe back.

Can-Can Kick: Hop on the right foot, and simultaneously bring the bent left knee up high in front. **Hop** again on the right foot, lightly touch the left foot on the floor next to the right, and kick the left foot into the air forward and up.

32 counts
8 times

Repeat the entire phrase while hopping (bouncing) on the right foot 4 times and tapping the left foot forward and to the side as described. Repeat the phrase again on each side.

Repeat to the left.

Repeat the two running in place phrases

With your feet separated, jump and land forward and backward a distance of about one foot. Alternate feet as you land in front and in back on each jump. Your arms can swing high in opposition to the leg movements.

Repeat on the other side.

Repeat the entire phrase by hopping on the right foot and sliding to the left.

Reverse.

Reverse.

Repeat 8 times. Reverse with opposite foot leading.

Repeat 4 times and then repeat on the other side. A more advanced version involves alternating sides after each kick.

INSTRUCTIONAL ACTIVITIES	TEACHING HINTS
Twist the body while using a bounce landing, and swing the arms in opposition overhead on each twist. The arms can also be swung from side to side at chest level.	
Skiers' jump: Jump to the right while twisting the body toward the left diagonal. Perform 8 times.	Reverse on the other side. For variety, jump twice on each side before changing directions.
Walk in place while moving arms from hips to overhead.	32 counts
Walk in place while stay near the hips, hands are flexed, and move away from the body and back towards the hips.	32 counts
Stretches and Isolations	
Head isolations Lift head up and down. Turn head to the right and then the left.	Repeat the set 4 to 8 times Caution: All head and neck exercises should be performed smoothly and in a relaxed manner. If the neck is allowed to arch or roll back, unnecessary tension could be placed on the cervical vertebrae.
Shoulder Circles In a slow, smooth manner, circle shoulders forward, up, back, and around 8 times.	Reverse the direction of the roll, and repeat it 8 times.
Rib Isolations While standing with good posture, place hands on hips (this helps keep hips from moving). Move ribs forward, back to center, to the side, back to center, to the back, back to center, to the other side, and back to center.	Repeat by reversing the direction of the rib isolations.
Rib Circles Perform rib circles the same way as the rib isolations, but in a continuous manner.	Perform them several times in each direction.
Hip Isolations While standing with good posture, slightly bend the knees. Now smoothly tilt the pelvis forward and then backward.	Repeat 8 times.
Hip Swings Tilt hips and pelvic area to the right and then the left.	Repeat 8 times. Be sure to execute these movements in a smooth, sustained manner.
Hip Circles While standing with good posture, slightly bend knees. Smoothly circle hips forward, to the side, to the back, and to the other side. Continue circling hips at least 8 times.	Reverse the direction and perform the hip circles the same number of times. Keep movements smooth and sustained. Jerking movements should be avoided.
Deep Lunge Begin in a standing position with good posture. With feet parallel, take a large step forward on one foot. Assume a deep lunge position, place hands on each side of the knee. The heel of the forward foot must remain on the floor, and the knee should be directly above the foot. Keep the extended back leg straight, with the toes of the foot pushing against the floor.	Hold this position for 20 seconds. You may want to repeat the entire exercise for each leg.
Now, straighten your forward bent leg and lift the toe up. Gently, without pulling, try to have your head touch your knee. This exercise will stretch your quadriceps, hamstrings, and the Achilles' tendon. Perform the exercise on your other leg.	

INSTRUCTIONAL ACTIVITIES	TEACHING HINTS

Hamstring Stretch

While lying on back with feet parallel, bend one leg and keep the other foot on the ground for support. Lift the straight leg up and try to keep the knee straight. Place hands under the thigh of the lifted leg. Hold the lifted leg under the thigh for a minimum of 15 seconds, preferably for 30 to 60 seconds.

This exercise stretches the hamstrings. Repeat on the other side.

Perform another set.

Quadriceps Stretch

Stand up with good posture. Keeping the supporting leg slightly bent, grasp the lower leg near the foot and gently pull foot toward buttocks.

Proceed carefully, as this exercise can place stress on your knee joint.

Repeat on each leg.

Calf Stretches

Perform either or both of the following calf exercises:

Perform a standing lunge by stepping forward with one foot so that both feet are approximately 1 to 2 feet apart. The front leg is bent, the back leg is straight with the toes facing forward.

Stand facing a wall, approximately 2 feet away from it. Keep the body in a straight line and lunge forward, place both hands on the wall about shoulder level. In the lunge position, the forward leg is bent, and the back leg is straight. There should be a stretch in the calf of the straight leg. If not, adjust the position until a stretch is felt.

Hold this position for 20 seconds. Repeat on the other leg. Repeat the set again.

Ankle Circles

While standing or sitting, circle each ankle 10 times in each direction. Repeat

Repeat the exercise on the other leg.

Ankle Raises

From a standing position in good posture, raise up on the balls of both feet. Hold for 4 counts, and then lower back to the floor in 4 counts.

Repeat 10 times. Do another set, holding for 2 counts in each position.

Heel Walking

Lift toes up and walk around the room on both heels.

This strengthens the tibialis muscles.

Sitting Straddle Side Stretch

Sit on the floor in a wide straddle position, with legs straight and toes pointed. Hold arms overhead, and stretch to the side. Hold this position for 10 seconds.

Variation 1: If the knee hurts, bend one leg so the foot faces the body as shown, and stretch over the extended leg.

Variation 2: Instead of holding both arms overhead, stretch one arm overhead and the other one toward the toes.

Repeat on the other side. Repeat the total exercise several times.

Sitting Straddle Forward Stretch

Sit on the floor in a wide straddle position. Let gravity pull the torso down, and lean the upper body forward. Be sure to bend from the hips.

Hold this position for 10 seconds. Sit up, and repeat the exercise.

Strengthening Exercises

Push-Up

Perform the maximum number of push-ups.

Repeat as many times as possible.

Reverse Push-Ups

Begin with weight supported on hands and feet with the back parallel to the floor. Fingers must point toward the heels. Shift most weight toward the shoulders. Lower the body halfway to the floor, and then straighten the elbows to return to the starting position.

This exercise strengthens triceps muscles.

Repeat as many times as possible.

INSTRUCTIONAL ACTIVITIES	**TEACHING HINTS**

Abdominal Curl-Ups

Donkey Leg Lifts

Begin on hands and knees, with weight supported on forearms. Keep head looking between hands. Lift a bent leg up to hip level. Lift leg in this position several inches, and then lower it to hip level. Keep hips parallel to the floor, and be sure not to lean to one side.

> Repeat this exercise at least 20 times on each leg. This exercise strengthens your gluteal muscles in the buttocks.

Side Leg Lifts

Begin lying on side. Have the arm closest to the floor supporting the head and have the top arm bent in front of the chest, with the palm on the floor. Lift the top leg straight up toward the ceiling, keeping it on a forward diagonal between 30°–45° from the body. Point the toe slightly towards the floor. Slowly lower the leg.

> This exercise works the abductor muscles located on the upper outside thigh.
>
> Repeat this exercise at least 20 times on each leg.

Bent Side Leg Lifts

Begin lying on side. Bend both legs. Bring the top leg up towards the chest, and place the knee and lower leg on the floor for support. Lift the top leg up, hold it there, then slowly lower it to the floor.

> Repeat this 20 times on each side.
>
> This exercise strengthens the abductor muscles.

Pelvic Lifts/Buttocks Exercise

Lie on back with knees bent, the soles of the feet on the floor, and hands by the sides. Keeping the lower back close to the floor, contract the abdominal muscles and gluteal muscles to tilt and lift the pelvis approximately 1 to 2 inches toward the ceiling.

> Repeat approximately 20 to 30 times.
>
> Caution: Do not lift the lower and middle back off the floor.

Slowly sit up.

Slowly stand up.

> Take deep breaths once sitting up.
>
> Take deep breaths while lifting the arms from by the sides to overhead.
>
> 8 counts alternating arms

Stretch the arms overhead.

Open the feet to "second position," feet parallel.

Stretch one arm overhead and towards the diagonal.

Take a full deep breath and exhale.

> Repeat on the other side.
>
> Repeat several times.

GAME (5 MINUTES)

Balance Tag

> **DPESS page 312**
> Select several "its."
> Rotate positions frequently.
> Select a balance position in which one is safe.

EVALUATION/REVIEW AND CHEER

Was the Aerobic Routine easier for you today since this was your second day?

What muscles were worked today?

What do you need to continue working on?

Cheer: 2, 4, 6, 8, Aerobics makes me feel great!

Juggling

OBJECTIVES:

The student will:

1. Run, change directions, pivot, evade other students, and assume poses during Rubber Band and Run and Change Direction Introductory Activities as directed by the instructor.
2. Demonstrate cooperation in Triangle plus 1 Tag and Foot tag activities following the instructions established by the instructor.
3. Participate in Parachute Fitness and Jump and Jog Fitness activities to improve their overall fitness.
4. Demonstrate Cascading, Reverse Cascading, and Column Juggling skills while using one, two, and three scarves and using form demonstrated by the instructor.

```
┌─────────────────────────┐
│  JUGGLING BLOCK PLAN    │
│      2 DAY UNIT         │
└─────────────────────────┘
```

Week #1	Day One	Day Two
Introductory Activity	Run and Change Direction	Rubber Band
Fitness	Jump and Jog Fitness	Parachute Fitness
Lesson Focus	Cascading Reverse Cascading Column Juggling	Review Juggling Additional challenges in Juggling
Game	Triangle plus 1 Tag	Help Me Tag

Juggling Lesson Plan 1

EQUIPMENT:

3 juggling scarves per student
5–6 cones
Instructional signs

Jump ropes for half the number of students in class
CD/cassette tape player and fitness CD/cassette tape

INSTRUCTIONAL ACTIVITIES	TEACHING HINTS

INTRODUCTORY ACTIVITY (2–3 MINUTES)

Run and Change Direction
Students run in any direction, changing directions on
  signal.

DPESS page 308
Scattered formation
Specify type of angle, i.e., right, obtuse, 45-degree.

FITNESS DEVELOPMENT (8–12 MINUTES)

Jump and Jog Fitness
One partner jumps rope at the cone, other jogs around the
  circle. Change roles.
Variations in moving around circle:
- Slide
- Carioca
- Power Skip

DPESS page 357
Use continuity music CD/cassette tape to signal activity
  change.
Set up 5–6 cones in a circle in gym or field area.
3 jump ropes at each cone

LESSON FOCUS (15–20 MINUTES)

Tossing One Scarf at a time
  Demonstrate tossing straight up and catching with one
  scarf in each hand.
Cascading
  Demonstrate with 1, then 2 scarves.
  Demonstrate **Three-scarf cascading.**
Reverse Cascading
  Demonstrate with 1, then 2 scarves.
  Demonstrate **Three-scarf reverse cascading.**
  Demonstrate with 1, then 2 scarves.
  Demonstrate **Three-scarf reverse cascading again.**
Column Juggling
  Demonstrate with 3 scarves.

DPESS pages 392–394

Proceed to 3 scarves only when 2 are mastered

Proceed to 3 scarves only when 2 are mastered

To perform three-scarf column juggling, begin with two
  scarves in one hand and one in the other hand

GAME (5 MINUTES)

Triangle plus 1 Tag
Triangle moves around to avoid getting leader tagged.

DPESS page 312

Use Whistle Mixer to make groups of 4.
Identify leader and tagger.
3 make triangle and hold hands.
Tagger tries to tag leader.

EVALUATION/REVIEW AND CHEER

What activity was the most challenging during fitness today?
Which juggling skills were the easiest to master?
Which juggling skills do you need to work on more and why?
What is the most important skill to practice in Triangle plus 1 Tag?
Cheer: 3, 2, 1, Juggling is fun!

Juggling Lesson Plan 2

EQUIPMENT:

3 juggling scarves per student	CD/cassette tape player
Parachute	Fitness music CD/cassette tape
Stuffed animal/chicken	

INSTRUCTIONAL ACTIVITIES	TEACHING HINTS

INTRODUCTORY ACTIVITY (2–3 MINUTES)

Rubber Band

Students move away from instructor performing a locomotor movement (jump, hop, slide, etc.). On signal, students run back to instructor.

DPESS page 309
Scattered formation
Use whistle for signals

FITNESS DEVELOPMENT (8–12 MINUTES)

Parachute Fitness

Jog: hold chute in right hand; Change directions, switch hands. Slide, hold chute with both hands.

Skip: hold chute with right hand. Change directions, switch hands. Freeze and shake chute.

Sit with bent legs under chute for curl-ups. Lay on right side, lift left leg up. Reverse.

Stand up and shake chute. Jog and lift chute up and down. Repeat.

DPESS page 351
Use music to make fitness fun and exciting.
Use signal to change task.
Keep all movements under control.

LESSON FOCUS (15–20 MINUTES)

DPESS pages 392–394

Review:

- **Cascading**
- **Reverse Cascading**
- **Column Juggling**

Demonstrate Showering

Showering is more difficult than cascading because of the rapid movement of the hands.

Start with two scarves; one in the right hand and one in the other

Additional Cascading Juggling Challenges

While cascading, toss a scarf under one leg.

While cascading, toss a scarf under one leg.

While cascading, instead of catching one of the scarves, blow it upward with a strong breath of air.

Begin cascading by tossing the first scarf into the air with a foot. Lay the scarf across the foot and kick it into the air.

Try juggling three scarves with one hand. Do not worry about establishing a pattern; just catch the lowest scarf each time.

Juggle three scarves while standing side by side with inside arms around each other.

Additional Column Juggling Challenges

While doing column juggling, toss up one scarf, hold the other two, and make a full turn. Resume juggling.

GAME (5 MINUTES)

Help Me Tag

Students touching stuffed animal are safe.

Can be 3 people touching animal

Must pass animal in 30 seconds

Students about to be tagged call for help and the animal needs to be passed to them for safety.

DPESS page 312
Use Whistle Mixer to create groups of 3–5.
You need 3–5 taggers.
You need 3 people in center of area holding a stuffed animal in safe area.

EVALUATION/REVIEW AND CHEER

What muscles were used during fitness?

Which juggling skills were the most challenging today?

Which juggling skills were easier to master today than yesterday?

Cheer: 5, 4, 2, Juggling is cool!

Kickboxing

OBJECTIVES:

The student will:

1. Demonstrate agility and listening skills while participating in the Move and Change Direction Introductory Activity.
2. Participate in the Circuit Training Fitness activities following directions and using form demonstrated by the instructor.
3. Demonstrate the Boxer's stance placing the dominant foot to the rear of the front foot and using form demonstrated by the instructor.
4. Demonstrate the Boxer's center jog stance using form demonstrated by the instructor.
5. Demonstrate the Jab, Cross, Uppercut, Hook, Block and Flutter Jabs using the right and left hand and form demonstrated by the instructor.
6. Demonstrate the basic kicks of front, side, and roundhouse leading with both the right and left foot and using form demonstrated by the instructor.
7. Demonstrate the routine presented by the instructor to the music provided and use form demonstrated by the instructor.
8. Participate in the Wheelbarrow relay games demonstrating cooperation and good sportsmanship while following directions.

```
KICKBOXING BLOCK PLAN
2 DAY UNIT
```

Two Day Unit Plan	Day One	Day Two
Introductory Activity	Move and Change Directions	Bean Bag Challenges
Fitness	Circuit Training	Squad Leader Exercises
Lesson Focus	Stance Punches and Blocks Kicks	Review Basic Moves Teach Kickboxing Routine
Game	Wand Activities	Addition Tag

Kickboxing Lesson Plan 1

EQUIPMENT:

Cones for each station
Jump ropes at each required station
CD/cassette tape player

Signs for each station
Fitness music CD/cassette tape with timing as listed
1 wand per person

INSTRUCTIONAL ACTIVITIES	TEACHING HINTS

INTRODUCTORY ACTIVITY (2–3 MINUTES)

Move and Change Direction

Scattered formation

DPESS page 308

Students run in any direction, and change direction on signal given by the instructor.

FITNESS DEVELOPMENT (8–12 MINUTES)

Circuit Training

Jump rope station
Upper body stretching
Jump rope station
Lower body stretching
Jogging in place station
Push-up and reverse push-up station
Jumping jacks and mountain climber station
Curl-up station
Run around the area station
Side leg lifts
Jump rope station
Leg and back flexibility station
Stuttering/quick running in place station
Sit and reach station
Backwards running around the area station

DPESS page 348

Create a music CD/cassette tape with 30–40 seconds of music followed by 5–10 seconds of silence CD/tape to change stations.

Create signs for each circuit training station clearly indicating expectations.

INSTRUCTIONAL ACTIVITIES	**TEACHING HINTS**

LESSON FOCUS (15–20 MINUTES)

Basic Skill Introduction & Demonstrations

Boxer's stance

Hands held chin high. Dominant hand slightly behind the opposite hand. Weight on balls of the feet. dominant foot to the rear of the front foot.

Boxer's center jog stance

Punches and blocks:
- Jab
- Cross

- Uppercut

- Hook

- Blocks

- Flutter jabs

Basic Kicks
- Front

- Side

- Roundhouse

DPESS page 361

Scattered formation so students see demonstrator.

Most punches require a weight transfer and a pivot off the rear foot.

Bounce on both feet with the hands up to the chin. Feet even, parallel, and shoulder width apart.

Lead arm snaps forward and back.

Rear arm used with a shoulder turn and a pivot on the rear foot.

Uppercut involves dropping the knee and starting a circular windmill motion with the arm followed by rotating the hips and extending the knee upward as the punch comes up and forward.

Performed with either arm. Involves a slight drop of the arm and a rounded hooking motion to hit the side of the target.

Involve moving either arm upward in an L shape to block a punch.

Flutter jabs are done from the center jog stance and involve a burst of continuous jabs.

Involves a step with the opposite foot followed by bringing the knee up with a flexed ankle and extending the kick forward.

Right side kick: Step sideways on R foot, cross over L foot. Bring up R knee, and extend kick to the side.

Step forward with opposite foot, raise kicking leg to a flexed position, pivot on rear foot, and explode the kick forward with the toes pointed.

GAME (5 MINUTES)

Wand Activities

Wand Whirl

Wand Kick over

Wand Walk Down

Wand Reaction Time

DPESS 402

Everyone has a Wand.

EVALUATION/REVIEW AND CHEER

Ask the students questions to review the elements of the stance, punches and blocks and basic kicks.

Ask review questions discussing the challenges of the Circuit Training and Wand activities.

Ask which activities were the most challenging and why they were challenging.

Cheer: 3, 6, 9, Kickboxing is fine!

Kickboxing Lesson Plan 2

EQUIPMENT:

CD/cassette tape player

Aerobics music CD/cassette tape

1 bean bag per student

Instructional cards with exercises listed for Squad Leaders

INSTRUCTIONAL ACTIVITIES	TEACHING HINTS

INTRODUCTORY ACTIVITY (2–3 MINUTES)

Bean Bag Challenges

Toss the bean bag overhead and catch it

Try catching on different body parts, such as shoulder, knee, and foot.

Toss the bean bag, make a half-turn, and catch it.

Try making a different number of turns (full, double).

Toss, clap the hands, and catch. Try clapping the hands a specified number of times.

Clap the hands around different parts of the body.

DPESS page 360

FITNESS DEVELOPMENT (8–12 MINUTES)

Squad Leader Exercises

Plan exercises covering the following:

    Two exercises for the arm-shoulder girdle area

    Two for the abdominal region

    One exercise for the legs

    Three exercises for flexibility

    Two–three minutes of continuous movement

DPESS page 346

Provide squad leaders with instructional cards listing the exercises you would like them to lead.

Play aerobics music CD/cassette tape during fitness.

The leader can add additional exercises that you have taught in class previously.

LESSON FOCUS (15–20 MINUTES)

Review Basic Movements from Lesson 1:

- Stances
- Punches and jabs
- Basic Kicks

DPESS page 361

Scattered formation

Routine:

- Boxer's jog with bobbing, weaving, jabs and blocks.
- Left jabs and right jabs
- Left hooks and right hooks
- Left uppercuts and right uppercuts
- Left side kicks and right side kicks
- Left roundhouse kicks and right roundhouse kicks
- Left combo kicks and right combo kicks

Use an Aerobics Music CD/cassette tape.

GAME (5 MINUTES)

Addition Tag

DPESS page 312

Select several "its."

Play the game 2–3 times.

EVALUATION/REVIEW AND CHEER

What body parts were worked today during the Fitness section?

Which challenges were the most difficult with the Bean Bag Introductory Activities?

Which activities are the most challenging in Kickboxing?

What is fun about Addition Tag?

Cheer: Kickboxing, yeah!

Pilates Mat

OBJECTIVES:

The student will:
1. Participate in the Move and Change Locomotion introductory activity following the instructions given by the instructor.
2. Participate in the Move and Perform a Stretch introductory activity following the instructions given by the instructor.
3. Participate in the Walk and Jog fitness activity continuously moving to the best of her ability.
4. Participate in the Pilates mat movements presented in class using form demonstrated by the instructor.
5. Participate in the game Zipper demonstrating cooperation and good sportsmanship while following the rules of the game.
6. Participate in the game Musical Hoops demonstrating cooperation and good sportsmanship while following the rules of the game.

PILATES MAT BLOCK PLAN
2 DAY UNIT

Two Day Unit Plan	Day One	Day Two
Introductory Activity	Move and Change Locomotion	Move and Perform a Stretch
Fitness	Walk and Jog	Combine fitness and lesson focus today to focus on Pilates movements
Lesson Focus	Basic Beginner Pilates Mat Movements	Review Basic Beginner mat movements and continue with additional Pilates movements
Game	Zipper	Musical Hoops

Pilates Mat Lesson Plan 1

EQUIPMENT:

1 individual mat/towel per student
Aerobics music CD/cassette tape

CD/cassette tape player

INSTRUCTIONAL ACTIVITIES	TEACHING HINTS

INTRODUCTORY ACTIVITY (2–3 MINUTES)

Move and Change the Type of Locomotion
Students move using a specified locomotor movement.
On signal, they change to another type of movement.

DPESS page 308
Scattered formation
Specify the locomotor movements.
Challenges can be given to do the movements forward, backward, sideways, or diagonally.

FITNESS DEVELOPMENT (8–12 MINUTES)

Walk and Jog
Walk and jog continuously for 5–8 minutes.

DPESS page 347
Use an Aerobics music CD/cassette tape to motivate the walking and jogging.
Allow student to move at his/her own pace.

LESSON FOCUS (15–20 MINUTES)

Basic Beginner Movements
Posture and arms
Lift and straighten the spine as though resting against an imaginary wall
Bend the elbows at a 90-degree angle to protect the shoulder in "its" socket
Lift shoulders in a circular motion up and back, move arms back and down as shoulders move down, so it feels as if shoulder blades are sliding down the spine.
Raise the bent arms overhead and end with arms in starting position. Repeat.

DPESS page 363
Scattered formation
Each student on towel/mat
Sit cross-legged in good posture. Inhale. Exhale.

Roll Up
Lie on back, legs straight, arms stretched above head, shoulders down.
While breathing out, slowly roll forward, lifting the spine off the mat one vertebra at a time.

Lie on back with legs straight and arms stretched above head, shoulders down.

Lie on back with legs straight and arms stretched above head, shoulders down.
Keep back flat on the floor, slowly lift arms toward the ceiling as breathe in.
Breathe out and slowly roll up and forward, lifting spine off mat one vertebrae at a time. Head remains straight, eyes focused forward. Stomach remains taut, not crunched.

Breathe in again, stretch spine and arms over legs, hands toward toes. Breathe out while slowly rolling back down to the floor.

Breathe in again while stretching out over legs. Breathe out while slowly rolling back down to the floor.

While breathing in, roll up again to begin the second repetition. Repeat several times.
Keep back flat on floor; slowly lift arms toward the ceiling while breathing in.
Head remains straight, eyes focused forward, arms move forward toward feet. Stomach remains taut, not crunched.
Without a pause, breathe in, roll up again, to begin the second repetition.
Repeat several times.

Spinal rotation
Slowly rotate upper body to the left and then right.

Sit in slight straddle position with the legs extended and arms out to sides.

INSTRUCTIONAL ACTIVITIES	TEACHING HINTS
The Hundred On back with legs between a 90-degree to 120-degree angle. Lift shoulders and arms up slightly, exhale 5 times pressing the hands down and then 5 times pressing the hands upward with palms down.	Increase until this sequence can be done 10 times for one hundred breaths.
Abdominal strengthener Lie on back with hands behind the head and knees flexed or hands on thighs sliding up during the movement. Exhale and curl-up slowly using just the abdominal muscles.	Repeat several times. Keep chin tucked.
Single-leg stretch Lie back with one leg extended about 12 inches off the floor. Flex the other leg and bring the knee to the chest. Hold the flexed leg at the tibia and raise the shoulders slowly.	Hold the position while rotating the position of the legs and changing the hand touch from tibia to tibia.

GAME (5 MINUTES)

Zipper Players make a single-file line. Each student bends over, reaches between the legs with the left hand, and grasps the right hand of the person to the rear. On signal, the last person in line lies down, the next person backs over the last person and lies down until the last person lies down, and then immediately stands and reverses the procedure.	DPESS page 407 Use Whistle Mixer to create several groups. The first team to zip and unzip the zipper is declared the winner.

EVALUATION/REVIEW AND CHEER

Which Pilates mat movements were the most challenging?

What muscles were used during class today?

Was there anything about the game Zipper that was difficult to accomplish? If so, what?

Cheer: Pilates does a body good!

Pilates Mat Lesson Plan 2

EQUIPMENT:

One hoop per student   Music and CD/cassette tape player for Musical Hoops

INSTRUCTIONAL ACTIVITIES	TEACHING HINTS

INTRODUCTORY ACTIVITY (2–3 MINUTES)

Move and Perform a Stretch

Run throughout the area.

On signal, stop and perform a designated stretching activity.

DPESS page 308

See Chapter 16 for a comprehensive list of stretching exercises.

A list of stretches that covers all body parts can be posted, and students can perform a different stretch after each signal.

COMBINE FITNESS DEVELOPMENT AND LESSON FOCUS TODAY (20 MINUTES)

Review all of the basic beginner movements from Day 1.

DPESS page 363

Add the following movements:

Double straight leg

Lie on back with hands behind head and legs pointed toward the ceiling while held tight together.

Lift the chin and shoulders slightly off the mat and lift the legs about one foot. Keep the lower back tight to the floor.

Lower chin, shoulders, and legs.

Repeat 5–6 times.

Forward spine stretch and roll-ups

Sitting position with legs and arms extended forward. Stretch forward and exhale.

Add the roll-up by slowly going backward to the mat with the arms extended forward.

Repeat 5–6 times

Gently roll down to the floor and back up to the extended position.

Pelvic Tilt

Lie on back with the arms extended, palms down, and knees bent.

Lift the pelvic girdle upwards using the abdominal and gluteal muscles.

Take 4 counts to lift the pelvis, hold for 4 counts.

Repeat several times.

Back strengthener

All-fours position. Lift and extend the opposite arm and leg and hold the position several seconds and then switch arms and legs.

Repeat several times.

Total rest pose

All-fours position.

Push the hips to heels, stomach to thighs, head down on floor. Slowly extend arms forward with palms down and flat on the floor.

Hold for a 4–6 counts.

Sit up onto knees then repeat.

INSTRUCTIONAL ACTIVITIES	TEACHING HINTS

GAME (5 MINUTES)

Musical Hoops

DPESS page 310

Hoops are spread over the floor space with each student standing inside a hoop. The locomotor movement can be changed each round.

This activity is similar to musical chairs. Hoops are spread over the floor space with each student putting one foot or two feet in a hoop (depending on how many hoops are available). Play a musical CD/tape with random pauses. The teacher collects some of the hoops during the music so that some students will be eliminated when the music stops.

Play a musical CD/cassette tape with random pauses. The teacher collects some of the hoops during the music so that some students will be eliminated when the music stops. The eliminated students go to the perimeter and perform a designated stretch or some type of exercise until the music stops and then get back in the game.

EVALUATION/REVIEW AND CHEER

Were there any activities that were particularly challenging today? Which ones? Why?

In what way do Pilate's movements make you feel good?

What was fun about musical hoops?

Cheer: Pilates makes me strong. Yeah!